J2EE Web Services Using BEA WebLogic

Hewlett-Packard® Professional Books

HP-UX

Cooper/Moore	HP-UX 11i Internals
Fernandez	Configuring CDE
Keenan	HP-UX CSE: Official Study Guide and Desk Reference
Madell	Disk and File Management Tasks on HP-UX
Olker	Optimizing NFS Performance
Poniatowski	HP-UX 11i Virtual Partitions
Poniatowski	HP-UX 11i System Administration Handbook and Toolkit, Second Edition
Poniatowski	The HP-UX 11.x System Administration Handbook and Toolkit
Poniatowski	HP-UX 11.x System Administration "How To" Book
Poniatowski	HP-UX 10.x System Administration "How To" Book
Poniatowski	HP-UX System Administration Handbook and Toolkit
Poniatowski	Learning the HP-UX Operating System
Rehman	HP-UX CSA: Official Study Guide and Desk Reference
Sauers/Ruemmler/Weygant	HP-UX 11i Tuning and Performance
Weygant	Clusters for High Availability, Second Edition
Wong	HP-UX 11i Security

UNIX, Linux

Mosberger/Eranian	IA-64 Linux Kernel
Poniatowski	Linux on HP Integrity Servers
Poniatowski	UNIX User's Handbook, Second Edition
Stone/Symons	UNIX Fault Management

Computer Architecture

Evans/Trimper	Itanium Architecture for Programmers
Kane	PA-RISC 2.0 Architecture
Markstein	IA-64 and Elementary Functions

Networking/Communications

Blommers	Architecting Enterprise Solutions with UNIX Networking
Blommers	OpenView Network Node Manager
Blommers	Practical Planning for Network Growth
Brans	Mobilize Your Enterprise
Cook	Building Enterprise Information Architecture
Lucke	Designing and Implementing Computer Workgroups
Lund	Integrating UNIX and PC Network Operating Systems

Security

Bruce	Security in Distributed Computing
Mao	Modern Cryptography: Theory and Practice
Pearson et al.	Trusted Computing Platforms
Pipkin	Halting the Hacker, Second Edition
Pipkin	Information Security

Web/Internet Concepts and Programming

Amor	E-business (R)evolution, Second Edition
Apte/Mehta	UDDI
Chatterjee/Webber	Developing Enterprise Web Services: An Architect's Guide
Kumar	J2EE Security for Servlets, EJBs, and Web Services

Little/Maron/Pavlik	Java Transaction Processing
Mowbrey/Werry	Online Communities
Tapadiya	.NET Programming

OTHER PROGRAMMING

Blinn	Portable Shell Programming
Caruso	Power Programming in HP OpenView
Chaudhri	Object Databases in Practice
Chew	The Java/C++ Cross Reference Handbook
Grady	Practical Software Metrics for Project Management and Process Improvement
Grady	Software Metrics
Grady	Successful Software Process Improvement
Lee/Schneider/Schell	Mobile Applications
Lewis	The Art and Science of Smalltalk
Lichtenbelt	Introduction to Volume Rendering
Mellquist	SNMP++
Mikkelsen	Practical Software Configuration Management
Norton	Thread Time
Tapadiya	COM+ Programming
Yuan	Windows 2000 GDI Programming

STORAGE

Thornburgh	Fibre Channel for Mass Storage
Thornburgh/Schoenborn	Storage Area Networks
Todman	Designing Data Warehouses

IT/IS

Anderson	mySAP Tool Bag for Performance Tuning and Stress Testing
Missbach/Hoffman	SAP Hardware Solutions

IMAGE PROCESSING

Crane	A Simplified Approach to Image Processing
Gann	Desktop Scanners

J2EE Web Services Using BEA WebLogic

Anjali Anagol-Subbarao

www.hp.com/hpbooks

Pearson Education

Prentice Hall Professional Technical Reference

Upper Saddle River, New Jersey 07458

www.PHPTR.com

Library of Congress Publication in Data: 2004108498

Publisher HP Books: William Carver
Editor in Chief: Karen Gettman
Acquisitions Editor: Jill Harry
Editorial Assistant: Brenda Mulligan
Marketing Manager: Stephane Nakib
Cover Designer: Alan Clements
Managing Editor: Gina Kanouse
Senior Project Editor: Kristy Hart
Copy Editor: Krista Hansing
Indexer: Angie Bess
Compositor: Julie Parks
Manufacturing Buyer: Dan Uhrig

Published by Pearson Education, Inc.
Publishing as Prentice Hall Professional Technical Reference
Upper Saddle River, New Jersey 07458

Prentice Hall offers excellent discounts on this book when ordered in quantity for bulk purchases or special sales. For more information, please contact U.S. Corporate and Government Sales, 1-800-382-3419, corpsales@pearsontechgroup.com. For sales outside the U.S., please contact International Sales, international@pearsoned.com.

Printed in the United States of America

First Printing October 2004

ISBN 0131430726

Pearson Education LTD.
Pearson Education Australia PTY, Limited.
Pearson Education Singapore, Pte. Ltd.
Pearson Education North Asia, Ltd.
Pearson Education Canada, Ltd.
Pearson Educatión de Mexico, S.A. de C.V.
Pearson Education—Japan
Pearson Education Malaysia, Pte. Ltd.

I dedicate this book

To my father

who inspired me to achieve what appeared impossible

and dared me to break new ground

and

To my mother

who instilled in me the desire to pursue excellence

and the value of perseverance

Contents

Acknowledgments

Murali Subbarao, my husband, for his painstaking efforts in reviewing every chapter not once, but several times, and for all the encouragement throughout writing this book.

Keoki Young, who reviewed all the chapters and helped me resolve the technical roadblocks I encountered while developing the examples.

Rajesh Pradhan, who gave me a lot of guidance and help in all aspects of web services, especially modeling and BPEL.

Ravindra Gore, who helped me with the examples and reviewed the chapters.

Chris Peltz, who reviewed the book and was always very helpful with all aspects of the book, especially HP OpenView and manageability products.

Dwight Mamanteo, who reviewed the book and gave excellent suggestions to make the book what it is today.

David Cooke (Ness Technologies) and Robert Husted (Requisite Technology), for reviewing the book and providing valuable comments to improve the quality of the content.

William Vambenepe, Tim Hall, Toral Mehta, Jeff Rees, Guy Randazzo, Pankaj Kumar, and Virginia Smith, who reviewed the content relating to HP OpenView products, WSDM, and LCM4WS.

Sankar Ram Sundaresan, for the SSA contribution.

Manjunath Ganimasty and Matt Cohen, for helping me with the technical material and technical roadblocks.

Louise Ng, for all the documentation on security and testing procedures.

Stephen Hood, who helped me with getting the latest information on WLI in this book.

Catherine Neal, who helped connect me with the right people at BEA and solved many technical roadblocks.

Deana Dipasquale, for the constant encouragement and support.

Jill Harry (acquisitions editor), who helped with this book from inception to production.

Kristy Hart (senior project editor) who helped this book through production.

Craig Flower, Sam Szteinbaum, Mauricio Cori, and Saumyendra Mathur for giving me an executive's perspective on web services.

Scott Dietzan, for taking time to write the foreword with his busy schedule.

Gary Fukumara, Jenena Hansson, Ian Bromehead, and Bala Balchandran, for helping to make the foreward a reality.

My friend, Rekha Belur, for all the encouragement and for the long runs that kept me sane while writing this book.

My sons, Anirudh and Mohith, who helped me with some of the figures and patiently waited until I got through this book.

About the Author

ANJALI ANAGOL-SUBBARAO has over a decade's experience in IT, including more than four years developing leading-edge Web services. She was among the first architects to build Web services in real-world business environments, and led the first Web services project of HP to integrate its consumer business operations with twelve of the largest retailers in the USA. She is now helping to architect and build the Web services infrastructure based on SOA for HP's global operations, and has four Web services patents pending.

Foreword

I remain convinced that service-oriented architecture (SOA) is at least a "next big thing." SOA is about delivering on the promise of best-of-breed IT by unleashing the *shared* business services that are currently bound up in monolithic and often isolated applications.

In my experience, there is nothing that does more to protect IT investment long-term than SOA: With SOA

- You can more closely align IT resources with their business functions.
- You can more easily deliver composite applications that provide unified, task-oriented views across the business (such as via automated business-process management or workflow).
- You can achieve greater application life-cycle flexibility by incrementally managing requirements and change.
- You can more easily deliver real-time business intelligence on the aggregate information flowing through your applications.

SOA can empower you to deliver more dynamic and cost-effective business systems by enabling an optimal "mix and match" across the spectrum of "buy" versus "build" and insourcing versus outsourcing.

One of BEA's competitors is fond of saying best of breed only works in dog shows. I find that view both depressing and somewhat offensive, but it is reflective of the reality that best of breed is much harder to achieve today than it ought to be. As an industry, we must make best-of-breed IT a reality. We do not have much choice:

- Applications are proliferating.
- Applications are becoming ever more specialized.
- Applications are being aggregated and customized to meet user demands.
- Applications are being outsourced and offshored.
- The pace of application change is accelerating.

SOA via the Web application platform is just in time!

SOA is founded on modular programming practice, and as such has been part of the vision for distributed computing with each iteration—from DCE to DCOM to CORBA to MQSeries to RDBMS stored procedures. But we as an industry have never quite gotten there in terms of practicing SOA at scale.

Why is the application integration that underlies SOA so hard? We developers have been quite successful at modular re-use within applications (procedures, objects, components, events ...). However, a look at the history of distributed computing suggests that we have done much less well at *inter*-application re-use. Each of the aforementioned architectures was at one time envisioned as being the universal SOA fabric (or bus) for interconnecting all applications. And each came up short. Why?

Application integration is simply a hard problem—if an application is code that is developed and deployed as a unit, then we can easily recognize that

- Applications are developed by different teams,
- Who work in different places,
- On different schedules, and
- Who don't talk to each other enough.

Most critically, there generally *is* no shared vision of precisely how a *customer* or *order processing* should be represented. So each team builds their own and hardwires it into their code. Exporting such "local" object models is inherently fragile.

My hope for XML and web services is that we can enshrine SOA once and for all within our application architectures. By defining or surfacing web-standard "service access points" for individual business operations, XML and web services will become the universal SOA fabric, replacing, over time, the existing *ad hoc* mix of proprietary and partially standard technologies for interconnecting applications.

One reason XML and web services have gained greater momentum than their distributed computing predecessors is that they have gained nearly universal industry support. Web services provide communications infrastructure for both synchronous (request/response) operations and asynchronous (message-oriented) operations within a single, unified framework. Web services is the first to meet integration and scalability challenges across enterprise application integration (EAI) and business-to-business interactions (B2B). Preceding technologies have never come close to achieving the critical mass required for a transitive closure of participants (that is, working with all of an enterprise's own business systems, the business systems of their partners, of their partners' partners, and so on).

Understanding how the different aspects of web services come together and support SOA in real-word situations and thus fulfill business requirements are critical for developers and architects. One of the values of this book is that it showcases a live implementation of SOA architecture at Hewlett-Packard using web services on BEA's WebLogic Platform. It goes through the lifecycle of web services by tracing this case study from the business requirements through to architecture, design, development, testing and management.

This book details out how the WebLogic platform is leading the effort in providing one end-to-end integration tool for developers to do Java/J2EE/web services development and integration with business processes and backend systems. The book is reflective of start-of-the-art innovations such as using Javadoc annotations for capturing metadata, transformations, business processes through BPELJ, and web services through Java web services (JWS), which are collectively being standardized through the JCP, OASIS, and W3C.

Those wishing to systematically transform their organizations with SOA based on XML and web services—specifically architects, developers, and technical project managers—will find this book useful to guide them through the lifecycle of a web service and help solve issues and problems. In all of my conversations with enterprise IT personel, implementation of SOA architecture with web services (especially the security, performance and complexity of their EAI/B2B requirements) reigns among their top concerns. This book makes it quite a bit easier to comprehend all the facets of web services. It's a reference book that architects, developers, and technical managers may well want to keep handy.

Scott Dietzen, Ph.D.

Chief Technology Officer BEA Systems

Introduction

About This Book

This book covers the implementation of J2EE web services using the BEA WebLogic Platform. It describes the lifecycle of activities for IT projects: design, development, deployment, and management. The concepts are peppered with lessons learned from a live implementation of web services at Hewlett-Packard with 12 large retailers in the United States.

Those who want to go beyond understanding concepts and actually implement web services will find this book a great reference. Special attention is given to topics encountered in large enterprises: business relevance, prototyping, methodologies, ties to existing infrastructure, testing, and manageability.

Who Should Read This Book?

This book is targeted to developers, senior architects, and IT project managers within IT departments of large enterprises. The typical buyers fits into one of the following groups:

- **Technical managers**—Those wanting to systematically transform their organizations to web services, the new IT paradigm, and those charged with the responsibility of managing web services projects.
- **Architects and programmers**—Those involved in developing web services. We assume that the reader is fluent with basic Java coding and has some experience with coding EJBs.

How Is This Book Organized?

The book is organized into four main sections. The first section, which consists of Chapters 1, 2, and 3, is a primer on web services and an introduction to J2EE and WebLogic Platform, in the context of web services. The second section, comprised of Chapters 4, 5, and 6, describes the process of designing web services using a service-oriented architecture framework and within a business context. The third section, consisting of Chapters 7–10, helps the reader learn the process of developing web services using WebLogic Workshop. It addresses how these web services are integrated with existing applications, databases, and enterprise information systems. It also covers the integration of web services with business processes by using WLI. The fourth and final section covered in Chapters 11–14 is dedicated to best practices for improving performance, security, testing, and management of web services.

You can use the following guide to understand which chapters are most relevant to your job function or role:

- **Technical manager**—Chapters 1–4, 13, and 14
- **Architect**—Chapters 1–6, 11,12, and 14
- **Developer**—Chapters 1–3 and 6–12

Here are the details of each chapter.

Chapter 1, "Introduction to Web Services"

This chapter looks at the significant developments in technologies that have taken place during the past two decades, leading up to the creation of web services technologies. It also looks at the standard organizations and consortiums that are shaping the creation of the web services specifications. Four primary standards are in the web services stack: XML, SOAP, WSDL, and UDDI. This chapter describes each one of these standards, along with Web Services Security, an important requirement of any web services implementation.

Chapter 2, "Essentials of J2EE"

If you are new to the J2EE applications development platform, this chapter is a good place to start. Here, you will learn the J2EE architecture and become acquainted with important terms and concepts that are relevant in the context of web services. Specifically, this chapter looks at the J2EE architecture, the J2EE services and APIs, and how to assemble a J2EE application. It then looks at the support for web services in the J2EE 1.4 specifications.

Chapter 3, "Introduction to WebLogic Platform"

This chapter introduces BEA's WebLogic Platform, a widely used application platform suite. This chapter describes how BEA's WebLogic Platform 8.1 supports the building and deployment of J2EE components and web services, and introduces the reader to WebLogic Server, WebLogic Workshop, WebLogic Integration, WebLogic Portal, and WebLogic JRockit.

Chapter 4, "Benefiting from SOA and Web Services"

In this chapter, you explore SOA and understand the value proposition of SOA and how SOA can be implemented through web services. You will see how organizations have already realized the benefits of using SOA and web services. This chapter describes a case study from a business unit at HP that adopted SOA and implemented it using web services.

Chapter 5, "Enabling Enterprise-Class Web Services"

This chapter closely looks at the factors to consider for enabling enterprise-class web services. Enterprise-class web services represent a level of technical and operational maturity consistent with the increasingly stringent requirements of today's enterprise. Toward building such web services, this chapter closely looks at designing interoperability, publishing an enduring web services contract, exposing the business tier components, and planning for a robust production environment. You will learn how the WebLogic Workshop web services framework abstracts the developer from the plumbing code required to build enterprise-class web services.

Chapter 6, "Designing Web Services"

In this chapter, you look into the details of designing web services through designing a real-world web service. This chapter looks at how to design a WSDL using XMLSPY. Next, taking this WSDL, it shows how to prototype the web service using WebLogic Workshop and then test it. You will also learn how to test a web service using different clients—Java, Apache, and .NET. Finally, this chapter talks about how to include versioning as part of the design of a web service.

Chapter 7, "Developing and Deploying Web Services"

This chapter describes the essentials of developing and deploying web services, and demonstrates how to do these using WebLogic Workshop. Here, you will look at adding to a web service a set of capabilities that are required in business environments. First, this chapter looks at enabling asynchronous communication using callbacks, conversations, buffering, and polling.

Then it talks about sending and receiving SOAP with attachments and ensuring interoperability with .NET implementations. It also shows how to transform XML Schemas to match with client environments using XQuery map and ECMAScript. After a web service is developed, you can publish and enable discovery of the web service using UDDI Explorer and a web service control. Finally, this chapter shows how to deploy the web service to a production environment using automatic and manual methods, and how to view and test this deployed web service.

Chapter 8, "Using Controls, Bindings, and Parsers"

In this chapter, you will look at the functions that support the building of web services. You will learn about using controls, XML-to-Java bindings, and XML parsing.

Control Frameworks are part of Web Logic Workshop, so here, you will see how to build custom controls, use built-in controls, and leverage ISV controls.

This chapter also describes how to use XML Beans in WebLogic Workshop to accomplish the conversion of XML to Java objects. In addition, it discusses the details of the StAX parser and compares it to two other parsers, DOM and SAX.

Chapter 9, "Connecting to a Distributed Environment"

In this chapter, you look at the next layer of technology that supports controls: EJBs and the Application Integration Framework. Here, you learn how to build EJBs in WebLogic Workshop. This chapter also covers the Application Integration Framework of WLI for integration to Enterprise Information Systems (EIS). The J2EE connector architecture specification defines how application servers such as WebLogic can be connected to EIS systems. You will also learn about the main components of the Adapter Development Kit.

Chapter 10, "Managing Business Processes"

In this chapter, you will learn how orchestration, choreography, and collaboration techniques are used for composing web services into a business process. You will also see how you can apply business process management (BPM) and B2Bi with web services. This chapter gives examples of how WebLogic Integration supports both BPM and B2Bi, and it looks at WLI examples for the BPM and ebXML messaging specifications.

Chapter 11, "Security of Web Services"

This chapter describes one of the biggest challenges for the implementation of web services: security. It reviews the security considerations—authentication, authorization, confidentiality, integrity, and nonrepudiation—required to properly secure an implementation. It also looks at how Two-Way SSL and other packaged security solutions, such as XML firewalls, can be used to ensure the security of web services.

This chapter also describes WS-Security and the emerging standards from Liberty Alliance and SAML. Finally, you will learn how Two-Way SSL and WS-Security can be used in WebLogic.

Chapter 12, "Enhancing the Performance of Web Services"

This chapter covers the factors that affect web services performance, how to track the performance bottlenecks, and how to improve performance in all the building blocks of web services. You first examine the inherent factors constraining the performance of a web service implementation: HTTP, XML, SOAP, and security. The chapter then describes how the HP OpenView Transaction Analyzer can help in identifying performance bottlenecks. You take a look at a variety of ways to improve the performance: SOAP implementation options, XML parsers, XML Beans, XML compression, XML and SSL accelerators, patterns and EJB tuning, and databases and JVM.

Chapter 13, "Testing of Web Services"

In this chapter, you will learn the unique requirements of testing web services and how you have to extend current traditional testing methods to test web services. The chapter discusses how to build a comprehensive test suite that covers unit, functional, integration, interoperability, regression, performance, load, and stress testing. Automated tools can be used effectively to test web services. Here, you get an introduction to some performance tools such as Empirix e-TEST and e-load and HP OpenView Internet Services.

Chapter 14, "Managing Web Services"

This chapter covers web services manageability. You will see why web services present a different challenge in manageability compared to traditional management. You will explore the manageability stack to see how you can meet the challenges of web services management, and you will explore the JMX architecture used in the WebLogic Platform with OpenView. In addition, you will examine the concepts of WS-Resource Framework, WS-Notification, WSDM, and grid computing, which are some of the efforts in the industry to have standard specifications for web services manageability. This chapter also looks at HP's strategy in the area of web services manageability and examines how Lifecycle for Management of Web Services (LCM4WS) helps you to manage the changes in the lifecycle of web services.

1

Introduction to Web Services

"Web services are based on a breakthrough architecture offering modularity, reusability, and extensibility of business transactions. By exposing back-end monolithic applications as services, it has helped us decrease by 50 percent our e-commerce storefronts while providing overall better customer experience and reduced costs."—Craig Flower, Vice President, eBusiness and Customer Operations IT, Hewlett Packard

We are living in one of the most exciting times for an IT professional. An interesting transformation is taking place in the design, development, and deployment of distributed applications. Today, we're seeing the emergence of an entirely new approach to corporate information systems: web services. This will provide significant cost savings to businesses while creating new opportunities for growth.

Scores of firms from the Internet era, such as Google, Amazon, and eBay, as well as blue-chip firms, such as Merrill Lynch, General Motors, and Dell Computer, are already transitioning to the new architecture. Instead of building, owning, and maintaining all of their own software, these companies are buying their information technologies as services provided over the Internet. They are building on their existing systems and connecting them to the web services architecture to gain immediate benefits. They are transforming applications that connect their organization to their customers or other companies to web services.

To appreciate this excitement, we look at the significant developments in technologies that have taken place during the past two decades, leading up to the creation of web services technologies. We also look at the standard organizations and consortiums that are shaping the creation of the web services specifications. Four primary standards exist in the web services stack: XML, SOAP, WSDL, and UDDI. We describe each one of these standards, along with web services security, an important requirement of any web services implementation.

Developments Leading up to Web Services

The development of applications in a distributed environment has been an important field ever since computing moved from centralized mainframe computers to networked computers—client/server and peer-networked workstations. During the past two decades, major developments in distributed technologies eventually led to the current dominant paradigm of web services (see Figure 1.1).

During the 1980s, the distribution of services across multiple workstations was a way to scale and organize the data center. Distributed services required both synchronous and asynchronous forms of communications. As a result, the prevalent architectures and operating systems of the period, such as DEC VMS, HP, and Sun UNIX variants, developed distributed messaging and remote procedure call (RPC) technologies.

At the very end of the 1980s, the distributed computing environment (DCE) emerged as a way to standardize the various competing RPC technologies. This effort consciously omitted messaging technologies and never attained widespread industry support. By this time, IT shops started to adopt object systems as the standard for software development because of benefits of maintainability and code reuse. As a result, the emerging distributed technologies took on a strong object flavor.

In the mid-1990s, the Common Object Request Broker Architecture (CORBA) came out of an industry consortium Object Management Group (OMG) effort to standardize on distributed procedure technology. It focused on requests to remote objects for cross-platform distributed applications. Because of its attempt to enable transparency of object state and lifecycle management, CORBA proved less scalable than messaging technologies and DCE. Microsoft brought forth its version of an object platform, the Component Object Model (COM) and the Distributed COM (DCOM) remote object protocol, but these failed to address the scalability issue.

In the late 1990s, e-mail and the web were proving themselves the most successful distributed architectures ever, and designers sought distributed development technologies that provided the looser coupling of messaging technologies and the ubiquity of the Internet. The popularity of Java led to its specialized Remote Method Invocation (RMI) protocol, and the niche successes of MQSeries led to Microsoft and Java messaging flavors.

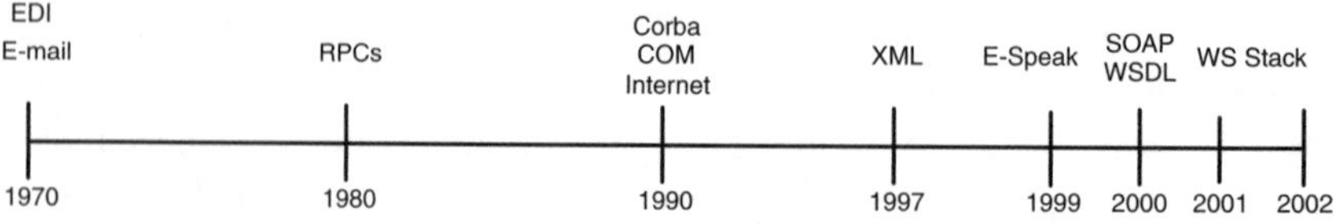

Figure 1.1 History of web services

As the new millennium approached, the stage was set for a new generation of distributed computing, based on information systems needs and experience with network technologies to date. The prevalent needs were these:

- Use of distributed operation within an application, and generic services across applications supporting both software developers and systems integrators
- Cross-platform support for data sharing
- High leverage of Internet infrastructure
- Capability to scale as the number of nodes, heterogeneity of nodes, and the complexity of each node's needs increase
- Support for internationalization to enable cross-border transactions
- Tools for software development and business workflow management
- Support for both the simple request/response exchanges and sophisticated orchestration, transaction, and security needs

In late 1999, the efforts at HP Labs to address the well-known technical and cost problems of distributed systems culminated in HP's e-Speak, which addressed most of these needs. e-Speak emerged as probably the first web services technology—and certainly the first commercially marketed web services technology. It used generic protocols such as HTTP and an XML data representation to treat all manner of networked systems as "e-services" into which one could rapidly plug data streams. e-Speak enabled service-to-service interaction similar to the present-day web services by allowing the registration, discovery, and interaction of dynamic web services. HP suppressed e-Speak in favor of the emerging web services specifications.

At about the same time, other early forms of web services based on HyperText Transfer Protocol (HTTP) and eXtensible Markup Language (XML) technologies started emerging, inspired not by the need for enterprise application integration (EAI), but rather for business-to-business transactions. In 1999, the Simple Object Access Protocol (now referred to by only its acronym, SOAP), a structured exchange of XML documents, was brought out by a small group of organizations, including Microsoft. SOAP superceded e-Speak because the organizations that brought it out worked to make it an industry standard. Soon afterward, IBM, Microsoft, and Ariba announced the Web Services Description Language (WSDL). They saw significant value in a standardized form for web services metadata to enable the processing of web services. The same trio was also merging its various proprietary discovery systems into Universal Description, Discovery, and Integration (UDDI), a system for directories (White Pages, Yellow Pages, and Green Pages) of web services.

The W3C Workshop on Web Services (WSWS), in April 2001, was a grand exercise in planning the future of web services. Until this time, web services was being developed outside the W3C, either at the grass roots level or by separate consortia such as UDDI.org. It seemed a natural move to have the W3C bring web services under the aegis of other web standards such as HTML and XML.

What Are Web Services?

The W3C web services architecture working group defines web services in the following manner:

> A web service is a software system designed to support interoperable machine-to-machine interaction over a network. It has an interface described in a machine-processable format (specifically, WSDL). Other systems interact with the web service in a manner prescribed by its description using SOAP messages, typically conveyed using HTTP with an XML serialization in conjunction with other web-related standards.

Four parts make up a web services stack:

- XML
- SOAP
- WSDL
- UDDI

You will learn more about XML, SOAP, WSDL, and UDDI in the following sections.

Platforms for Developing Web Services

J2EE and .NET are the most popular platforms on which developers are developing and deploying web services. .NET contains VB .NET, which is a version of the Visual Basic programming language, and C# (C sharp), which is an object-oriented language. The good news for proponents of web services is that both platforms equally support the existing web services standards. This book looks mainly at the J2EE web services and the interoperability of such services with web services developed on the .NET platform.

Web Services Standards Organizations

The foundation of web services architecture is built on industry standards. Two key standards bodies are driving the development of these standards: the World Wide Web Consortium (W3C) and the Organization for the Advancement of Structured Information Standards (OASIS). Another important organization is the Web Services Interoperability Organization (WS-I), which makes recommendations on applying and using existing standards:

- The W3C develops interoperable technologies—specifications, guidelines, software, and tools—to lead the web to its full potential. The core web services standards—XML, SOAP, WSDL, and UDDI—are W3C Recommendations. The W3C consists of more than 400 member organizations and provides a neutral meeting ground for the web community to find consensus and prevent the web from dissolving into mutually noninteroperable subwebs.

- OASIS is a not-for-profit global consortium that drives the development, convergence, and adoption of e-business standards. Members themselves set the OASIS technical agenda using a lightweight, open process expressly designed to promote industry consensus and unite disparate efforts. OASIS produces worldwide standards for security, web services, XML conformance, business transactions, electronic publishing, topic maps, and interoperability within and between marketplaces. OASIS has more than 600 corporate and individual members in 100 countries around the world. OASIS and the United Nations jointly sponsor ebXML, a global framework for e-business data exchange.
- WS-I is an open, industry organization chartered to promote web services interoperability across platforms, operating systems, and programming languages. The organization works across the industry and standards organizations to respond to customer needs by providing guidance, best practices, and resources for developing web services solutions that are interoperable. The Basic Profile specification that defines conformance and interoperability standards for web services implementations was developed through the WS-I. Other areas currently being pursued at the WS-I are security, workflow, reliable messaging, and attachments.

Web Services Standards

In this section, we look at the web services standards in detail—XML, SOAP, WSDL, and UDDI.

XML

XML is a W3C Recommendation that was announced in late 1997. It is a structured text format, a markup language, designed to describe data. XML is extensible. The tags in the markup language are not predefined, compared to other markup languages such as HTML. You can specify a set of tags to describe the data contained in a document using a Document Type Definition (DTD) or an XML Schema. In addition to enabling the definition of a document, DTDs and XML Schema provide a mechanism for validating XML documents. The tags describe the set of elements, attributes, structure, semantics, processes, and vocabulary for the document. An XML standard is created when there is agreement on a common DTD or schema. With a standard, documents can be exchanged, validated, and interpreted in a consistent manner.

XML is an open standard and continues to be influenced by a number of standards organizations. Today, more than 450 XML standard specifications are in place. Some of them are used widely, while others are used only within a small community. One interesting use of XML is to describe other standards specifications. For example, RosettaNet defines the partner interface processes (PIPs) using XML for companies to exchange data. Even the other web services standards, such as SOAP, WSDL, and UDDI, are described in XML.

DTD

DTDs provide the basic mechanism for describing a list of elements and attributes in a specific order and cardinality within a document. A DTD can be used to verify the validity of an XML document. DTDs have proliferated among early adopters of XML and standards organizations.

However, DTDs aren't capable of specifying data types, bounds for acceptable data ranges, inheritance of schema classes, and support for namespaces. For example, DTDs specify only that the `price` element should exist, but not what values are considered valid. Also, DTDs are not represented in XML syntax. DTDs are fairly compact formats, but large DTDs rapidly become unwieldy. For these reasons, DTDs are insufficient for most business and industrial-strength applications.

As an example, this is a DTD for requesting a price quote for a product by sending a product number (`productKey`):

```
<?XML version="1.0" encoding="UTF-8"?>
<!ELEMENT productKey (#PCDATA)>
```

This DTD is the response containing the price for the product:

```
<?XML version="1.0" encoding="UTF-8"?>
<!ELEMENT requestedPrice (#PCDATA)>
```

XML Schema

To address the inadequacies of DTDs, the XML Schema approach was adopted in May 2001 as a W3C Recommendation. XML Schema provides a more complex validation mechanism. An XML Schema defines elements, attributes, data types, inheritance rules and valid data ranges.

The following are examples for a request and response schema. The request schema sends a product key. The response schema sends back the price for the requested product key. Note the advantages that XML Schema have over DTDs.

This next XML Schema requests a price quote for a product. The type and the range are defined for the element. Here, the `productKey` is of type `xsd:string`, which is a defined type:

```
<?XML version="1.0" encoding="UTF-8"?>
<xsd:schema>
<xsd:element name="productKey" type="xsd:string" minOccurs="0"
➥maxOccurs="1"/>
</xsd:schema>
```

This XML Schema is the response containing the product price. Here, `requestedPrice` is of the type `requestedPriceType`, which is user defined:

```
<?XML version="1.0" encoding="UTF-8"?>
<xsd:element name="requestedPrice" type="requestedPriceType" minOccurs="0"
➥maxOccurs="1"/>
</xsd:schema>
```

This next XML Schema shows that the length of the element `GlobalBusinessIdentifier` is 12:

```
<xsd:element name="GlobalBusinessIdentifier" type="Length12Type"
➥minOccurs="0"/>
```

This XML Schema shows that the `GlobalSupplyChainCode` is a string and has the fixed value `INFORMATION TECHNOLOGY`:

```
<xsd:element name="GlobalSupplyChainCode" type="xsd:string" fixed=
➥"INFORMATION TECHNOLOGY" minOccurs="0"/>
```

DTDs are in wide use today, and it will take some time before they are replaced with the more robust XML Schema. You can learn more about XML Schemas at http://www.w3.org/XML/Schema.

XML Namespace

An XML document consists of a tree of elements. Elements are made up of the element type name and attributes. Both of these are needed to determine how to process the element. In XML 1.0 without namespaces, element type names and attribute names are unstructured strings. This is problematic in a distributed environment such as the web. One XML document might use `part` elements to describe parts of phones; another might use `part` elements to describe parts of computer. An XML application has no way of knowing how to process a part element unless it has some additional information external to the document.

With the XML namespaces recommendation, element type names and attributes names can be qualified with a universal resource identifier (URI). Thus, a document that describes parts of phones can use `part` qualified by one URI, and a document that describes parts of a computer can use `part` qualified by another URI:

```
<phones:part XMLns:phones="http://www.phones.com/XML"/>←URI
<computer:part XMLns:computer="http://www.computer.com/XML"/>
```

The role of the URI in a universal name is purely to allow applications to recognize the name. Avoidance of tag collision and reuse are two other benefits. Namespaces can be used to ensure that two elements that share the same name but have different definitions can coexist without collisions. As for reuse, it simply allows you to define elements in such a way that you can leverage them later.

SOAP

SOAP version 1.2 is a W3C Recommendation. SOAP provides a simple and lightweight mechanism for exchanging structured and typed information between peers in a decentralized, distributed environment. All SOAP messages are encoded using XML. This protocol is independent of runtime environments, so it works well in a heterogeneous environment for data transfer.

SOAP does not itself define any application semantics, such as a programming model or implementation-specific semantics; it defines a simple mechanism for expressing application semantics by providing a modular packaging model and encoding mechanisms for encoding data within modules. This means that SOAP can be used in a variety of systems, ranging from messaging systems to RPC (see the sidebar "RPC-Style Web Services").

RPC-Style Web Services

RPC-style web services are synchronous. This means that when a client sends a request, it waits for a response before doing anything else. A remote procedure call (RPC)–style web service is implemented using a stateless session EJB or using simple Java classes. It appears as a remote object to the client application.

The interaction between a client and an RPC-style web service centers on a service-specific interface. When clients invoke the web service, they send parameter values to the web service, which executes the required methods and then sends the return values. Because of this back-and-forth conversation between the client and the web service, RPC-style web services are tightly coupled and resemble traditional distributed object paradigms, such as RMI or DCOM.

Message-Style Web Services

Message-style web services are asynchronous. A client that invokes the web service does not wait for a response before it can do something else. The response from the web service, if any, can appear hours or days later. A message-style web service can be implemented using a JMS Message Listener, such as a message-driven bean or even a simple Java class.

Message-style web services are loosely coupled and document-driven; they are not associated with a service-specific interface. When a client invokes a message-style web service, the client typically sends it an entire document, such as a purchase order, instead of a discrete set of parameters. The web service accepts the entire document, processes it, and might or might not return a result message. Because no tightly coupled request-response occurs between the client and the web service, message-style web services promote a looser coupling between a client and a server.

A client can either send or receive a document to or from a message-style web service; the client cannot do both using the same web service.

SOAP Message

A SOAP message is an XML document. A SOAP message consists of three parts: the envelope, encoding rules, and HTTP bindings. Although these parts are described together as part of SOAP, they are functionally independent of each other. In particular, the envelope and the encoding rules are defined in different namespaces, to promote simplicity through modularity:

- The envelope is the top element of the XML document representing the message. The SOAP envelope defines an overall framework for expressing what is in a message, who should deal with it, and whether it is optional or mandatory. It contains the tag `ENVELOPE` as the root element. The envelope contains an optional SOAP header and a mandatory SOAP body.
- The header is optional. It contains the meta information about the message, such as user authentication information—name and password. The standard does not specify the content of the header. Vendors and developers can choose their own header data. The `mustUnderstand` attribute is an optional attribute that shows which headers require processing; an error is generated if these headers cannot be processed. All header entries must be qualified in a namespace.
- The body contains the actual message content (for example, a RPC request, RPC response, or an error message in case of a failure). If the envelope contains a header, the body must not be the first element within the envelope. There is a great deal of freedom in defining the contents of a SOAP body. The SOAP body, in turn, may contain an optional SOAP `Fault` element.
- The `Fault` tag contains the error data. It must appear in the envelope's body. It may contain several subelements: fault code, text code identifying the fault; the fault string, a human-readable description of the fault; the fault actor, a component of the system responsible for generating the error; the example client or server; and the detail, a section giving further details. If a `Fault` element is present, it must appear as a child element of the `Body` element. A `Fault` element can appear only once in a SOAP message.

```
<SOAP-ENV:Envelope>
<SOAP-ENV:Body>
        <SOAP-ENV:Fault>
             <faultcode>Client.ERR_SOAP</ faultcode>
             <faultstring>
                     Fatal error:not valid SOAP message
             </ faultstring>
        </SOAP-ENV:Fault>
     </SOAP-ENV:Body>
</SOAP-ENV:Envelope>
```

As an example, if a `placeOrderWebservice` receives a duplicate purchase order number, it is rejected as a SOAP fault. For example, the fault code could have a value of `01`, the fault string a value of duplicate PO, the fault actor a value of server, and the detail a value of PO number.

SOAP Encoding Rules

The SOAP encoding rules define a way to sequence application-defined data types. It is the most complex part of the SOAP standard. It relies heavily on data types and XML Schema. SOAP defines three data types:

- Simple types are analogous to Java primitives. They are derived directly from the XML Schema standards: string, base64binary, byte, integer, decimal, Boolean, and date.
- Structs are analogous to Java classes with only fields and no methods. They are used the way XML is typically used to encode object data, and they can be formally defined as XML Schema complex types.
- Arrays are analogous to Java arrays. SOAP arrays are specified using a special `SOAP-ENC: Array` tag. Arrays can have both simple types and structs.

The following example shows the SOAP envelope and body encapsulating the XML. Here, a request `GetProductPrice` is being made by providing the `productKey`. This XML can be validated against the XML Schema explained in the previous section:

- Envelope → `<SOAP-ENV:Envelope`
  `XMLns:SOAP-ENV="http://schemas.XMLSOAP.org/SOAP/envelope/"`
  `SOAP-ENV:encodingStyle="http://schemas.XMLSOAP.org/SOAP/encoding/">`
- Body → `<SOAP-ENV:cBody>`

```
        <m:GetProductPrice XMLns:m="Some-URI">
             <productKey>D7456</productKey>
        </m:GetProductPrice>
    </SOAP-ENV:Body>
</SOAP-ENV:Envelope>
```

SOAP HTTP Bindings

HTTP is the most common protocol used for SOAP messaging. The SOAP HTTP bindings give a standard mechanism for sending SOAP messages over HTTP. This follows the request/response structure typical of RPC. The SOAP Request is bound to the HTTP Request using the `POST` method. The SOAP Response is bound to the HTTP Response with the response code `2xx`, which signifies a successful response. SOAP Responses with error information use the HTTP response code `500`. The SOAP message itself is carried in the body of the HTTP message.

A SOAP action is a piece of information in the message header in front of the SOAP message. It indicates the intent of the message and allows your web service to do some processing that is separate from the processing of the actual SOAP content. SOAP actions let the web service filter the message in some appropriate way before processing the message. Here are a few examples of how a SOAP action can be used:

- As a form of firewall filter to validate an operation of the SOAP message
- To filter out and reject the message based on certain conditions, and thus avoid the overhead of processing the rest of the SOAP message
- As a form of load balancing to limit the requests for large amounts of database data during certain times or if requests are heavy

The following example shows how a SOAP request message is sent over the wire using the HTTP `POST` method:

- HTTP POST→ `POST /PriceQuote HTTP/1.1`

```
Host: www.pricequoteserver.com
Content-Type: text/XML; charset="utf-8"
Content-Length: 474
```

- SOAPAction→`SOAPAction: "http://www.openuri.org"`

```
<SOAP-ENV:Envelope
   XMLns:SOAP-ENV="http://schemas.XMLSOAP.org/SOAP/envelope/"
  SOAP-ENV:encodingStyle="http://schemas.XMLSOAP.org/SOAP/encoding/">
   <SOAP-ENV:Body>
      <m:GetProductPrice XMLns:m="http://www.openuri.org">
           <productKey>D7456</productKey>
       </m:GetProductPrice>
   </SOAP-ENV:Body>
</SOAP-ENV:Envelope>
```

This next example is of a successful response with a `200` code:

- Successful
  2xx code→ `HTTP/1.1 200 OK`

```
Content-Type: text/XML; charset="utf-8"
Content-Length: 474

<SOAP-ENV:Envelope
  XMLns:SOAP-ENV="http://schemas.XMLSOAP.org/SOAP/envelope/"
  SOAP-ENV:encodingStyle="http://schemas.XMLSOAP.org/SOAP/encoding/"/>
   <SOAP-ENV:Body>
       <m:GetProductPriceResponse XMLns:m="http://www.openuri.org">
           <requestedPrice>1034.5</requestedPrice>
       </m:GetProductPriceResponse>
   </SOAP-ENV:Body>
</SOAP-ENV:Envelope>
```

SOAP with Attachments

A SOAP message package contains a primary SOAP 1.1 message. It may also contain additional entities that have formats other than XML. Such additional entities are often informally referred to as attachments. A SOAP message might need to be transmitted together with attachments of various sorts, ranging from facsimile images of legal documents to engineering drawings. Such data often is in some binary format. On the Internet, most images are transmitted using either GIF or JPEG data formats. For example, a product catalog that has images can be sent as an attachment.

A SOAP message package is constructed using the Multipart/Related media type. The primary SOAP 1.1 message must be carried in the root body part of the Multipart/Related structure. The type parameter of the `Multipart/Related` media header always equals the `Content-Type` header for the primary SOAP 1.1 message (as in `text/XML`).

Referenced MIME parts must contain either a `Content-ID` MIME header or a `Content-Location` MIME header. It is strongly recommended that the root part contain a `Content-ID` MIME header and that, in addition to the required parameters for the Multipart/Related media type, the `start` parameter always be present. This permits more robust error detection.

The MIME Multipart/Related encapsulation of a SOAP message is semantically equivalent to a SOAP protocol binding, in that the SOAP message itself is not aware that it is being encapsulated. That is, nothing in the primary SOAP message proper indicates that the SOAP message is encapsulated .The following example shows a SOAP 1.1 message for a product catalog web service with an attached product image (`D7456.jpg`):

```
MIME-Version: 1.0
Content-Type: Multipart/Related; boundary=MIME_boundary; type=text/XML;
        start="<D7456.XML@productimages.hp.com>"
Content-Description: This is the optional message description.
```

```
--MIME_boundary
Content-Type: text/XML; charset=UTF-8
Content-Transfer-Encoding: 8bit
Content-ID: < D7456.XML@productimages.hp.com >

<?XML version='1.0' ?>
<SOAP-ENV:Envelope
XMLns:SOAP-ENV="http://schemas.XMLSOAP.org/SOAP/envelope/">
<SOAP-ENV:Body>
..
<theProductImage href="cid:D7456.jpgproductimages,hp.com"/>
..
</SOAP-ENV:Body>
</SOAP-ENV:Envelope>

--MIME_boundary
Content-Type: image/tiff
Content-Transfer-Encoding: binary
Content-ID: < D7456.jpg@productimages,hp.com >

...binary JPG image...
--MIME_boundary--
```

WSDL

The Web Services Description Language (WSDL) 1.1 is a W3C Note. WSDL enables applications to communicate with each other in an automated way. SOAP specifies the communication between a service requester and a service provider, and WSDL describes the network services offered by the provider (an endpoint). WSDL also be used as a recipe to generate the proper SOAP messages to access these services.

A WSDL document includes five elements in the definition of network services: `types`, `messages`, and `portType`, which are abstract definitions; and `binding` and `service`, which are concrete definitions. In WSDL, abstract definitions are separated from the concrete network deployment or data format bindings. This allows the reuse of abstract definitions:

- `types` give a precise description of the data types used in services. This is defined in the `<WSDL:types>` tag using XML Schema.

```
<?XML version="1.0"?>
<definitions name="PriceQuote"
     targetNamespace="http://example.com/pricequote.wsdl"
          XMLns:tns="http://example.com/pricequote.wsdl"
          XMLns:xsd1="http://example.com/pricequote.xsd"
         XMLns:SOAP="http://schemas.XMLSOAP.org/wsdl/SOAP/"
        XMLns="http://schemas.XMLSOAP.org/wsdl/">
</definitions>
```

In the following example, the `types` tag shows that `productKey` is a string and `price` is a float:

```
<types>
   <schema targetNamespace="http://example.com/pricequote.xsd"
          XMLns="http://www.w3.org/2000/10/XMLSchema">
       <element name="ProductPriceRequest">
          <complexType>
              <all>
                  <element name="productKey " type="string"/>
              </all>
          </complexType>
       </element>
       <element name="ProductPrice">
          <complexType>
              <all>
                  <element name="price" type="float"/>
              </all>
          </complexType>
       </element>
   </schema>
</types>
```

- `messages` are abstract descriptions of the data being exchanged. They define the structure of RPC method calls and responses. This is defined in the `<WSDL:messages>` tag. The following example shows in and out messages—`GetProductPriceInput` and `GetProductPriceOutput`:

```
<message name="GetProductPriceInput">
    <part name="body" element="xsd1:ProductPriceRequest"/>
</message>

<message name="GetProductPriceOutput">
    <part name="body" element="xsd1:ProductPrice"/>
</message>
```

- portType defines an abstract service. A portType must be mapped to a concrete application. It groups related messages, the request-response pairs. This is defined in the <WSDL:portType> tag. A portType is an abstract collection of operations. The messages are defined within operations. Four types of operations exist: one-way, in which the endpoint receives a message; request/response, in which the endpoint receives a message and sends a correlated message; solicit/response, in which the endpoint sends a message and receives a correlated message; and notification, in which the endpoint receives a correlated message. A port is defined by associating a network address with a reusable binding, and a collection of ports defines a service. In the following example, the portType defines the operation that is GetProductPrice:

```
<portType name="PriceQuotePortType">
    <operation name="GetProductPrice">
        <input message="tns:GetProductPriceInput"/>
        <output message="tns:GetProductPriceOutput"/>
    </operation>
</portType>
```

- binding maps a portType to a message protocol such as SOAP or HTTP. This is defined in the <WSDL:binding> tag. SOAP bindings can be RPC style or document style. The most typical use is RPC style, in which standard encoding is used. You use the document style for transmitting XML documents, with no encoding or in literal form. In the following example, the binding shows that the web services are document/literal: The style is document and the use is literal:

```
<binding name="PriceQuoteSOAPBinding" type="tns:PriceQuotePortType">
    <SOAP:binding style="document"
    ➥transport="http://schemas.XMLSOAP.org/SOAP/http"/>
    <operation name="GetProductPrice">
        <SOAP:operation SOAPAction="http://example.com/GetProductPrice"/>
        <input>
            <SOAP:body use="literal"/>
        </input>
        <output>
            <SOAP:body use="literal"/>
        </output>
    </operation>
</binding>
```

- service lists the address of the concrete implementations of the web service. The address information is specific to the binding type. There is a great deal of flexibility in the service definition. Multiple services might be implementing the same abstract port types, such as load balancing. A single service might have ports that support many abstract port types. `<WSDL:port>` specifies the name of the concrete port and the binding used by the port. `<SOAP:address>` describes the protocol-specific address information. In the following example, the web service name is `ProductPriceService` and the URL to request this service is http://example.com/productPrice:

```
<service name="ProductPriceService">
    <documentation>My first service</documentation>
    <port name="productPricePort" binding="tns:PriceQuoteSOAPBinding">
       <SOAP:address location="http://example.com/productPrice "/>
    </port>
</service>
```

UDDI

Universal Description, Discovery, and Integration (UDDI) is a specification defined by UDDI.org. UDDI is a searchable directory of businesses and their web services. It is a key building block that enables enterprises to quickly and dynamically discover and invoke web services both internally and externally. The specification defines a SOAP-based programming protocol based on HTTP for registering and discovering web services. UDDI acts like a service broker, enabling service requesters to find a suitable service provider. Its design is analogous to a phone book. It contains support for Yellow Pages, White Pages, and Green Pages:

- **Yellow Pages**—Businesses organized by industry, product category, or geographic region. Searches can be performed to locate a business.
- **White Pages**—Information about a service provider, including address, contact, and known identifiers.
- **Green Pages**—Technical information about web services that are exposed by a business, such as information on how to communicate with the web service.

The main application of UDDI is for registration of web services by businesses. Using the UDDI discovery services, businesses individually register information about the web services that they expose for use by other businesses. This information can be added to the UDDI business registry by using tools that make use of the programmatic service interfaces described in the UDDI API Specification. An XML file is used to describe a business entity and its web services. To get access to the UDDI services, use the UDDI directory, which exposes a set of APIs in the form of a SOAP-based web service. You can search and browse information found in a UDDI registry.

The UDDI XML Schema defines four core types of information that developers need to bind to web services:

- **Business entity**—You can provide information about the company publishing the web service. This information includes at least the name of the company, but it might also give information about discovery URLs, the services offered, and information on how to contact a person from that company (address, phone number, e-mail address, and so on). Each business entity may contain multiple business services.
- **Business service**—Using this data structure, you can describe a service in business terms. You must specify at least a name and one binding template for each business service. You can specify more than one binding templates.
- **Binding template**—A binding template structure describes how to get access to a service. These so-called access points represent URLs. One type of binding element is a tModel.
- **tModel (technical model)**—tModels are used to describe a technical specification, such as wire protocols, interchange formats, or sequencing rules. They can be used to determine compatibility between service providers and service requesters. Two mandatory attributes exist within a tModel:
    1. `tModelKey`—This attribute serves as a unique identifier among all the tModels. If you want to update an existing tModel, you have to provide the key of that model.
    2. `name`—This attribute is used to provide a meaningful name for the tModel.

WS-Security

Security is one of the biggest issues facing web services, and it has become a barrier for adoption of web services at many organizations. The OASIS standards body has a technical committee that looks at WS-Security specifically for web services. WS-Security has three different documents: SOAP Message Security, Username Token Profile, X.509 Token Profile.

The *SOAP Message Security* document describes enhancements to SOAP messaging to provide message integrity and single-message authentication. SOAP extensions can be used when building secure web services to implement message content integrity and confidentiality. This document specifies an abstract *message security model* in terms of security tokens combined with digital signatures to protect and authenticate SOAP messages. Message integrity is provided by XML Signature in conjunction with security tokens to ensure that modifications to messages are detected. The integrity mechanisms are designed to support multiple signatures, potentially by multiple SOAP roles, and to be extensible to support additional signature formats.

Message confidentiality leverages XML encryption in conjunction with security tokens to keep portions of a SOAP message confidential. The encryption mechanisms are designed to support additional encryption processes and operations by multiple SOAP roles.

We talk about WS-Security in detail in Chapter 11, "Security of Web Services," and show how WebLogic implements the WS-Security specifications.

Summary

Looking at the history of technology developments for distributed applications, we realize that web services are one of the most important developments of recent times. Web services have evolved through the work of many leading technology firms and have since been refined and standardized through the work of standards organizations and consortiums such as the W3C, OASIS, and the WS-I.

The components of the web services stack are XML, SOAP, WSDL, and UDDI. XML is a markup language designed to describe data using tags in a DTD or XML Schema. By using XML namespaces, you can reuse tags across different applications, as well as avoid tag collision. SOAP provides a simple messaging mechanism for exchanging structured and typed information between peers in a distributed environment. WSDL describes the services offered by a provider, enabling a requestor to access these services through an exchange of the proper SOAP messages. UDDI is a searchable directory of businesses and their published web services. WS-Security addresses how to deal with security challenges in developing and deploying web services.

In the next chapter, we look at the J2EE development platform for applications and the support it offers for the development of web services.

2
Essentials of J2EE

If you are new to the J2EE applications development platform, this chapter is a good place to start. Here, you will learn the J2EE architecture and become acquainted with important terms and concepts that are relevant in the context of web services. Specifically, we look at the J2EE architecture, the J2EE services and APIs, and how to assemble a J2EE application. We then look at the support for web services in the J2EE 1.4 specifications. That said, a full discussion of J2EE is beyond the scope of this book. You can find additional sources of information at the end of this chapter.

Overview of J2EE

The Java 2 Platform, Enterprise Edition (J2EE) is a component-based platform for the design, development, assembly, and deployment of enterprise applications. The J2EE platform offers the following capabilities:

- Multitiered distributed application model
- Capability to reuse components
- Integrated XML-based data interchange
- Unified security model
- Flexible transaction control

Many vendors offer application servers built with J2EE. Solutions built with J2EE components are platform independent and are not tied to the products and application programming interfaces (APIs) of any one vendor. This gives you the advantage of choosing the products and components that best meet your business and technological requirements.

Here is a quick historical note about the developments of J2EE. In the mid-1990s, engineers at Sun Microsystems developed several Enterprise APIs using Java that provided enterprise-level services for server-side deployments. These services included naming and lookup services, transaction services, database connectivity, and the Enterprise JavaBeans (EJB) 1.0 API. The first EJB-based application servers were built using these services and highlighted many problems with the Enterprise APIs. Each of the Enterprise APIs was related, yet each was being developed independently. Sun was not communicating the typical purpose of the Enterprise APIs together as a suite, and the specifications themselves were not very intertwined. Also, each of the Enterprise APIs was evolving separately and had new versions coming out all the time. This made it somewhat difficult to program using EJB because EJB depends on those Enterprise APIs. What versions of each API should be used? This was unspecified, which led to nonportable code between application server vendors.

Realizing the problems with Enterprise APIs, Sun Microsystems took a major leap forward by issuing the J2EE platform. This platform bundled the Java Enterprise APIs in a complete development platform for enterprise-class server-side deployments in Java. J2EE version 1.4 is the latest version of the platform. It has Java APIs that let you write your web services entirely in the Java programming language.

The J2EE Architecture

Normally, thin-client multitiered applications are hard to write because they involve many lines of intricate code to handle transaction and state management, multithreading, resource pooling, and other complex low-level details. The component-based and platform-independent J2EE architecture makes J2EE applications easy to write because business logic is organized into reusable components.

The J2EE application model divides enterprise applications into three fundamental parts: components, containers, and connectors (see Figure 2.1). Components are the key focus of application developers. The containers and connectors are typically implemented by system vendors to conceal complexity and promote portability.

Containers intercede between clients and components, providing services transparently to both, including transaction support and resource pooling. Container mediation allows many component behaviors to be specified at deployment time instead of in program code.

Connectors sit beneath the J2EE platform, defining a portable service API to plug into existing enterprise vendor offerings. Connectors promote flexibility by enabling a variety of implementations of specific services.

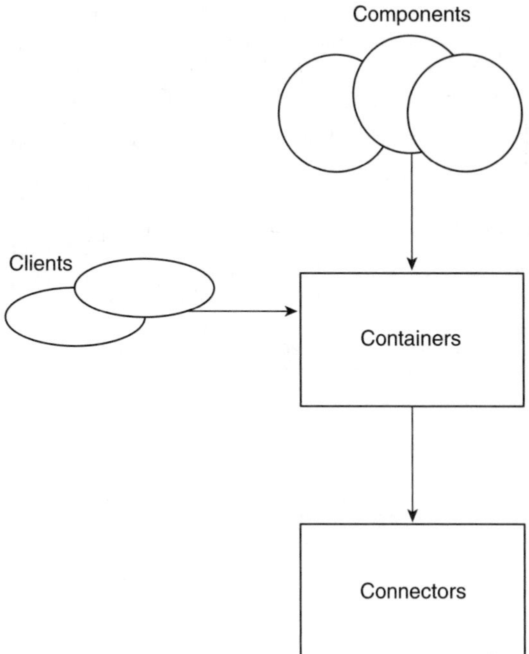

Figure 2.1 Components, containers, and connectors

J2EE Components

The J2EE platform uses a multitiered distributed application model. The tiers are the various information systems—client, web, business, and database—that interact with each other.

- Client-tier components are end user–oriented applications and run on the client machine.
- Web-tier components extend the traditional HTTP web server through Java Servlets and Java Server Pages.
- Business-tier components provide the business logic and run on the J2EE server.
- Enterprise information system (EIS)–tier software contains back-end database components and runs on the database server.

Using the J2EE approach, you divide an application into J2EE components, one for each tier (see Figure 2.2). A component is a self-contained functional software unit that is assembled into a J2EE application with its related classes and files. J2EE components communicate with other J2EE components.

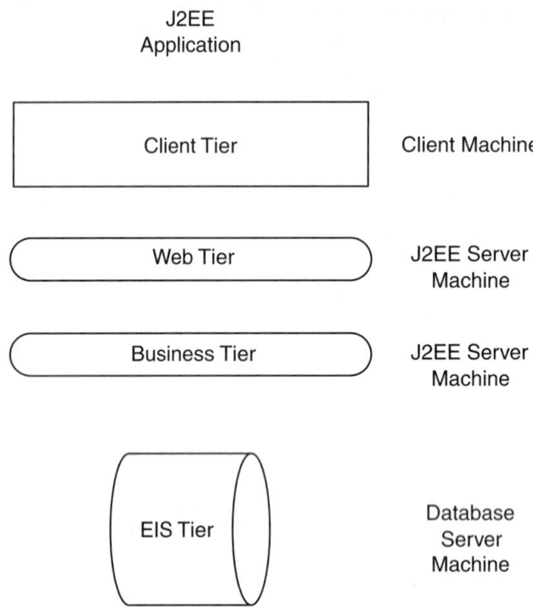

Figure 2.2 A multitiered J2EE application divided into tiers

Although a J2EE application can consist of the three or four tiers, J2EE multitiered applications are generally considered to be three-tiered applications because they are distributed over three different locations: client machines, the J2EE server machine, and the database or legacy machines at the back end. Three-tiered applications that run in this way extend the standard two-tiered client and server model by placing a multithreaded application server between the client application and back-end storage. Table 2.1 gives more details of three-tier applications.

Table 2.1 J2EE Components

Components	**Where They Run**	**Examples**
Client tier	On the client machine	Application client, web client, or applet
Web tier	On the web server	Java Servlet or Java Server Pages (JSP) components
Business tier	On the application server	Enterprise JavaBeans (EJB) components, simply called enterprise beans

We look at each tier in further detail shortly.

Client-Tier Components

A J2EE client can be a web client or an application client.

A J2EE application client runs on a client machine and provides a way for users to handle tasks that require a richer user interface than can be provided by a markup language such as HTML. It typically has a graphical user interface (GUI) created from Swing or Abstract Window Toolkit (AWT) APIs, but a command-line interface is certainly possible. (See Figure 2.3.)

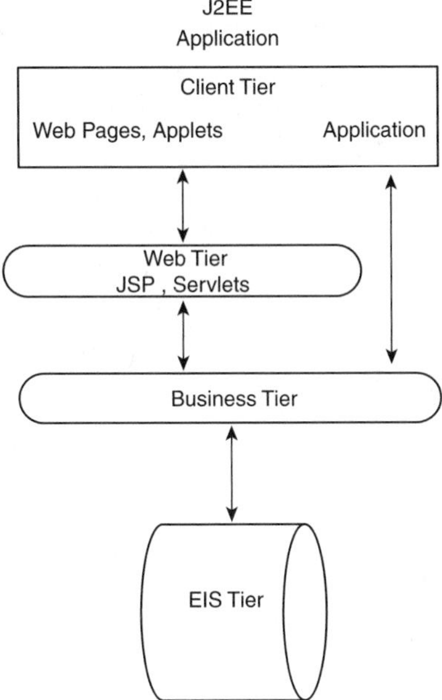

Figure 2.3 Client-tier components

Application clients interact directly with enterprise beans running in the business tier. However, if application requirements warrant it, a J2EE application client can open an HTTP connection to establish communication with a servlet running in the web tier.

A web client consists of two parts: dynamic web pages containing various types of markup language, such as HTML and XML, which are generated by web components running in the web tier, and a web browser, which renders the pages received from the server. Dynamic web pages build the content during runtime.

Web clients are used in many e-commerce types of applications today, and consumers use them on a daily basis. A web client is sometimes called a thin client. It enables fast response to the consumer. Thin clients usually do not do things such as query databases, execute complex business rules, or connect to legacy applications. When you use a thin client, heavyweight operations such as these are offloaded to enterprise beans in the business tier executing on the J2EE server. This way, they can leverage the security, speed, services, and reliability of J2EE server-side technologies.

A web page received from the web tier can include an embedded applet. An applet is a small client application written in the Java programming language that executes in the Java Virtual Machine installed in the web browser. However, client systems likely need the Java plug-in and possibly a security policy file for the applet to successfully execute in the web browser.

Web-Tier Components

J2EE web components are used for creating a web client component. They can be either servlets or JSP pages (see Figure 2.4).

Web components enable cleaner and more modular application design because they provide a way to separate application programming from web page design.

Servlets are Java programming language classes that dynamically process requests and construct responses. Java Servlet technology lets you define HTTP-specific servlet classes. Servlets separate the presentation from the business logic. A servlet class extends the capabilities of servers that host applications accessed by way of a request-response programming model. Although servlets can respond to any type of request, they are commonly used to extend the applications hosted by web servers.

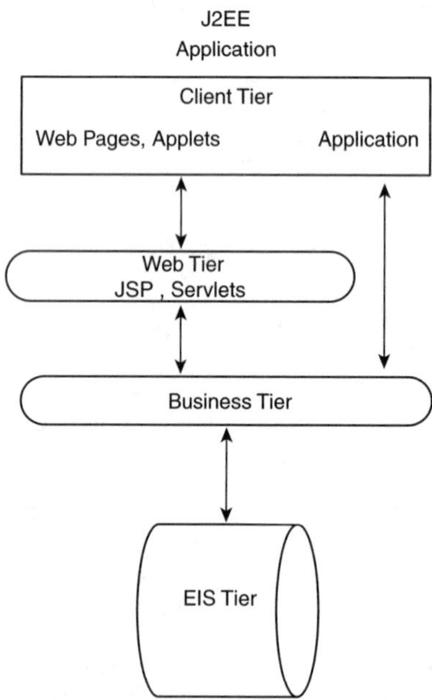

Figure 2.4 Web-tier components

Java Server Pages (JSPs) are text-based documents that execute as servlets but allow a more natural approach to creating static content. JSP lets you put snippets of servlet code directly into a text-based document. A JSP page is a text-based document that contains two types of text: static template data, which can be expressed in any text-based format, such as HTML, WML, or XML, and JSP elements, which determine how the page constructs dynamic content. JSP is just a cleaner way of doing servlets because your HTML and JavaScript are in an HTML document instead of coded in a Java class like many servlets do. It's also an easier way to separate presentation logic from business logic. Custom tags (XML tags) let you add programming logic to what is essentially still just an HTML document.

Static HTML pages, applets, and server-side utility classes are bundled with web components during application assembly but are not considered web components by the J2EE specification.

Business-Tier Components

The programming code that solves or meets the needs of a particular business domain, such as banking, retail, or finance, is the enterprise beans running in the business tier. Figure 2.5 shows how an enterprise bean receives data from client programs, processes it, and sends it to the enterprise information system tier for storage.

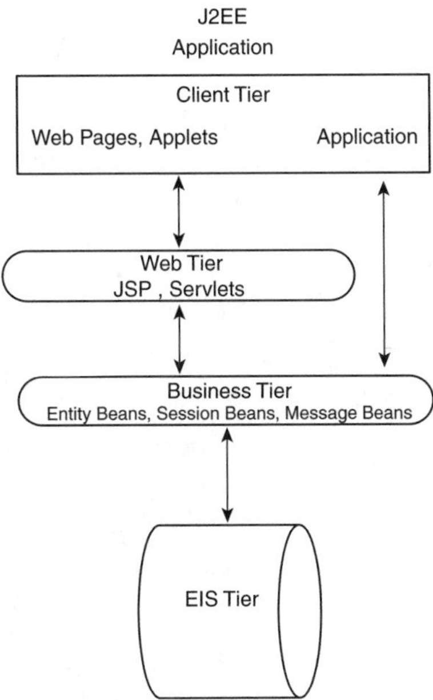

Figure 2.5 Business-tier components

An enterprise bean also retrieves data from storage, processes it, and sends it back to the client program. J2EE application components might need access to enterprise information systems for database connectivity.

An enterprise bean is a body of code with fields and methods to implement modules of business logic. You can think of an enterprise bean as a building block that can be used alone or with other enterprise beans to execute business logic on the J2EE server. Enterprise beans often interact with databases.

Three kinds of enterprise beans exist: session beans, entity beans, and message-driven beans. Usually, you use session beans and entity beans in tandem. Entity beans come in two flavors, differentiated by the party responsible for persisting the data to and from the database:

- Container-managed persistence (CMP) entity beans delegate the responsibility for persisting data to the container that's managing the bean.
- Bean-managed persistence (BMP) entity beans delegate that responsibility to the bean itself and, hence, to the programmer.

One of the benefits of entity beans, particularly CMP entity beans, is that you do not have to write any SQL code or use the JDBC API directly to perform database access operations; the EJB container (described later in this chapter) handles this for you. However, if you override the default container-managed persistence for any reason, you need to use the JDBC API. We talk about JDBC in the "J2EE Services and APIs" section. Message-driven beans offer a simple way to build EJB components that asynchronously respond to messages from clients and other beans.

The J2EE 1.4 application server includes an implementation of the EJB 2.1 specifications. The new features for EJB 2.1 allow stateless session beans to implement web service endpoints. In earlier versions, an extra servlet layer was needed to achieve the same functionality. Web service clients cannot access stateful session beans, entity beans, and message beans. Provided that it uses the correct protocols (SOAP, HTTP, WSDL), any web service client can access a stateless session bean through a servlet, whether or not the client is written in the Java programming language. (See Table 2.2.)

Table 2.2 Entity Beans

	Session Beans	**Entity Beans**	**Message-Driven Beans**
Persistence	Short lived; created and exist during session	Persistent	Same as session bean
Interface	Exposed interface and are callable	Exposed interface and are callable	Are not callable
Messaging	Synchronous	Synchronous	Asynchronous

Enterprise Information System Tier

The term *enterprise information system tier* refers to the enterprise information system software. It includes enterprise infrastructure systems such as enterprise resource planning (ERP), mainframe transaction processing, database systems, and other legacy information systems. J2EE application components might need access to enterprise information systems.

J2EE Containers

You install J2EE application components in J2EE containers. Each J2EE application component has a corresponding J2EE container. A container manages the execution of the component installed in it. See Figure 2.6.

You install application client components in an application client container. The application clients and the application client container run on the client. You install applets in an applet container. This container consists of a web browser and a Java plug-in running on the client together. You install JSP page and servlet components in a web container. Web components and the web container run on the J2EE server. You install enterprise bean components in an EJB container. Enterprise beans and the EJB container run on the J2EE server.

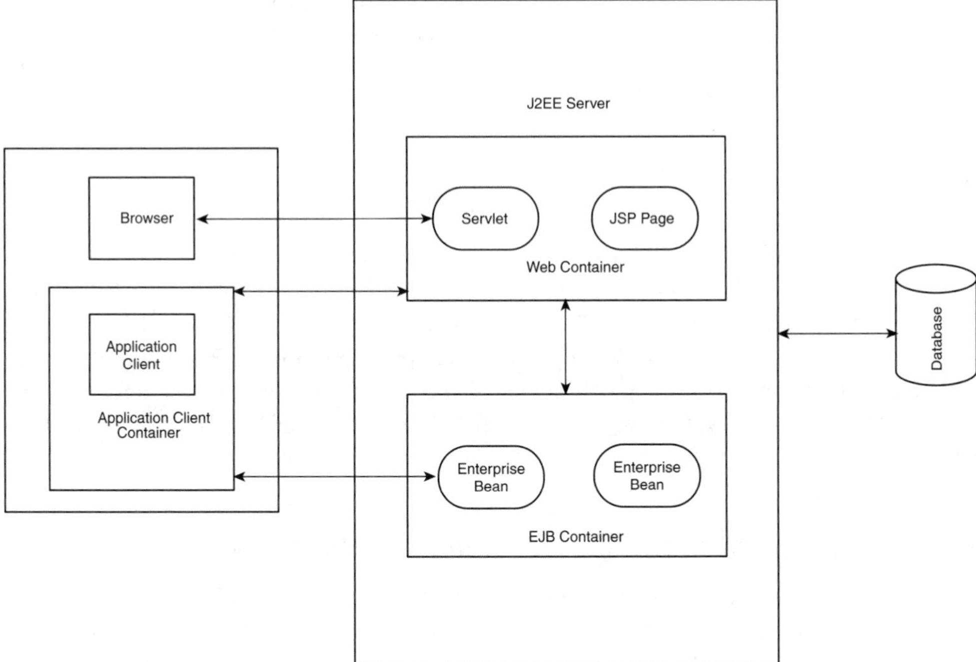

Figure 2.6 J2EE server and containers

The J2EE server provides underlying services in the form of a container for every component type. Because you do not have to develop these services yourself, you are free to concentrate on solving the business problem at hand.

Container Services

Containers are the interface between a component and the low-level platform-specific functionality that supports the component. Before a client, web, or business component can be executed, it must be assembled into a J2EE application and deployed into its container.

The assembly process involves specifying container settings for each component in the J2EE application and for the J2EE application itself. Container settings customize the underlying support provided by the J2EE server, which includes services such as security, transaction management, Java Naming and Directory Interface (JNDI) lookups, and remote connectivity. The fact that the J2EE architecture provides configurable services means that application components within the same J2EE application can behave differently based on where they are deployed.

The container also manages nonconfigurable services such as enterprise bean and servlet lifecycles, database connection resource pooling, data persistence, and access to the J2EE platform APIs. Although data persistence is a nonconfigurable service, the J2EE architecture lets you override container-managed persistence by including the appropriate code in your enterprise bean implementation when you want more control than the default container-managed persistence provides. You might use bean-managed persistence to implement your own finder (search) methods or to create a customized database cache.

J2EE Services and APIs

J2EE has a robust suite of middleware services that make life very easy for server-side application developers. The J2EE Software Development Kit (SDK) provides core APIs for writing J2EE components, core development tools, and the Java Virtual Machine (see Figure 2.7).

These J2EE services and APIs give you a unified application model across tiers with enterprise beans and a simplified response and request mechanism with JSP and servlets. The J2EE APIs enable systems and applications integration. We now explore in more detail the APIs in the J2EE SDK.

Java Authentication and Authorization Service (JAAS)

JAAS provides a way for a J2EE application to authenticate and authorize a specific user or group of users to run it. The J2EE security model lets you configure a web component or enterprise bean so that only authorized users access system resources. It implements a Java version of the standard Pluggable Authentication Module (PAM) framework and extends the access-control architecture of the J2EE Platform in a compatible fashion to support user-based authorization. The PAM library is a generalized API for authentication-related services that allows a system administrator to add new authentication methods simply by installing new PAM modules and to modify authentication policies by editing configuration files.

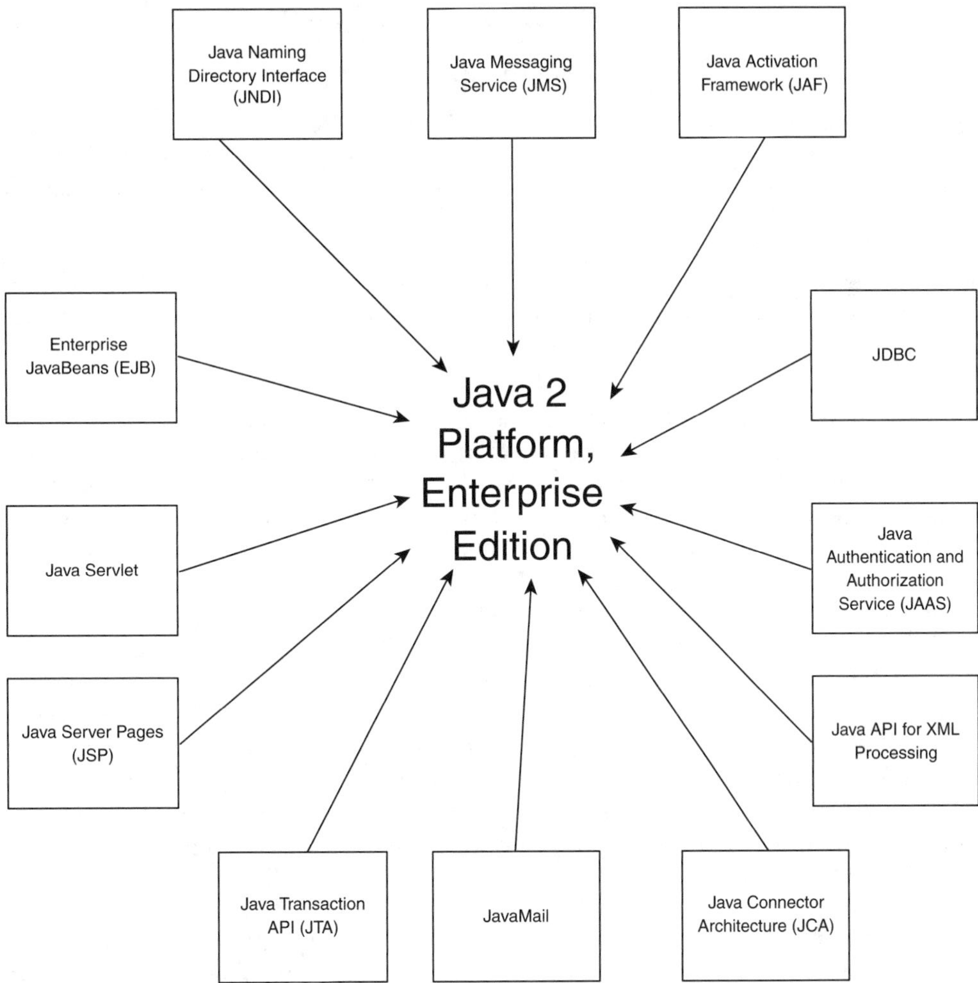

Figure 2.7 J2EE services and APIs

The latest release of the J2EE SDK, version 1.4, provides a means of enforcing access controls based on where code came from and who signed it. The need for such access controls derives from the distributed nature of J2EE. For instance, a remote applet can be downloaded over a public network and then run locally.

J2EE, however, lacks the means to enforce similar access controls based on who runs the code. To provide this type of access control, the J2EE security architecture requires additional support for authentication for determining who's actually running the code, as well as extensions to the existing authorization components to enforce new access controls based on who was authenticated. The JAAS framework augments the Java 2 platform with such support.

Java API for XML Processing (JAXP)

JAXP enables applications to parse and transform XML documents independent of a particular XML processing implementation. Programs and tools can generate XML documents that other programs and tools can read and handle. JAXP gives users a great deal of flexibility in how they use the APIs. For example, JAXP code can use various tools such as the Simple API for XML (SAX), the Document Object Model (DOM), the Streaming API for XML (StAX), and the XML Stylesheet Language for Transformations (XSLT) for processing an XML document. Implementers have flexibility as well. JAXP defines strict compatibility requirements, to ensure that all implementations deliver the standard functionality, but they also give developers a great deal of freedom to provide implementations tailored to specific uses.

The SAX protocol is an event-driven, serial-access mechanism for accessing XML documents. This is the protocol that you will want to use when programming servlets and network-oriented programs to transmit and receive XML documents; it's the fastest and least memory-intensive mechanism that is currently available for dealing with XML documents. There are a few drawbacks with using the SAX protocol. While parsing the document, you can't back up to an earlier part of the document or rearrange it any more than you can back up a serial data stream or rearrange characters that you have read from that stream. It is harder to visualize the XML document. The SAX protocol requires a lot more programming than DOM.

The DOM mechanism is a garden-variety tree structure, in which each node contains one of the components from an XML structure. The two most common types of nodes are *element nodes* and *text nodes*. Using DOM functions lets you create nodes, remove nodes, change their contents, and traverse the node hierarchy. If you are writing a user-oriented application that displays an XML document and possibly modifies, it you will want to use the DOM mechanism. However, even if you plan to use DOM exclusively, there are several important reasons for familiarizing yourself with the SAX model:

- **Same error handling**—When parsing a document for a DOM, the same kinds of exceptions are generated, so the error handling for JAXP SAX and DOM applications are identical.
- **Validation error handling**—By default, the specifications require that validation errors be ignored. If you want to throw an exception in the event of a validation error (and you will probably want to), you need to understand how the SAX error handling works.
- **Conversion of existing data**—In DOM, you can use a mechanism to convert an existing data set to XML. However, taking advantage of that mechanism requires an understanding of the SAX model.

DOM provides APIs that allow random access and manipulation of an in-memory XML document. However, this comes at a very high cost: performance. For very large documents, you might be required to read the entire document into memory before taking appropriate actions based on the data.

The StAX software offers a pull parser that gives client applications full control over the parsing process. A client application can decide at any time to discontinue the parsing process, and no tricks are required to stop the parser. This is ideal for screening purposes. StAX gives parsing control to the programmer. It allows an application developer to ask for the next event (pull the event) instead of handling the event in a callback. This gives a developer more procedural control over the processing of the XML document. The Streaming API also allows the programmer to stop processing the document, skip ahead to sections of the document, and get subsections of the document. The StAX specification is covered by JSR 173 and is being led by BEA.

To use SAX, a programmer writes handlers: objects that implement the various SAX handler APIs that receive callbacks during the processing of an XML document. The main benefits of this style of XML document processing are that it is efficient, flexible, and relatively low level. Programmers must keep track of the current state of the document in the code each time they process an XML document, so they cannot iteratively process it. Another drawback to SAX is that the entire document needs to be parsed at one time.

We talk in detail about StAX and its comparison to SAX and DOM in Chapter 8, "Using Controls, Bindings, and Parsers." In Chapter 12, "Enhancing Performance of Web Services," we compare the performance of these parsers.

XSLT defines mechanisms for addressing XML data and for specifying transformations on the data, to convert it into other forms. JAXP includes an interpreting implementation of XSLT called Xalan.

J2EE Connector Architecture (J2CA)

As your business moves toward e-business, integration with existing enterprise information systems (EIS) becomes important. You will need to integrate your existing EIS with new web-based applications. This will extend the reach of your EIS to support business-to-business (B2B) transactions. Most EIS vendors and application server vendors use nonstandard vendor-specific architectures to provide connectivity between application servers and EIS. Before J2CA was defined, no specification for J2EE addressed the problem of providing a standard architecture for integrating heterogeneous EIS.

Now J2EE tool vendors and system integrators use J2 CA to create resource adapters for access to EIS from any J2EE product. A resource adapter is a software component that allows J2EE application components to access and interact with the underlying EIS. Because a resource adapter is specific to its EIS, there is typically a different resource adapter for each type of database or EIS. JCo is one example of a connector from a J2EE product to the SAP application. Based on J2 CA, it allows for remote function calls (RFC) to be made to SAP Business APIs (BAPIs) from the J2EE product.

Java Database Connectivity (JDBC) API

The JDBC API lets you invoke SQL commands from Java programming language methods. You use the JDBC API in an enterprise bean when you override the default container-managed persistence (CMP) or have a session bean access the database. With CMP, the container handles database access operations, and your enterprise bean implementation contains no JDBC code or SQL commands. You can also use the JDBC API from a servlet or JSP page to access the database directly without going through an enterprise bean.

The JDBC API has two parts: an application-level interface used by the application components to access a database, and a service provider interface to attach a JDBC driver to the J2EE platform. JDBC is database-agnostic, so you can switch databases with little or no changes in your code.

Java Message Service (JMS)

Enterprise messaging is now recognized as an essential tool for building enterprise applications. Enterprise messaging provides a reliable, flexible service for the asynchronous exchange of critical business data and events throughout an enterprise. The JMS API adds to this a common API and provider framework that enables the development of portable, message-based applications in the Java programming language. JMS is a messaging standard that allows J2EE application components to create, send, receive, and read messages. It enables distributed communication that is loosely coupled, reliable, and asynchronous. Sun Microsystems developed the JMS API, working in close cooperation with leading enterprise messaging vendors.

The JMS API is an integral part of the J2EE 1.4 platform. The JMS API works with the message-driven bean, which enables the asynchronous consumption of messages. You can use messaging with components using J2EE APIs for developing applications. You can easily add new behavior to a J2EE application with existing business events by adding a new message-driven bean to operate on specific business events. The J2EE EJB container architecture, moreover, enhances the JMS API in two ways:

1. Allows concurrent consumption of messages
2. Provides support for distributed transactions so that database updates, message processing, and connections to EIS using the J2EE CA can all participate in the same transaction context

JMS API version 1.1 is incorporated into the J2EE 1.4 specification. Version 1.1 provides common interfaces that enable you to use the JMS API in a way that is not specific to either the point-to-point or the publish-subscribe domain. Also, a foreign JMS provider can be integrated with the application server using J2EE CA. You access the JMS provider through a resource adapter.

Java Transaction API (JTA)

JTA provides a standard interface for demarcating transactions. The J2EE architecture provides a default autocommit to handle transaction commits and rollbacks. With an autocommit, any other application viewing data will see the updated data after each database read or write operation. However, if your application performs two separate database-access operations that depend on each other, you will want to use the JTA API to demarcate where the entire transaction begins, rolls back, and commits.

Java Naming and Directory Interface (JNDI)

JNDI provides naming and directory functionality. It provides applications with methods for performing standard directory operations, such as associating attributes with objects and searching for objects using their attributes. Using JNDI, a J2EE application can store and retrieve any type of named Java object.

Because JNDI is independent of any specific implementations, applications can use JNDI to access multiple naming and directory services, including existing naming and directory services such as LDAP, NDS, DNS, and NIS. This allows J2EE applications to coexist with legacy applications and systems.

JavaMail API

J2EE applications can use the JavaMail API to send e-mail notifications. The JavaMail API has two parts: an application-level interface used by the application components to send mail, and a service provider interface. The J2EE platform includes JavaMail with a service provider that allows application components to send Internet mail.

JavaMail uses the JavaBeans Activation Framework (JAF). The JavaMail API supports Multipurpose Internet Mail Extension (MIME) types, which is a standard Internet mail extension mechanism. MIME enables e-mail systems to support mail content other than plain text, such as XML documents or images. It provides standard services to determine the type of an arbitrary piece of data, encapsulate access to it, discover the operations available on it, and create the appropriate JavaBeans component to perform those operations.

Security and J2EE

By using J2EE, application programming developers do not need to understand the specific implementation details of application security. The J2EE insulation is done in a way that applications are portable, therefore allowing them to be deployed in diverse security environments.

Security for components of web services is provided by their containers. A container provides declarative and programmatic security.

To access an application from an external source, the application can use *declarative security* to express an application's security structure, including security roles, access control, and authentication requirements. *Programmatic security* is embedded in an application and is used to make security decisions.

J2EE applications consist of components that can contain both protected and unprotected resources. *Authentication* and *authorization* provide controlled access to protected resources. Authentication is a process that verifies the identity of a user, device, or other entity in a computer system, to allow access to resources in a system. When the authentication is done, authorization determines what this entity can access.

Authorization and authentication are not required for an entity to access unprotected resources.

Assembling a J2EE Application

After the components and containers are developed, they have to be put together to create a J2EE application. Then during runtime, the Java application classes must be loaded in proper sequence.

Packaging

J2EE components are packaged separately and bundled into a J2EE application for deployment. A J2EE application is composed of one or more enterprise bean, web, or application client component modules.

A J2EE application and each of its modules have their own deployment descriptor. A deployment descriptor is an XML document with a `.xml` extension that describes a component's deployment settings. An enterprise bean module deployment descriptor, for example, declares transaction attributes and security authorizations for an enterprise bean. Because the deployment descriptor information is declarative, it can be changed without modifying the bean source code.

A J2EE application with all of its modules is delivered in an Enterprise Archive (EAR) file. An EAR file is a standard Java Archive (JAR) file with a `.ear` extension.:

- A JAR file is used to package a EJB.
- A WAR file is used to package a web component.

Using modules and EAR files makes it possible to assemble a number of different J2EE applications using some of the same components.

Classloader

A classloader allows a Java application to load new classes at runtime. Within a Java application, there is a hierarchy of classloaders. The bootstrap classloader is the first in a sequence. It's responsible for loading all of the JVM's internal classes, as well as the classes in the java.* package. The extensions classloader, a child of the bootstrap classloader, loads all the JARs in the JDK's ext directory. The system classloader is a child of the extensions classloader (often called the classpath classloader); it loads all the classes in the classpath environment variable or those specified using the `-classpath` command-line switch. Any classloaders created by an application (such as WLS) are children of the system classloader.

To load a class, the classloader first checks to see if the class is already resident in memory. If the class isn't loaded, the classloader asks its parent to load the class. This leads to requests being propagated up the classloader hierarchy to the bootstrap classloader. The bootstrap classloader then tries to load the file; if it can't, the request goes back down the hierarchy until a classloader is found that can load the class (see Figure 2.8). If no classloader can load the class, a `ClassNotFoundException` is thrown.

In WebLogic servers, the application classloader loads all the classes explicitly associated with the EAR file and the classes in the EJB JAR files. The WebLogic server creates new classloaders for the web applications. In turn, these are responsible for loading any classes and libraries associated with the web application. If a class is uniquely defined in a WAR file, it isn't accessible to other classloaders.

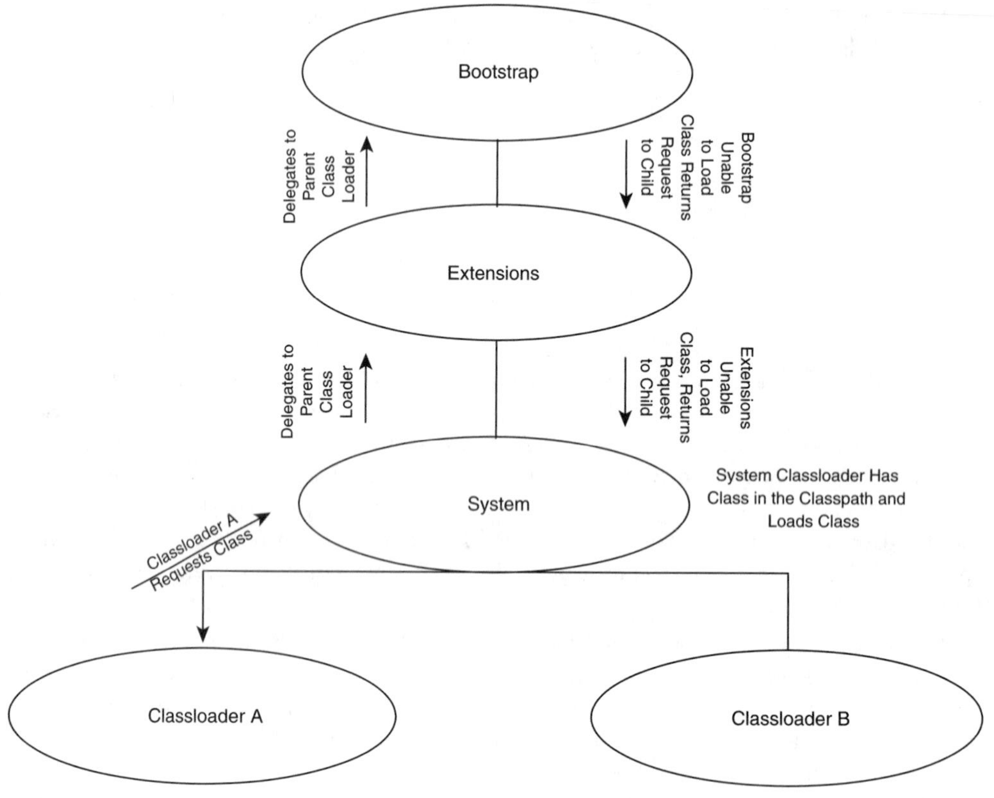

Figure 2.8 Classloader sequence

Web Services Support in J2EE

All of the J2EE platform elements, such as the J2EE architecture, components, containers, and APIs, are described through documents called J2EE Specifications. J2EE Specifications updates are done through the Java Specification Request (JSR) process. The JSR is submitted through the Java Community Process (JCP, http://www.jcp.org/en/home/index), which includes forming an expert group from companies and individuals. A draft specification is submitted for public review and eventual vote. JSR 151 produced the J2EE 1.4 Specification, which includes many individual specifications:

JSR109: Web services

JSR153: EJB 2.1

JSR 154: Java Servlets 2.4

JSR 152: Java Server Pages (JSP) 2.0

JSR 112: Java Standard Tag Library (JSTL) 1.0

JSR 914: Java Messaging Service (JMS) 1.1

JSR 112: J2EE Connector Architecture (JCA) 1.5

JSR 77: J2EE management

JSR 88: J2EE deployment

Thus, several JSRs are used to build a J2EE Specification. In the following section, we talk in more detail about the J2EE 1.4 Specification.

J2EE 1.4 Specification

Included in J2EE 1.4, the latest J2EE Specification, are Java APIs for XML that let you write your web services entirely in the Java programming language. Perhaps the most important feature of the Java APIs for XML is that they all support industry standards, thus ensuring interoperability. The various network interoperability standards groups, such as W3C and OASIS, have been defining standard ways of doing things so that businesses that follow these standards can make their data and applications work together. The J2EE 1.4 will fully support guidelines being promoted by WS-I for interoperability. Complying with the WS-I 1.0 basic profile specification has been made an absolute requirement for all J2EE 1.4 products released by vendors.

In the following sections, we give a high-level review of the Java APIs for XML: JAX-RPC, JAXR, JAXB, JAXM, and SAAJ.

Java API for XML-Based RPC (JAX-RPC)

JAX-RPC provides the core API for developing and deploying web services on the Java platform. JAX-RPC offers several benefits for developers:

- Ease of development of web services endpoints and clients. Using JAX-RPC, you can develop a web service endpoint using either the Servlet or EJB component model. JAX-RPC enables JAX-RPC clients to invoke web services developed across heterogeneous platforms and then enables these web service endpoints to be invoked by heterogeneous clients. A JAX-RPC client can use stubs-based, dynamic proxy, or dynamic invocation interface (DII) programming models to invoke a heterogeneous web service endpoint.
- Support for XML, SOAP, and WSDL standards. This makes JAX-RPC a key technology for web services–based integration.
- Standard API developed under the Java Community Process.
- Support for WSDL tools. JAX-RPC provides support for WSDL-to-Java and Java-to-WSDL mapping functionality. This can help create the clients to invoke the web service from the WSDL. On the other side, if you created a web service in Java using JAX-RPC, the WSDL can be generated from the Java code.

- RPC programming model with support for attachments. You can use the RPC programming model to develop web service clients and endpoints without being exposed to the complexity of the underlying runtime mechanisms (for example, SOAP protocol-level mechanisms such as marshalling and unmarshalling). A JAX-RPC runtime system abstracts these runtime mechanisms for the web services programming model. JAX-RPC provides support for document-based messaging. Using JAX-RPC, any MIME-encoded content can be carried as part of a SOAP message with attachments. This enables the exchange of XML documents, images, and other MIME types across web services. This simplifies SOAP-based web services development.
- Support for the SOAP message-processing model and extensions through the SOAP message handler functionality. JAX-RPC requires SOAP over HTTP for interoperability. You can build SOAP-specific extensions to support security, logging, and any other facility based on the SOAP messaging.
- Secure web services. JAX-RPC supports HTTP-level session management and SSL-based security mechanisms. You can develop secure web services.
- You can develop SOAP-based interoperable and portable web services using JAX-RPC. You can also develop and deploy JAX-RPC web services on J2EE 1.4 containers and Servlet container.

A client uses the WSDL document (that describes the service) to import the service. A WSDL-to-Java mapping tool generates a client-side stub class for the service and its ports. You can also use the dynamic proxy mechanism instead of a generated stub class to invoke a remote method on a service endpoint.

The JAX-RPC programming model describes how a client looks up and invokes a remote method on a service endpoint.

The following code snippet shows an illustrative example of how a client invokes a remote method on the imported product catalog service. This example uses a generated stub class:

```
javax.xml.rpc.Service service =
➥ServiceFactory.newInstance().createService(...);
com.example.ProductCatalogProvider pcp = (com.example.ProductCatalogProvider)
➥service.getPort(ProductCatalogProvider.class);
float productPrice = pcp.getLastproductPrice(.D7456.);
```

Java API for XML Messaging (JAXM)

The JAXM package enables applications to send and receive document-oriented XML messages using a pure Java API. JAXM implements SOAP 1.1 with Attachments messaging. JAXM messages are exchanged between a client, the sender, and a final service, the recipient. JAXM message exchanges support for both asynchronous and synchronous communication. JAXM is not part of the J2EE 1.4 specifications.

The JAXM API consists of two main packages: javax.xml.soap and javax.xml.messaging. The former provides basic SOAP support, and the latter provides messaging support built on top of SOAP. The package javax.xml.soap provides APIs for creating and manipulating SOAP messages, with or without attachments. In addition to these, the package provides the `SOAPConnectionFactory` and `SOAPConnection` classes. JAXM clients should use these classes to participate in point-to-point, synchronous interactions with a web service.

On the other side, the package javax.xml.messaging consists of APIs for writing JAXM services that can participate in both point-to-point (`ReqRespListener`) interactions and one-way (`OnewayListener`)-style messaging

JAXM Versus JAX RPC

JAXM and JAX-RPC are both based on SOAP 1.1 with attachments and can be represented in the following manner. Table 2.3 shows the comparison between JAXM and JAX RPC.

Table 2.3 JAXM Versus JAX RPC

JAX-RPC	JAXM
Procedure call	Document-driven
Synchronous	Asynchronous and synchronous
Marshalling and unmarshalling of parameters between Java objects and XML	

Java API for XML Registries (JAXR)

JAXR provides a standard way to access business registries such as UDDI and share information with a unified JAXR information model, which describes content and metadata within XML registries. With JAXR, you can use a single, easy-to-use abstraction API to access a variety of XML registries. An XML registry is an enabling infrastructure for building, deploying, and discovering web services. Currently, there are a variety of specifications for XML registries, including, pre-eminently, the ebXML (electronic business XML) Registry and Repository standard, which is being developed by OASIS and U.N./CEFACT, and the UDDI specification version 2.0, which is being developed by a vendor consortium.

JAXR provides metadata capabilities for classification and association, as well as rich query capabilities. As an abstraction-based API, JAXR gives you the capability to write registry client programs that are portable across different target registries. This is consistent with the Java philosophy of write once, run anywhere.

The registry can be queried using various `find` methods defined by the `BusinessQueryManager` interface that supports business-oriented searches. Clients can use three essential find `methods` to search registries according to JAXR:

- `findOrganizations` returns all organizations in the registry that match the search criteria specified. Here is an example of a message signature to `findOrganizations`:

```
public BulkResponse findORganizations(
....java.util.Collection find.Qualifiers,
....java.util.Collection namePatterns,
....java.util.Collection classifications,
....java.util.Collection specifications,
....java.util.Collection externalIdentifiers,
....java.util.Collection externalLinks) throws JAXRException
```

- `findServices` returns the services provided by the organization.
- `findServiceBindings` returns service bindings supported by the organization containing technical information about accessing the specific interface of the service.

Java Architecture for XML Binding (JAXB)

Java Architecture for XML Binding (JAXB) provides an API and tools that automate the mapping between XML documents and Java objects. This helps developers by providing an efficient and standard way to map XML to Java code. JAXB makes XML easy to use by compiling an XML Schema into one or more Java technology classes. The combination of the schema-derived classes and the binding framework enables developers to perform the following operations on an XML document:

- Unmarshal XML content into a Java representation
- Access, update, and validate the Java representation against a schema constraint
- Marshal the Java representation of the XML content into XML content

When using JAXB, developers do not have to be experts in XML. JAXB is an alternative to using XML parsing. XML Beans, which can be used to do XML binding in BEA WebLogic, has functionality that sits on top of JAXB API. We talk more about XML Beans in Chapter 10, "Managing Business Processes."

SOAP with Attachments API for Java (SAAJ)

SOAP with Attachments API for Java (SAAJ) is an offshoot of JAXM. The SAAJ API provides low-level support to the JAX-RPC by enabling JAX-RPC to create and send SOAP messages, with or without attachments, and also to consume SOAP messages. The various interfaces and classes that comprise SAAJ are bundled in the java.xml.soap package and are available directly to J2EE application developers if the higher-level JAX-RPC APIs aren't sufficient.

Following are the main features of SAAJ that you can tap into as needed by importing the java.xml.soap package into your application and using the corresponding interfaces and classes that it contains. Specifically, you can use SAAJ for the tasks listed here:

- Creating a SOAP message; populating it with content, such as a message header, body data, and attachments; and sending the message to a specific endpoint using a point-to-point connection. Attachments can include any type of content, including XML fragments, which SAAJ can create; or documents such as XML files, images, proprietary documents, and so forth.
- Adding parts to a SOAP message, and accessing or modifying parts of a message. SAAJ can also create SOAP fault information, and access or modify fault information.
- Extracting SOAP message contents and sending SOAP request-response messages.

Summary

The J2EE platform is composed of a suite of standard services, application programming interfaces (APIs), protocols, and data formats that together provide the functionality necessary for developing, deploying, and maintaining distributed multitiered applications. The tiers are the various information systems—client, web, and business tiers—that interact with each other. The client tier can be built with application clients, web clients, or applets. The web tier can be built with Java Servlet technology or JSP. The business tier is made of EJBs.

The J2EE Platform provides standards services for a reliable security model (JAAS), simplified interoperability (JCA), easy database connectivity (JDBC), reliable distributed messaging (JMS), a variety of naming and directory services (JNDI), mail (JavaMail API), transaction integrity (JTA), XML parsing (JAXP), and web services.

The J2EE 1.4 platform services provide complete support for standard XML-based web services. In particular, the Java APIs for XML built into J2EE 1.4 (JAX-RPC, JAXR, JAXB, JAXM, and SAAJ) enable developers to create enterprise applications that can produce and consume XML web services based on SOAP/HTTP and WSDL. J2EE also provides support for standard XML registries, such as the popular UDDI and ebXML registries, enabling a J2EE application to publish the various web services so that other applications can find and use them.

A thorough understanding of J2EE is required before developing the web services. From experience, we have learned that building the business logic (EJBs) is a large part of creating a complete web service. With the inclusion of web services support in the J2EE specification, a clear grasp of J2EE will help, for a faster and robust implementation.

So far, in the first two chapters, you have learned about the web services specifications and J2EE application-development platform specifications for web services. The next chapter focuses on the basics of the BEA WebLogic application server, a vendor tool for developing web services applications on the J2EE Platform using BEA WebLogic.

References

- JDBC 3.0: http://java.sun.com/products/jdbc/
- JNDI 1.2: http://java.sun.com/products/jndi
- JAXP 1.1: http://java.sun.com/j2se/1.4/docs/guide/xml/jaxp/index.html
- JAAS 1.0: http://java.sun.com/products/jaas
- Enterprise Java Beans (EJB) 2.1: http://java.sun.com/products/ejb
- Servlet 2.4: http://java.sun.com/products/servlet
- Java Server Pages (JSP) 2.0: http://java.sun.com/products/jsp
- Java Message Service (JMS) 1.1: http://java.sun.com/products/jms
- Java Transaction API (JTA) 1.0: http://java.sun.com/products/jta
- Java Mail 1.3: http://java.sun.com/products/javamail
- Java Beans Activation Framework (JAF) 1.0: http://java.sun.com/beans/Glasgow/jaf.html
- Java API for XML Parsing (JAXP) 1.2: http://java.sun.com/xml
- J2EE Connector Architecture 1.5: http://java.sun.com/j2ee/connector
- Web services for J2EE 1.1: http://jcp.org/jsr/detail/109.jsp, http://jcp.org/jsr/detail/151.jsp, http://www-3.ibm.com/software/solutions/webservices/pdf/websvcs-0_3-pd.pdf
- Java API for XML-Based RPC (JAX-RPC) 1.0: http://java.sun.com/xml/jaxrpc
- SOAP with Attachments API for Java (SAAJ) 1.1: http://java.sun.com/xml/saaj
- Java API for XML Registries (JAXR) 1.0: http://java.sun.com/xml/jaxr

3

Introduction to WebLogic Platform

In the first two chapters, we talked about web services and J2EE. To develop and deploy web services with J2EE, you need an application server platform. The platform should support J2EE components and the web services specifications of XML, SOAP, and WSDL. The BEAs WebLogic Platform is a widely used application platform suite. BEA WebLogic Platform combines a rich web services framework with a service-oriented development model to enable Service Oriented Architecture (SOA). This chapter describes how the BEAs WebLogic Platform supports the building and deployment of J2EE components and web services.

Building Blocks of the WebLogic Platform

The BEA WebLogic Platform is a unified, simplified, and extensible platform for developing, deploying, and managing enterprise applications. It is a standards-based platform supporting both the J2EE and web services specifications, and it offers a rich framework for integrating with third-party application packages. These two characteristics make it easy to rapidly build, deploy, manage, and integrate enterprise-class web services using the BEA WebLogic Platform. The following three main advantages of using the WebLogic Platform are as follows:

- A single runtime framework for your entire software platform. This framework abstracts complexity from the underlying software, simplifying the development of complex tasks and enhancing developer productivity for all aspects of the project.
- A unified and simplified management architecture, empowering developers and administrators to realize business objectives in a environment that is populated by distributed, heterogeneous technologies and platforms.
- A highly reliable, available, scalable, extensible standards-based and high-performing foundation—WebLogic Server—enabling you to incorporate flexibility, extensibility, and choice into your IT solutions.

In summary, the WebLogic Platform makes it easier and faster to design, develop, test, and deploy web services compared to the competitor's products. The platform consists of five major building blocks: WebLogic Server, WebLogic Workshop, WebLogic JRockit, WebLogic Integration, and WebLogic Portal. Figure 3.1 shows the WebLogic Platform with the building blocks.

We look at all of these modules in detail in this chapter.

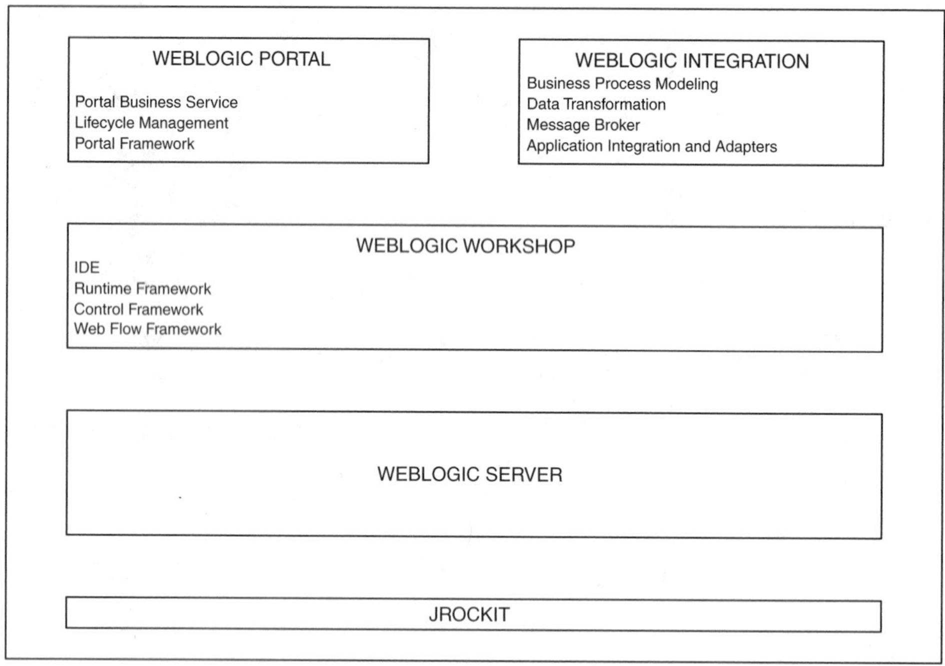

Figure 3.1 Building blocks of the WebLogic Platform

WebLogic Server

WebLogic Server is the platform foundation, providing the core services to ensure a reliable, available, scalable, and high-performing execution environment for your platform. Figure 3.2 shows the core services provided in WebLogic Server:

- **J2EE container**—WebLogic Server implements J2EE version 1.3 technologies. It supports JSP, Java Servlet, EJB, JCA, JDBC, and JNDI.
- **High availability**—WebLogic Server allows you to group WebLogic Server instances into clusters. This enables high scalability, availability through failover, and load balancing to the web application platform.

- **Connectivity**—WebLogic Server enables an integrated, robust, and pluggable messaging architecture for integrating diverse applications in a loosely coupled, asynchronous manner. The services included are JMS and web services, which make software application resources available to distributed clients over a network in a standardized way.
- **Presentation services**—WebLogic Server provides services for managing interactions with desktop clients, web browsers, wireless devices, and other client types. In addition to being an application server, WebLogic Server includes a fully functional, high-performance web server for responding to browser HTTP requests for web content.
- **Operations administration and management**—WebLogic Server offers a framework for managing the application development, deployment, and runtime environments. It includes a web-based Administration Console through which you can perform all the core management tasks. You can start, stop, monitor, and configure system resources; monitor and evaluate system performance; balance load on servers or connection pools; detect and correct problems; and deploy web applications, EJBs, or other resources.
- **Security service**—WebLogic Server provides a single security framework for all applications deployed on the platform. It enables you to control and track access to system resources. The security features supported include access control, cryptography-based privacy, user authentication, policies and roles, Secure Sockets Layer (SSL), and digital certificates.

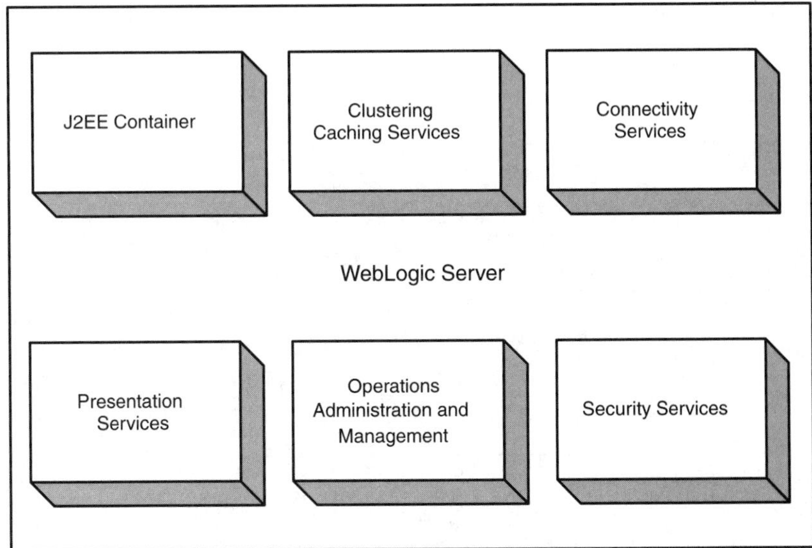

Figure 3.2 Core services in WebLogic Server

WebLogic Workshop

WebLogic Workshop is a unified, integrated development framework that makes it easy for developers to build powerful enterprise-class J2EE applications. It has a rich, intuitive user interface that makes it easy to build, test, and deploy J2EE applications. It uses a unified architecture that makes it possible for developers to learn only a single programming model for building and integrating the full suite of WebLogic Platform applications, including web services, web applications, portals, and workflows.

WebLogic Workshop makes it easy to create and deploy web services that adhere to web service standards: SOAP and WSDL. It provides XML Beans and XQuery mapping capabilities, which make it easy for you to access, process, and format XML-based data and documents. Its architecture supports key web services needs such as asynchrony, loose coupling, business-level documents, enhanced security, and reliable messaging.

EJBs make a good foundation for layering web services. WebLogic Workshop provides a built-in control, called the EJB control, that makes it easy to use an existing, deployed EJB from your application. WebLogic Workshop also enables you to create new EJBs.

The WebLogic Workshop architecture includes two basic components, depicted in Figure 3.3.

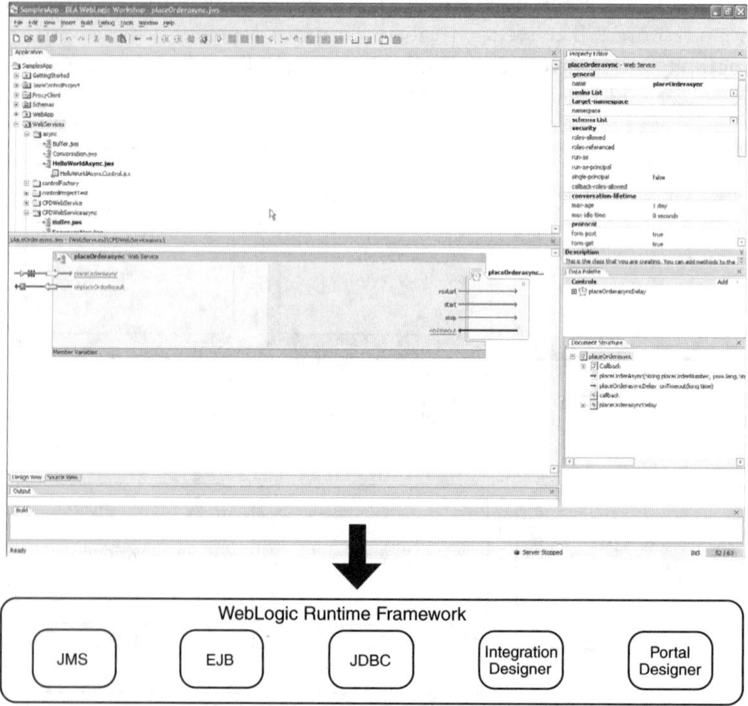

Figure 3.3 WebLogic Workshop architecture

Workshop Integrated Development Environment

The Workshop Integrated Development Environment (IDE) is a visual development environment that you can use for building, testing, and debugging all WebLogic Platform applications. Using the Workshop IDE, you can encapsulate business logic and produce Java code. You can easily connect to enterprise resources such as databases and EJBs, and specify runtime application behavior without writing a lot of code. The Workshop IDE provides two views of your application: source view and design view (see Figure 3.4). The source code that you create in the Workshop IDE is easily accessible and is always synchronized with the design view, thereby enabling you to work with visual designers in the design view or with powerful code-editing features in the source view. In addition, the Workshop IDE includes several features, such as multilanguage debugging and source code control integration.

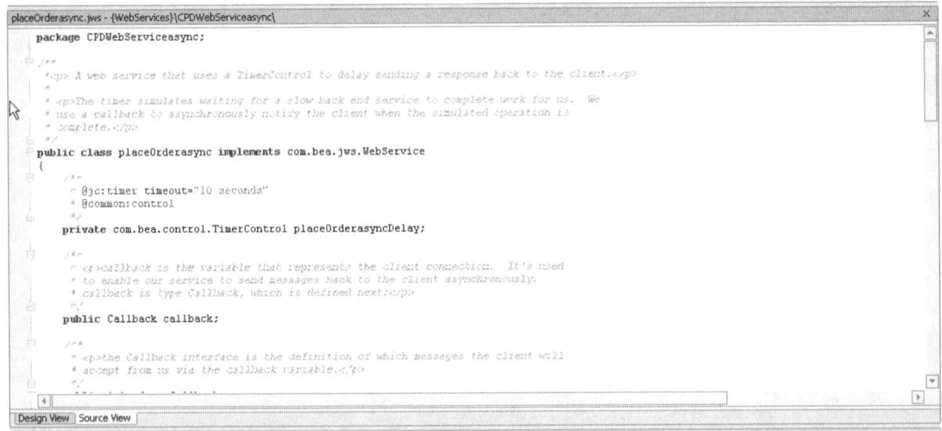

Figure 3.4 Workshop IDE views

Java controls provide a powerful means of abstracting code so that the developer can focus on handling events and calling methods instead of writing complex object-oriented J2EE infrastructure code. A Java control is a component that has a predefined set of methods, events, and properties that encapsulate business logic (see Figure 3.5). For example, a control can perform a database query, receive a JMS message, or execute business logic and return a result to the Workshop application. Controls are reusable and shorten delivery because they can be leveraged from templates.

A *designer* is a collection of Workshop IDE controls and graphical tools, and the Workshop runtime framework infrastructure that enables a developer to build, test, and deploy a specific category of applications in WebLogic Workshop (see Figure 3.6). For example, most WebLogic applications have at least some integration requirements, and integration projects typically involve the use of process workflow and data transformation. To enable the easy development of such applications, WebLogic Workshop provides designers that enable you to create workflows and data transformations.

Figure 3.5 Workshop IDE Java controls

Figure 3.6 Workshop IDE designer

Workshop Runtime Framework

The Workshop runtime framework is a standard J2EE application that runs on top of WebLogic Server. The files created by WebLogic Workshop are `.jws` files, which is a standard Java source file with special javadoc-style annotations prefixed with `@jws:`. The runtime framework interprets the annotated code created in the Workshop IDE and automatically implements the appropriate J2EE components, such as EJB, JSP, and JDBC connections, required to build the specified application.

The runtime framework automates all the low-level plumbing details involved with the J2EE application infrastructure. By using this framework, as a developer, you can focus on application logic instead of infrastructure code, component configuration, and deployment details.

WebLogic Control Framework

WebLogic Workshop provides a Control Framework that enables a developer to easily connect to and use databases, back-end systems such as ERP or legacy systems, custom or vendor applications, and web services with Java controls. These controls wrap up other controls and add business logic to create reusable, composite components that expose business operations. In addition, you can automatically generate web service wrappers to a control without any coding. Java controls hide the J2EE complexity in connecting to any of these. They are used in WebLogic Workshop applications from either the web services or web applications, or Portal or Integration applications. You can create your own custom Java controls or use Java controls from BEA partners. Actional Corp., Blue Titan Software Inc., Salesforce.com Inc., E.piphany Inc., Documentum Inc., and FileNet Corp. are among the 50 ISVs that have built controls and extensions that enable developers to link functionality from their products with Java applications being developed in WebLogic Workshop. The WebLogic Control Framework is part of JSR 181.

BEA WebLogic Workshop ships with the following controls:

- **EJB control**—EJBs can be invoked through local control objects. The EJB control contains the code for JNDI lookups, object creation, and casting steps.
- **Database control**—Enterprise databases are integrated via JDBC through the Database control. SQL maps allow the developer to indicate how their Java parameters should be replaced in the query.
- **Web service control**—These controls are interoperable with any .NET or Java web service. The control can import web services from their WSDL files, which can be local or dynamically picked up from UDDI server.
- **JMS control**—This control enables publishing and subscribing to queues. The client listens on this JMS control via callbacks defined in the client.
- **J2EE CA Adapter control**—Enterprise applications and legacy systems can be accessed via J2EE CA adapters, which are controlled by J2EE CA controls. J2EE CA interfaces are integrated with Java through XML maps.
- **Timer control**—Scheduling for responses and requests can be managed through this control, which triggers the web service periodically to enable it to send status updates to the client, poll a data source, or establish a timeout on a request to a resource.

Web Flow Framework

The Web Flow Framework is a visual representation of presentation scenarios. The Web Flow Framework is based on Struts, an open-source framework for building web applications based on the Model-View-Controller (MVC) design paradigm. WebLogic Workshop facilitates the Web Flow Framework, which extend the Struts framework to provide a simplified development model with numerous additional features.

The Web Flow Framework provides a dramatically simpler single-file programming model that enables developers to focus on the code, see a visual representation of the overall application flow, and easily navigate among pages, actions, and form beans. The framework also provides a number of wizards to automate common tasks and visualize tag libraries. This abstracts the developers from learning the complexities of the low-level Struts architecture.

WebLogic Workshop's out-of-the-box data-binding tags and wizards make it extremely easy to create rich, dynamic pages within the framework. These features enable the binding of UI components to numerous data contexts; the data may come from any source—a database, a web service, an EJB, a custom application, and so on.

It also leverages WebLogic Workshop's streamlined iterative development model with automated deployment. Integrated testing shows you the results of your code change immediately. Finally, the framework facilitates automated state management, nested Java Page Flows, and powerful exception handling.

Project Beehive

BEA has launched Project Beehive, is an open-source project. Beehive includes support for JSR 175 metadata annotations, which we talked about in the "Workshop Runtime Framework" section. It also covers the Java controls framework for creating and consuming J2EE components. It has a simplified web services programming framework and the Struts-based Java Page Flow technology for creating web-based user interfaces and applications

XML Beans, which is already part of Apache open source, can be used with Beehive to deliver XML to Java binding.

WebLogic JRockit

WebLogic JRockit is a high-performance Java Virtual Machine (JVM) optimized for server-side performance and scalability. WebLogic JRockit is supported by all WebLogic Platform components and is fully integrated into the WebLogic Platform package. Some of the benefits of using JRockit include increased performance and support for the 32-bit and 64-bit Intel architecture for both Windows and Linux environments.

WebLogic Integration

One of the essential requirements of enterprise applications is the capability to exchange business-critical information in real time and to link business processes. This integration of data and processes needs to take place between applications within the enterprise or with those of the business partners. WebLogic Integration (WLI) leverages WebLogic Server as the underlying deployment environment. WLI uses the Control Framework, which includes custom controls developed by more than 50 ISV partners and through J2EE CA adapters. WebLogic Integration builds on the J2EE CA specification in its application integration framework by providing a standards-based architecture for hosting J2EE CA-based adapters from legacy mainframe applications, such as CICS, to packaged applications, such as PeopleSoft, Siebel, and SAP.

WebLogic Integration, shown in Figure 3.7, is a complete solution for developing, deploying, and integrating applications and business processes from within and across the enterprise.

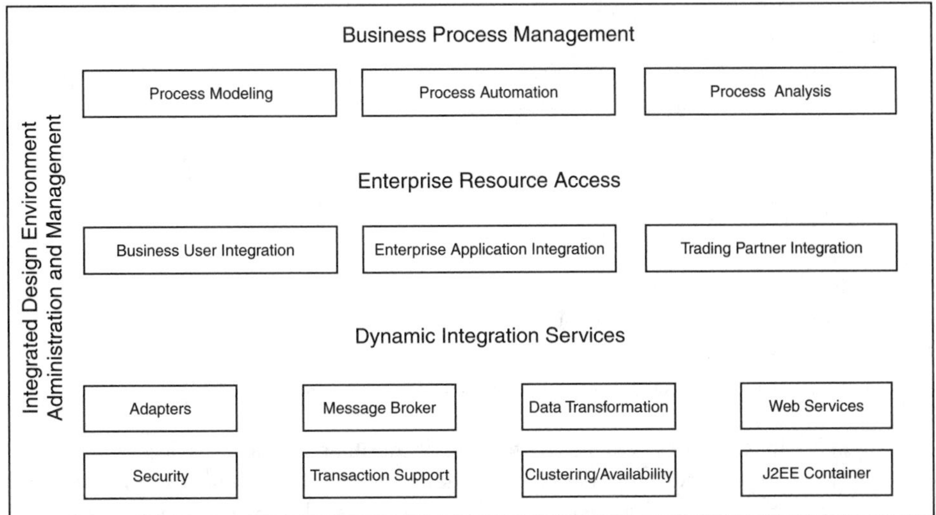

Figure 3.7 WebLogic Integration

WebLogic Integration is tightly integrated with WebLogic Workshop. It provides a simplified design and runtime environment that includes support for business process modeling, data transformation, messaging brokering, and application integration:

- **Business process modeling (BPM)**—An enterprise can be regarded as a set of business services orchestrated to model a business process. Using BPM, you can model, run, and maintain business processes that span multiple internal systems, cross-enterprise applications, external resources, and human decision makers.

The BPM component supports synchronous and asynchronous communications, and stateless and stateful processes.

- **Data transformation**—WebLogic Integration supplies components and tools to support the three main categories of data transformation: binary to XML, XML to XML, and XML to binary.
- **Message broker**—This allows applications to communicate in a loosely coupled, anonymous manner using a publish-and-subscribe communication mechanism. Publishers can publish messages, and subscribers, business processes, or other back-end resources can access these messages. Neither publishers nor subscribers need to be defined beforehand with respect to each other. This is loose coupling. At runtime, you can add new publishers and new subscribers.
- **Application integration and adapters**—The application integration functionality simplifies the integration of existing internal enterprise systems with each other and with new e-business applications. Applications can be linked using a set of J2EE CA-based adapters. Custom adapters can be added using an Adapter Development Kit. All of the adapters are exposed to the WebLogic Workshop IDE via the Application View control for configuring the adapter and defining the relevant high-level business operations and events. J2EE resources such as JMS, EJB, databases (JDBC), and JCA can be linked using a set of controls.

WebLogic Portal

WebLogic Portal is an enterprise portal platform that enables you to easily produce and manage customized portal environments. Using this platform, you can develop portals for accessing customer, partner, and employee information and applications. WebLogic Portal includes the following for the development and administration of portal applications:

- **Portal business services**—This is a core set of modular business services that support enterprise portal and application development. These services improve the developers' ability to build custom portals and the administrators' ability to tailor the portal user experience.
- **Lifecycle management**—WebLogic Portal offers functionality and tools tailored to specific users, including application developers, JSP developers, HTML and graphic designers, system administrators, portal administrators, and business analysts.
- **Unified Portal framework**—This framework is composed of several components that support the development of a flexible user interface to provide secure access to content, applications, and business processes. Portals for different departments in the same enterprise can be developed using this framework. This can be facilitated by incorporating runtime entitlement and personalization rules to make the

portal dynamic, thus presenting itself differently depending upon who has logged in, events fired, and the time or day. The framework enables you to develop reusable portal components such as personalization rules, content rules, user profiles, users, and portlets using WebLogic Workshop. From these components, you can create portals by combining components during deployment.

Support for Web Services

We have described all the modules of the WebLogic Platform. Of these modules, the two essential building blocks for web services are WebLogic Workshop for creating and running web services and WebLogic Server for deploying these web services. Now let us look at the explicit support provided by the WebLogic Platform for SOAP, WSDL, which creates web service clients and deploys web services.

Support for SOAP in WebLogic Server

WebLogic erver includes its own implementation of both the SOAP 1.1 and SOAP 1.1 with Attachments specifications. Along with support for the SOAP specifications, it comes with a fully integrated SOAP server to send and receive SOAP messages. You can use these SOAP implementations to create clients that invoke web services. WebLogic Server supports both the tightly coupled, synchronous, RPC-style web services, and the loosely coupled, asynchronous, message-style web services.

Support for WSDL in WebLogic Server

WebLogic Server supports the WSDL 1.1 implementation. Developers need the WSDL that describes the web service for clients that invoke a WebLogic web service. WebLogic Server automatically generates the WSDL of a deployed web service. You access the WSDL of a web service through a special URL. Workshop also enables you to build a control for service from a WSDL file.

Support for Creating Web Service Clients

WebLogic Server can automatically generate a thin Java client. The Java client JAR file includes all the classes needed to invoke a web service, such as the Java client API classes and interfaces, a parser to parse the SOAP requests and responses, and the Java interface to the EJB. Client applications that use this Java client JAR file do not need to include the full WebLogic Server JAR file on the client computer.

Building and Deploying Web Services

BEA WebLogic Workshop lets application developers rapidly create, test, and deploy enterprise-class web service applications. WebLogic Workshop offers the following specific capabilities for web services development and deployment:

- Integrated development framework for web services
- Visual representation of web services with two-way code editing
- Integrated web service test and debugging environment
- Automated application deployment on WebLogic Server
- Simplified access to J2EE APIs and resources with WebLogic Workshop Control Architecture (controls include access to EJBs, legacy applications, message queues, databases, and web services)
- Support for XML-to-Java and Java-to-XML mapping for loosely coupled application logic

The WebLogic web services runtime component is a set of servlets and the associated infrastructure needed to create a web service. One element of the runtime is a set of servlets that handle SOAP requests from a client. You do not need to write these servlets; they are automatically included in the WebLogic Server distribution. Another element of the runtime is an Ant task that generates and assembles all the components of a WebLogic web service.

Workshop generates 100 percent standard J2EE components, and ongoing standards and community initiatives are in progress to ensure that annotated code files (such as Java web services and Java Page Flows) are fully portable at the source level.

Summary

The BEAs WebLogic Platform is a unified, simplified, and extensible platform for developing, deploying, and managing enterprise applications. It offers five building blocks for creating these applications: WebLogic Server, WebLogic Workshop, WebLogic JRockit, WebLogic Integration, and WebLogic Portal.

WebLogic Server is the foundation, providing core services to ensure a reliable, available, scalable, secure, and highly performing execution environment. WebLogic Workshop is an integrated development environment. It includes a runtime framework to automate the low-level plumbing details of the application infrastructure, a Control Framework to work with Java controls, and a Web Flow Framework for visual representation of presentation scenarios. Its rich user interface makes it easy to create and deploy web services. WebLogic JRockit is a high-performance JVM optimized for server-side performance and scalability. WebLogic

Integration is a simplified design and runtime environment with support for business process modeling, data transformation, message brokering, and application integration. WebLogic Portal enables you to produce and manage customized portal environments.

BEA WebLogic Platform provides a set of "utilities" and runtime capabilities to build, expose, and access web services, shielding developers from needing additional expertise in XML, SOAP, and WSDL.

4

Benefiting from an SOA and Web Services

"Many of the off-the-shelf packages are monolithic and do not provide a service-oriented architecture of modular services which demand-side partners can pick and choose from. We face the challenge of achieving expediency of deployment and maintaining business agility."
—Mauricio Cori, IT Manager, eBusiness and Customer Operations IT, Hewlett-Packard Co.

With any new technology, there is always a lot of skepticism, especially from business managers. The claims made by vendors for new technologies don't always translate into business benefits. New technologies also mean large new investments and a long time until one can see business benefits.

A service-oriented architecture (SOA), and its implementation through web services, offers a different proposition. Unlike many other technologies, web services enable a pragmatic solution that requires minimal investment at the beginning and delivers business results quickly. It addresses the critical needs that businesses face—flexibility and collaboration—better than any other technology architectures.

In this chapter, we explore an SOA so that you understand its value proposition and how it can be implemented through web services. You will see how organizations have already seen the benefits of using an SOA and web services. We also describe a case study from a business unit at HP, which adopted an SOA and implemented it using web services.

Understanding the SOA

In its Web Service Glossary, the W3C defines an SOA as "a set of components which can be invoked, and whose interface descriptions can be published and discovered" (see Figure 4.1). This definition covers the primary attributes of an SOA; its semantics definition is as follows:

"A set" means a collection of services that are designed to work together and are based on common infrastructure and semantics.

"Of components" means that it is modular and implemented as components.

"Can be invoked" means that one can call the services.

"Whose interface descriptions" means that the interface can be described succinctly.

"Can be published and discovered" shows that the producer of the service be separated from the user of the service. The term *discovered* implies that they can be registered in a registry.

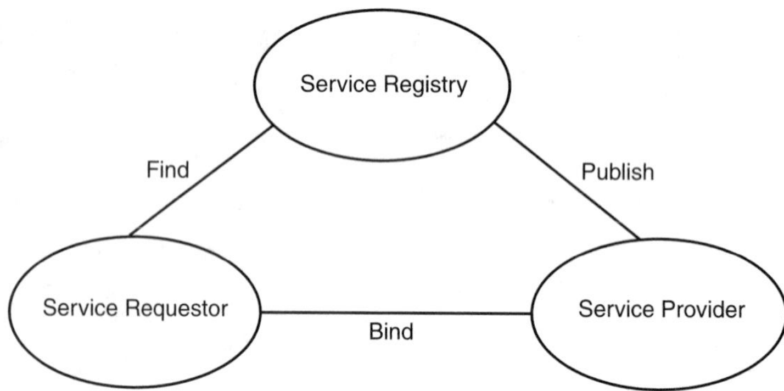

Figure 4.1 Service-oriented architecture

Service-oriented architectures are not a new thing. Before the evolution of DCOM or Object Request Brokers (ORBs), earlier SOA development was based on the CORBA interface definition language (IDL), the COM/DCOM Microsoft IDL, the Customer Information Control System (CICS) common area, and other specifications.

Architecture

An SOA enables the nonintrusive reuse of services in new runtime contexts. An SOA is more than any particular set of technologies, such as web services. Let us take a closer look at the main features of an SOA.

In SOA architecture, all functions are defined as services. This includes business functions such as creating and changing orders, the lower-level functions that these business functions might have, and system service functions. Each service has a service interface. The interface is the contract to identify the services and rules to access the service. All input data and response data and all exception conditions must be listed in the interface. Metadata must be provided in the interface to identify the purpose and function of the service.

All services are abstracted from the logic that achieves the results for the services. For example, if a service accesses an ERP system today and the ERP system is changed tomorrow, there is no effect on the service itself. The service interface must have sufficient information for a service to be identified (that is, found and understood) and used, without considering its internal design and content.

An SOA facilitates loose coupling by separating the producer of the service from the consumer of the service. In an SOA, a service is designed with loose coupling, which means that services are designed for no particular service consumer. The information carried by the service is agnostic to the purpose and technical or business objectives of the service consumer.

The interfaces are "invokable." Therefore, at an architectural level, it is irrelevant whether the services are local or remote. The interface is the key and is the focus of the calling application. It defines the required parameters and the nature of the result. Thus, it defines the nature of the service, not the technology used to implement it. It is the system's responsibility to effect and manage the invocation of the service, not that of the calling application. This allows two critical characteristics to be realized: 1) The services are truly independent, and 2) they can be managed.

The service contracts are designed to be coarsely grained where the interactions package several function calls and responses into fewer but larger messages. The service contracts correspond to the granularity of activities and subprocesses within end-to-end business processes.

Infrastructure

To have a running model of an SOA, the infrastructure is as important as the architecture. Several aspects of the infrastructure are important:

- Security from end to end and the capability to provide such critical services as message authentication, authorization, confidentiality, integrity, and nonrepudiation are critical expectations of the underlying infrastructure. These security policies need to be applied across a variety of services instead of being from point to point.
- Services deployed should be allowed to be redeployed. They should be capable of being moved around the network for performance, redundancy, availability, or other reasons.
- Use dynamic rerouting for control over the interaction between clients and services by routing client requests to different services depending on specified criteria (message content, security context, or external rules). This rerouting might require the message content to be transformed to a new format. It could also be based on data within the XML document itself. For example, messages can be examined for customer class; gold customers could be routed to a specific server to ensure the fastest response time.

- A services management infrastructure is needed to ensure performance, reliability, availability, operational management, and lifecycle management of new versions of the service. Agents are provisioned at intermediary nodes to enable message interception, inspection, filtering, and policy-driven processing at the most appropriate nodes. Operations staff should be able to monitor and manage the infrastructure, set and monitor SLA conditions, track message flow between clients and services, generate alerts, and handle exception conditions.
- A mapping/transformation is needed so that the middleware layer can transform diverse schema representations to a single data model.
- In business process management (BPM) technology, new business processes that orchestrate existing services can be created very rapidly. This enables the enterprise to quickly react to changing environments. The next step is to create composite applications that consist of new application logic code leveraging these services. This approach enables new business functionality to be deployed more rapidly than with traditional approaches.

Using Web Services to Implement an SOA

The web services framework can be built on the SOA architecture and aligned to the attributes of an SOA. Web service protocols are just one way to implement an SOA, although they are probably the best way. Web services facilitate an SOA by providing a better interface technology in which to make the services available. Besides platform independence, web services provide a richer specification and go on to provide a more complete set of protocols for security, transactions, orchestration, and so on. These protocols will also provide a mechanism to better express some key SOA principles, such as contracts, SLA, and pre/post conditions, which were rarely provided by existing interface mechanisms.

Defining the Service Interface

When WSDL is used for defining a service interface, the service is a web service. A typical SOA application-development process starts with the definition of the interface and follows with the development of service-implementation software. WSDL supports this type of process. You can create WSDL first, and many tools are available to do this; we show how WSDL can be modeled in Chapter 6, "Designing Web Services."

Implementing the Service Interface

At runtime, a service interface is rendered as a pair of programs: 1) the service interface stub and 2) the service interface proxy. This pair of programs implements the service interface. Both these programs can be generated by a development tool or can be created first and then used in the tool. A typical example has the stub as a Java servlet and the proxy as a Visual Basic component.

The service interface stub is deployed on the server, local to the service implementation, and interacts with the service implementation using local communication methods and data encoding that is appropriate to the service implementation.

The service interface proxy is deployed local to the service consumer and interacts with the service consumer using local communication methods and data encoding that is appropriate to the implementation of the service consumer. Any new runtime application can access the service via its interface proxy, delivering the nonintrusive runtime reuse of services.

When SOAP is used in service stub and service proxy communication, the service is a web service. Theoretically, the generated pair of interface stub and proxy modules can use XML, a SOAP message envelope, HTTP, message-oriented middleware (MOM), or shared memory to pass the service interface parameters.

Registering the Services

Another important aspect of SOA architecture is the registration of services in a registry so that the consumer of the service can discover the service. Web services implement this through UDDI. Services are discovered by querying the UDDI server and accessing the WSDL documents for the services. By using a central registry, client applications can dynamically discover and bind to services. The UDDI server and protocol are reasonably generic. For a service architecture, the UDDI component provides a central service agency that knows about all the services within its domain. Whenever a service requestor needs to access or locate a service, the UDDI server is queried for information. UDDI provides a variety of ways to search the registry.

Factors Driving the Business Decision

The advent of web services has produced a fundamental change in how businesses are looking at IT. The success of many web services projects has shown that you can implement an SOA through web services technologies. An SOA examines not only your application architecture, but also the basic business problems you are trying to solve. From a business perspective, web services is no longer just another technology, but a matter of developing an application architecture and framework that help solve business problems in a coherent and repeatable way.

Businesses are implementing SOA architecture through web services to achieve numerous benefits that an SOA brings. Business executives who have understood the opportunities that lie ahead with web services are already reaping the benefits of their recent implementations. Case studies have shown that the deciding factors for using web services were 1) the potential business benefits and the 2) return on investment (ROI) that can be realized from such an implementation. Other goals included streamlining operations, reducing human intervention, redirecting staff to more productive tasks, and driving down operations costs. Actual benefits included low implementation time and minimal development and implementation cost by leveraging legacy systems and by reusing the modules already developed. New revenues have been achieved by reaching customers in new ways.

Going Live with Web Services: HP Case Study

To understand how an SOA architecture can be used to create business impact, let us look at a case study from Hewlett-Packard. We use examples from this case study throughout the book.

The Consumer Partner Direct program at HP provides consumers the ability to purchase HP desktop PCs and notebooks, along with peripherals, from a retailer's website or in-store kiosk. Consumers can customize their orders and have the product built per the order and shipped to the address of their choice.

In response to dramatic changes in the competitive environment that are forcing shorter product lifecycles, lower profit margins, and better-informed consumers, the consumer business activity is rapidly moving to the web. For HP and other companies selling consumer products, this means that they need to sell directly or through retailers to end consumers through the web. For selling configure-to-order PCs to consumers, the website can be represented in a simple manner, as shown in Figure 4.2. Four functions describe the business process: product representation, product availability and configuration, shopping basket, and purchase transaction.

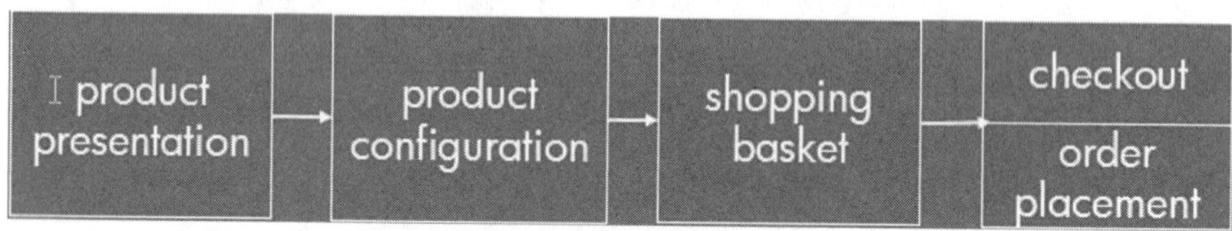

Figure 4.2 Configured-to-order PC website

Each of these functions is provided on the website, and they require integration with the business partners' IT systems. For example, to provide product representation, product catalogs need to be passed from HP to the retailer. For product configuration and availability, HP must check information such as availability and lead time from the factory. If a product requires an order to be placed on HP to a manufacturer, integration is needed with the partners' relevant IT systems.

Challenges Faced

Historically, implementing new business models within HP's Consumer Business Unit or engaging new business partners required a high degree of customization. It was time consuming and costly, and it drastically limited HP's capability to rapidly respond to changing market conditions. To sell these PCs through the web, HP had set up different architectures for catering to retailers, according to the retailer's size and IT capabilities. The larger retailers wanted from HP only data such as product catalog data and the capability to place orders on HP. The smaller retailers wanted HP to build, manage, and support the entire website. Some retailers wanted to manage some of the web pages and let HP manage the rest. Figure 4.3 illustrates these architectures.

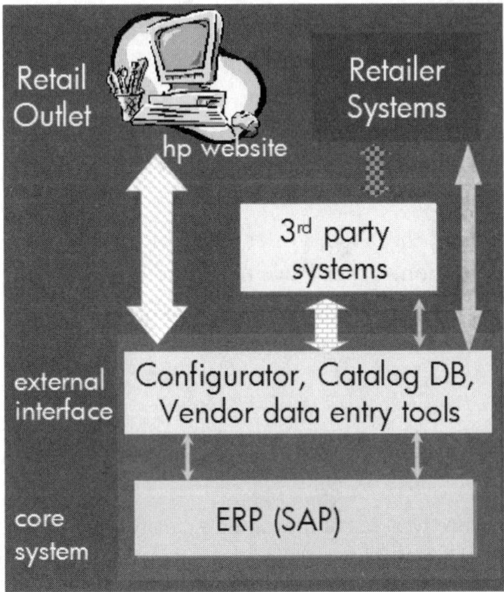

Figure 4.3 Custom pipes

Because of the need to establish these custom pipes with each retailer, it took a long time to enable online ordering of new retailers. There were support issues and lost revenues. HP needed to change this situation to facilitate revenue increase, improve total customer satisfaction, and decrease IT costs. There was an urgent need to create a highly agile and adaptive architecture that would provide a significant advantage over its less responsive competitors.

Goals of the Project

A project team at HP analyzed the problem and formulated the goals that the solution had to meet. This was translated into the capabilities that the solution architecture ought to facilitate:

- A flexible and modular architecture that should cater to the needs of every retailer, regardless of size, and offer a menu of services that retailers could pick and choose from.
- An architecture that could be layered on the ERP systems already in place and could be linked with the highly diverse legacy environment at HP. It should facilitate the integration of disparate systems between the retailers and HP and within HP.
- Support for real-time transactions, to facilitate faster delivery times for customers.
- The capability to leverage the expertise of retailers because they are closer to their customers and have a better understanding of their needs. The retailer should control the look and feel of the website and could use promotions for up-selling or cross-selling.
- Support for functions of the "Place Order" process as services: Product Catalog, Configuration Information, Order Placement, and Order Status.
- An adaptive architecture that should improve the organization's capability in reacting to changes in business requirements.

Web Services Solution

HP used the SOA architecture to achieve the stated goals for the project and used web services as an implementation vehicle. The first step was to create a prioritized set of real-time web services that would deliver the critical functionality to its partners. The initial web service offerings were Product Catalog, Validate Config, Place Order, and Order Status:

- Product Catalog enables retailers to request real-time product and price changes from HP.
- Validate Config is used by consumers when they are on the website to get HP to verify the configuration they have selected.
- Place Order enables retailers to place real-time orders on HP.
- Order Status enables retailers to retrieve status information.

The high-level architecture used for this project is shown in Figure 4.4. The web services were layered across a multivendor environment, including BEA, SAP, Oracle, and Microsoft. The order fulfillment system, which takes purchase orders and gives order status, is an ERP system from SAP. The product catalog and configuration databases facilitate the product, price, and configuration information. The web services were exposed through the BEA platform. On the client side, stubs were created from the WSDL for all these clients. The retailers had disparate systems: Microsoft .NET, Visual Basic, BEA, Web Methods, and Axis.

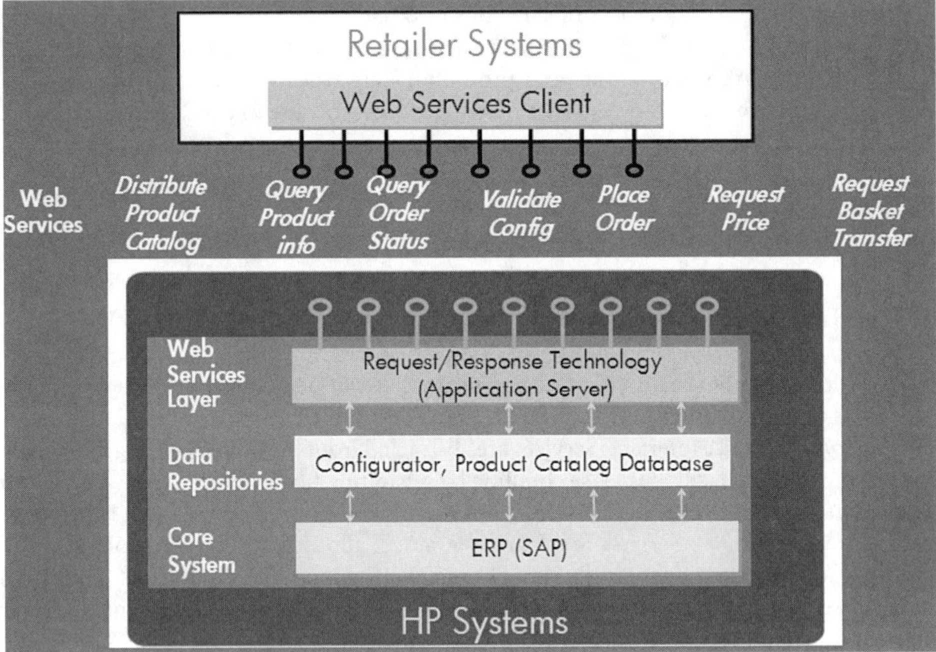

Figure 4.4 Web services architecture

How these web services were designed and developed is covered in the following chapters.

Benefits of the Solution

One of the key success metrics was the time it took for recently signed retailers to become fully operational. HP can now get a new retailer up and running in three to five months, compared to the six to nine months it took previously. The team can quickly accommodate any retail partner's business model and get that partner operational in a very short period of time.

The utilization of a standards-based, modular approach has provided many additional benefits to HP, including a simplified administration model, significant returns from module reuse, and the capability to offer a broad portfolio of market-proven web services. The comprehensive library of web services has almost eliminated the need to create unique solutions for new retailers.

The investment in legacy components has been leveraged without compromising the overall performance of new or existing applications. For example, some of the retailers were already set up on EDI links into HP's existing SAP systems. These EDI linkages were leveraged and translated to web services.

HP is benefiting from a greatly lowered total cost of ownership (TCO) for the Consumer Direct Program. The configure-to-order PC business has seen an increase in revenue. Orders are delivered up to 24 hours faster compared to real-time transactions; batch processes are conducted once a day. Also, the website and promotions are tailored to customers because the retailer, who is in sync with the customer needs, now controls the website. This has increased the total customer satisfaction.

Overall, the solution has enabled HP to provide an increasingly compelling set of offerings to attract new retail partners.

Summary

The W3C defines an SOA as a set of components that can be invoked and whose interface descriptions can be published and discovered. In an SOA architecture, every function is defined as a service with a service interface. Services are abstracted from the underlying logic that delivers the result. An SOA facilitates loose coupling by separating the producer of the service from the consumer of the service. Services are "invokable;" therefore, it is irrelevant whether the service is local or remote. Services are coarsely grained, allowing several function calls to be packaged into fewer messages. Finally, an SOA enables the reuse of components. End-to-end security, a services-management infrastructure, and business process management are the important capabilities that the underlying infrastructure ought to provide in an SOA.

Web services are the probably the best way to implement an SOA. WSDL is used for defining a service interface. The interface is implemented using a service interface stub and a service interface proxy, and SOAP is used for the communication between the stub and the proxy. UDDI facilitates the registration and discovery of the SOA implementation.

Businesses are implementing an SOA architecture through web services to reap the benefits that an SOA brings. The deciding factors for using web services are 1) the potential business benefits and the 2) return on investment (ROI) that can be realized from such an implementation. The case study from HP provides a real-life example of how one business has benefited from implementing an SOA using web services.

5

Enabling Enterprise-Class Web Services

In the last chapter, we talked about the business requirements and the business reasons for choosing a web services architecture for the solution. Before you start designing the web services to meet these business requirements, you have to take a close look at the factors to be considered for enabling enterprise-class web services. Enterprise-class web services represent a level of technical and operational maturity that is consistent with the increasingly stringent requirements of today's enterprise. As we progress toward building such web services, in this chapter, we take a close look at designing interoperability, publishing an enduring web services contract, exposing the business-tier components, and planning for a robust production environment.

The WebLogic Workshop web services framework abstracts the developer from the plumbing code required to build enterprise-class web services. WebLogic Workshop combines the visual development environment with the runtime framework to help developers and nondevelopers effectively and efficiently build these services.

Designing Interoperability

The two dominant web services development platforms are on J2EE and .NET. Most often, the client accessing the web services cannot be predetermined. Therefore, it is important to make certain design choices—choice of standards, WSDL design, and SOAP messaging style—that enhance the interoperability of the web services implementation across different platforms.

Conforming to Standards

Using the web services standards—XML, WSDL, SOAP, and UDDI, as well as WS-Security (security), Web Services Distributed Management (manageability), and the Business Process Execution Language (orchestration)—strictly as defined by the standard bodies is a necessary requirement for interoperability. Following the recommendation from bodies such as the WS-I not only improve interoperability, but it also facilitates fast implementation with business partners.

Standards are important at all levels of web services communication. By using a standard way of exchanging data using XML, choosing a common SOAP message protocol, and describing services through WSDL, you enable the users of your service to communicate with your application regardless of the platform they are using. This approach helps you to integrate your web services with those of your business partners without relying on proprietary vendor technology.

In WebLogic Workshop, exposing an operation through these standards is extremely easy. Workshop introduces a simple javadoc-based annotation `@jws:operation` for marking up standard Java code. If you simply put this annotation before a method in a standard Java class file, Workshop exposes that method as a web service that fully supports the web services standards.

Designing WSDL First

In general, designing the WSDL first is the right way to start your web services. The WSDL represents the contract between you and the user of your service. Not unlike the real world, the contract needs to be well crafted. It needs to spell out in the clearest possible terms what the service offers—and, ideally, what it does not do.

Most often, developers seldom design the WSDL because many SOAP implementations provide tools to automatically generate a WSDL file from a COM object or Java class files. Surprisingly, this can cause issues of interoperability between different Java application servers and between .NET and Java implementations. This is because the automatically generated WSDLs might not be interpretable across different platforms. For example, some application servers cannot use WSDLs that have imported or included XML Schemas. Designing the WSDL first and then creating the web service avoids the issue.

The recommendation is that you generate WSDL using techniques based on the Unified Modeling Language (UML) or using WSDL editors (see Figure 5.1). We cover in detail how to design WSDL using XMLSPY, a WSDL editor, in the next chapter.

WSDL modeling in UML can be another way of creating WSDL rather than using WSDL editors. The Object Management Group (OMG) has established a Model Driven Architecture (MDA) and Unified Modeling Language (UML) for modeling software applications. UML is a graphical language for specifying, visualizing, constructing, and documenting software systems. Because of its wide acceptance and capabilities, UML is the natural choice for any modeling activities. UML profiles provide a generic extension mechanism for building UML models in particular domains such as Web Modeling Profile, XSD Schema Profile, and Business Profile Modeling. A *profile* consists of stereotypes, constraints, and tagged values that allow modeling of all WSDL definitions.

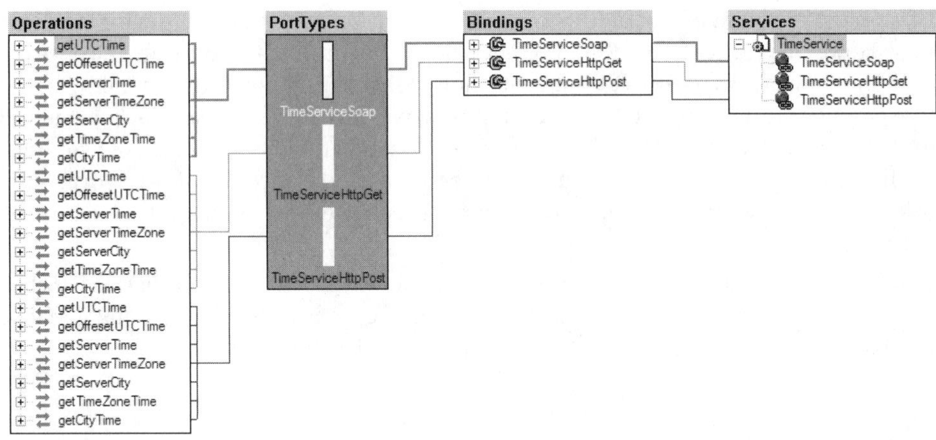

Figure 5.1 XMLSPY, a sample WSDL editor

Deriving from the MDA, the modelling of the WSDL can be divided into a platform-independent model (PIM) and a platform-specific model (PSM). A WSDL file has two sections, the abstract section and the bindings section. The PIM represents the abstract section of the WSDL. This includes `Definitions`, `Service`, `PortType(s)`, `Messages`, `Parts`, and `PartType(s)`. The PSM completes the bindings section of the WSDL. The elements modelled here include `Service`, `Ports`, and `Binding(s)`.

Selecting SOAP Messaging

The style, or binding style, decision controls how the elements just under the SOAP body are constructed. The two choices are RPC and document. The use, or encoding, concerns how types are represented in XML. The two choices are literal and SOAP encoded. Literal follows an XML Schema definition. SOAP encoded follows special encoding rules detailed in the SOAP 1.1 specification to produce XML that can contain references pointing within the message. The WS-I Basic Profile Version 1.0a specification recommends the use of literal encoding; it actually discourages the use of SOAP encoding.

Theoretically, you should be able to mix and match any of the styles and uses for SOAP messaging. However, practically, the RPC-encoded and document-literal choices are the ones used. In addition, many web service platforms don't directly support RPC-literal. WebLogic Workshop uses document-literal as its default message format, but it also supports the RPC-encoded message format. To specify the message format that a web service uses to communicate with the web service control, you can set the `soap-style` attribute of the `@jc:protocol` annotation to `document` for the document-literal message format or `rpc` for the SOAP-RPC format.

RPC-encoded seemed reasonable in a world without XML Schema. Now that XML Schema is here to stay, document-literal is quickly becoming the de facto standard among developers and toolkits, thanks to its simplicity and interoperability results.

Styles: Document and RPC

Document style indicates that the SOAP body contains an XML document. In this approach, you the send XML document as is. The sender and receiver must agree on the format of the document ahead of time. Here is an example of a document-style message:

```
<SOAP-ENV: Envelope xmlns:SOAP-
➥ENV=http://schemas.xmlsoap.org/soap/envelope/
➥xmlns:SOAP-ENC="http://schemas.xmlsoap.org/soap/encoding/"
➥mlns:xsi="http://www.w3.org/2001/XMLSchema-instance"
➥xmlns:xsd="http://www.w3.org/2001/XMLSchema">
     <SOAP-ENV:Body>
          <m:inValidateConfig xmlns:m="http://production.psg.hp.com/types">
               <m:Config>
                    <m:Model/>
                    <m:Cstic/>
               </m:Config>
               <m:User AccountID=0000000000>
                    <m:Password>String</m:Password>
               <m:IpcVersion>OLD</m:IpcVersion>
               <m:ConfigID>String</m:ConfigID>
          </m:inValidateConfig>
     </SOAP-ENV:Body>
</SOAP-ENV:Envelope>
```

Observe that all elements are defined within the same namespace. With a document-style web service, you are free to define the XML however you want because all the XML is explicitly specified.

RPC style indicates that the SOAP body contains an XML representation of a method call. RPC style uses the names of the method and its parameters to generate structures that represent a method's call stack. Here's an example of a RPC-style message:

```
    <SOAP-ENV:Body>
        <m:validate xmlns:m="local
➥host:7001/services/validate" SOAP-ENV:encodingStyle=
➥"http://schemas.xmlsoap.org/soap/encoding/">
            <in0 xsi:type="xsd:string">String</in0>
        </m:validate>
    </SOAP-ENV:Body>
</SOAP-ENV:Envelope>
```

RPC relies on some rules. Observe that the root element is qualified with a namespace, but the child element uses an unqualified name. The root element is named after the operation: `validate` for a SOAP request and `opNameResponse` for a SOAP response. Each child is a parameter, or a return value named `opNameReturn`.

The binding style is specified in the WSDL. There actually is a style attribute that can be `RPC` or `Document` in the `<soapbind:binding>` element, which is the `<wsdl:binding>` element's first child. Table 5.1 illustrates the differences between `RPC` and `Document`.

Table 5.1 Binding Style in a WSDL

	RPC	**Document**
`<soapbind:binding>` element	`style="rpc"`	`style="document"`
`<wsdl:part>` element(s)	`<part>` element can be many; each contains a "type" attribute.	Only one `<part>` element containing an "element" attribute.
`<wsdl:part>` element(s) explained	Specify the type so that the SOAP engine can use RPC rules to make it either a parameter or a return value.	The SOAP body has an XML element that is fully specified in `<wsdl:types>`.

Use: Literal and Encoding

The use, or encoding, concerns how types are represented in XML. The two choices are literal and SOAP encoded. Literal follows an XML Schema definition. SOAP encoded follows special encoding rules detailed in the SOAP 1.1 specification (section 5) to produce XML that can contain references pointing within the message. Now to compare the literal and encoded use, let's compare the example from the document style that also uses the literal with another example showing the encoding use.

Here's the literal use:

```
<m:User AccountID=0000000000>
        <m:Password>xyz </m:Password>
<m:User>
```

Here's the encoding use:

```
< AccountID xsi:type ="xsd:string">0000000000</ AccountID r>
<Password xsi:type="xsd:string">xyz</Password>
```

SOAP encoding automatically maps all eligible fields to elements, not attributes. With the literal use of an XML Schema, on the other hand, you can specify what items are attributes and what items are elements. In the previous example, the simple `AccountID` field can be written more compactly as an attribute.

Now we can examine how use is specified in the WSDL. Table 5.2 shows the difference in literal versus encoded in the WSDL document.

Table 5.2 Use/Encoding Specified in a WSDL

	Encoded	**Literal**
`<soapbind:body>` use attribute	`use="encoded"`	`use="literal"`
Other `<soapbind:body>` attributes	`encodingStyle="http://schemas.xmlsoap.org/soap/encoding/"`	—

Publishing Enduring Web Services Contracts

A web service contract, usually expressed via a WSDL, describes the relationship between the web services that you publish and the manner in which an external client can interact with them. These touch upon what XML messages to expect, what business operations you can perform, and what XML messages you generate. You can do so without letting the other party know about the technical details of your application and how they change over time. By the same token, you can use other developers' public contracts to consume their applications without needing to know the details or even the language and platform they use to implement their web service.

These contracts can be made more durable by following certain principles, such as loose coupling, XML strategy selection, and versioning.

Integrating Through Loose Coupling

An important aspect of web services design is to ensure that the web services are loosely coupled. Web services are loosely coupled when you separate the internal implementation from the interface exposed to the user of your service. The web service has an interface defined by the WSDL that is exposed to the outside world. The internal implementation of a web service is the specific application server that it runs on or the EJBs that do the business logic. If you need to change your application server, the user of the service is not affected because there is a change only to the internal implementation. When this is ensured, the user of the web service does not need to get involved in testing changes unless the interface changes as defined by the WSDL. You might still want to test with the client even if the WSDL doesn't change, to make sure that SLAs and performance requirements can still be met.

Using the WSDL, however, is not enough to guarantee loose coupling. If your WSDL is automatically generated from the code and you change the code, the WSDL changes, thus making it tightly coupled to the code. WebLogic Workshop provides XQuery Maps which is a simple, declarative way of describing how your Java code relates to the WSDL of your web service. If your Java code changes over time, you can change your XQuery Map so that your WSDL stays intact. XQuery Map maps the Java code to your WSDL. When the Java code changes, the mapping can be alerted to keep the WSDL the same. This enables you to truly realize the promise of loose coupling. WebLogic also provides the facility of modeling the WSDL in XMLSpy and then importing it into WebLogic Workshop. With this WSDL, you can create a web service in WebLogic Workshop. See Figures 5.2 and 5.3 for an illustration of the modeling and importing of WSDL.

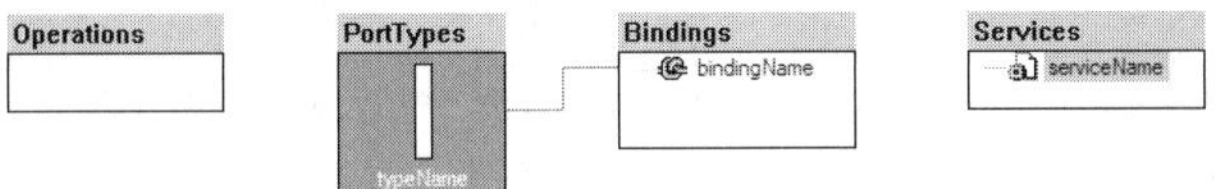

Figure 5.2 Modeling of WSDL

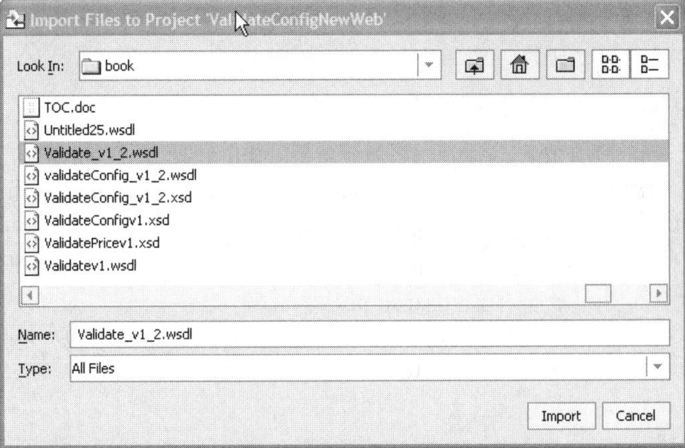

Figure 5.3 Importing of WSDL in WebLogic Workshop

Here is an example of using an XQuery map in WebLogic Workshop. The start and end of the XML map is shown by the annotation:

```
 * @jws:operation
 * @jws:parameter-xml xml-map::
 *    < order>
 * <item xm:multiple="String name in nameA,
➥int amount in amountA, float price in priceA">
 *          <name>{name}</name>
 *          <amount>{amount}</amount>
 *          <price>{price}</price>
 *       </item>
 *    </order>
 * ::
 * @jws:return-xml xml-map::
 *    <totalPrice>{return}</totalPrice>
 * ::
 */
 public float getTotalPrice(String [] nameA,
➥int [] amountA, float [] priceA)
 {
      float totalPrice = 0.0f;
      if( nameArr != null )
      {
           // for each item, compute subtotal and add to total
          for (int i = 0; i < nameArr.length; i++)
           {
                totalPrice += amountArr[i] * priceArr[i];
           }
       }
       return totalPrice;
 }
```

This map specifies that the `getTotalPrice` Java method receives an XML document that contains an order with multiple line items, each with a name, amount, and price. These fields are extracted from the XML message and mapped into Java arrays. Similarly, the float value that is returned from the method is placed in the context of a simple XML document that has a `<totalPrice>` tag.

Choosing an XML Strategy

XML is the messaging standard for web services. You have to choose the right strategy for handling XML messages in web services, depending on how the web services you are designing fit into the overall application.

The XML strategy that you will use depends on two criteria. One is whether you have any application logic and whether you are exposing the application logic. The second criterion is whether the interface to the web service you are developing has a predefined XML Schema and whether you want to define your own.

This can lead to four different strategies for handling XML Schemas:

- **Defined application logic and predefined XML Schema**—In this case, the strategy that you use is mapping between defined incoming messages to fields in your internal data types. XQuery maps in WebLogic Workshop can be used to map the data.
- **No internal classes and predefined XML Schema**—If schemas are defined in the WSDL file, you should import the WSDL in WebLogic Workshop and let XML Beans accept the schema file and return a set of Java classes that a developer can conveniently leverage to process any XML document that conforms to the original schema file. Having schema definitions at the core of the XML Beans system provides a variety of benefits. For example, when you first receive an XML document for processing, you can validate the data based on the schema definition. Any time you manipulate the XML document via the schema-inspired Java classes, the XML Beans system can always ensure that all changes remain consistent with the prevailing schema definition. This unambiguously disallows the creation of invalid XML documents.
- **When internal classes are defined and the schema is not defined, you should define your schema according to your internal classes.** If both are not defined, first define the schemas and then derive the Java classes from there. This follows the concept of designing WSDL first, as described in the earlier section.

Versioning New Releases

You need to consider versioning of your web service to facilitate managing multiple versions of a web service. Versioning should minimize code replication and maximize code reuse. It should also put a logical and manageable naming paradigm in place. This allows for upgrades and improvements to be made to existing web services, while continuously supporting previously released versions of that web service.

Two areas should be considered for versioning a web service: the public interface, as described by the WSDL file, and the web service implementation, including its conversational state.

Versioning the Public Interface

You can version the public interface—specifically, your WSDL—in different ways:

- Use a different endpoint for your service:

```
<wsdl:service name="Validate_v1_2">
        <wsdl:port name="Validate" binding="tns1:ValidateSoapBinding">
            <wsdlsoap:address location="localhost:7001/ValidateConfigNewWeb/
➥ValidateConfigNew/validate_v1_2ControlTest.jws"/>
        </wsdl:port>
    </wsdl:service>
```

In this example, you can change to the next version `validate_v1_3` by changing the address of the endpoint for the service as follows:

```
<wsdlsoap:address location="localhost:7001/ValidateConfigNewWeb
➥/ValidateConfigNew/validatev_1_3ControlTest.jws"/>
```

In this approach, the XML Schema does not change and there is no change in your SOAP message. The advantage in this option is that you can insulate your users from changing schemas. The drawback is that there is no reference to the version `validate_v1_2` within the SOAP message, so you cannot use management tools that can direct the message to the right version:

```
<SOAP-ENV:Body>
        <m:inValidateConfig xmlns:m="http://production.psg.hp.com/types">
            ...
    </SOAP-ENV:Body>
```

- Use a date stamp as part of the target namespace of your XML Schema. This is in compliance with the W3C XML Schema specification. The disadvantage here is that your schema changes every time the version changes. The advantage of this approach is that you can see the version in your SOAP messages, and you can write code or use management tools to direct the web service to the right version, according to the SOAP message:

```
<SOAP-ENV:Body>
        <m:inValidateConfigv1_2
➥xmlns:m="http://production.psg.hp.com/types/2004/02/04">
            ...
    </SOAP-ENV:Body>
```

- Add new operations to the WSDL and support old ones until the user moves to the new operation. You can add new operations to the public interface of a web service to reflect the new versions, keeping the existing operations. The advantage of doing so is that you do not disrupt clients that rely on the web service. By adding new operations and making them known to clients, you can gradually shift clients over to a new set of operations, but you should leave the original operations intact for backward compatibility. For example, the `operation` section of the WSDL will look as shown here:

```
<wsdl:operation name="validateConfig">
        <wsdlsoap:operation soapAction="validate_v1_2"/>
        <wsdl:input>
            <wsdlsoap:body use="literal"/>
        </wsdl:input>
        <wsdl:output>
            <wsdlsoap:body use="literal"/>
        </wsdl:output>
    </wsdl:operation>
    <wsdl:operation name="validatePrice">
        <wsdlsoap:operation soapAction=" validate_v1_3 "/>
        <output>
            <wsdlsoap:body use="literal"/>
        </output>
        <input>
            <wsdlsoap:body use="literal"/>
        </input>
    </wsdl:operation>
```

The `types` section of the WSDL will look as shown here:

```
<wsdl:types>
        <xsd:schema targetNamespace="http://production.psg.hp.com/types"
➥xmlns="http://production.psg.hp.com/types" elementFormDefault="qualified">
            <xsd:include schemaLocation="ValidateConfigv1_2.xsd"/>
            <xsd:include schemaLocation="ValidateConfigv1_3.xsd"/>
        </xsd:schema>
    </wsdl:types>
```

The SOAP message for each of the operations will look as shown next. Again, you can use management tools to direct messages to different versions:

```
<SOAP-ENV:Body>
        <m:inValidateConfigv1_2 xmlns:m="http://production.psg.hp.com/types">
            ...
    </SOAP-ENV:Body>
<SOAP-ENV:Body>
        <m:inValidateConfigv1_3 xmlns:m="http://production.psg.hp.com/types">
            ...
    </SOAP-ENV:Body>
```

- Use UDDI and versioning UDDI in conjunction with WSDL to provide for versioning. The UDDI data model is rich enough that the current best practices can be enhanced to include service versioning. A given service can advertise more than one interface that represents its different versions. Different interfaces have different tModels. The service can reference the tModel for each of the interface in its `tModelInstanceDetails` collection. `tModelInstanceDetails` is a class that has `tModelKey` as a mandatory attribute.

Versioning the Implementation

WebLogic Workshop uses Java serialization to persist the state associated with web service requests and conversations. For this reason, the primary requirement for supporting versioned implementations is maintaining backward serialization compatibility. Specifically, it must be possible to load state into the current version of a class that was stored using any older versions of that class.

Versioning Lifecycle

Understanding the versioning lifecycle will help you to implement the new versions of your web service and deprecate the older versions effectively. First, you need to put together a plan for the lifecycle of the web services you are supporting. The main aspects of the plan of the versioning lifecycle are listed here:

1. Your plan should contain the frequency of the release of your versions. For example, you could release one version per year. Consider how many versions of the web service you want to support in parallel.
2. The plan should also contain the time frame for your users to move to the new version. This would be the same as the time you would support an older version after the new one is released.
3. Consider using a pilot for the new version of the web services with an early release of version.

4. Consider releasing new functionality and conformance to new web service specifications only through this versioning strategy, as with software releases.
5. Communicate the versioning strategy to the users of your web service.

After you lay out the versioning strategy for each version, follow these steps to release each version of your web service:

1. Make changes to the services that you are supporting, as detailed in the previous sections.
2. Do unit and functional testing of the service.
3. Deploy the new service either through new WSDLs for users of the service or to UDDI registries.
4. Notify the consumers of your new service and pilot the new service with one of your consumers.
5. Run the new and old versions in parallel for the time frame you have allocated in your versioning plan.
6. Notify the consumers of the date when the old service is obsoleted.
7. Remove the old service version from descriptions, registries, and so on to keep new consumers from discovering and using the old web service. Remove the functional behavior of the old service; return only an appropriate error message.
8. Retire the old service. Physically remove the old service version.

Effectively Using Business-Tier Systems

Web services are usually built on existing business-tier systems. To effectively interface with these systems, you have to take into consideration the communication, frequency of interaction, and degree of exposure to the business components. For example, a purchase order web service must effectively interface with the underlying ERP systems.

Facilitating Asynchronous Communication

Web services can be designed to be synchronous or asynchronous in nature. In synchronous mode, a web service implements a call-and-response RPC mode of interaction. Here, when the service is invoked, the business logic behind the web service executes the logic while the client is waiting for a response. For example, this can be used in getting price quotes and stock quotes.

For complex processes such as orders and order changes, processing might take minutes or even days to complete. This is particularly true when the web service implementation depends on batch processing or manual steps that require human intervention. This is an asynchronous web service. The client does not wait for the response to do the next steps. It either checks back periodically to see if the process is completed on the web service producer side, or acts as a listener to any updates.

Web services standards include the infrastructure and mechanisms on which asynchronous operations can be based. Handling web services interactions asynchronously is useful to accommodate user interactions, legacy IT systems, and partner IT systems. In these instances, systems must not block one another, and relevant systems and data must be easy to connect. This is also essential for scalability.

To effectively build composite, asynchronous applications, Workshop provides a model for web service conversations. A *conversation* is a series of message exchanges in both directions that are related and share some context. The Workshop framework automatically manages a unique ID for each conversation, and messages in a conversation are related through a conversation ID. In addition, any class member variables are automatically persisted and available later as the conversation continues. To use conversations in Workshop, methods must be annotated as starting, continuing, or finishing a conversation. To start a conversation, you can use the following tag:

```
* @jws:operation
* @jws:conversation phase="start"
```

SOAP conversation is a SOAP- and WSDL-based specification that defines long-running and asynchronous interactions between SOAP-based senders and receivers.Workshop web service conversations enable you to easily build asynchronous web services without having to write the underlying infrastructure typically associated with these types of applications (see Figure 5.4).

Figure 5.4 Asynchronous web service

Using a Coarsely Grained Approach

Much of the design of a web service interface involves designing the service's operations. After you determine the service's operations, you define the parameters for these operations, their return values, and any errors or exceptions that they can generate. That is, you define the method signatures of the service.

You should define the web service's interface for optimal granularity of its operations. Although finely grained service operations, such as an operation to browse a catalog by categories, products, or items, offer greater flexibility to the client, they also result in greater network overhead and reduced performance. More coarsely grained service operations, such as returning catalog entries in a set of categories, reduce network overhead and improve performance, although they are less flexible. Generally, you should consolidate finely grained operations into more coarsely grained ones to minimize expensive remote method calls. The key benefits of coarsely grained web services are that they provide a uniform interface, reduce coupling, increase manageability and reusability, centralize security management and transaction control, and improve performance.

With WebLogic Workshop, the XML documents that you exchange are business-level documents, such as entire invoices or purchase orders. The coarsely grained web services can access finely grained business logic through the control framework of WebLogic Workshop. You can have web services, such as purchase orders, that access finely grained controls for business logic such as EJB controls and database controls.

Exposing Business Logic Components

The Model-View-Controller (MVC) architecture is one of the well-known architecture frameworks used in many web-based applications. The MVC design is modular, separating the key components of the architecture:

- **Model**—Contains data required by the application
- **View**—Manages the presentation of the data to the user
- **Controller**—Acts as an intermediary between the client and the data

The MVC approach (see Figure 5.5) can allow an organization to expose multiple interfaces to the same set of data. For example, consider a web service in which EJBs provide the data from a database (Model), JSPs are used to present the data (View), and servlets mange the interface between the client and the data (Controller). Now, if the client device changes from a browser to a PDA, the View can be changed from HTML to WML without affecting the EJBs and servlets. Also, if web services can be considered as just another View on the model, a web services presentation can easily be plugged into an existing MVC architecture. In this case, instead of HTML or WML being sent back to the client application, the web services View would construct XML or SOAP messages through interactions by interacting with the Controller.

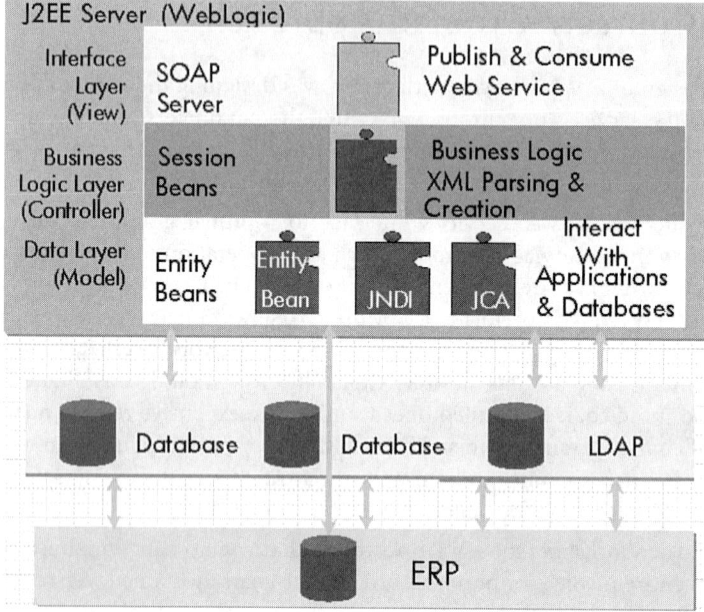

Figure 5.5 MVC architecture

A Java class or an EJB can perform the business logic for fulfilling a web service request. The EJBs that support web services are session- and message-driven beans. Stateless session beans facilitate RPC-style web services that result in component operation invocations. Message-driven beans facilitate document-oriented web services. They do asynchronous messaging through a JMS consumer. Java classes can also be used for the business logic and are simpler to implement.

WebLogic Workshop has a Controls Framework with many built-in controls, such as database, EJB, and web service, that can wrap the back-end components and help expose them as web services. We talk more about the Controls Framework in Chapter 8, "Using Controls, Bindings, and Parsers."

The Web Flow Framework is a visual representation of presentation scenarios in WebLogic Workshop. The web flow framework is based on Struts, which is based on the MVC design paradigm. WebLogic Workshop facilitates the Web Flow Framework, which extends the Struts framework to provide a simplified development model with numerous additional features.

Companies such as HP are using frameworks such as SSA, which is described in the accompanying sidebar to build well-designed robust, scalable, and extensible web services. SSA complements standard J2EE web service toolkits such as WebLogic Workshop and helps HP IT in creating a consistent, repeatable approach to developing web services in J2EE.

Shared Services Architecture

The Shared Services Architecture (SSA) is a framework based on J2EE standards that was developed at HP to meet developers' needs for reusable services. The first version of the SSA was released in the year 2000, and support for creating web services was added in 2002. The SSA was developed by and is maintained by a small team within HP IT; it is the corporate standard framework for all internal Java-based web services development.

As we have discussed in this chapter, there is more to programming of web services, in production, you need modular, reusable, high-performance web services. This is where the SSA framework codifies the use of best practices, including design patterns, into a ready-to-use architecture and offers a robust, flexible framework for implementing enterprise-class web services.

The SSA offers developers a set of higher-level abstractions such as Request, Result, Feature, and Business Policy that developers can start with instead of having to start with a clean slate for every new service that they implement.

The SSA offers help in several areas:

- Designing and developing a layered service implementation
- Developing a modular, reliable, scalable, high-performance service
- Designing and developing a modular, easily repurposable user experience implementation
- Enforcing business rules in an easy-to-change fashion
- Dealing with error handling and metrics gathering
- Providing scalability and availability, ERP/legacy integration, authentication, and authorization
- Specifying and controlling the overall flow and calling service components at predefined points in time using predefined interfaces. Conceptually, this is very similar to what other frameworks such as Struts offer for building web UIs in Java.

The SSA architecture complements the frameworks, describes the overall structure of a shared service, and provides a design blueprint for organizing a service, including the logical layers that a service is recommended to have, and the responsibilities of those layers.

continues

As complements of the core SSA framework itself, there are several plug-ins, utilities, and tools. The plug-ins expand the base functionality available in SSA and are analogous to web browser plug-ins. The list of available plug-ins includes the Apache Axis and the WebLogic SOAP plug-in for exposing SSA services as web services with different web services toolkits. The utilities include APIs for logging, metrics gathering, and lifecycle management. The tools include development tools such as code-generation wizards and deployment tools such as scripts and Ant build files.

Several key business benefits are associated with using SSA, including faster time to market, reduced total cost of ownership (TCO), reduced support costs, improved developer productivity, and improved capability to react to change. The SSA framework presently is being used in HP's identity-management solution for external users, HP Passport. It allows all external users to HP to be registered through web services built with the SSA framework in the BEA WebLogic plug-in. The SSA framework has helped make this solution robust and scaleable. It has high performance and is very flexible in adding operations to the existing web services.

Planning a Robust Production Environment

Enterprise-class web services require application servers to provide clustering, caching, transaction coordination, messaging, high-performance XML processing, database connection pooling, and other features that have made J2EE the de facto standard for enterprise computing. WebLogic Workshop is built on top of WebLogic Server. As a developer, you can automatically leverage much of the robustness of the WebLogic Server platform (see Figure 5.6).

In addition to leveraging the robust foundation provided by WebLogic server, you need to pay particular attention to security, scalability, peformance, and manageability to ensure a robust production environment.

Security

Securing the web services that you build is an important aspect of building enterprise-class web services. You can use traditional techniques such as two-way SSL. However, there is performance degradation using two-way SSL because the whole message will be encrypted even though only parts of it might need to be encrypted. For example, you might want to encrypt just the customer name, address, and credit-card information in a purchase order, not the purchase order items and their descriptions.

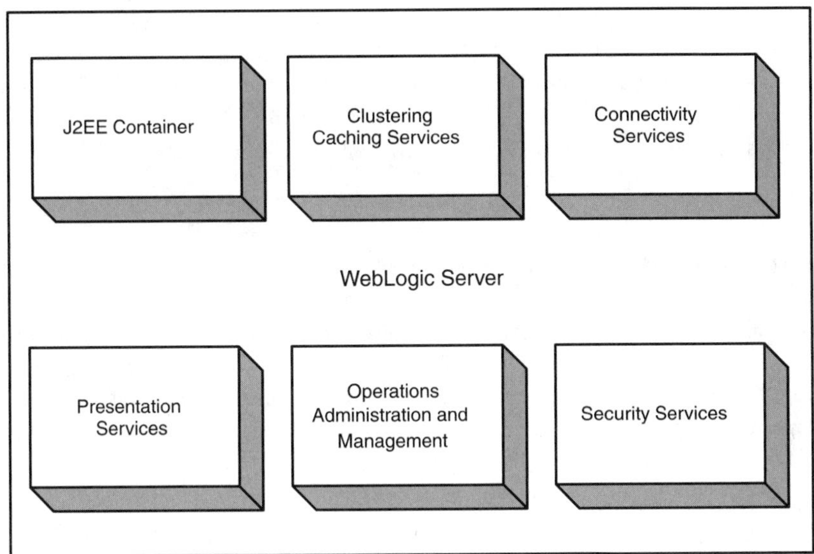

Figure 5.6 WebLogic Server

WS-Security secures the SOAP message. The OASIS Technical Committee has ratified a specification with a standard set of SOAP extensions that can be used when building secure web services to implement message content integrity and confidentiality.

WS-Security is controlled using policy files. One part of a WS-Security policy determines the security requirements for SOAP messages coming into a web service or web service control. This part of the policy determines the security mechanisms for an inbound SOAP message to pass the security gate. The other part of a WS-Security policy determines the security enhancements to be added to outgoing SOAP messages before they are sent out to the client. This part of the policy file determines the kinds of security mechanisms that a web service or a web service control adds to SOAP messages.

In WebLogic Workshop, WS-Security policies are configured in WSSE files, an XML file with the `.wsse` extension. The `<wsSecurityIn>` element describes the security requirements for incoming SOAP messages; the `<wsSecurityOut>` element describes the security enhancements added to outgoing SOAP messages.

To apply a WS-Security policy to a web service, add the annotations `@jws:ws-security-service` and `@jws:ws-security-callback` to the web service file. If the web service communicates synchronously with its clients, you need to use only the `@jws:ws-security-service` annotation. If the web service sends callbacks to its clients, you must use both annotations. The Web Service CallBack Protocol (WS-CallBack) specification consists of the `CallBack` SOAP header and an associated WSDL definition. WS-CallBack is used to dynamically specify where to send asynchronous responses to a SOAP request:

```
/**
 * @jws:ws-security-service file="MyWebServicePolicy.wsse"
 * @jws:ws-security-callback file="MyWebServicePolicy.wsse"
 */
public class MyWebService implements com.bea.jws.WebService
```

Scalability and Performance

Enterprise-class web services need to be scalable and to perform at an optimum level. WebLogic Server provides clustering, caching, transaction coordination, messaging, high-performance XML processing, and database connection pooling, which makes the web services running on it highly scalable. You can improve your performance by tuning the WebLogic Server and by using JRockit instead of Sun JVM as your JVM (covered in detail in Chapter 12, "Enhancing Performance of Web Services").

Manageability

Management of web services is extremely important in an enterprise-class implementation. You need to establish the way you want to manage your web services while designing your web services. This is crucial to the success of business operations. Applications today are increasingly distributed, complex, and integral to the enterprise. For example, fault analysis now often involves gathering and reporting information across many applications, services, and platforms. As applications have grown more complex, so have their manageability needs.

BEA WebLogic with HP's OpenView uses Java/J2EE management via JMX. To manage the web services, WebLogic Server leverages Java Management Extensions (JMX). JMX defines a standard for developing managed beans (MBeans). The first step is to develop the MBeans as a wrapper to your Java web service that you want to manage and monitor. Then you need to register this MBean in the WebLogic JMX Server. JMX Server is responsible for decoupling management applications from the managed resources. It is important to note that MBeans are always accessed via the methods of the MBeanServer interface.

HP enhances the WebLogic Server management world by providing a WebLogic Server–specific Smart Plug-In (SPI) module that integrates the management of the WebLogic Server and any associated applications that depend on it. This SPI integrates several sources of information into one screen. Simultaneously, it gathers data from any supplied MBeans, performs calculations on that data to be more meaningful to the end operator, and brings filtered application logging messages to bear on the management task

This provides highly desirable management integration. Many IT operations departments want to monitor the health of their computers, networks, application servers and any applications that depend on them from the same console and using the same familiar tools.

Web services manageability goes beyond Java/J2EE management via JMX. In practice, this means that IT operations can deploy and configure your application, monitor its health and performance, predict and reduce failure, and analyze, correct, and report failures. At the business level, this means that your enterprise users can do more than just monitor: They can control and adapt your web service based on management data received.

The importance of a standardized management model for web services has driven industry leaders in web services and management technologies and applications to form a technical committee in OASIS called the Web Services Distributed Management (WSDM) Technical Committee.

Web services manageability is defined by this committee as a set of capabilities for discovering the existence, availability, health, performance, and usage (as well as the control and configuration) of a web service within the web services architecture. This implies that web services can be managed using web services technologies.

Web Services Networking

Functions such as load balancing, failover, routing, and monitoring and access control can also be done by an intermediary (see Figure 5.7). This unburdens each producing and consuming entity of the web service. This intermediary can also do the function of translation, as with messaging protocols, formats of XML messages, and security standards. They can also manage versioning of web services by directing consumers of the web service to different versions. All web service messages are routed first to the intermediary, where network policy is enforced. This class of solutions is called web services networking. Blue Titan and Grand Central are two vendors that offer such a capability. We cover web services manageability in detail in Chapter 14, "Managing Web Services."

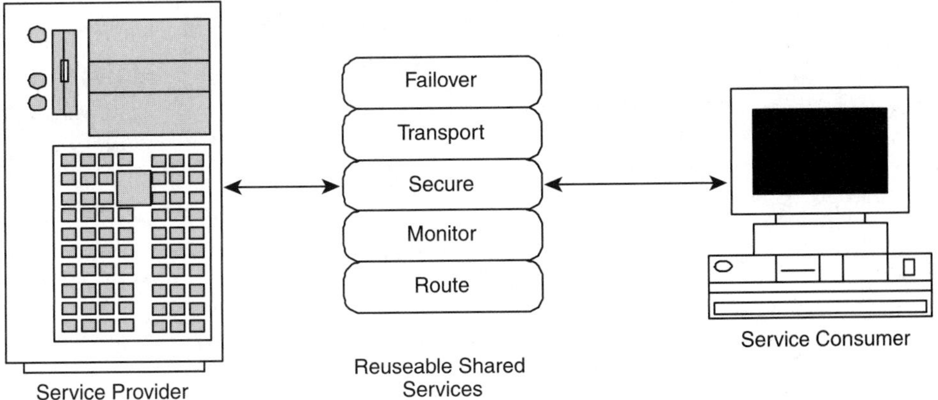

Figure 5.7 Web services networks

Summary

In this chapter, we focused on the considerations for enabling enterprise-class web services. These are web services that meet the level of technical and operational maturity consistent with the increasingly stringent requirements of today's enterprise.

J2EE web services must be designed for interoperability. This requires conforming to the specifications of XML, SOAP, WSDL, UDDI, and WS-I interoperability recommendations; designing the WSDL before implementing SOAP; and using document-literal as the SOAP messaging format.

Web services are published via WSDL. These represent contracts between the consumer and the producer of web services. To make these contracts durable, it is important to integrate using loose coupling, choose the right XML strategy, and use either versioning of the public interface or versioning of the implementation.

Web services are typically layered on top of enterprise business systems. To effectively interface with these business systems, we recommend using asynchronous communication using Workshop's web service conversations, using WebLogic's control framework to develop coarsely grained web services for reduced network overhead and improved performance, and using WebLogic's control framework and the MVC architecture to wrap the back-end components and help expose them as web services.

Security, scalability, and manageability considerations are crucial for enterprise-class web services. WS-Security secures SOAP messages and can be implemented using WebLogic Workshop through WS-Security policy files. Leverage the robust foundation of the WebLogic Server and improve performance by fine-tuning the WebLogic Server and using JRockit as the JVM. Use BEA WebLogic along with HP OpenView to manage web services. The former leverages JMX for developing MBeans, used for managing and monitoring web services. The latter offers the WebLogic Server–specific Smart Plug-In module for enhanced management capabilities. Intermediaries called Web Services Networks offload load balancing, failover, routing, monitoring, and access control from the web services infrastructure.

6

Designing Web Services

In this chapter, we look into the details of designing web services. Validate Config is an example of a real-world web service that we talked about in the HP case study in Chapter 4, "Benefiting from an SOA and Web Services." Throughout this chapter, we use a step-by-step approach to design this web service. We look at how to design a WSDL using XMLSPY. You will learn how to specify both the abstract and the concrete definitions of a WSDL, and you will learn how to validate the completed WSDL.

Next, using this WSDL, we show how you create the web service JWS files using WebLogic Workshop and test it. You will also learn how to test a web service using different clients: Java, Apache, and .NET. Finally, we talk about how to include versioning as part of the design of a web service.

Designing WSDL with XMLSPY

Often, developers develop the web services first and then use toolkits to create the WSDL. Because the WSDL is the contract between the provider of the service and the user of the service, you should do this the other way around: Model the WSDL first and then develop the web services for the WSDL.

Not all web services toolkits support the same WSDL message-binding options. .NET toolkits might not easily interpret WSDLs from Java toolkits because of inconsistencies in each vendor's implementation of WSDL, SOAP specifications, and compliance to WS-I basic profile. Therefore, interoperability is difficult or impossible to enforce if developers do not understand WSDL, do not know what WSDL definitions their toolkits will generate from their server-side native interfaces by default, or do not know how to customize their toolkits' behavior.

If you do not have the tools to model, another way is to let the web service toolkit create the WSDL and then manually add parts that the toolkit does not add, such as SOAP headers. Also test the WSDL with the WS-I tool and correct for errors and warnings, such as having a one-to-one relationship between messages and operations. Testing with the WS-I tool is described in Chapter 13, "Testing of Web Services."

XMLSPY WSDL Editor

XMLSPY from Altovo is a WSDL editor that ships along with WebLogic Workshop. A WSDL editor enables you to edit, visualize, and validate any WSDL file. WSDL is ideally suited as an interface definition language (IDL) for architecting web service applications, as shown in Figure 6.1.

By first building an interface for both the client and the server, you, as a programmer, can implement your programming contract using any language or operating system, thus avoiding interoperability problems.

XMLSPY has a WSDL documentation-generation utility that makes it easy for a web service developer to document and publish a web service's interface to business partners, other developers, or the public. Any WSDL file can be easily annotated and then published into a Microsoft Word or HTML output file, as shown in Figure 6.2.

example

`ValidateConfig` Web Service

The `ValidateConfig` web service is a real world web service that we use as an example throughout this chapter to show how to design a web service. This web service can be published by a PC manufacturer and consumed by an online retailer when a consumer is purchasing a PC. The service offer is to validate the correctness of the configuration of the PC that the consumer has selected. When the configuration is correct, it means that the PC manufacturer can indeed manufacture the selected PC.

The online retailer sends the components that make up a PC as input to the `ValidateConfig` web service. The PC manufacturer sends as output through the web service information on whether the configuration is correct and, if it is not correct, the error.

In this chapter, we show the process of designing the `ValidateConfig` web service in a step-by-step manner. We design the WSDL in XMLSPY. The web service that we design here is *document literal* with one operation. We show how to add new operations to this WSDL and how these appear over the wire. We also show how versioning can be done at design time.

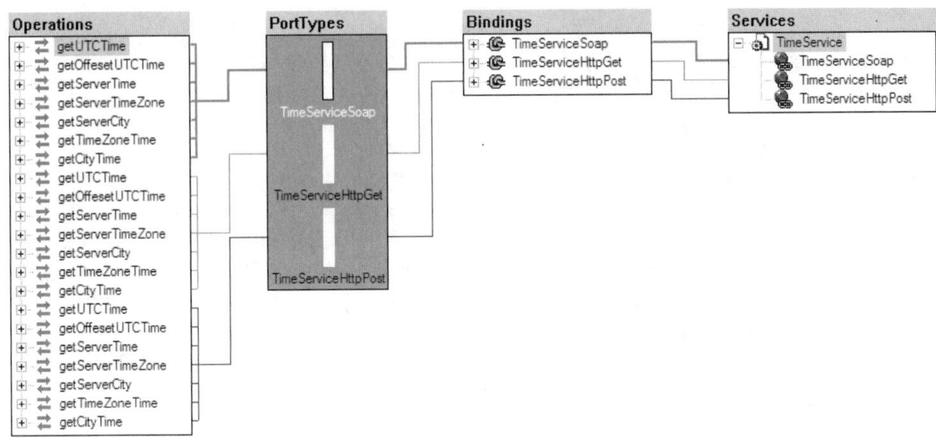

Figure 6.1 Defining the interface using WSDL

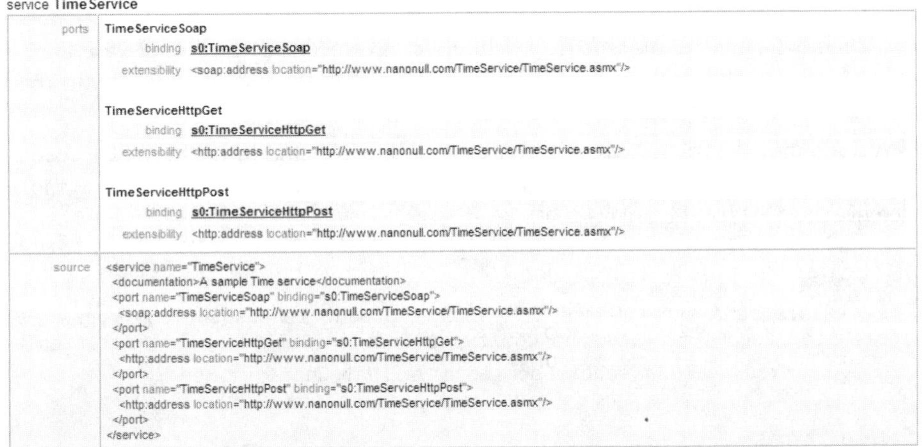

Figure 6.2 Annotating a WSDL file

Designing a web service starts with creating the WSDL. The WSDL describes the network services that the service provider (an endpoint) offers and is used as a recipe to generate the proper SOAP messages to access these services. A WSDL document includes three abstract definitions: types, messages and port type, and two concrete definitions: binding and service.

First, create the WSDL skeleton using XMLSPY (see Figure 6.3). The main components are Operations, PortTypes, Bindings, and Services.

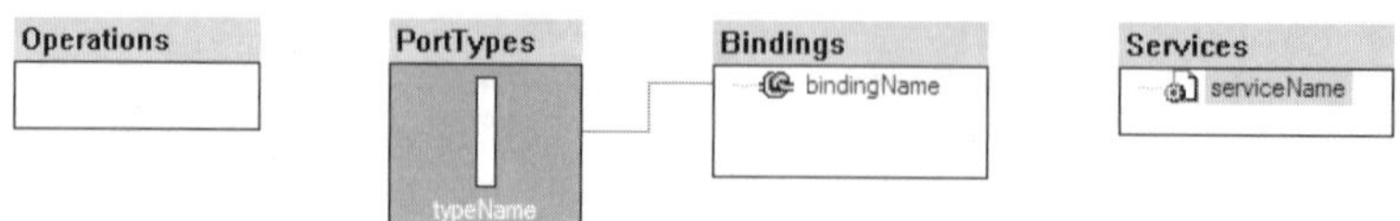

Figure 6.3 WSDL skeleton

In XMLSPY, you can see how to create a skeleton WSDL file, create a service and associate ports to this service, and associate a connection address to the binding. Next, we discuss how to add input and output messages, as well as their associated parameters; add messages to operations; and define the binding type. At the end, we show how to validate the WSDL.

Specifying Types

Next, you need to complete the types section of the WSDL. For this, you need the target namespace and the XML Schema definitions. The target namespace for the example is http://production.psg.hp.com/types.

The schemas for the `ValidateConfig` web service are already defined, so we use the XML strategy of creating the web service from the WSDL. We later describe how we do this by importing the WSDL into WebLogic Workshop.

To include the schema in XMLSPY, you can use Edit schema from the WSDL menu, as shown in Figure 6.4. You can either have the XSD embedded in the WSDL or use `xsd:include` to reference the XSD (see Figure 6.4):

```
<wsdl:types>
        <xsd:schema targetNamespace="http://production.psg.hp.com/types"
➥xmlns="http://production.psg.hp.com/types" elementFormDefault="qualified">
            <xsd:include schemaLocation="ValidateConfigv1.xsd"/>
        </xsd:schema>
    </wsdl:types>
```

import	loc: http://schemas.xmlsoap.org/soap/encoding/	ns: http://schemas.xmlsoap.org/soap/encoding/
include	loc: ValidateConfig_v1_2.xsd	

Figure 6.4 Include of schema

This pulls all the data types into the WSDL, as shown in Figure 6.5.

Each WSDL file imports the XML Schema for the data structure expected. In an RPC-encoded style of SOAP exchange, this is a simple process: Merely define the data type of each of the method arguments. Because there are generally only a few method arguments, this is a short definition list.

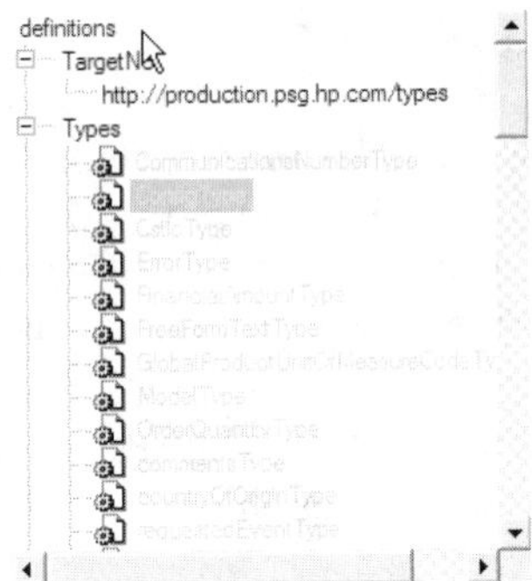

Figure 6.5 Types in WSDL

However, when you are using document-literal-style SOAP, an entire XML dataset is exchanged. Therefore, the data structure definition can be quite large. In this type of implementation of document-literal-style services, each data structure is imported into the corresponding WSDL file for external reference.

Moving forward, the industry standard is increasingly embracing a document-literal style of SOAP exchange, and each released version of a web service implementing this will import the data structure of XML exchanged for that service.

Specifying Services

Now you define the concrete definitions of the WSDL, the Service and the Port. In the services window, change the generic name Service to a `Validate_v1_2`. Add `Validate` as a port to the service. In the `location` field, enter the connection address of this service: `localhost:7001/Validate_v1_2`. This is the URL where your service is located. The WSDL now has the Service section as follows and as shown in Figure 6.6:

```
<wsdl:service name="Validate_v1_2">
        <wsdl:port name="Validate" binding="tns2:ValidateSoapBinding">
            <wsdlsoap:address location="localhost:7001 /validatev_1_2 "/>
        </wsdl:port>
</wsdl:service>
```

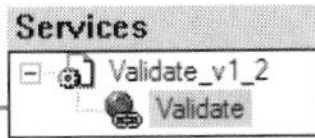

Figure 6.6 WSDL with service definition

Specifying portTypes

Next, you need to create the remaining two abstract definitions of the WSDL: portTypes and Messages. Change the generic name of the portType to `ValidateService` in the portType window. This changes the portType name in all associated portType windows. A portType is an abstract collection of operations. So next you define the operations that make up the `ValidateService` portType.

You can append operations to the portType. This creates a new operation in the Operations window and links the portType window to the Operations window, as shown in Figure 6.7. Call the operation `validateConfig`.

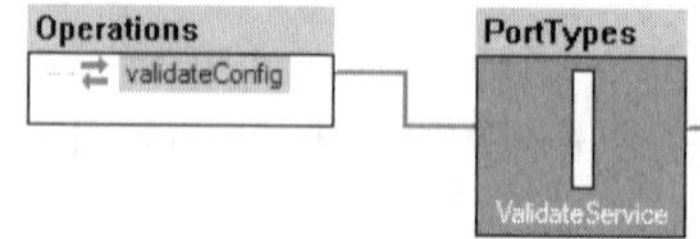

Figure 6.7 portType to Operations window

Specifying Messages

At this point, you need to add input and output messages to an operation. Call the input and output messages `validateRequest` and `validateResponse`. These messages define the abstract messages of the WSDL. These messages need to be connected to the incoming and outgoing schema through the part name. Add the part name `validateRequest` and `validateResponse` to the input and output messages, and connect it to the schemas `tns2: inValidateConfig` for `validateRequest` and `tns2: outValidateConfig` for the `validateResponse` part name, as shown Figure 6.8.

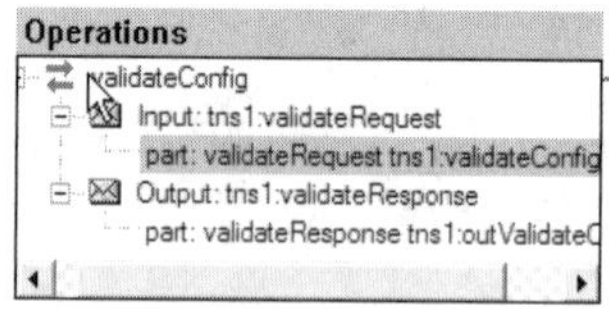

Figure 6.8 Part name

The abstract section of the WSDL then looks like this:

```
<wsdl:message name="validateRequest">
        <wsdl:part name="validateRequest"
➥ element="tns2:inValidateConfig"/>
    </wsdl:message>
```

```
    <wsdl:message name="validateResponse">
        <wsdl:part name="validateResponse"
➥ element="tns2:outValidateConfig"/>
    </wsdl:message>
    <wsdl:portType name="ValidateService">
        <wsdl:operation name="validateConfig">
            <wsdl:input message="tns2:validateRequest"/>
            <wsdl:output message="tns2:validateResponse"/>
        </wsdl:operation>
    </wsdl:portType>
```

Specifying Bindings

Next, you define the bindings. The binding section connects the abstract section to the concrete section of the WSDL. Call the binding `ValidateSoapBinding`. It has the operation `validateConfig` attached to it. This connects the abstract section to the binding. To connect the binding to the portName, select `ValidateSoapBinding` as the binding name. The other parameters of binding that you need to select are the type of binding, which is SOAP, use is literal, and style is document and transport uri is http://schemas.xmlsoap.org/soap/http. See Figures 6.9 and 6.10.

Figure 6.9 Binding: use

The binding section of the WSDL looks as follows:

```
    <wsdl:binding name="ValidateSoapBinding" type="tns2:ValidateService">
        <wsdlsoap:binding style="document"
➥transport="http://schemas.xmlsoap.org/soap/http"/>
    <wsdl:operation name="validateConfig">
```

```
            <wsdlsoap:operation soapAction="validate_v1_2"/>
            <wsdl:input>
                <wsdlsoap:body use="literal"/>
            </wsdl:input>
            <wsdl:output>
                <wsdlsoap:body use="literal"/>
            </wsdl:output>
        </wsdl:operation>
    </wsdl:binding>
```

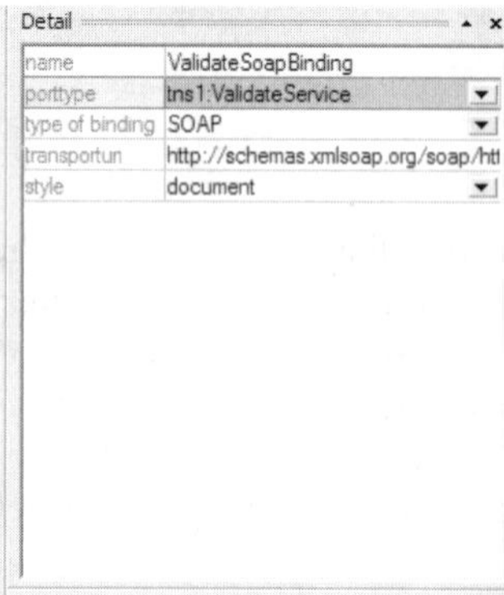

Figure 6.10 Binding: type, style

Validating the Completed WSDL

Now you need to validate the WSDL file. Press F8 to validate the file. You can now use the WSDL file as the basis of a web service. Here is the completed WSDL:

```
<wsdl:definitions xmlns="http://schemas.xmlsoap.org/wsdl/"
➥xmlns:soapenc="http://schemas.xmlsoap.org/soap/encoding/"
➥xmlns:wsdl="http://schemas.xmlsoap.org/wsdl/"
➥xmlns:wsdlsoap="http://schemas.xmlsoap.org/wsdl/soap/"
➥xmlns:xsd="http://www.w3.org/2001/XMLSchema"
➥xmlns:tns2="http://production.psg.hp.com/types"
➥xmlns:ns="http://production.psg.hp.com/types"
➥targetNamespace="http://production.psg.hp.com/types">
    <wsdl:types>
        <xsd:schema targetName
➥space="http://production.psg.hp.com/types"
➥xmlns="http://production.psg.hp.com/types"
➥elementFormDefault="qualified">
```

```
            <xsd:include schemaLocation="ValidateConfig_v1_2.xsd"/>
        </xsd:schema>
    </wsdl:types>
    <wsdl:message name="validateRequest">
        <wsdl:part name="validateRequest" element="tns2:inValidateConfig"/>
    </wsdl:message>
    <wsdl:message name="validateResponse">
        <wsdl:part name="validateResponse" element="tns2:outValidateConfig"/>
    </wsdl:message>
    <wsdl:portType name="ValidateService">
        <wsdl:operation name="validateConfig">
            <wsdl:input message="tns2:validateRequest"/>
            <wsdl:output message="tns2:validateResponse"/>
        </wsdl:operation>
    </wsdl:portType>
    <wsdl:binding name="ValidateSoapBinding" type="tns2:ValidateService">
        <wsdlsoap:binding style="document"
➥transport="http://schemas.xmlsoap.org/soap/http"/>
        <wsdl:operation name="validateConfig">
            <wsdlsoap:operation soapAction="validate_v1_2"/>
            <wsdl:input>
                <wsdlsoap:body use="literal"/>
            </wsdl:input>
            <wsdl:output>
                <wsdlsoap:body use="literal"/>
            </wsdl:output>
        </wsdl:operation>
    </wsdl:binding>
    <wsdl:service name="Validate_v1_2">
        <wsdl:port name="Validate" binding="tns2:ValidateSoapBinding">
            <wsdlsoap:address location="localhost:7001/ validatev_1_2 "/>
        </wsdl:port>
    </wsdl:service>
</wsdl:definitions>
```

Adding Operations to the WSDL

You can generate a SOAP message from this WSDL file to test it. Notice in the SOAP message that the root element is not the operation name. This is typical of a document-literal service and shows how it differs from an RPC-encoded service. In a document-literal service, the operation is not passed as the root element of the SOAP Body:

```
<SOAP-ENV:Envelope xmlns:SOAP-ENV="http://schemas.xmlsoap.org/soap/envelope/"
➥xmlns:SOAP-ENC="http://schemas.xmlsoap.org/soap/encoding/"
➥xmlns:xsi="http://www.w3.org/2001/XMLSchema-instance"
➥xmlns:xsd="http://www.w3.org/2001/XMLSchema">
    <SOAP-ENV:Body>
        <m:inValidateConfig
➥xmlns:m="http://production.psg.hp.com/types/02/04/2004">
            <m:Config>
                <m:Model/>
                <m:Cstic/>
            </m:Config>
            <m:AccountID>0000000000</m:AccountID>
            <m:Password>String</m:Password>
            <m:IpcVersion>OLD</m:IpcVersion>
            <m:ConfigID>String</m:ConfigID>
        </m:inValidateConfig>
    </SOAP-ENV:Body>
</SOAP-ENV:Envelope>
```

WebLogic Server needs the operation name as the root element to call the right method for the web service. You can provide the mapping of the operation to the root element through the Ant file used to deploy your web service. In the next chapter, when we discuss the deployment of web services, you will learn how the operation can be interpreted from the root element of the SOAP Body.

The other challenge is how you handle more than one operation in a document-literal service. For example, imagine that you want to add another operation, `validatePrice`, to the WSDL. Let us assume that the input schema is the same for both the operations. However, the output messages for each operation are different.

The challenge here is that because the input schemas are the same, they will send the same root element in the SOAP message, and your web service will not be capable of recognizing which operation to call. To solve this issue, you can define two different input SOAP messages in your WSDL, but the messages refer to the same schema.

In the example, WSDL with two operations, `validateConfig` and `validatePrice`, looks as follows. As you can see, each operations input message is different, but when you look at the input schemas, they are the same.

The WSDL looks as follows:

```
<wsdl:types>
    <xsd:schema targetNamespace="http://production.psg.hp.com/types"
➥xmlns="http://production.psg.hp.com/types"
➥elementFormDefault="qualified">
        <xsd:include schemaLocation="ValidateConfigv1.xsd"/>
        <xsd:include schemaLocation="ValidatePricev1.xsd"/>
    </xsd:schema>
```

```
    </wsdl:types>
<wsdl:message name="validateRequest">
        <wsdl:part name="validateRequest" element="tns2:inValidateConfig"/>
    </wsdl:message>
    <wsdl:message name="validateResponse">
        <wsdl:part name="validateResponse" element="tns2:outValidateConfig"/>
    </wsdl:message>
    <wsdl:message name="validateinPrice">
        <wsdl:part name="validateinPrice" element="tns2:inValidatePrice"/>
    </wsdl:message>
    <wsdl:message name="validatePrice">
        <wsdl:part name="validatePrice" element="tns2:outValidatePrice"/>
    </wsdl:message>
    <wsdl:portType name="ValidateService">
        <wsdl:operation name="validateConfig">
            <wsdl:input message="tns2:validateRequest"/>
            <wsdl:output message="tns2:validateResponse"/>
        </wsdl:operation>
        <wsdl:operation name="validatePrice">
            <wsdl:output message="tns2:validatePrice"/>
            <wsdl:input message="tns2:validateinPrice"/>
        </wsdl:operation>
    </wsdl:portType>
```

Schemas look as follows for `inValidateConfig`:

```
<xsd:element name="inValidateConfig">
        <xsd:complexType>
            <xsd:sequence>
                <xsd:element name="Config" type="ConfigType"/>
                <xsd:element name="AccountID" type="AccountIDType"/>
                <xsd:element name="Password"
➥type="xsd:string" minOccurs="0"/>
                <xsd:element name="IpcVersion" type="IPCVersionType"/>
                <xsd:element name="ConfigID"
➥type="xsd:string" minOccurs="0"/>
                <!-- unique per xaction -->
            </xsd:sequence>
        </xsd:complexType>
</xsd:element>
```

and `inValidatePrice`:

```
<xsd:element name="inValidatePrice">
        <xsd:complexType>
            <xsd:sequence>
                <xsd:element name="Config" type="ConfigType"/>
                <xsd:element name="AccountID" type="AccountIDType"/>
                <xsd:element name="Password"
➥type="xsd:string" minOccurs="0"/>
                <xsd:element name="IpcVersion" type="IPCVersionType"/>
                <xsd:element name="ConfigID"
➥type="xsd:string" minOccurs="0"/>
                <!-- unique per xaction -->
            </xsd:sequence>
        </xsd:complexType>
</xsd:element>
```

SOAP messages on the wire `validateConfig` look as follows:

```
<SOAP-ENV:Envelope xmlns:SOAP-ENV="http://schemas.xmlsoap.org/soap/envelope/"

xmlns:SOAP-ENC="http://schemas.xmlsoap.org/soap/encoding/"
➥xmlns:xsi="http://www.w3.org/2001/XMLSchema-instance"
➥xmlns:xsd="http://www.w3.org/2001/XMLSchema">
    <SOAP-ENV:Body>
        <m:inValidateConfig
➥xmlns:m="http://production.psg.hp.com/types/02/04/2004">
            <m:Config>
                <m:Model/>
                <m:Cstic/>
            </m:Config>
            <m:AccountID>0000000000</m:AccountID>
            <m:Password>String</m:Password>
            <m:IpcVersion>OLD</m:IpcVersion>
            <m:ConfigID>String</m:ConfigID>
        </m:inValidateConfig>
    </SOAP-ENV:Body>
</SOAP-ENV:Envelope>
```

For `ValidatePrice`, it looks like this:

```
<SOAP-ENV:Envelope xmlns:SOAP-ENV="http://schemas.xmlsoap.org/soap/envelope/"

xmlns:SOAP-ENC="http://schemas.xmlsoap.org/soap/encoding/"
➥xmlns:xsi="http://www.w3.org/2001/XMLSchema-instance"
➥xmlns:xsd="http://www.w3.org/2001/XMLSchema">
```

```
    <SOAP-ENV:Body>
        <m:inValidatePrice
➥xmlns:m="http://production.psg.hp.com/types/02/04/2004">
            <m:Config>
                <m:Model/>
                <m:Cstic/>
            </m:Config>
            <m:AccountID>0000000000</m:AccountID>
            <m:Password>String</m:Password>
            <m:IpcVersion>OLD</m:IpcVersion>
            <m:ConfigID>String</m:ConfigID>
        </m:inValidatePrice>
    </SOAP-ENV:Body>
</SOAP-ENV:Envelope>
```

As you can see, the root elements are different for the two SOAP messages, so WebLogic Server can direct the client to two different operations.

Prototyping Using Workshop

After you have designed the WSDL in XMLSPY, you can import it into WebLogic Workshop. In Workshop, you can rapidly prototype a web service using the WSDL and also test it to verify that you are getting the right response from the web service.

Main Components of Workshop

Let's look at the basic concepts that you need to know to begin building web services with WebLogic Workshop. A WebLogic Workshop application is a set of projects, libraries, and resources that are related in some way. Your web service project (and other projects you're working on) is contained in this application. You can build multiple web services within a single web service project. At deployment time, a WebLogic Workshop application is compiled into a J2EE EAR file.

Creating a Web Service from the WSDL

Let's walk through the steps of converting a WSDL to a web service using the `ValidateConfig` example:

1. First, you need to create a new application in WebLogic Workshop called `ValidateConfig`. When you create an application, use the default application.

2. Create a web service project and, within that, a web services folder. You will see under the project that you also have a WEB-INF file. We talk more about this folder in the section on creating proxies and also in the deployment of web services in the next chapter.
3. Import the WSDL to the Web Services folder.
4. Right-click on the WSDL and create a web service from it. The web service is created as a JWS file, as shown in Figure 6.11.

In the source view, it creates the Java code for the web service, as shown in Figure 6.11.

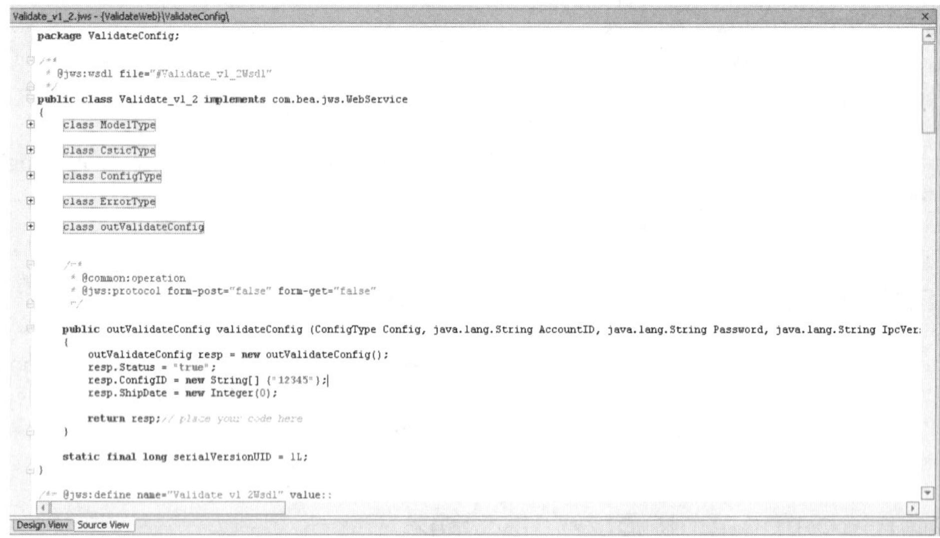

Figure 6.11 Web service in source view

In the web service source view, you will see that there is a section that reads "Place code here." Here, you put the business logic.

You can also create a web service from the WSDL using BEA WL command-line tools and Ant tasks. You can use the `wsdl2Service` Ant task, which uses an existing WSDL file and generates the Java interface that represents the implementation of your web service based on the WSDL file, the Java exception class for user-defined exceptions specified in the WSDL file, and the `web-services.xml` file that describes the web service.

The template includes the method signatures that correspond to the operations in the WSDL file. Write a Java class that implements this interface so that the methods function as you want. The `wsdl2Service` Ant task generates a Java interface for only one web service in a WSDL file (specified by the `<service>` element). If you have more than one service, use the `serviceName` attribute to specify a particular service so that the `wsdl2Service` Ant task can generate a Java interface for that service.

The wsdl2Service Ant task does *not* generate data type mapping information for any non-built-in data types used as parameters or return values of the operations in the WSDL file. If your WSDL uses non-built-in data types, you must first do the data type and then point the typeMappingFile attribute of the wsdl2Service Ant task to the types.xml file generated by the autotype Ant task.

Web Service as JWS Files

In Workshop, JWS files represent the web services. Let's take a close look at JWS files.

A JWS file contains syntactically correct Java. However, a JWS file also has attributes that allow it to take advantage of WebLogic Workshop's powerful facilities for web services. It contains javadoc annotations specific to WebLogic Workshop that enable or access features in the WebLogic Workshop runtime. It has the .jws extension, which, when it appears in a URL, indicates to WebLogic Server that the file should be handled as a web service. A JWS file contains only the logic that you need to implement your web service. The underlying infrastructure, protocols, and web service lifecycle management are handled automatically by the WebLogic Workshop runtime.

A JWS file contains the package statement, import statements, the class declaration, member variables, control instances, the JWSContext object, a callback interface, inner classes, methods, and internal methods.

The package statement specifies the Java package in which the classes and objects in this file reside. The package is dictated by the directory in the project within which the JWS file is located. It contains the following package statement:

```
package validate;
```

WebLogic Workshop manages the package statement for you. For example, if you move a JWS file from one directory to another using the Application pane, WebLogic Workshop updates the package name in the moved file.

A JWS file must include the declaration of a single top-level public class. The name of your web service is the name of this class:

```
public class Validate_v1_2 implements com.bea.jws.
 {
     ...
}
```

The implements com.bea.jws clause indicates that this class is a web service. The WebService Java interface is a marker interface only; it declares no methods.

The term *method* refers to a method that is exposed to clients of your service. A method is exposed to the client when it is marked with the @common:operation annotation. Methods that are exposed to the client must be declared with the public access modifier.

The `@jws:protocol` annotation specifies which protocols and messages formats the web service can receive. The web service can then listen on the specified protocols and understands these messages. The default behavior for a JWS file is to enable SOAP with document-literal formatting of method calls via `http-post` and `http-get`. Therefore, in the following example, you see `form-post ="false"` and `form-get = "false"`. The other protocols are `http-soap`, `http-soap12` (SOAP 1.2 messages), `http-xml` (XML messages), `jms-soap`, `jms-soap12` (JMS over SOAP 1.1 and 1.2), `jms-xml` (XML messages), and `soap style`, which can be specified as `document` or `rpc`.

Because we are prototyping, we put in a default return value for the purposes of testing the web service:

```
/**
      * @common:operation
      * @jws:protocol form-post="false" form-get="false"
      */
     public outValidateConfig validateConfig
➥ (ConfigType Config, java.lang.String AccountID,
➥java.lang.String Password, java.lang.String
➥IpcVersion, java.lang.String ConfigID)
     {
          outValidateConfig resp = new outValidateConfig();
          resp.Status = "true";
          resp.ConfigID = new String[] {"12345"};
          resp.ShipDate = new Integer(0);

          return resp;
          // place your code here
     }

     static final long serialVersionUID = 1L;
}
```

Testing the Web Service Using Workshop

WebLogic Workshop provides a test environment for the web services you develop. This environment is called test view. You begin testing the web service by using the Start button to start the web service.

Test view provides a way for you to invoke a web service's methods from a browser and view the XML messages that are exchanged. Test view keeps a log of all the activity during the test. You can use the logs to examine the details of the interaction between the client and web service at any point.

Test view can be reached directly via the Start or Start with Debug actions in WebLogic Workshop's user interface. However, you can also enter test view directly by entering the URL of your web service in the address bar of a browser.

In the test browser, use the Test XML tab, shown in Figure 6.12. In the figure, you see the SOAP request, in which the SOAP body has the incoming schema. As you can see, the root element is not the operation name.

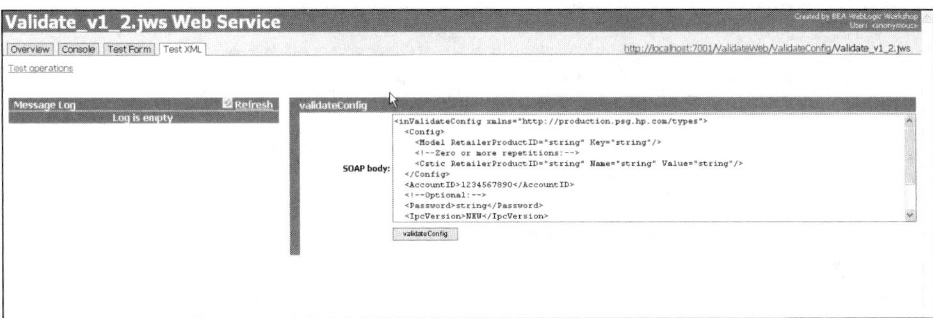

Figure 6.12 Incoming SOAP message

When you click `validateConfig`, you will see the SOAP response, as shown in Figure 6.13.

Service Response

Submitted at Saturday, May 15, 2004 8:01:27 PM PDT

```
<SOAP-ENV:Envelope xmlns:SOAP-ENV="http://schemas.xmlsoap.org/soap/envelope/" xmlns:xsd="http://www.w3.org/2001/XMLSchema"
  xmlns:xsi="http://www.w3.org/2001/XMLSchema-instance">
  <SOAP-ENV:Body>
    <ns:outValidateConfig xmlns:ns="http://production.psg.hp.com/types">
      <ns:Status>true</ns:Status>
      <ns:ConfigID>12345</ns:ConfigID>
      <ns:ShipDate>0</ns:ShipDate>
    </ns:outValidateConfig>
  </SOAP-ENV:Body>
</SOAP-ENV:Envelope>
```

Figure 6.13 Incoming and outgoing SOAP message

The SOAP response contains the outgoing schema. It has a status that indicates whether the configuration is correct. If there is an error, a SOAP fault is sent back. In the example, you can see an error stating that the `invalidateConfig` element could not be resolved (see Figure 6.14).

Service Response

Submitted at Saturday, January 31, 2004 8:02:12 PM PST

```
<SOAP-ENV:Envelope xmlns:SOAP-ENV="http://schemas.xmlsoap.org/soap/envelope/" xmlns:xsd="http://www.w3.org/2001/XMLSchema" xmlns:xsi="http://www.w3.org/2001/X
  instance">
  <SOAP-ENV:Body>
    <SOAP-ENV:Fault>
      <faultcode xmlns:fc="http://www.bea.com/2003/04/jwFaultCode/">fc:JWSError</faultcode>
      <faultstring>
        Could not resolve method with element 'http://production.psg.hp.com/types:inValidateConfig' as top element.
        </faultstring>
      <detail>
        <jwErr:jwErrorDetail xmlns:jwErr="http://www.bea.com/2002/04/jwErrorDetail/">
          com.bea.wlw.runtime.core.request.RequestValidationException: Could not resolve method with element
          'http://production.psg.hp.com/types:inValidateConfig' as top element.
          at com.bea.wlw.runtime.jws.request.SoapRequest.getDispMethodFromStream(SoapRequest.java:669)
          at com.bea.wlw.runtime.jws.request.SoapRequest.<init>(SoapRequest.java:423)
          at com.bea.wlw.runtime.jws.request.XmlRequest.validateTarget(XmlRequest.java:174)
          at com.bea.wlw.runtime.core.bean.SyncDispatcherBean.invoke(SyncDispatcherBean.java:65)
          at com.bea.wlw.runtime.core.bean.SyncDispatcher_k1mrl8_EOImpl.invoke(SyncDispatcher_k1mrl8_EOImpl.java:100)
          at com.bea.wlw.runtime.core.dispatcher.Dispatcher.remoteDispatch(Dispatcher.java:161)
          at com.bea.wlw.runtime.core.dispatcher.Dispatcher.dispatch(Dispatcher.java:49)
          at com.bea.wlw.runtime.core.dispatcher.HttpServerHelper.executePostRequest(HttpServerHelper.java:703)
          at com.bea.wlw.runtime.core.dispatcher.HttpServer.doPost(HttpServer.java:49)
          at javax.servlet.http.HttpServlet.service(HttpServlet.java:760)
          at javax.servlet.http.HttpServlet.service(HttpServlet.java:853)
          at weblogic.servlet.internal.ServletStubImpl$ServletInvocationAction.run(ServletStubImpl.java:971)
          at weblogic.servlet.internal.ServletStubImpl.invokeServlet(ServletStubImpl.java:402)
          at weblogic.servlet.internal.ServletStubImpl.invokeServlet(ServletStubImpl.java:305)
          at weblogic.servlet.internal.WebAppServletContext$ServletInvocationAction.run(WebAppServletContext.java:6354)
          at weblogic.security.acl.internal.AuthenticatedSubject.doAs(AuthenticatedSubject.java:317)
          at weblogic.security.service.SecurityManager.runAs(SecurityManager.java:118)
          at weblogic.servlet.internal.WebAppServletContext.invokeServlet(WebAppServletContext.java:3635)
          at weblogic.servlet.internal.ServletRequestImpl.execute(ServletRequestImpl.java:2585)
          at weblogic.kernel.ExecuteThread.execute(ExecuteThread.java:197)
          at weblogic.kernel.ExecuteThread.run(ExecuteThread.java:170)

          </jwErr:jwErrorDetail>
      </detail>
    </SOAP-ENV:Fault>
  </SOAP-ENV:Body>
</SOAP-ENV:Envelope>
```

Figure 6.14 SOAP fault

Next, if you go to the Overview tab, you can click on Complete WSDL to get the WSDL for the web service.

Testing the Web Service Using a Client

After you have designed/prototyped the web service, it is a good idea to test it with a web service client. You can create the web services clients in different ways. We discuss the following:

- Java proxy from a JSP
- Separate Java application
- Customized Java proxy
- Apache client
- .NET client

Java Client

You can create a Java proxy for the web service and give it to the user of your web service. We first discuss how to create a Java proxy in WebLogic. Using the Java proxy for a web service requires different steps, depending on whether you use it from within WebLogic Server (as in a JSP or servlet) or from outside WebLogic Server (as in a standalone Java application).

First, create the Java proxy from a JSP. You can get the Java proxy from the test browser in the Overview tab, as shown in Figure 6.15. Save the file to the WEB-INF/lib directory of the web application that you want to use.

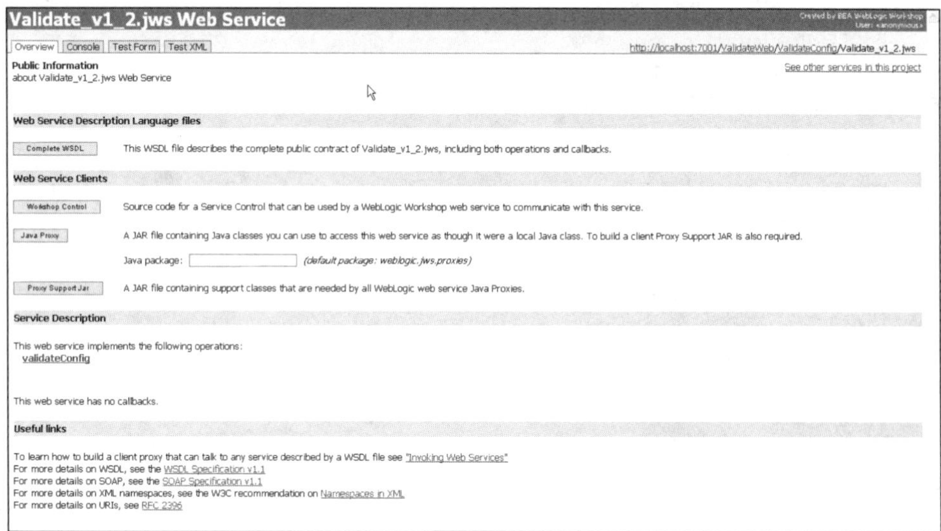

Figure 6.15 Java proxy

Create a new application called clientJSP, and create a JSP called `ValidateJSP`. Save the JAR file to the WEB-INF directory of this JSP file. In your JSP file, add an import of the web service proxy package, as shown here:

```
<%@ page import="weblogic.jws.proxies.*" %>
```

Create an instance of the proxy class as shown next. Use the name of the web service with `_Impl` appended to the end to get the generic proxy class:

```
<% Validate_v1_2_Impl proxy = new Validate_v1_2_Impl(); %>
```

The generic proxy returns protocol-specific proxies that, in turn, contain the actual interface of the web service proxy.getValidateService. In this example, we would like to use a SOAP proxy:

```
<% ValidateService vs = proxy.getValidateService(); %>
```

Call the appropriate methods on the protocol-specific proxy, as shown here for the example:

```
<%
InValidateConfig req = new InValidateConfig();
req.setAccountID("1234");
req._unsetConfigID();
req.setPassword("password");
req.setIpcVersion(IPCVersionType.NEW);
OutValidateConfig resp = vs.validateConfig(req);%>
```

Now, to create a separate Java application, obtain the Java proxy JAR file as described earlier. Save the JAR file to a location that is convenient for your Java application. Also save the proxy support JAR file from the test browser in the same place as the Java proxy file.

Use the proxy classes as described in the previous procedure for JSPs. The following is an example of a Java client using the Validate_v1_2 service:

```
import weblogic.jws.proxies.*;
public class Main
{
    public static void main(String[] args)
    {
        try
        {
          Validate_v1_2_Impl proxy = new Validate_v1_2_Impl();

            ValidateService vs = proxy.getValidateService();
            InValidateConfig req = new InValidateConfig();
req.setAccountID("1234");
req._unsetConfigID();
req.setPassword("password");
req.setIpcVersion(IPCVersionType.NEW);
OutValidateConfig resp = vs.validateConfig(req);
        }
        catch (Exception e)
        {
            e.printStackTrace();
        }
    }
}
```

Compile your source while making sure that you include the saved JAR files in your class path. Run your Java application, including the two JAR files on your class path.

When you want to customize a generated Java proxy, remember that WebLogic Workshop uses WebLogic Server's clientgen tool to generate the Java proxy for a web service, based on the web service's WSDL file. You can use the clientgen tool directly if you want to customize the generated Java proxy. The clientgen tool accepts several command-line parameters. The only parameter set by WebLogic Workshop when generating a Java proxy from test view is the `packageName` parameter, which is always set to `weblogic.jws.proxies`.

To run the clientgen Ant task directly and automatically generate the web service-specific client JAR file, first set the environment. On Windows NT, execute the `setEnv.cmd` command, located in your domain directory. The default location of WebLogic Server domains is `BEA_HOME\user_projects\domains\domainName`, where `BEA_HOME` is the top-level installation directory and `domainName` is the name of your domain.

On UNIX, execute the `setEnv.sh` command, located in your domain directory. The default location of WebLogic Server domains is `BEA_HOME/user_projects/domains/domainName`. Next, create a file called `build.xml` that contains a call to the `clientgen` Ant task:

```
<project name="buildWebservice" default="generate-client">
   <target name="generate-client">
      <clientgen wsdl="
➥http://localhost:7001/services/placeOrderWebService?WSDL"
                  packageName=" services.placeOrderWebService.client"
                  clientJar=" services.placeOrderWebService.client.jar"
/>
   </target>
</project>
```

Execute the Ant task or tasks specified in the `build.xml` file by typing `ant` in the same directory as the build.xml file.

When you run the `clientgen` Ant task using the preceding `build.xml` file, the Ant task creates a client JAR file (called `services/placeOrderWebService _client.jar`) that the client application uses to invoke the web service described by the http://localhost:7001/services/placeOrderWebService?WSDL. It packages the interface and stub files in the myapp .myservice.client package.

Apache Client

If the user of your service is using another application server, such as Apache, you can give the user of the service the WSDL. Apache Axis uses WSDL2Java in Apache to create the Java proxy. From these Java proxies, the user can create a client to call your web service. Shown here is an example of a Java client generated using WSDL2Java in Apache:

```
public class VCTester {

    public static void main(String[] args) {
        try
        {
            Validate_v1_2 validate_v1_2 = new Validate_v1_2Locator();

            ValidateService validateServicePort
➥= validate_v1_2.getValidate();

            _inValidateConfig invalidateConfig = new _inValidateConfig();

            AccountIDType accountID = new AccountIDType();
            accountID.setValue("0000000000");

            ConfigType config = new ConfigType();
            CsticType cstic= new CsticType();
            cstic.setName("cstic");
            cstic.setRetailerProductID("productid");
            cstic.setValue("value");

            ModelType model = new ModelType();
            model.setKey("key");
            model.setRetailerProductID("retailerProductId");

            config.setModel(model);
            CsticType[] csticList = new CsticType[1];
            csticList[0] = cstic;
            config.setCstic(csticList);

            invalidateConfig.setAccountID(accountID);
            invalidateConfig.setConfig(config);
            invalidateConfig.setConfigID("1234");
            invalidateConfig.setIpcVersion(IPCVersionType.NEW);
            invalidateConfig.setPassword("password");


            _outValidateConfig outValidateConfig = (_outValidateConfig)
➥validateServicePort.validateConfig(invalidateConfig);

            System.out.println("Hi");

        }
        catch(Exception excp)
```

```
        {
            excp.printStackTrace();
        }
    }
}
```

.NET Client

To create a .NET client, you can use `WSDL.exe` from the .NET Framework. You can also create the .NET client from Visual Studio environment. One point to keep in mind is that when you do an include or import of a schema in your `wsdl.exe`, the .NET Framework is more forgiving than Visual Studio in creating the client. There is a behavioral difference between using the Add Web Reference Wizard in Visual Studio 2003 and using `wsdl.exe` to generate web service proxy classes. Following is an example of a .NET client in C#:

```
using System;
using System.Xml;
using System.Web.Services.Protocols;
namespace Project3
{
    /// <summary>
    /// Summary description for VCTest.
    /// </summary>
    public class VCTest
    {
        public VCTest()
        {
            //
            // TODO: Add constructor logic here
            //
        }

        public static void Main(String[] args)
        {
            try
            {

                Validate_v1_2 validate = new Validate_v1_2();

                validate.Url = "http://localhost:7001
➥/services/Validate_v1_2"; (here the /services can be below validate.Url but
I am not able to format it and also all the following lines)
```

```
                    inValidateConfig invalidateConfig = new inValidateConfig();

                    invalidateConfig.AccountID = "0000000000";
                    invalidateConfig.ConfigID = "ConfigID";
                    invalidateConfig.IpcVersion = IPCVersionType.NEW;
                    invalidateConfig.Password = "password";

                    ConfigType config = new ConfigType();
                    CsticType cstic = new CsticType();
                    cstic.Name = "csticname";
                    cstic.RetailerProductID = "RetailerProductId";
                    cstic.Value = "csticvalue";

                    CsticType[] csticArr = new CsticType[1];
                    csticArr[0] = cstic;
                    config.Cstic = csticArr;

                    ModelType model = new ModelType();
                    model.Key = "modelkey";
                    model.RetailerProductID = "retailerProductId";
                    config.Model = model;

                    invalidateConfig.Config = config;

                    outValidateConfig response = vali
➥date.validateConfig(invalidateConfig);


                    System.Xml.Serialization.XmlSerializer xmlSerializer = new
➥System.Xml.Serialization.XmlSerializer(typeof(outValidateConfig));
                    System.IO.StreamWriter myFile = new
➥System.IO.StreamWriter("C:\\CPD\\dotnet\\Project2\\VC-output-a.xml");
                    xmlSerializer.Serialize(myFile, response);
                    myFile.Close();



                    Console.WriteLine(response.ConfigID);
               }
               catch(SoapException soapExcp)
               {
                    Console.WriteLine(soapExcp.Actor);
                    Console.WriteLine(soapExcp.Code);
                    Console.WriteLine(soapExcp.Detail);
                    Console.WriteLine(soapExcp.Message);
```

```
                Console.WriteLine(soapExcp.ToString());
            }
            catch(Exception e)
            {
                Console.WriteLine(e.StackTrace);
                Console.WriteLine(e.Message);
                Console.WriteLine(e.Source);
            }
        }
    }
}
```

Design for Versioning

While designing, you also need to consider how you will version the web service when it is in production. Let us see how to use the versioning capability in WebLogic Workshop to version the sample web service that you created earlier. WebLogic Workshop handles both aspects of versioning: the first is the versioning of the interface, and the second is the versioning of the implementation itself.

Versioning the Interface

We talked in the previous chapter about different ways of versioning the web services interface. Here, you will see how to add new operations to the web service in WebLogic Workshop and use versioning to deal with existing operations.

Consider that a new version of the `ValidateConfig` service has a new element, `PriceType`, in the outgoing schema, and the XSD is now `ValidateConfig_v1_3. xsd`. Include this in the WSDL `Validate_v1_2.wsdl`. Then add a new operation, `validateConfigv3`, to `Validate_v1_2.wsdl`, as described earlier in this chapter. Import the new WSDL to Workshop and create the new service `Validate_v1_2.jws`, which now has two operations. Figure 6.16 shows the web service with the two operations.

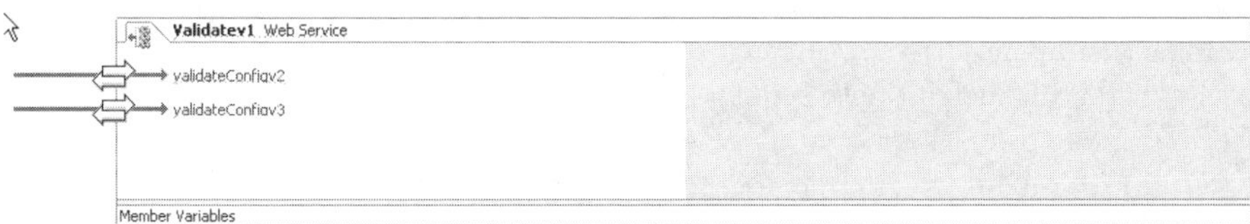

Figure 6.16 Web service with two operations

Instead of importing the WSDL again, you can add a method called `validateConfigv3` to `Validate_v1_2.jws`. The method needs to be qualified to implement the new schema element. Then import the schema to the Schemas directory and include it in the WSDL. An example of including price type is shown here:

```
public outValidateConfig validateConfigv3(ConfigType
➥Config, java.lang.String AccountID, java.lang.String
➥Password, java.lang.String IpcVersion, java.lang.String ConfigID)
    {
        outValidateConfig resp = new outValidateConfig();
        resp.Status = "true";
        resp.ConfigID = new String[] {"12345"};
        resp.PriceType = new String[] {"acquistion"};
        resp.ShipDate = new Integer(0);

        return resp;
    }

    static final long serialVersionUID = 1L;
```

Versioning the Implementation

For versioning of the implementation, WebLogic Workshop uses Java serialization. The `ServiceCompatible` changes are described in the Java Serialization Specification and include changing the implementation of a method, adding new methods, and adding new instance variables. Certain types of changes are not compatible between versions. They include changing the type of a variable and moving a class within an inheritance hierarchy. You should avoid making these kinds of changes if you want to maintain backward compatibility.

This way of versioning is known as hot-fix versioning because although there can be multiple earlier versions of an implementation, there can be only one current version of an implementation. Deploying an updated version of a class creates the new current version. At that point, all conversational instances that receive requests for that service will use the current version, regardless of which version was used to process any earlier requests.

Web services created in WebLogic Workshop include a default field, `serialVersionUID`, for tracking binary compatibility between web service versions. In the web service we have created, you can see that the default field is included:

```
public outValidateConfig validateConfig (ConfigType
➥Config, java.lang.String AccountID, java.lang.String
➥Password, java.lang.String IpcVersion, java.lang.String ConfigID)
```

```
{
    ...
}

static final long serialVersionUID = 1L;
```

In the property editor, you can see the `serialVersionUID` (see Figure 6.17). This value remains constant as long as subsequent revisions of the web service maintain binary compatibility. The Java Virtual Machine uses this value, and you should not modify it.

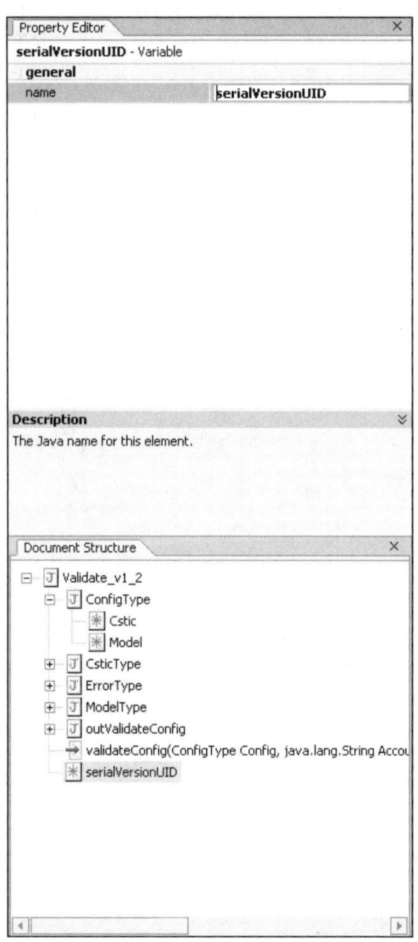

Figure 6.17 `SerialVersionUID` in the property editor

If WebLogic Workshop detects that a class does not have a `serialVersionUID` field but is being serialized as part of a request to a web service, WebLogic Workshop generates a warning message.

Summary

The first step in designing a web service is to create the WSDL. For interoperability reasons, we strongly recommend that you design WSDL instead of letting toolkits automatically produce it. XMLSPY has a WSDL editor and comes bundled with BEA WebLogic Workshop. Starting from a WSDL skeleton, the main steps in creating a WSDL are to specify the types, services, portTypes, messages, and bindings; to validate the completed WSDL; and, optionally, to also add new operations to the WSDL.

WebLogic Workshop allows for quick prototyping of a web service from WSDL. You create JWS files to represent the web service. JWS files take advantage of Workshop's powerful facilities for web services. You can use Workshop to test the web service you create. We suggest that you also test the web service using Java clients, Apache clients, and .NET clients.

It is important to look at versioning during design. You have to consider versioning at two levels: versioning the interface and versioning the implementation.

This chapter provided a detailed example of designing the `ValidateConfig` web service from a real-world web services implementation.

After we have designed the web services, the next step is to develop them. We cover this topic in the following chapter.

7 Developing and Deploying Web Services

"Web services do not try to reinvent the wheel but layer on top of the functions already available." —Saumyendra Mathur, Americas IT Manager, Supply Chain IT, Hewlett-Packard Co.

In this chapter, we describe the essentials of developing and deploying web services, and demonstrate how to do these using WebLogic Workshop. In the previous chapter, you learned how to design the WSDL and prototype the web service. Here, we look at adding to a web service a set of capabilities that are required in business environments. As a developer, you can be more efficient in developing web services by following some of the techniques described in this chapter.

First, we look at enabling asynchronous communication using callbacks, conversations, buffering, and polling. Then we talk about sending and receiving SOAP with attachments and how to ensure interoperability with .NET implementations. We also show how to transform XML Schemas to match with client environments using XQuery map and ECMAScript. After a web service is developed, we cover how to publish and enable discovery of the web service using UDDI Explorer and web service control. Finally, we show how to deploy the web service to a production environment using automatic and manual methods, and how to view and test this deployed web service.

Building an Asynchronous Web Service

When a client makes a request from a web service, if the web service doesn't return a response right away, the client might be left waiting for it, incapable of continuing other operations. This wait is not desirable in many business situations because many steps in a business process take time to complete. For example, when an order is placed on an enterprise, internal credit checks and inventory checks need to be completed. Therefore, an immediate response cannot be given to the party placing the order. The desired behavior is for the client to proceed with other operations after the web service request is made. Only when the request has been processed by the web service provider and a response is ready does the client need to revert attention to the result of this previously placed web service request. We look at a business situation in which such asynchronous behavior is needed and show you how to build asynchronous web services in WebLogic Workshop. We use real-world examples (see the accompanying sidebar) throughout the chapter to demonstrate the use of concepts described.

Figure 7.1 shows an order fulfillment scenario. First, the client—a retailer here—places the order on the partner, a computer vendor. After receiving the order, the partner needs to do credit checks and inventory checks. When these are complete, there is a communication from the partner to the client acknowledging that the order has been placed. After the shipment, which corresponds to the order, has been made, the partner sends a shipment notification to the client and sends the invoice. The client sends a payment to the partner, marking the completion of the order fulfillment transaction.

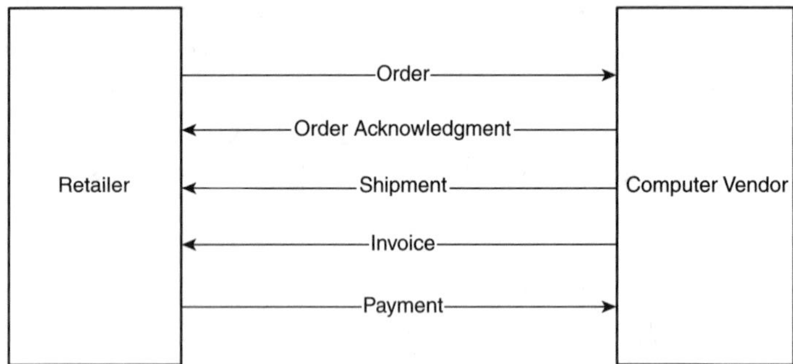

Figure 7.1 Asynchronous communications in order fulfillment scenario

example

`PlaceOrder` Web Service

The `PlaceOrder` web service is a real-world web service. This is the same `placeOrder` web service we talked about in the HP case study. This web service can be published by a PC manufacturer and consumed by an online retailer at the time a consumer is placing an order for a PC. This web service enables consumers of this web service to place an order with the producer of the web service. Asynchronous communication is necessary to complete many order-fulfillment tasks, such as credit checks and inventory checks.

First, you create the `PlaceOrder` web service in WebLogic Workshop, as described in Chapter 6, "Designing Web Services," and name it `placeOrder.jws`. Add a method `placeOrderAsync`.

Note that you can design the `placeOrder` web service and prototype it similar to the `validateConfig` web service. The `placeOrder` web service is used here to depict a real-world asynchronous web service.

In WebLogic Workshop, you implement asynchronous communication for your web service by specifying callbacks, conversations, buffering, and polling. We describe where and why these features are used in the following sections.

Callbacks

Callbacks notify a consumer of your web service that an event has occurred or that the results of the consumer's request are ready. To receive callbacks, the calling client must be operating in an environment in which a web service is running on a web server. If the client does not meet this requirement, it is most likely not capable of receiving callbacks from your web service. We talk about polling later in this chapter, regarding clients that cannot handle callbacks.

In the `PlaceOrder` web service, the web service client has to be notified of events such as when an order is placed, when a client's request cannot be fulfilled, when an order cannot be placed due to credit check failure, or when not enough inventories of parts are available to fulfill the order. To enable this asynchronous communication, you need to add one or more callbacks to the web service.

To add a callback in WebLogic Workshop, right-click on the web service in design view (see Figure 7.2) and add a callback. Name it `placeOrderResult`.

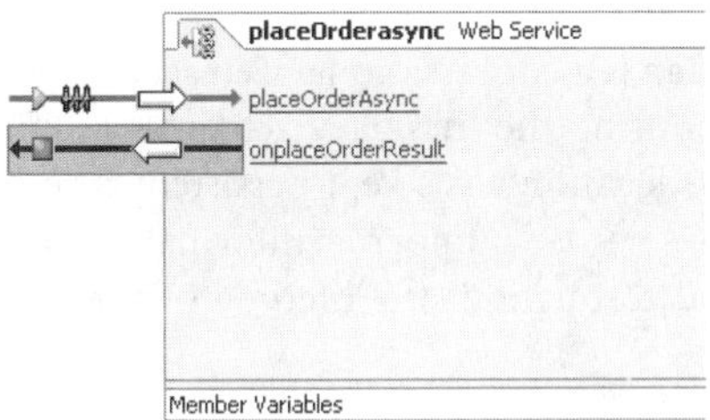

Figure 7.2 Callback in `PlaceOrder` web service

In source view, you will see the following code for the callback:

```
public Callback placeOrderCallback;
public interface Callback
```

```
    {.....
.......}
```

placeOrderCallback is the variable that represents the client connection. It is of type Callback and is used to enable the method placeOrderAsync to send messages back to the client asynchronously. The Callback interface is the definition of the messages that the client will accept from the PlaceOrder web service via the placeOrderCallback variable. placeOrderResult is the message that is sent back to the client some time after the client initiates the operation and all the checks on the order are done:

```
public interface Callback
    { public void placeOrderResult(......);
}
```

Next, you need to correlate the responses sent via the callback placeOrderResult to the client request made using the method placeOrderAsync.

Conversations

A web service and a client might communicate multiple times to complete a single task. Also, multiple clients might communicate with the same web service at the same time. *Conversations* provide a straightforward way to keep track of data between calls and to ensure that the web service always responds to the right client. Conversations maintain state between calls to the web service; they keep track of the data associated with a particular client between calls. Conversations also make your web service more robust because they write state-related data to disk and enable recovery from failures.

Conversations help to persist data across multiple communications by uniquely identifying a communication between a client and a web service.

In our example, placeOrder is a conversational web service that keeps track of which order belongs to which customer during the message exchanges required by the business process. Data such as the purchase order number is kept persistent throughout the conversation. The web service stores the purchase order number as information tied to the conversation so that it can be retrieved as needed throughout the lifetime of the message exchange between the client and the web service.

Conversation Context

WebLogic Server maintains the aspects of a conversation that regulate its life span. When a client calls a service operation that is annotated to start a conversation, WebLogic Server creates a conversation context through which it can correlate calls to and from the service and persist its state-related data. The conversation context contains a conversation ID, the maximum idle time, the conversation maximum age, and the web service state.

The conversation correlates the client's requests and the web service response by means of a conversation ID. This is a unique identifier that is generated when the client initiates a conversation with the service. Through this conversation ID, you can relate the web service callback to the right client request. The maximum idle time is the amount of time that can elapse between method invocations before your web service conversation automatically ends. The conversation maximum age is the maximum time that a conversation instance can exist before it is terminated by WebLogic Server. The web service state relates to all of the data that is being tracked at a particular moment for the client. This state information is useful for persisting data during the conversation.

You can write code to control and respond to these aspects of a conversation at runtime using methods and callbacks exposed by the JwsContext interface.

To set the maximum lifetime of the conversation and idle time of conversation, go to design view for the web service and, in the property editor, enter this information in the `conversation-lifetime` property, as shown in Figure 7.3. You can set both the `max-age` and the `max-idle-time`.

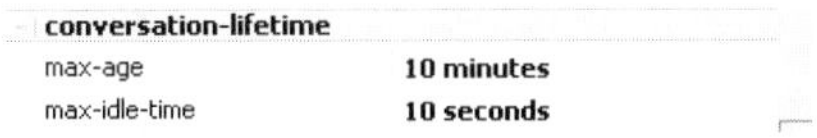

conversation-lifetime	
max-age	10 minutes
max-idle-time	10 seconds

Figure 7.3 Conversation lifetime property

In source view, you will see this javadoc:

```
@jws:conversation-lifetime max-idle-time="10 seconds" max-age="10 minutes"
```

Conversation Phase

When you apply a conversation phase attribute to a method or callback, you identify that it has a role in conversations. The method that requests the web service and the callback that responds to the web service request have roles defined by the `phase` attribute. There are four values for the `phase` attribute:

- The `start` value creates a new conversation context and an accompanying unique conversation ID, saves the service's state, and starts its idle and age timers.
- The `continue` value specifies that the conversation is in progress. Each call to a `continue` method saves the service's state and resets its idle timer.
- The `finish` value finishes the conversation.
- The `none` value specifies that a call to this method or callback has no meaning in the context of the conversation.

In our `placeOrder` web service example, to indicate that the method `placeOrderAsync` is the start of a conversation, you need to set the `phase` attribute of the `conversation property` for that method to start. This can be done in design view in WebLogic Workshop by selecting the method and using the property editor, as shown in Figure 7.4.

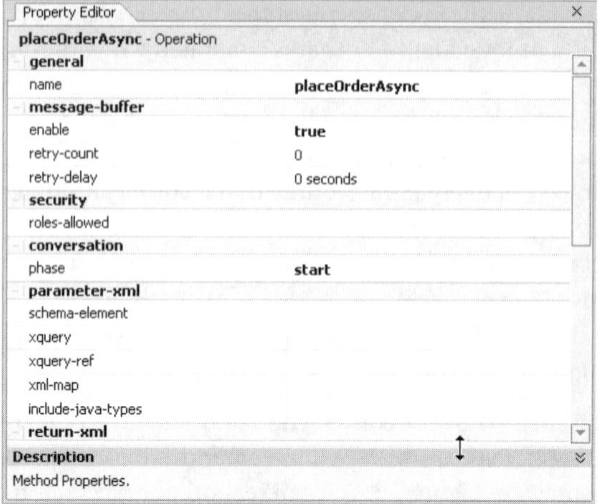

Figure 7.4 Conversation `phase` attribute

WebLogic Workshop uses `start`, `continue`, and `finish` of conversation in design view and the annotation in source view:

```
@jws:conversation phase="start"
@jws:conversation phase="continue"
@jws:conversation phase="finish"
```

To show that the callback is the finish of the conversation, change the value of the conversation `phase` attribute to finish in the property editor. Add the following in source view to let the client know that the order was successfully placed in the service provider's system:

```
public void placeOrder()
    callback.placeOrderResult("Order placed");
    return;
```

Testing the Conversation

Now you can test the `placeOrder` web service for asynchronous communication using callbacks and conversations. See Figure 7.5.

```
SOAP body:
<placeOrderAsync xmlns="http://www.openuri.org/">
  <!--Optional:-->
  <placeOrderNumber>string</placeOrderNumber>
  <!--Optional:-->
  <productNumber>string</productNumber>
  <!--Optional:-->
  <Quantity>3</Quantity>
  <!--Optional:-->
  <CustomerNumber>string</CustomerNumber>
  <!--Optional:-->

placeOrderAsync  starts a conversation
```

Figure 7.5 `placeOrder` message

The following code brings together the code snippets shown earlier. You can execute this code in WebLogic Workshop to test its behavior:

```
package placeOrderWebService;

public class placeOrder implements com.bea.jws.WebService
{
     public Callback placeOrderCallback;
     public interface Callback
     {
           * @jws:conversation phase="finish"
           */
          public void placeOrderResult(String placeOrder);
     }
      * @common:operation
      * @jws:conversation phase="start"
      */
     public void placeOrderAsync(String placeOrderNumber,
➥java.lang.String productNumber, java.lang.Integer Quantity, java.lang.String
➥CustomerNumber, java.lang.String CustomerName)
     {
          callback.placeOrderResult("Order placed");
          return;
     }
}
```

When you run the test, you will observe the following:

The conversation ID and the callback location are in the SOAP header of the `placeOrderAsync` SOAP message. The SOAP body carries the order details, such as order number, product number, quantity, customer number, and customer name (see Figure 7.6).

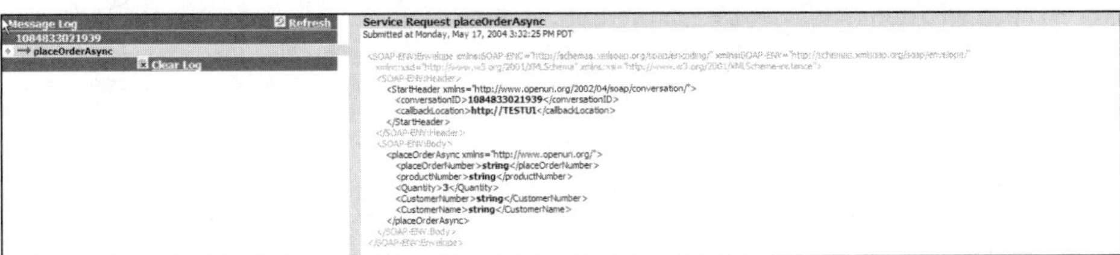

Figure 7.6 `placeOrderResult`

The SOAP message for the callback `placeOrderRequest` has the conversation ID in the SOAP header and the "Order Placed" message in the SOAP body. See Figure 7.7.

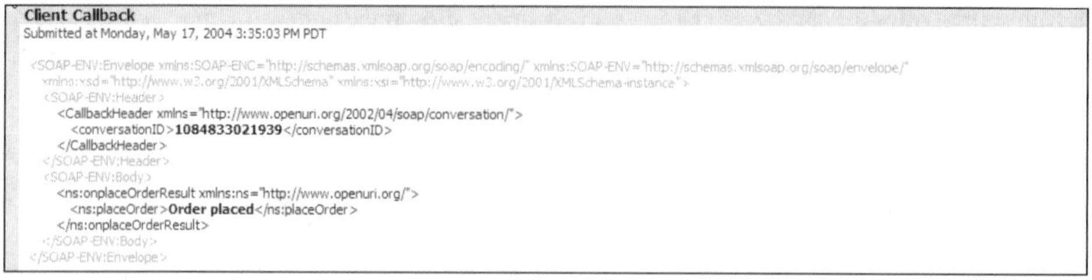

Client Callback

Submitted at Monday, May 17, 2004 3:35:03 PM PDT

```
<SOAP-ENV:Envelope xmlns:SOAP-ENC="http://schemas.xmlsoap.org/soap/encoding/" xmlns:SOAP-ENV="http://schemas.xmlsoap.org/soap/envelope/"
  xmlns:xsd="http://www.w3.org/2001/XMLSchema" xmlns:xsi="http://www.w3.org/2001/XMLSchema-instance">
  <SOAP-ENV:Header>
    <CallbackHeader xmlns="http://www.openuri.org/2002/04/soap/conversation/">
      <conversationID>1084833021939</conversationID>
    </CallbackHeader>
  </SOAP-ENV:Header>
  <SOAP-ENV:Body>
    <ns:onplaceOrderResult xmlns:ns="http://www.openuri.org/">
      <ns:placeOrder>Order placed</ns:placeOrder>
    </ns:onplaceOrderResult>
  </SOAP-ENV:Body>
</SOAP-ENV:Envelope>
```

Figure 7.7 `Client Callback`

Clients and Conversations and Callbacks

Clients need to send information about conversations, and callback URLs are transmitted through SOAP headers. For the start of a conversation, the client needs to send a conversation ID, which is a string with no format restrictions. The conversation ID must be unique on the server hosting the target web service, however. Clients can use a combination of the client machine's hostname, IP address, process ID, clock time, or other data that in combination is unique to that client. If the conversation ID is not unique on the server, a SOAP fault is returned.

To receive callbacks from the web service, the client must send a second SOAP header specifying the URL to which callback messages should be sent. The general form of the SOAP headers for a `start` method is as follows:

```
<SOAP:Header>
    <StartHeader xmlns="http://www.openuri.org/2002/04/soap/conversation/">
        <callbackLocation>Callback_URL</callbackLocation>
        <conversationID>Conversation_ID</conversationID>
    </StartHeader>
</SOAP:Header>
```

When you call a `continue` or `finish` method, you pass only the conversation ID. If the specified conversation ID does not identify an existing conversation on the target server, a SOAP fault is returned:

```
<SOAP:Header>
   <ContinueHeader xmlns="http://openuri.org/2002/04/soap/conversation/">
       <conversationID>Conversation_ID</conversationID>
   </ContinueHeader>
</SOAP:Header>
```

Buffering

Buffering is a mechanism for sending an acknowledgment to a client's request without waiting for the web service to finish all its processing. This is useful when a client invokes the web service and waits for a reply before continuing with its execution. However, the client doesn't wait for the web service to completely process the request. An example is a client expecting an acknowledgment for receipt from a service provider of a purchase order. This acknowledgment is sent before the service provider completes credit and inventory checks required for accepting this purchase order.

Buffering can be turned on for method or callback in a web service, provided that the method or callback's parameters can be serialized and the return type is void. It is important to understand that when you add message buffers, the queues that provide the buffering always exist on your end of the wire. There are no configuration actions such as message buffering in client's infrastructure.

Adding Message Buffer to a Method

If you add a message buffer to a method, incoming messages are buffered on the local machine. The method invocation returns to the client immediately. This prevents the client from waiting until your web service processes the request. Because the buffering occurs on your end of the wire, the client still must wait for the network roundtrip, even though it will return a void result. But the client does not have to wait for your web service to process the message.

Adding Message Buffers to a Callback

When you invoke a callback, your web service acts as the caller. That is, your service sends an outgoing message to the client, which responds with an incoming message containing the callback's return value.

If you add a message buffer to a callback of a web service, outgoing messages are buffered on the local machine and the callback invocation returns immediately. This prevents your service from having to wait while the message is sent to the remote server and the void response is received. In other words, your web service doesn't have to wait for the network roundtrip to occur.

To add a buffer to our example on the method `placeOrderAsync`, in design view in the property editor for `message-buffer`, set `enable` to `true`, as shown in Figure 7.8.

This adds the following annotation in source view:

```
@common:message-buffer enable="true"
```

This is displayed with the icon of a spring in design view, as shown in Figure 7.9.

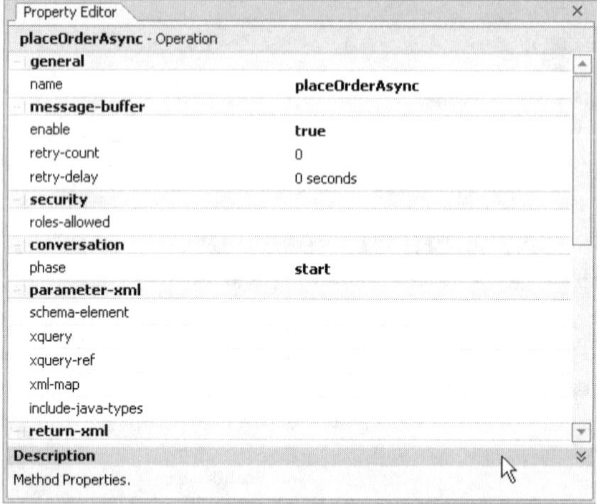

Figure 7.8 Message buffer for a method

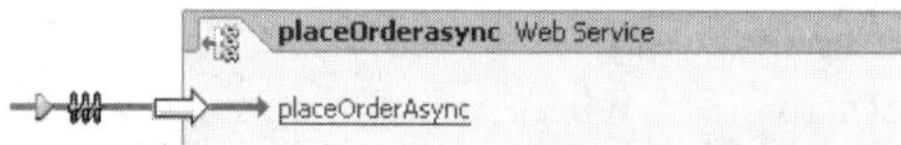

Figure 7.9 Design view for buffer

Polling as an Alternative to Callbacks

You can expose polling methods in addition to callbacks so that a client that can't accept callbacks can use it. Clients operating from behind firewalls might not be capable of receiving asynchronous callbacks. If a client can accept callbacks, it must send a `callbackURL` as part of any `start conversation` method invocation. The `callbackURL` is available via the `getCallbackLocation` method of the `jwsContext` interface, which is available in all WebLogic web services:

```
private String callbackURL = null;
```

This variable holds the `callbackURL` of the client. If the client does not supply a `callback` URL, callbacks cannot be sent to the client. If the client can't accept callbacks, it can use the polling interface `getRequestStatus` to get the current state. It can use `terminateRequest` when the client is done using the web service. The sample code is shown here:

```
public class placeOrderConversation {
/**
* @common:operation
```

```
* @jws:conversation phase="start"
*/
public void startRequest()
{
...
}
/**
* @common:operation
* @jws:conversation phase="continue"
*/
public String getRequestStatus()
{
...
}
/**
* @common:operation
* @jws:conversation phase="finish"
*/
public void terminateRequest()
{ }
}
```

To do polling, a client uses the `startRequest` method to initiate a request from a conversational web service. It calls `getRequestStatus` periodically to check on the result. The `getRequestStatus` method returns an indication that the request is pending until the request is complete. The next time the client calls `getRequestStatus` after the request is complete, the result is returned to the client. The client then calls `terminateRequest` to finish the conversation.

Using SOAP with Attachments

When using asynchronous and synchronous web services, there might be a need to send attachments across the wire. For example, this might be needed when sending images of products from a product catalog. Web services facilitate this through attachments to the main message. The SOAP specification defines SOAP attachments as a way to include Multipurpose Internet Mail Extensions (MIME) data in or associated with SOAP messages. MIME messages can contain text, images, audio, video, or other application-specific data. The Java API includes the javax.activation package, which can decode MIME messages and provide application access to the operations that are possible on each type of content.

WebLogic Workshop's SOAP attachment support is based on the SOAP messages with Attachments specification. WebLogic Workshop supports SOAP attachments only for web service method invocations that arrive via HTTP. To support SOAP attachments, a web service method must support the `http-soap` or `http-soap12` protocols. You specify the protocols that a web service supports using the `@jws:protocol` annotation.

Sending a SOAP Attachment

In the `PlaceOrder` web service, we want to send back a product image, `productJPEG`, as an attachment in the SOAP response confirming that the order has been placed for a certain product. To do this, import `javax.activation.DataHandler` and `javax.activation.FileDataSource`, and add the method `getFileAsAttachment`, as shown in this code:

```
package placeOrderWebService;


import javax.activation.DataHandler;
  import javax.activation.FileDataSource;

  public class placeOrder implements com.bea.jws.WebService

  {
    static final long serialVersionUID = 1L;

    /**
    * @common:operation
    * @jws:protocol form-get="false" form-post="false"
    */
    public DataHandler getFileAsAttachment(String productjpeg)
    {
      return(new DataHandler(new FileDataSource(productJPEG)));
    }
  }
```

When you test this web service, you will see the product JPEG sent as an attachment in response to the web service request. According to the SOAP with Attachments specification, it will look like this:

```
MIME-Version: 1.0
Content-Type: Multipart/Related; boundary=MIME_boundary; type=text/xml;
        start=""
Content-Description: This contains product image.
```

```
--MIME_boundary
Content-Type: text/xml; charset=UTF-8
Content-Transfer-Encoding: 8bit
Content-ID: <product.xml@sample.org>

<?xml version='1.0' ?>
<SOAP-ENV:Envelope
xmlns:SOAP-ENV="http://schemas.xmlsoap.org/soap/envelope/">
<SOAP-ENV:Body>
<productimage http =" http://example.org/productJPEG.jpg "/>
</SOAP-ENV:Body>
</SOAP-ENV:Envelope>

--MIME_boundary
Content-Type: image/jpeg
Content-Transfer-Encoding: binary
Content-Location: 'http://sample.org/productJPEG.jpg

fd a5 8a 29 aa 46 1b 24
--MIME_boundary--
```

Receiving a SOAP Attachment

The code for creating a web service that receives a SOAP attachment is similar to the code described previously for sending a SOAP attachment. You have to include an argument of type `javax.activation.DataHandler` in the method's signature, as shown here in a web service named `SoapAttachmentService.jws`:

```
import javax.activation.DataHandler;

public class SoapAttachmentService implements com.bea.jws.WebService
{
  static final long serialVersionUID = 1L;

  /**
  * @common:operation
  * @jws:protocol form-get="false" form-post="false"
  */
```

```
    public String soapAttachment(DataHandler dh)
    {
      return("***Service received DataHandler of
    ➥type: " + dh.getContentType());
    }
  }
```

The preceding example returns a string containing the content type of whatever MIME message it receives as an attachment.

In both examples, the `form-get` and `form-post` attributes of the `@jws:protocol` annotation have been set to `false`. The `HTTP GET` and `FORM POST` operations have no way to convey SOAP attachments. To access a web service that accepts SOAP attachments, clients must send and be capable of receiving raw SOAP messages.

SOAP Attachments in the Real World

As we have described, you can send and receive attachments in a web service. However, the challenge is interoperating with a .NET implementation when using attachments.

At present, there are two specifications for attachments: SOAP with Attachments and WS-Attachments. As we said earlier, WebLogic Workshop supports SOAP with Attachments. Microsoft .NET supports WS-Attachments, which is based on Direct Internet Message Encapsulation (DIME) rather than MIME packaging. DIME is a lightweight, binary message format that can be used to encapsulate one or more application-defined payloads of arbitrary type and size into a single message construct.

Working with attachments can cause a lot of interoperability problems because of mixed J2EE and .NET environments. One way to avoid these problems is either to not use attachments or to embed the data within the SOAP message. The following is an example of embedding the `productJPEG` file we talked about in the section on "Sending a SOAP Attachment" embedded in the XML:

```
m:data xmlns:m= 'http://example.org/productJPEG.jpg'>
    <productimage>/aWKKapGGyQ=</productimage>
  </m:data>
```

In this example, the `productimage` element contains a base 64 string that represents the following octet sequences:`fd a5 8a 29 aa 46 1b 24.`

The other way is to negotiate with your partner to use one specification. However, this might be not practical because you most probably will have .NET and J2EE clients, and your J2EE clients will be using application servers from different vendors that might or might not support DIME.

Future Approach for Dealing with Binary Data

The W3C XML Protocol Working Group is defining a new approach for sending binary data with SOAP messages, called the Message Transmission Optimization Mechanism (MTOM).

MTOM proposes selectively encoding portions of the SOAP message using different encoding systems. MTOM is an abstract feature; the concrete implementation of MTOM is defined in the XML-Binary Optimized Packaging (XOP) specification.

In XOP/MTOM, the attachments are included within the SOAP message infoset, but they are encoded differently, enabling numerous optimizations. The binary data is typically encoded using MIME multipart–related messages.

It's really useful to keep the binary data in the SOAP message infoset rather than sending it as a separate attachment. For one thing, when data is within the infoset, it means that it operates within the constraints of the SOAP processing model. In other words, you can control the processing of the infoset using SOAP headers. For example, you can use WS-Security for authentication, authorization, message integrity, and message confidentiality for information within the infoset. But WS-Security can't be used to secure attachments.

WebLogic and DIME Attachments

When you are using WebLogic to create web services and you need to send DIME because you have to work with .NET clients, you might want to check out the LGPL-licensed Java DIME package at `http://onionnetworks.com/developers/index.php`. Onion Networks is open source and has downloads of Java DIME libraries. It has `dimeGenerator` and `dimeParser` classes.

First, implement a servlet filter with the `HttpServletRequestWrapper` and `HttpServletResponseWrapper` classes that uses the generator and parser from the package. Next, change the `Content-type` header to `text/xml` (refer to the SOAP example for an attachment, shown earlier) by using the methods on `HttpServletRequestWrapper`. Then remove everything but the contents of the DIME record with the SOAP message in it, and change the `Content-length` header using the methods on `HttpServletRequestWrapper`.

Transforming XML Messages

In some web services implementations between business partners, the client business partner consuming the web service defines the service interface and, therefore, accepts only the XML Schema that it has defined. The provider of the web service might already have this web service in production or might have functionality using existing Java classes. This means that the provider's output schema might not be the same as the one that the client is expecting.

For example, your web service might be used by a client that expects an XML message format that is specific to its industry but that differs from what your service is designed to handle.

For example, in the retail industry, Wal-Mart generally sets the format. To do business with Wal-Mart, you have to handle its format rather than requiring Wal-Mart to conform to yours.

XQuery Map

As shown in Figure 7.10, by default, WebLogic Server translates XML messages to and from the types in your Java declaration according to a "natural" map—a format in which the parts of your Java declaration match the contents of the message. You can override natural mapping with an XQuery map, and create a translation layer that handles the format of your client's request messages while allowing your implementation code to remain unchanged.

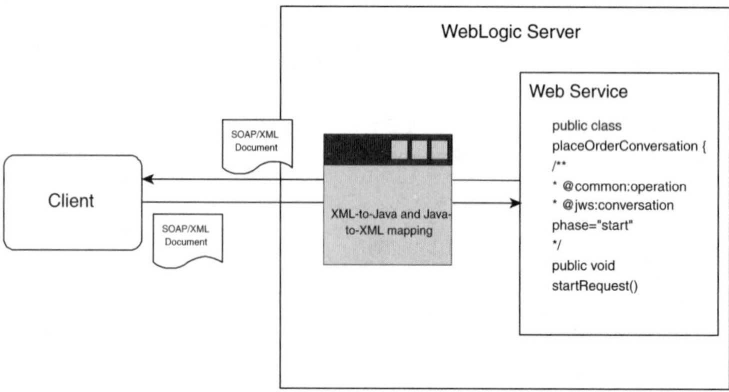

Figure 7.10 Natural map

XQuery maps provide a way for you to reshape the XML messages that web services send or receive. Applying an XQuery map enables you to change the format of a message dictated by the WSDL into the format that you want to use in your Java program (see Figure 7.11).

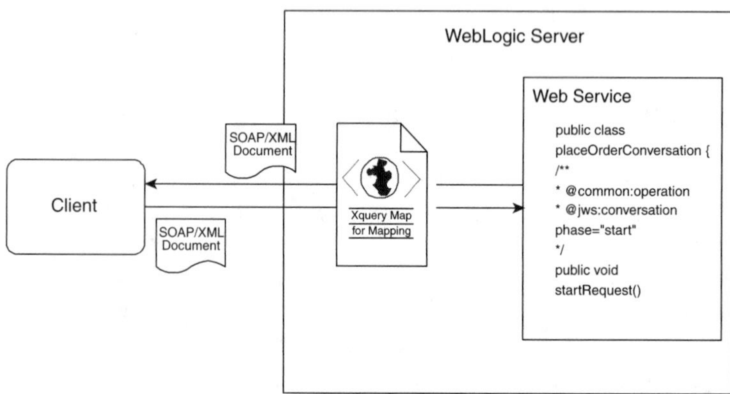

Figure 7.11 XQuery map

Another reason for using XML transformation is to provide a layer for loose coupling between your web service and its clients. Again, the XML format represented by the XQuery map is used for your web service's public face to the world. You can change the underlying Java code without breaking the contract with clients.

For the `ValidateConfig` example described in Chapter 6, the outgoing schema looks as follows:

```
<xsd:element name="outValidateConfig">
        <xsd:complexType>
                <xsd:sequence>
                      <xsd:element name="Status"
                      type="TrueFalseType"/>
                      <xsd:element name="Error" type="ErrorType"
                      minOccurs="0"/>
                      <xsd:element name="ConfigID"
                      type="xsd:string" minOccurs="0" maxOc
                      curs="unbounded"/>
                      <xsd:element name="ShipDate"
                      type="AtLeast1Type" minOccurs="0"/>
                </xsd:sequence>
        </xsd:complexType>
</xsd:element>
```

However, the client wants a slightly different XML Schema, shown here:

```
<xsd:element name="outValidateConfig_Cust">
              <xsd:complexType>
                     <xsd:sequence>
```

The client needs `Result` instead of `Status`:

```
                            <xsd:element name="Result"

                             type="TrueFalseType"/>
                            <xsd:element name="Error"

                             type="ErrorType" minOccurs="0"/>
```

The client needs `Config_Number` instead of `ConfigID`:

```
<xsd:element name="Config_Number" type="xsd:string" minOc
➥curs="0" maxOccurs="unbounded"/>
```

The client needs `Shipping_Date` instead of `ShipDate`:

```
<xsd:element name="Shipping_Date" type="AtLeast1Type" minOccurs="0"/>
```

The client wants an Extra element `Delivery_Date`:

```
<xsd:element name="Delivery_Date" type="AtLeast1Type" minOccurs="0"/>
                    </xsd:sequence>
                </xsd:complexType>
        </xsd:element>
```

You can address this mismatch by using XML transformation. To do the XML transform, you need to import the customer-specific XSD to the Schemas file. XML Beans are automatically created. We talk about XML Beans in detail in the next chapter. The XQuery map maps specific XML element content and XML attribute values to Java method parameters and return values. To create the XQuery map, in design view, click the outgoing method; in the property editor, in the section labeled `parameter-xml`, locate the `xquery` property. In the dialog box, select the schema `ValidateConfig_v1cust.xsd` to which you want to map your schema. Edit the XQuery as shown in Figure 7.12, and map the elements from source schema to target schema.

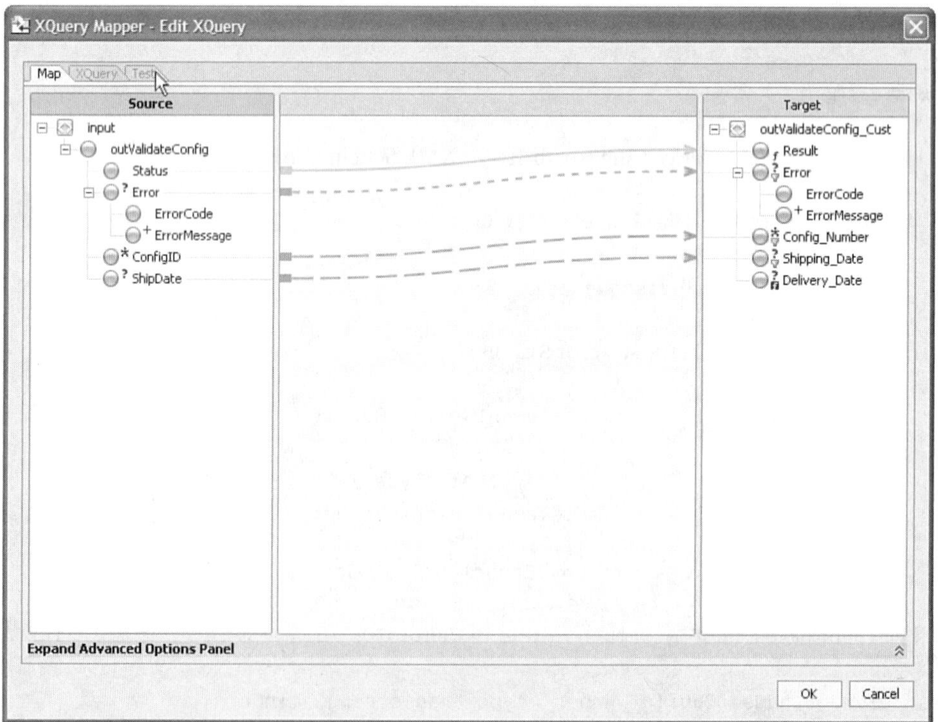

Figure 7.12 Editing the XQuery map

Solid lines indicate that a data conversion function is applied to the mapping. Table 7.1 lists the mappings between the source schema and the target schema.

Table 7.1 Mapping Source Schema to Target Schema

Source Schema	**Target Schema**
Error	Error
ConfigID	Config_Number
ShipDate	Shipping_Date
	Delivery_Date

`Shipping_Date` refers to the number of days before the order ships. `Delivery_Date` is related to `Shipping_Date`. `Delivery_Date` refers to the days that either a ground shipment or a FedEx shipment takes to reach the destination. You can either set a default number of days for `Delivery_Date` or write a script to calculate `Delivery_Date` from `Shipping_Date`. To set a default for `Delivery_Date`, select the Functions tab within the Advanced Options panel and enter `10` as a default (see Figure 7.13).

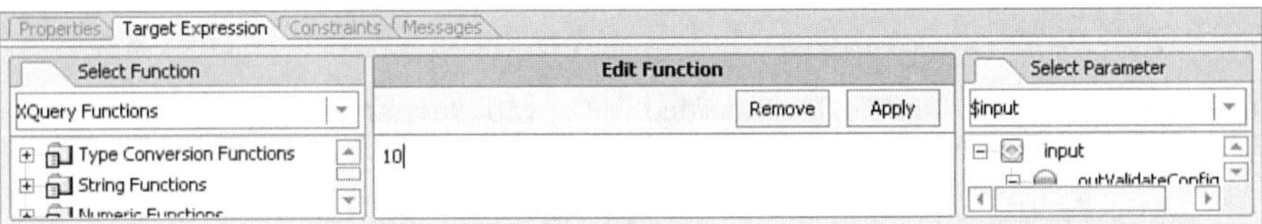

Figure 7.13 Setting default values in XQuery map

ECMAScript

ECMAScript is an open, internationally accepted scripting language specification. JavaScript is an implementation of the ECMAScript specification. WebLogic Workshop uses ECMAScript to handle dramatic differences between natural mapping and required formats. You will see here how you can use ECMAscript to calculate the delivery days.

In our example, you can add a script to calculate the shipment days by writing a function in ECMAScript and then referring to the function from the XML map. First, create an XScript file with which a XML scripting file called `deliverydate.jsx` and write the following ECMAScript to calculate `Delivery_Date`:

```
function calDeliveryDate(shipdate)
{
   {
    deliverydate = Math.ceil(Math.pow(shipdate,1) + Math.pow(number,1)));
    return deliverydate;
  }
}
```

In source view, the XQuery map looks as follows:

```
* @jws:parameter-xml schema-element="ns0:outValidateConfig_Cust"
* @jws:return-xml schema-element="ns0:outValidateConfig_Cust" xquery::
* declare namespace ns0 = "http://production.psg.hp.com/types"
*
* <ns0:outValidateConfig_Cust>
*       <ns0:Result>{ data($input/ns0:outValidateConfig/ns0:Status)
➥}</ns0:Result>
*       {
*            for $Error in $input/ns0:outValidateConfig/ns0:Error
*            return
*                  <ns0:Error>{ $Error/@* , $Error/node()}</ns0:Error>
*       }
```

Here, you can see that `ConfigID` is mapped to `Config_Number`:

```
{
*     for $ConfigID in $input/ns0:outValidateConfig/ns0:ConfigID
*     return
*           <ns0:Config_Number>{ data($ConfigID) }</ns0:Config_Number>
*}
*{
*     for $ShipDate in $input/ns0:outValidateConfig/ns0:ShipDate
*     return
*           <ns0:Shipping_Date>{ data($ShipDate) }</ns0:Shipping_Date>
*}
```

This is how the default value of `10` is set for `Delivery_Date`:

```
*       <ns0:Delivery_Date>10</ns0:Delivery_Date>
* </ns0:outValidateConfig_Cust>
* ::
*/
```

Edit the XQuery map to add the previously written ECMAScript as shown in Figure 7.14. The figure shows how to call the ECMAScript from the XQuery map.

```
    <ns0:Delivery_Date>{Validate_v1_2JWS.DeliverydateScript.calcDeliveryDate(data($inputns0:outValidateConfig/ns0:ShipDate))} </ns0:Delivery_Date>
</ns0:outValidateConfig_Cust>
```

Figure 7.14 Calling ECMAScript from the XQuery map

Now you can test the web service to see the outgoing message. You can see in Figure 7.15 that the XML format is as expected by the client and that it also has the calculated `Delivery_Date`.

Service Response
Submitted at Saturday, May 15, 2004 7:31:25 PM PDT

```
<SOAP-ENV:Envelope xmlns:SOAP-ENV="http://schemas.xmlsoap.org/soap/envelope/" xmlns:xsd="http://www.w3.org/2001/XMLSchema"
 xmlns:xsi="http://www.w3.org/2001/XMLSchema-instance">
  <SOAP-ENV:Body>
    <typ:outValidateConfig_Cust xmlns:typ="http://production.psg.hp.com/types">
      <typ:Result>yes</typ:Result>
      <typ:Config_Number>1234</typ:Config_Number>
      <typ:Shipping_Date>1234</typ:Shipping_Date>
      <typ:Delivery_Date>1241.0</typ:Delivery_Date>
    </typ:outValidateConfig_Cust>
  </SOAP-ENV:Body>
</SOAP-ENV:Envelope>
```

Figure 7.15 Test results from XQuery map

Discovering Web Services Through UDDI

So far, we have talked about developing web services in Workshop. WebLogic also has the facility to discover web services in private and public UDDI registries and to use these web services.

WebLogic Server provides a basic browser-based tool for keeping a private registry of web services and their WSDL files. You can access this UDDI by going to the following URL:

```
http://localhost:7001/uddiexplorer/index.jsp
```

UDDI Explorer

You need to start the WebLogic examples server before you access the URL. Figure 7.16 shows the UDDI Explorer. In the left pane, you can view the following functions:

- **Search Public Registries**—Enables you to perform searches using various search parameters, such as business name and key, as shown in Figure 7.17. You can maintain the public registries via Setup UDDI Directory.

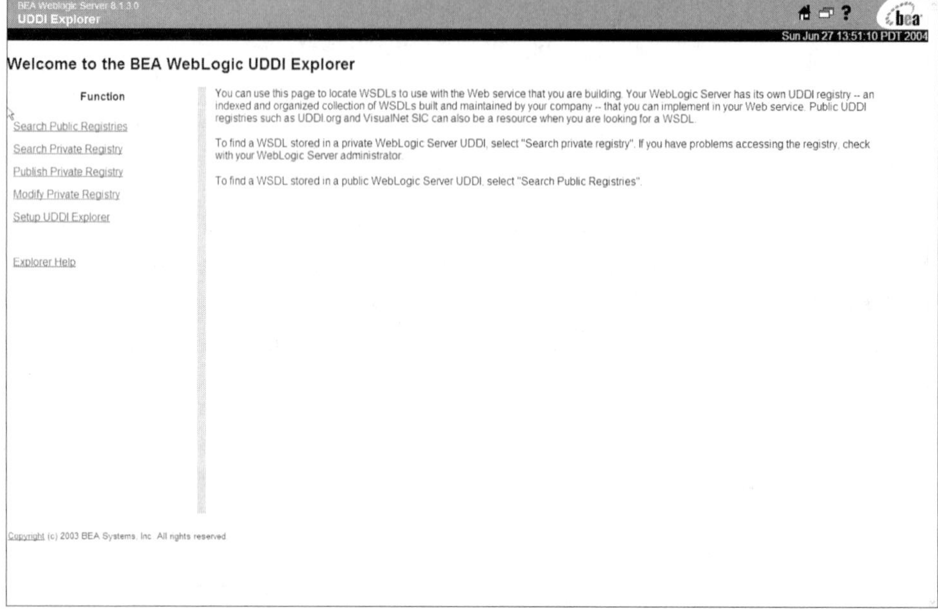

Figure 7.16 UDDI Explorer

Figure 7.17 Public registry

- **Search Private Registries**—Provides a starting point for finding existing projects and services.
- **Publish to Private Registry**—Helps you publish your web service to the private registry. You can log in with the default user ID/password (weblogic/weblogic) and enter your WSDL and other information (see Figure 7.18).
- **Modify Private Registry Details**—Enables you to add new projects and edit existing projects.
- **Set Up UDDIDirectory Explorer**—Enables you to select the private registry that you want to browse or manage and maintain a list of public UDDI registries.

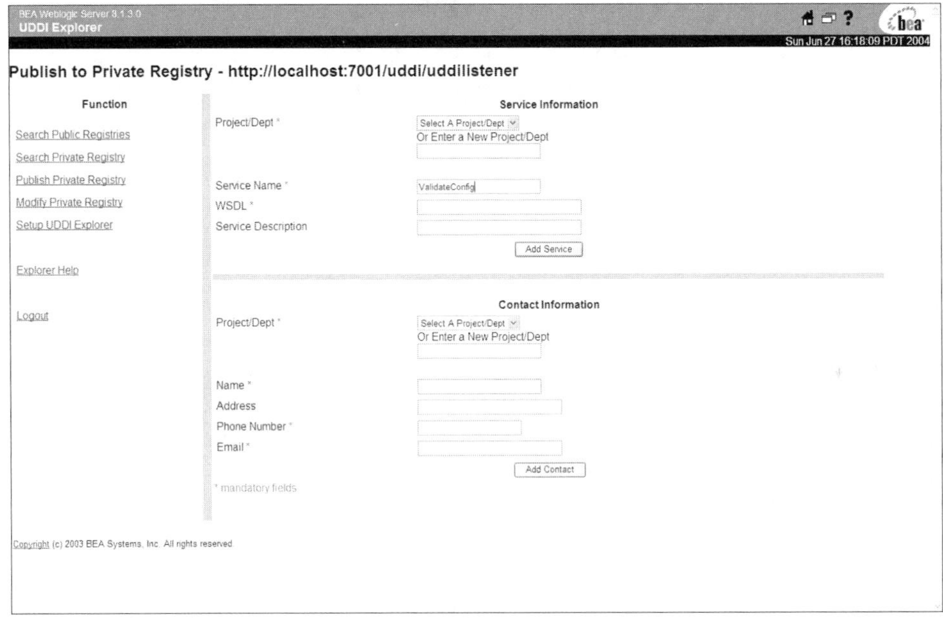

Figure 7.18 Publish to a private registry

Web Service Control

You can use a WSDL from the private or public registry and create a web service control in WebLogic Workshop. A web service control makes it easy to access an external web service from a WebLogic Workshop application. A web service control can be created from a web service that publishes a WSDL file.

The following steps show how to create a web service control. In design view, using the Insert menu, select Controls, Web Service.

In the Step 1 pane, enter the UDDIWebService that your web service will use to reference the control you are about to create from the WSDL. In the Step 2 pane, click Create a New Web Service Control to Use and provide a JCX name called `UDDIWebServiceControl`. In the Step 3 pane, click UDDI. This button opens the UDDI Explorer, a web application that enables you to browse both public and private registries for web services stored as WSDL files (see Figure 7.19).

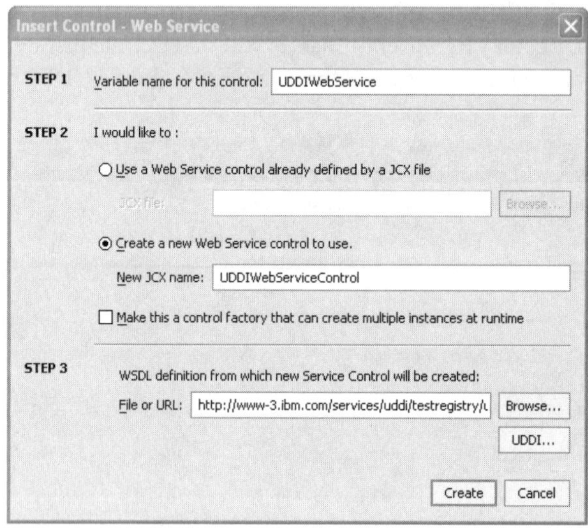

Figure 7.19 Web service control from web service in UDDI registry

Use the Search a Public Registry and Search a Private Registry links to locate a WSDL. When you find the WSDL file that you want to use as a web service control, copy the URL for the WSDL and it into the File or URL box, and click Create.

A JCX file is created in the same directory as the web service to which it was being added, and a reference to that control is added to your web service. This control can now be used to access the web service represented by the WSDL.

Deploying to Production Environment

You can deploy to a production server the web services that you created in WebLogic Workshop. When you are deploying an entire application, you have EAR files; when you are deploying a specific project within an application, you have a JAR file.

To deploy the Validate application, which contains the `ValidateConfig` web service, select from the menu bar Build, Build EAR. WebLogic Workshop compiles an EAR file and places it in the application's root directory, which is the same directory that holds your application's work file. When you compile an EAR file using Build EAR, a wlw-manifest.xml file is produced and placed in the application's META-INF directory. This wlw-manifiest.xml file lists the server resources that must be created on the production server for the application EAR to run successfully (see Figure 7.20).

Figure 7.20 Deployment of the Validate application

Values specified in a project's WEB-INF/wlw-config.xml file, such as hostname, http-port, and https-port, are hard-coded into the EAR file. The result is an EAR file that can be run only on the machine named in the wlw-config.xml file. WEB-INF/wlw-runtime-config.xml enables the administrator to configure runtime parameters of web resources on a production server. This XML file addresses the hard-coded issues.

You can also use the wlwBuild.cmd command-line tool. wlwBuild.cmd is somewhat more flexible, in that you can set flags to build a JAR file for a specific project instead of building an EAR file for the entire application.

EAR files can be deployed to WebLogic Server using the WebLogic Server console. To use the WebLogic Server console to deploy an EAR file, start the console, expand the Deployments node in the left pane, right-click the Applications node, and select Deploy a New Application (see Figure 7.21).

Manual Creation of Server Resources

The wlw-config.xml file lists the JMS queues and database tables that need to be manually created on the target WebLogic Server for the application to run properly.

Required database tables are indicated by a <con:conversation-state-table /> tag. These tables are used by web services to store conversational state. For each occurrence of the <con:conversation-state-table /> tag in the wlw-manifest.xml file, you must create a corresponding data table on WebLogic Server.

Automatic Assembly Using the servicegen Ant Task

If you have web services that have not been developed in WebLogic Workshop, you can assemble a WebLogic web service using Ant tasks in two ways: 1) using the servicegen Ant task to do all the assembly steps automatically, and 2) using a variety of narrowly focused Ant tasks for manual assembly. Ant is a Java-based build tool that uses XML-based configuration files (called build.xml by default) to execute tasks written in Java.

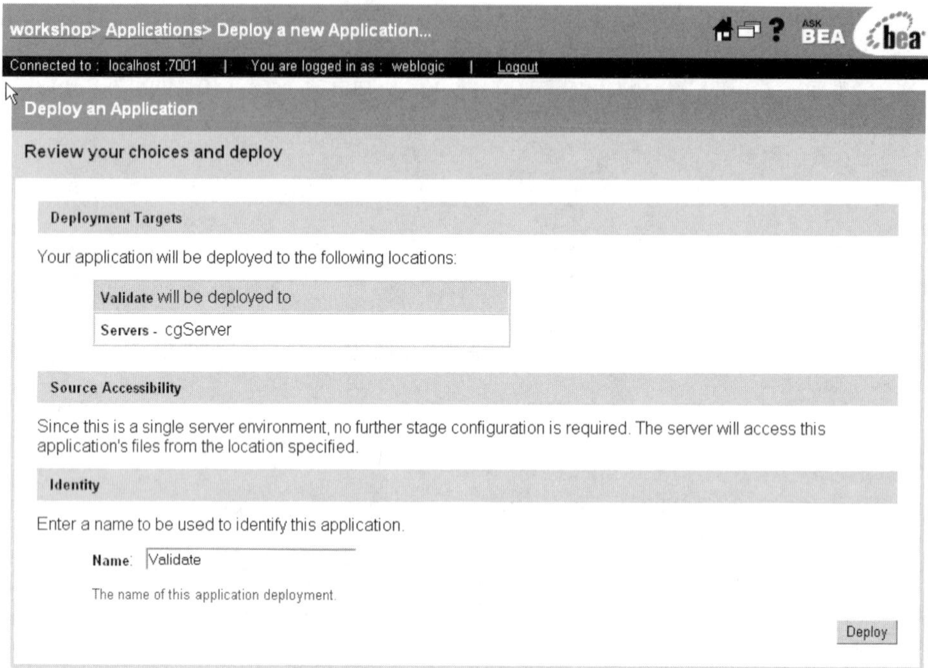

Figure 7.21 Deployment console

The Apache Ant Project provides many useful Ant tasks for packaging EAR, WAR, and EJB JAR files. For more information, see http://jakarta.apache.org/ant/manual/.

The `servicegen` Ant task performs all assembly steps for you. It takes as input an EJB JAR file, for EJB-implemented web services, or a list of Java classes, for Java class-implemented web services. It introspects the Java code and converts all public methods into web service operations. It looks for all data types that are not built in that are used as return values for the methods. Next it creates a `web-services.xml` deployment descriptor file based on this information and the attributes of the Ant task. It automatically generates all the components that make up a WebLogic web service and packages them into a deployable EAR file. Optionally, it creates the serialization class that converts the data that is not built in between its XML and Java representations and XML Schema representations of the Java objects, and it updates the `web-services.xml` file accordingly

The Ant task generates the web services EAR file in the staging directory, which you can then deploy on WebLogic Server.

Manual Assembly Using Ant Tasks

Typically, the `servicegen` Ant task is adequate for assembling most WebLogic web services. However, if you want more control over how your web service is assembled, you can use a set of narrowly focused Ant tasks, such as `autotype`, `source2wsdd`, and `wspackage`, to manually assemble a WebLogic web service. For example, you can use wspackage to generate the `web-services.xml` file, and then you can update this file manually if you want to add more information.

As we discussed in Chapter 6, the SOAP message generated by the client in a doc-literal implementation does not pass the operation as the root element of the SOAP body. WebLogic Server needs the operation name, so you can use the `wspackage` Ant task to create the `web-services.xml`, where you can show the correlation between the operation name and the root element, as shown here:

```
<?xml version="1.0" encoding="UTF-8"?>
<web-services>
<web-service useSOAP12="false" exposeWSDL="true" targetName
➥space="http://production.psg.hp.com/types"
➥name="Validate_v1_2" style="document" uri="/Validate_v1_2">
            <types>
                  <xsd:schema
➥xmlns:xsd="http://www.w3.org/2001/XMLSchema"
➥xmlns:stns="http://production.psg.hp.com/types" element
➥FormDefault="qualified" attributeFormDefault="qualified" targetName
➥space="http://production.psg.hp.com/types">
                        <xsd:element type="xsd:anyType"
➥name="inValidateConfig" nillable="true">
 </xsd:element>
                        <xsd:element type="xsd:anyType"
➥name="outValidateConfig" nillable="true">
 </xsd:element>
                  </xsd:schema>
            </types>

...
    Operation name→     <operations>
                  <operation name="validateConfig"
➥method="validateConfig(org.w3c.dom.Document)" component="jcComp0">
                        <params>
                              <param style="in" xmlns:p1="http://
➥production.psg.hp.com/types"
Root element→type="p1:inValidateConfig" location="body"
➥name="document" class-name="org.w3c.dom.Document">
            </param>
```

```
                                        <return-param
➥xmlns:p2="http://production.psg.hp.com/types"
➥type="p2:outValidateConfig" location="body"
➥name="result" class-name="org.w3c.dom.Document">
            </return-param>
                         </params>
                    </operation>
            </operations>
      </web-service>
```

Viewing and Testing the Assembled Web Service

Every web service deployed on WebLogic Server has a home page. From the home page, you can view the WSDL that describes the service, test each operation to ensure that it is working correctly, and view the SOAP request and response messages from a successful test of an operation.

For example, assume that you used the following `build.xml` file to assemble a WebLogic web service using the `servicegen` Ant task:

```
<project name="partnerdirect" default="build-ear">
  <target name="build-ear">
       <servicegen
          destEar="placeOrderWebService.ear"
          warName="placeOrder.war"
          contextURI="services">
          <service
               ejbJar="placeOrderEJB.jar"
               targetNamespace="http://production.psg.hp.com/types"
               serviceName="placeOrderWebService"
               serviceURI="/placeOrderWebService"
               generateTypes="True"
               expandMethods="True" >
          </service>
      </servicegen>
  </target>
</project>
```

Assuming that the service is running on a local host at the default port number, the URL to invoke the web service home page is this:
`http://localhost:7001/services/placeOrderWebService`

The URL to get the automatically generated WSDL of the web service is this:
`http://localhost:7001/services/placeOrderWebService?WSDL`

Summary

In this chapter, we covered the essentials of developing and deploying web services.

Most business processes require asynchronous communication. Four different elements are involved while building asynchronous web services in WebLogic Workshop. In each case, the client can continue with its operation after making the web service request, without waiting for the request to be completely processed. Callbacks notify a consumer of a web service when an event has occurred. When a web service and a client need to communicate multiple times to complete a single task, conversation is a useful technique to uniquely identify the dialogue. Buffering creates a synchronous handshake, or an acknowledgment, while enabling asynchronous behavior for the processing of the web service request. Polling is an alternative to callbacks.

Information such as text, images, audio, video, or application-specific data can be sent and received as a SOAP attachment. When working with .NET environments, because of interoperability reasons, it is better for data to be part of the XML payload rather than an attachment.

XML transformations are a necessity when a web service needs to adhere to a client format of the XML Schema. These transformations can be done using XQuery maps. ECMAScript can be used when there are dramatic differences between the source schema and the target schema.

WebLogic has the facility to enable registering the web service in private and public UDDI registries. UDDI Explorer and web service controls are two ways to enable discovery in a UDDI.

For deployment to a production environment, use Ant tasks, which can be either automated or manually changed. You can deploy your application or project from Workshop.

8

Using Controls, Bindings, and Parsers

In the last chapter, you learned how web services are built. In this chapter, you look at the functions that support the building of web services. You will learn about using controls, XML-to-Java bindings, and XML parsing.

WebLogic Workshop has Control Frameworks, which is a way to encapsulate business logic and to access enterprise resources such as databases, message queues, and timers, and to expose them as web services. This chapter describes how to build custom Controls, use built-in Controls, and leverage ISV Controls.

An important aspect of enabling web services is the translation of XML to Java objects. One way to achieve this is to bind XML to Java. This chapter describes how to use XML Beans in WebLogic Workshop to accomplish this. Another way is to convert XML to Java objects using XML parsers. Later, you'll learn about the details of the StAX parser and compare it to two other parsers: DOM and SAX. The decision of whether to use XML-to-Java binding or an XML parser depends on the actions you want to take with the XML document and the architecture of your environment. This chapter examines the right approach to use under different circumstances.

Using Workshop Control Framework

In your web service, you need to encapsulate business logic and connect to enterprise resources such as databases and JMS queues. You use Java Controls to do both.

Using the Control Framework, you can combine data and business logic from different resources and provide a business-level document at the web service level. By keeping the business logic in the custom Controls, you separate the business logic from the web service itself and practice the MVC pattern of keeping the View separate from the Model and the Controller.

Three types of Controls exist: custom Java Controls, built-in Java Controls, and extensible Controls. For enterprise-class web services, custom Java Controls offer the best approach for encapsulating complex business logic and connecting to diverse enterprise resources. The custom Java Control, in turn, connects to built-in Java Controls such as the database Control, the JMS control, and the timer control. The built-in controls are part of the Control Framework provided by WebLogic Workshop.

Consider an example of how to build a custom Control that uses a database Control and an EJB Control, and how to organize them using local Controls and Control projects. This example continues with the `validatev1_2` web service example from Chapter 6, "Designing Web Services."

First, you create a custom Control and have `validatev_1_2` access this Control for the business logic. The `validatev_1_2` service performs two functions. It takes as input a product configuration defined by the configID and accountID. It gives back a `valid` or `not valid` configuration status for the configID, and it returns the `ship_date` for the accountID. To enable these functions, you need to connect to a database Control and an EJB Control. Second, you create a database Control to get a `ship_date` for the given accountID. Third, you create an EJB Control to get the status of the configuration by passing the configID.

Building a Custom Control

First, create a new application for the custom Control with a new Java control project. Call the custom Control `VCImpl`. `Impl` indicates that the file contains the implementation code for your control. Two files are created: a Java Control Source (JCS) file and a JAVA file. The JCS file contains the implementation code for your Java Control. The JAVA file contains the public interface for the underlying implementation code, with a list of methods that users can call to access the functionality contained within the underlying implementation code. WebLogic Workshop automatically maintains the JAVA file as you edit the JCS file. A JCS file is what WebLogic Workshop calls a *regular* control. It does not provide a customizable interface—that is, the interface is already defined when an application developer adds it to an application. In this way, a regular control is like a library of reusable code. Regular Controls have the annotation of `jcs`:

```
* @jcs:jc-jar label="VC"
```

Next, add the method `validate` to the custom Control. The `validatev1_2` web service uses the `validate` method to invoke the business logic provided by the custom Control. See Figure 8.1.

Figure 8.1 Custom Control

Building a Database Control

Next, you add a database Control to the VC custom Control. The database Control provides access to a database containing `ship_dates` for accountIDs. You can access a relational database through a database Control from your application. Using the database Control, you can issue SQL commands to the database, which accesses the database through the JDBC driver. You must specify a data source that is configured in WebLogic. In this example, it is `cgdatasource`. The database Control automatically performs the translation from database queries to Java objects so that you can easily access query results.

You will create a new Java class called `record.java`. The `Record` class is a Java object that represents an individual record within a database. In particular, it represents an individual record of the validate table in the database. This is the code to add to `record.java`:

```
package validate;

public class Record
{
    public String ship_Date;
}
```

Create a database Control file that queries the validate table and then returns a `Record` object containing the results of the query. Next, create a database Control file, called `ShipDateDB.jcx`. *JCX* stands for Java Control extension. A JCX file extends one of Workshop's prebuilt control classes. In this case, it is the `com.bea.control.DatabaseControl` class, which offers easy access to a database. Most of the built-in Controls provided with WebLogic Workshop are customizable Controls—that is, when you add a new built-in Control to a project, WebLogic Workshop generates a JCX file that extends the Control. In some cases, such as with the database Control or the JMS control, you can customize the control by adding or editing methods defined in the JCX file. WebLogic Workshop customizes the EJB Control for you based on the EJB that the Control will be accessing. See Figure 8.2.

Figure 8.2 Database Control

Now you add a method named `getShipDate` to the database Control file `ShipDateDB.jcx`. Then you add a SQL query to the method in the property editor, as shown here:

```
SELECT SHIP_DATE FROM VALIDATE WHERE ACCOUNT_ID={accountId}
```

In the Java pane, this change is reflected in the method:

```
public Record getShipDate(String accountId)
```

In source view, the code shows that by passing the accountID, you get the `ship_date` from the database table validate:

```
package validate;

import com.bea.control.*;
import java.sql.SQLException;

*
 * @jc:connection data-source-jndi-name="cgDataSource"
 */
public interface ShipDateDatabase extends DatabaseControl,
➥com.bea.control.ControlExtension
{
     static final long serialVersionUID = 1L;

    /**
     * @jc:sql statement="SELECT SHIP_DATE FROM
➥ VALIDATE WHERE ACCOUNT_ID={accountId}"
     */
    public Record getShipDate(String accountId);
}
```

You must add code to modify the method `validate` to call the database Control. Note that `ship_date` is the shipment days, as explained in Chapter 7, "Developing and Deploying Web Services":

```
    public String validate(String accountId)
    {
        Record rec = ShipDateDB.getShipDate(accountId);
        if ( rec == null)
        {
            rec.ship_Date = "12";
        }

        return rec.ship_Date;
    }
```

Building an EJB Control

Next, you add an EJB Control to the custom Control. You can create EJB Controls either from EJBs provided in WebLogic or from EJBs that you have created in WebLogic. This section looks at an example of a session bean, `ConfigvSession`, that was created in WebLogic. You will see how this session bean is created in WebLogic in Chapter 9, "Connecting to a Distributed Environment."

Before an EJB Control can be added to a web service project, the compiled home and remote interfaces for the EJB must be in the project. The JAR file containing the home and remote interfaces is already within the Libraries folder of the application. To create an EJB Control to represent an EJB, you must know the names of the home and business interfaces. The EJB Control uses either the EJB's local interfaces or the remote interfaces. After you have created an EJB Control, you can invoke a target EJB method via the EJB Control by invoking the method with the same signature on your EJB Control. The EJB Control automatically manages locating and referencing the EJB instance, and it directs method invocations to the correct instance of the target EJB. Whether you must first create an instance of the target EJB using the EJB's `create` method depends on whether the EJB Control references a session or an entity bean.

In this example, the `ConfigvSession` EJB is designed to validate the configuration by taking a configID and returning the validity status of the configuration. To access the `ConfigvSession` bean, you add an EJB Control.

Enter values as shown in Figure 8.3. You can use server EJBs or application EJBs. The `jndi-name` value `ejb.ConfigvSession` is automatically entered. The home interface, `ValidateEJBFolder.ConfigvSessionLocalHome`, and the bean interface, `ValidateEJBFolder.ConfigvSessionLocal`, values are added automatically. For synchronous communication, you select stateless session beans, as has been done in this example. For asynchronous communication, you select message-driven beans.

You must change the `validate` method of the custom Control to include the result from the EJB:

```
public result validate(String accountId, String configid)
    {
        result rs = new result();

        rs.record = ShipDateDB.getShipDate(accountId);
        rs.Status = ValidateEJB.getStatus(configid);
        String status = ValidateEJB.getStatus(configid);
        Record rec = ShipDateDB.getShipDate(accountId);


        return rs;
    }
```

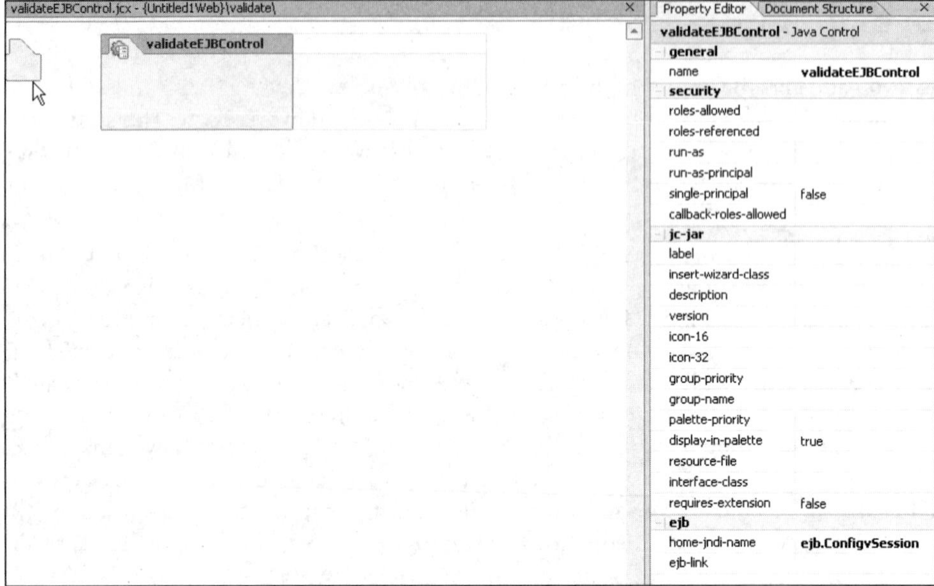

Figure 8.3 EJB Control

Now it is time to test the `validate_v1_2` web service and how it accesses the custom Control. Give the inputs accountID as `1234567890` and configID as `100`, as shown in Figure 8.4.

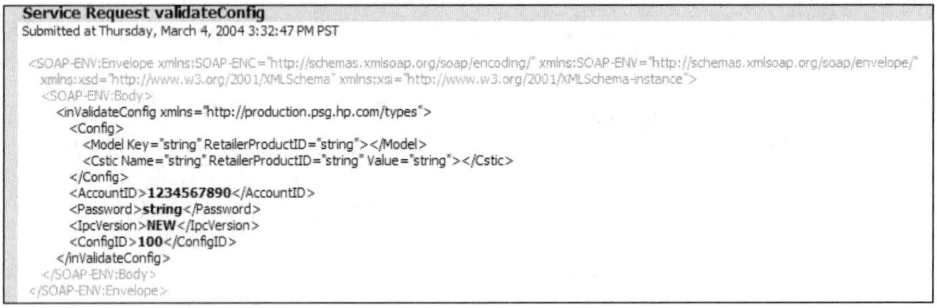

Service Request validateConfig

Submitted at Thursday, March 4, 2004 3:32:47 PM PST

```
<SOAP-ENV:Envelope xmlns:SOAP-ENC="http://schemas.xmlsoap.org/soap/encoding/" xmlns:SOAP-ENV="http://schemas.xmlsoap.org/soap/envelope/"
  xmlns:xsd="http://www.w3.org/2001/XMLSchema" xmlns:xsi="http://www.w3.org/2001/XMLSchema-instance">
  <SOAP-ENV:Body>
    <inValidateConfig xmlns="http://production.psg.hp.com/types">
      <Config>
        <Model Key="string" RetailerProductID="string"></Model>
        <Cstic Name="string" RetailerProductID="string" Value="string"></Cstic>
      </Config>
      <AccountID>1234567890</AccountID>
      <Password>string</Password>
      <IpcVersion>NEW</IpcVersion>
      <ConfigID>100</ConfigID>
    </inValidateConfig>
  </SOAP-ENV:Body>
</SOAP-ENV:Envelope>
```

Figure 8.4 Input message

The output is shown in Figure 8.5 where you see the return `ship_date` and the validation status.

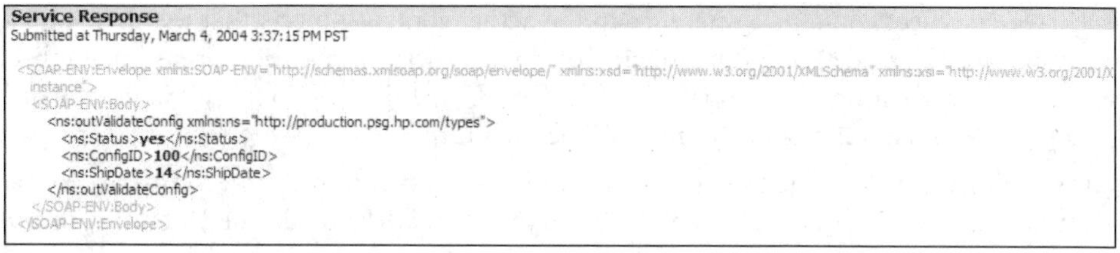

Service Response
Submitted at Thursday, March 4, 2004 3:37:15 PM PST

```
<SOAP-ENV:Envelope xmlns:SOAP-ENV="http://schemas.xmlsoap.org/soap/envelope/" xmlns:xsd="http://www.w3.org/2001/XMLSchema" xmlns:xsi="http://www.w3.org/2001/X
  instance">
  <SOAP-ENV:Body>
    <ns:outValidateConfig xmlns:ns="http://production.psg.hp.com/types">
      <ns:Status>yes</ns:Status>
      <ns:ConfigID>100</ns:ConfigID>
      <ns:ShipDate>14</ns:ShipDate>
    </ns:outValidateConfig>
  </SOAP-ENV:Body>
</SOAP-ENV:Envelope>
```

Figure 8.5 Output message

Using an ISV Control

In addition to the Java Controls embedded in WebLogic Workshop itself, Workshop offers extensible Controls. Extensible Controls enable developers to create reusable components of business logic as modules that can be integrated with any enterprise resource, ISV application, or piece of business logic. This makes it easy for ISVs to package and distribute them as standard JAR files. The ISV Java Controls make it possible to connect to ISV applications while protecting the developer's abstraction from most of the complexity of the infrastructure. As a result, developers can largely focus on procedural Java instead of J2EE or other vendor-specific APIs.

Sample ISV Control

When you want to add an ISV Control to your business process or expose it as a web service, you can go to the Add Control menu and add an ISV Control from vendors such as Documentum or Blue Titan. WebLogic Workshop includes a Help menu item labeled Premiere Component Gallery, which provides a link so that users can browse the component gallery to select the ISV controls that they want to download. To make the controls visible in the WebLogic Workshop IDE, all you need to do is place the control files (zipped) in the <bea_home>\ext_components directory.

ISV controls are provided as control stubs, which make these controls available to end users without requiring them to install the implementation files for those controls on their machines. When an end user selects a control from this menu, the implementation files for that control are downloaded to the user's machine. This allows the users to have the latest version of the control.

Consider an example of adding a Documentum Business Object Control to a project and exposing it as a web service. The Control connects to the Documentum Inbox Service Based Object (SBO). The web service created from the Control counts the number of items in the user's inbox. The SBO is used to implement service interfaces to the content-management functionality of Documentum. The capability to subscribe to content is actually accomplished by creating a new object associated with the user who wants to subscribe to the content; this newly created object contains a reference to the actual content objects that the user wants to "subscribe" to. The underlying functionality of this "subscription" procedure is accomplished using core Documentum functionality; the interface to this functionality for developers is through the Subscription SBO delivered by Documentum.

After you have downloaded the Control stub for Documentum Business, you need to add the Documentum JAR files to the WebLogic Server classpath and add the Documentum JAR files to the classpath for the WebLogic Workshop IDE.

Next, create a new Documentum Business Object Control called `inbox` (see Figure 8.6). It uses the SBO object `Inbox`. Select Use Control Generated SessionManager with the Following Identity, and complete the security credentials for the registered identity for your Docbase.

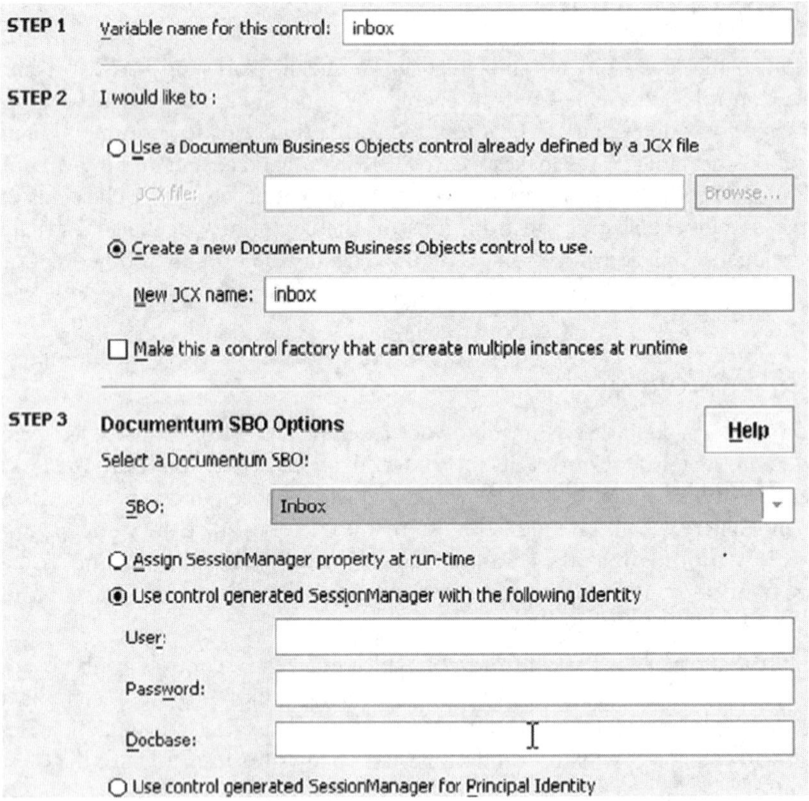

Figure 8.6 Insert Documentum Business Object Control

The Control is displayed on the IDE, listing the methods available for the `Inbox` SBO and the SessionManager. You can create a web service from this Control and test it, as shown in Figure 8.7. You will see the number of items in the `inbox`.

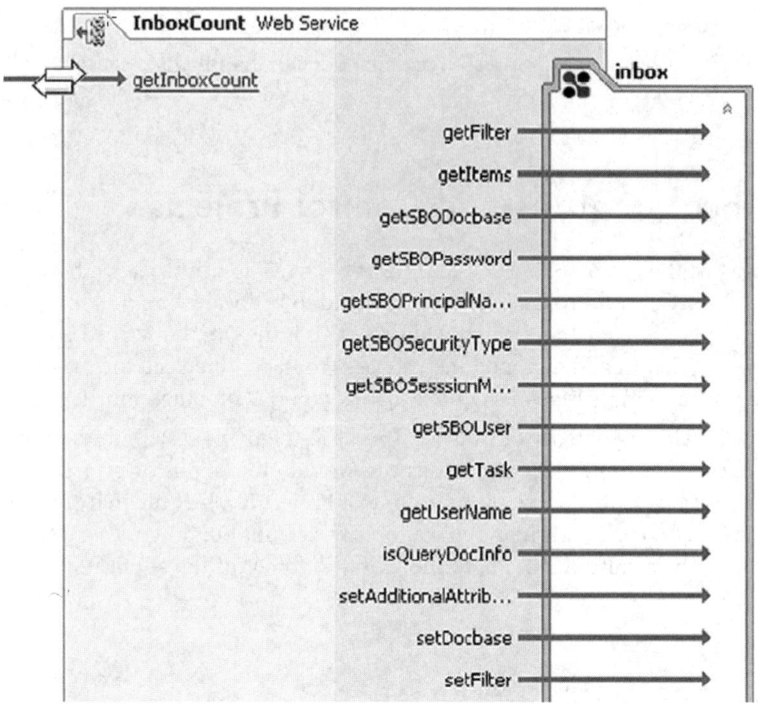

Figure 8.7 Testing `Inbox` web service

Developing an ISV Control

Extensible Controls can be developed through the Extensibility Development Kit provided by WebLogic Workshop, which includes a package called the Control Development Kit. The kit provides tools for incorporating advanced features into Java controls. ISVs can use these features to make their Java controls highly customizable by end users or to provide sophisticated property editors that are not required by all applications.

The Control Development Kit includes sample code and documentation that demonstrate and describe the advanced features of the Java control architecture. Using the samples as a guide, Controls can be built that have the following features:

- In design view, code is included that handles specific user actions.
- The Controls can use the Property Editor to define properties especially for custom data types.
- To validate custom property attributes in both the Property Editor and source code, use a class.

- To guide the end user, use a Custom Control Insert Wizard.
- For efficient management of resource dependencies, handle lifecycle callback events.

Using Local Controls and Control Projects

You can organize the custom Controls in different ways. The Controls can be set up as either Local Controls or Control Projects. A Control is said to be local when its source files reside in the same project as the code that uses the Control. This is the simplest way to use Java Controls. You can create a JCS file, add methods and callbacks to it, and then call the methods from code in the same project. This is most likely the way that you will organize your Java Controls.

You can also group related Controls and package them for distribution among multiple projects. You create a Control Project just as you would other kinds of projects, and then you add files for your Controls. The result of a Control Project is a JAR file that you can distribute for use in any WebLogic Workshop application. By default, building a Control Project automatically copies the resulting JAR file to the Libraries folder of the application containing the project.

Controls and Software Reuse

Controls allow the reuse of software code (that is, software components), basically the reuse of EJBs, databases, web services, and components from ISVs. You need to look at this reuse beyond just the ease of programming. Controls as reusable components can be a business success enabler to the organization and can bring about savings, software quality, and a shorter time to market. The right architecture allows applications and components to evolve gracefully and provides guidelines for implementing software engineering reuse processes. In his book *Software Reuse: Architecture, Process, and Organization for Business Success* (Addison-Wesley, 1997), Ivar Jacobson says that introducing effective reuse into a software-engineering business requires a concerted and systematic effort by both management and software developers to overcome the business, process, organizational, and technical impediments that often hinder effective reuse.

There needs to be a systematic transition to a reuse business, combining business-engineering techniques with change management and reuse-specific guidelines. Economic, process, and product measures also should be used to manage trade-offs and progress flow. Organizational and technical infrastructure changes also are needed to support a reuse business.

Binding Java to XML Using XML Beans

A web service communicates with clients and with many resources via XML messages. In many cases, it is necessary to translate back and forth between XML and the Java method or callback arguments inside your web service. Outgoing method calls need their Java parameters translated into the appropriate XML data types; likewise, incoming XML messages need their data translated into the appropriate Java method parameter types.

XML Beans, a technology used throughout WebLogic Workshop, provides powerful, natural, and very easy translation between XML data and Java types. A major objective of XML Beans has been to be applicable in *all* nonstreaming (in-memory) XML programming situations. The following are advantages of XML Beans for handling XML:

- You can access XML very expediently.
- Without losing access to the original XML structure, XML Beans provides a Java object-based view of XML data.
- Other APIs must take the XML apart. Unlike the other APIs, XML Beans handles the entire XML document instance as a whole. The XML data is stored in memory as XML.
- Within Workshop, you just drop an XSD into your project, and the XML Beans are created and available throughout the entire EAR. The integrity of the XML is not lost.

Other options for handling XML include using XML programming interfaces such as DOM or SAX, or an XML marshalling/binding tool such as JAXB. Because it lacks strong schema-oriented typing, navigation in a DOM-oriented model is more tedious and requires an understanding of the complete object model. JAXB provides support for the XML Schema specification but handles only a subset of it; XML Beans supports all of it. Also, by storing the data in memory as XML, XML Beans can reduce the overhead of marshalling and unmarshalling.

Three major APIs are provided for using XML Beans.

- `XmlObject`—The Java classes that are generated from an XML Schema are all derived from `XmlObject`. These provide strongly typed getters and setters for each of the elements within the defined XML. Complex types are, in turn, `XmlObjects`. Simple types turn into simple getters and setters with the correct Java type.
- `XmlCursor`—From any `XmlObject`, you can get an `XmlCursor`. This provides efficient, low-level access to the XML Infoset (that is, the XML Information Set). It is a W3C Recommendation that attempts to define a set of terms that other W3C specifications, as well as specifications from other organizations, can use to refer to the information chunks in a well-formed XML document. A cursor represents a position in the XML instance. You can move the cursor around the XML

instance at any level of granularity you need, from individual characters to tokens.

- SchemaType—XML Beans provides a full XML Schema object model that you can use to reflect on the underlying schema meta information.

Understanding XML Beans

The starting point for XML Beans is XML Schema. The XML Schema specification provides a rich data model that enables you to express structure and constraints on your data. For example, an XML Schema can enforce Control over how data is ordered in a document or constraints on particular values (for example, the product price has to be more than $100). This capability to enforce rules can be accomplished in Java by writing custom code. XML Beans honors schema constraints.

The schema and XML for outValidateConfig are shown here. Take a look at how it is converted to XML Beans and the processing that you can do on the XML Beans.

This is the schema for outValidateConfig:

```
<xsd:element name="outValidateConfig">
        <xsd:complexType>
            <xsd:sequence>
                <xsd:element name="Status" type="TrueFalseType"/>
                <xsd:element name="Error" type="ErrorType" minOccurs="0"/>
                <xsd:element name="ConfigID" type="xsd:string" minOccurs="0"
➥maxOccurs="unbounded"/>
                <xsd:element name="ShipDate" type="AtLeast1Type"
➥minOccurs="0"/>
            </xsd:sequence>
        </xsd:complexType>
</xsd:element>
```

This is the XML for outValidateConfig:

```
<ns:outValidateConfig xmlns:ns=http://production.psg.hp.com/types>
    <ns:Status>yes</ns:Status>
<ns:ConfigID>1234< /ns:ConfigID >
<ns:ShipDate>24</ns:ShipDate >
</ns:outValidateConfig>
```

Here, you see that you have one complex type of element, outValidateConfig. In a schema, a complex type is one that defines an element that can have child elements and attributes.

The sequence element nested in the complex type lists its child elements. Because `outValidateConfig` is at the top of the schema, it is a global type.

Within a complex type such as `outValidateConfig`, you use simple types such as `ConfigID` and complex types such as `Status`. The simple type is also a built-in type. A built-in type is part of the schema specification. Forty-six built-in types are defined in the specification. Table 8.1 shows the built-in types; you can get more information on these built-in data types at http: //e-docs.bea.com/workshop/docs81/doc/en/core/index.html.

Table 8.1 Built-In Schema Types, XML Bean Type, Natural Java Type

Built-In Schema Type	XML Bean Type	Natural Java Type
xs:anyType	XmlObject	com.bea.xml.XmlObject
xs:anySimpleType	XmlAnySimpleType	String
xs:anyURI	XmlAnyURI	String
xs:base64Binary	XmlBase64Binary	byte[]
xs:boolean	XmlBoolean	boolean
xs:byte	XmlByte	byte
xs:date	XmlDate	java.util.Calendar
xs:dateTime	XmlDateTime	java.util.Calendar
xs:decimal	XmlDecimal	java.math.BigDecimal
xs:double	XmlDouble	double
xs:duration	XmlDuration	com.bea.xml.Gduration
xs:ENTITIES	XmlENTITIES	String
xs:ENTITY	XmlENTITY	String
xs:float	XmlFloat	float
xs:gDay	XmlGDay	java.util.Calendar
xs:gMonth	XmlGMonth	java.util.Calendar
xs:gMonthDay	XmlGMonthDay	java.util.Calendar
xs:gYear	XmlGYear	java.util.Calendar
xs:gYearMonth	XmlGYearMonth	java.util.Calendar
xs:hexBinary	XmlHexBinary	byte[]
xs:ID	XmlID	String
xs:IDREF	XmlIDREF	String

Table 8.1 Continued

Built-In Schema Type	XML Bean Type	Natural Java Type
`xs:IDREFS`	`XmlIDREFS`	`String`
`xs:int`	`XmlInt`	`int`
`xs:integer`	`XmlInteger`	`java.math.BigInteger`
`xs:language`	`XmlLanguage`	`String`
`xs:long`	`XmlLong`	`long`
`xs:Name`	`XmlName`	`String`
`xs:NCName`	`XmlNCNAME`	`String`
`xs:negativeInteger`	`XmlNegativeInteger`	`java.math.BigInteger`
`xs:NMTOKEN`	`XmlNMTOKEN`	`String`
`xs:NMTOKENS`	`XmlNMTOKENS`	`String`
`xs:nonNegativeInteger`	`XmlNonNegativeInteger`	`java.math.BigInteger`
`xs:nonPositiveInteger`	`XmlNonPositiveInteger`	`java.math.BigInteger`
`xs:normalizedString`	`XmlNormalizedString`	`String`
`xs:NOTATION`	`XmlNOTATION`	Not supported
`xs:positiveInteger`	`XmlPositiveInteger`	`java.math.BigInteger`
`xs:QName`	`XmlQName`	`javax.xml.namespace.QName`
`xs:short`	`XmlShort`	`short`
`xs:string`	`XmlString`	`String`
`xs:time`	`XmlTime`	`java.util.Calendar`
`xs:token`	`XmlToken`	`String`
`xs:unsignedByte`	`XmlUnsignedByte`	`short`
`xs:unsignedInt`	`XmlUnsignedInt`	`long`
`xs:unsignedLong`	`XmlUnsignedLong`	`java.math.BigInteger`
`xs:unsignedShort`	`XmlUnsignedShort`	`int`

When you compile XML Schema, the resulting API is made up of two categories of types: built-in types that mirror those in the schema specification and others that are generated from user-derived schema types. To compile the XML Schema, import it into the schemas directory in WebLogic Workshop; it then creates the XML Beans.

XML Beans Hierarchy

When you examine the XML Beans, you will see that there is a hierarchy to represent the schema. At the top of the hierarchy is `XmlObject`, the base interface for XML Beans types. Beneath this level, there are two main type categories: generated types that represent user-defined schema types, and included types that represent built-in schema types.

Support for User-Defined Types

The compiled XML Schema gives two generated XML Beans interfaces: `OutValidateConfigDocument` and `OutValidateConfigDocument.OutValidateConfig`, which is similar to the `InvalidConfigDocument` and `InValidConfigDocument.InValidateConfig`. See Figure 8.8.

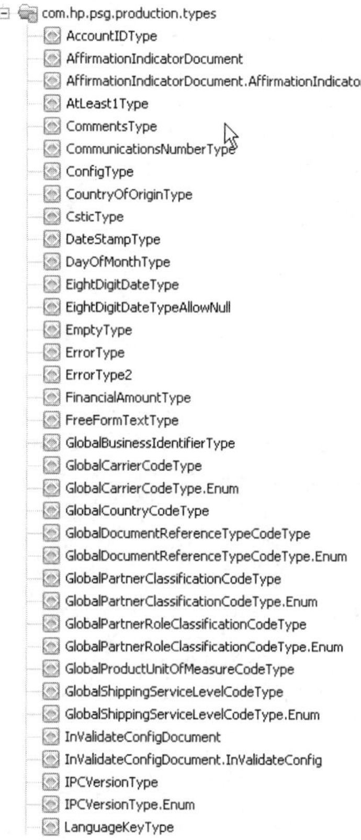

Figure 8.8 XML Beans in WebLogic Workshop

From the schema point of view, the generated `outValidateConfig` interface represents the complex type you see inside the schema's `outValidateConfig` element declaration. Looking at the XML instance, you can see that this complex type translates into a sequence of four elements: `Status`, `Error`, `ConfigID`, and `ShipDate`. The `OutValidateConfig` interface exposes methods such as `getStatus` and `setStatus` to set the value of the `status` element.

The `outValidateConfigDocument` interface, on the other hand, represents the `outValidateConfig` document that contains the root `outValidateConfig` element. XML Beans creates a special "document" type for global element types. A document type provides a way for you to get and set the value of the underlying type, here represented by `outValidateConfig`. The `outValidateConfig` element is considered a global element because it is the root element and can be referenced from anywhere else in the schema. To set or get the value of the user-defined types, `get` and `set` methods are provided.

The following bit of Java code illustrates how you might use these interfaces to set the `Status`, `ShipDate`, and `ConfigID` contained in the XML:

```
public static OutValidateConfigDocument setReply() throws Exception
    {
        OutValidateConfigDocument docXML =
➥OutValidateConfigDocument.Factory.newInstance();
        OutValidateConfig quoteXML = docXML.addNewOutValidateConfig();
        quoteXML.setStatus("yes");
        quoteXML.setShipDate("1234");
        quoteXML.addConfigID("1234");
        return docXML;
}
```

This code loads the XML and converts the `parse` method's return value to an `outValidateConfigDocument` instance. It uses the `factory` class to define the new instance. It then uses this instance to get an instance of `outValidateConfig`. With the `outValidateConfig` instance, the code sets the status.

Support for Built-In Types

In addition to types generated from a given schema, XML Beans provides 46 Java types that mirror the 46 built-in types defined by the XML Schema specification. XML Beans provides `XmlString`, `XmlDecimal`, and `XmlInt` for `xs:string`, `xs:decimal`, and `xs:int`. Each of these also inherits from `XmlObject`, which corresponds to the built-in schema type `xs:anyType`.

XML Beans provides a way for you to handle XML data as these built-in types. Where your schema includes an element whose type is `xs:int`, XML Beans provide a generated method designed to return an `XmlInt`. A method also returns a natural Java type such as an `int`. You can write code to return the quantity element's value, but return it as different types.

The following is an example to return a simple XML type:

```
XmlInt xmlQuantity = lineitems[j].xgetQuantity();
```

The following is an example to return a natural Java type:

```
int javaQuantity = lineitems[j].getQuantity();
```

Both get methods navigate to the `quantity` element; the `getQuantity` method goes a step further and converts the element's value to the most appropriate natural Java type before returning it. XML Beans also validates the XML as you work with it.

Using XQuery and XPath Expressions

With XML Beans, you can use XQuery and XPath to query XML for specific pieces of data. XQuery is a powerful and convenient language designed for processing XML data. That means not only files in XML format, but also other data, including databases whose structure (nested, named trees with attributes) is similar to XML. The first thing to note is that, in XQuery, everything is an expression that evaluates to a value. An XQuery program or script is a just an expression. For example, 3+4 is a complete, valid XQuery program that evaluates to the integer 7.

In the following example, using XQuery, you can return all the configurations whose status is `yes`, which corresponds to a valid configuration:

```
outValidateConfigDocument doc = outValidateDocument.Factory.parse(ns);
```

This line declares the namespace:

```
String nsText = "declare namespace ns =
'http://production.psg.hp.com/types'";
```

This code declares the expression:

```
String pathText = "$this/ns:outValidateConfig [ns:status= yes]";
String queryText = nsText + pathText;
```

Here, the `execQuery` method is used:

```
XmlCursor itemCursor = doc.newCursor().execQuery(queryText);
System.out.println(itemCursor.xmlText());
```

This code creates a new cursor at the start of the document. From there, it uses the `XmlCursor` interface's `execQuery` method to execute the query expression. In this example, the method's parameter is an XQuery expression that navigates through the `outValidateConfig` element and retrieves those status elements whose value is equal to `yes`. The `$this` variable refers to the current position.

You can also use the `selectPath` method to execute XPath expressions. The `selectPath` method is optimized for XPath, which is used to identify particular parts of XML documents. XPath lets you write expressions that refer to the document's elements, child elements, and attributes of elements. XPath indicates nodes by position, relative position, type, content, and several other criteria.

If you want to find out which configurations return a status of `yes`, you can capture the XPath expression in this way:

```
String queryExpression =
    "declare namespace ns = http://production.psg.hp.com/types"+
    "$this/"$this/ns:outValidateConfig/ns:status[contains(., '(yes)')]"
```

You can then retrieve the configuration and assign it to the generated type with code such as the following:

```
/*
 * Retrieve the matching configurations and assign the results
➥to the corresponding
 * generated type.
 */
StatusType[] status =
➥(StatusType[])outValidateconfigDoc.selectPath(queryExpression);
```

Using XML Cursors

In addition to providing a way to execute XQuery expression, XML cursors offer a fine-grained model for manipulating data. The XML cursor API is a way to point at a particular piece of data. The XML cursor defines a location in XML where you can perform actions on the selected XML.

First, the cursor moves to the desired location in the XML document. When the cursor is at the location you're interested in, you can perform a variety of operations with it. For example, you can set and get values, insert and remove fragments of XML, copy fragments of XML to other parts of the document, and make other fine-grained changes to the XML document.

The following example uses an XML cursor to navigate to the `outValidateConfig` element's `Status` child element:

```
outValidateConfigDocument doc =
    outValidateConfigDocument.Factory.parse(ns);
```

```
XmlCursor cursor = doc.newCursor();
cursor.toFirstContentToken();
cursor.toFirstChildElement();
cursor.toFirstChildElement();
System.out.println(cursor.getText());

cursor.dispose();
```

After loading the document, the code creates a cursor at its beginning. Moving the cursor a few times takes it to the nested `Status` element. There, the `getText` method retrieves the element's value.

Parsing XML

The last section looked at XML Beans and how it achieves XML-to-Java binding. XML parsing is another important technique when you are working with XML documents. Efficient parsing of XML documents is becoming increasingly critical as XML gets adopted more widely. It is very important to have an efficient way to parse XML data, especially in applications that are intended to handle large volumes. Improper parsing can result in excessive memory usage and processing times that can hurt scalability.

Using the StAX Parser

Streaming API for XML (StAX) is a parsing technique that uses an event-driven model and uses a pull model for event processing. The StAX parser returns events as requested by the application. StAX also provides user-friendly APIs for read-in and write-out. As its name suggests, StAX is best used for a streaming model, unlike XML Beans, whose main purpose is for non-streaming models.

Consider an example of `productcatalog.xml` to understand the workings of a StAX parser:

```
<productcatalog>
  <productID ="D7456">
    <desc > printer </desc >
    <type> laser</type >
    <price>450.00</price>
  </productID >
  <productID ="C65478">
    <desc >PDA </desc >
    <type >wireless </type>
    <price>650.00</price>
  </book>
</productcatalog>
```

In Figure 8.9, you can see how a StAX parser reads the XML when an application requests an event. It returns the event to the application. StAX includes factories for creating the StAX reader and writer so that applications do not have to reference an implementation.

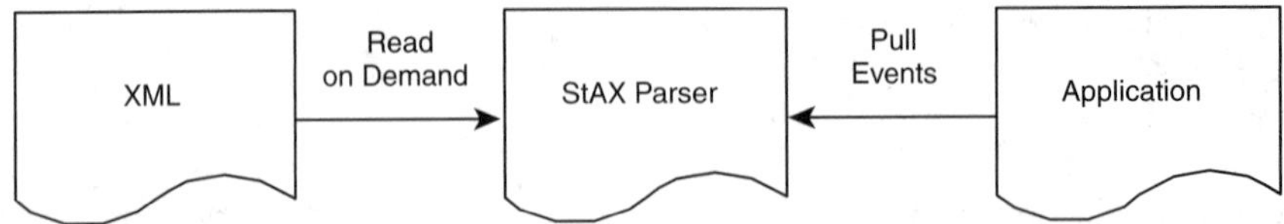

Figure 8.9 StAX parser

StAX has two parsing models. The cursor model, like SAX, returns events. The iterator model returns events as objects but has the additional overhead of object creation. The following examples show how the two models are used to print product catalog description:

```
XMLStreamReader reader = XMLInputFactory
  .newInstance().createXMLStreamReader(
    new FileInputStream("productcatalog.xml"));
while(reader.hasNext()) {
      int eventType = reader.next();
      if (eventType == XMLEvent
.START_ELEMENT && reader.getLocalName()
.equals("desc")) {
     reader.next();
     System.out.println(reader.getText());
      }
}
```

In this example, first the reader is set up. Then the application requests the next event, using the `reader.next()` method call. The StAX parser moves the cursor to the next event position. If this event indicates the start of an element named `desc`, the application code calls `reader.next()` one more time, to advance the cursor. Then, using the `reader.getText()` method, it obtains the text for the `desc` element, which, in this example, is printer.

The following example uses the iterator model, in which the events are returned as objects:

```
XMLEventReader eventReader =
  XMLInputFactory.newInstance()
    .createXMLEventReader(
       new FileInputStream("productcatalog.xml"));
while(eventReader.hasNext()) {
      XMLEvent event = eventReader.next();
```

```
      if (event instanceof StartElement &&
  ((StartElement)event).getLocalName()
.equals("desc"))
  {
  System.out.println( ((Characters)eventReader.next())
  .getData());
    }
}
```

In this example, the application requests the next event, which makes the StAX parser advance to the next event position and return the corresponding event object. The application can access the contents through the `event` object, using the `getData()` method, which returns the book title information.

StAX gives more Control of XML parsing to the programmer, in particular by exposing a simple iterator-based API and an underlying stream of events. Methods such as `next()` and `hasNext()` allow an application developer to ask for the next event, or pull the event, rather than handle the event in a callback. StAX also enables the programmer to stop processing the document at any time, skip ahead to sections of the document, and get subsections of the document.

Both the iterator and cursor APIs can be thought of as iterating over a set of events. An XML document is broken down into the following event granularity by both the cursor and event iterator API. See Table 8.2.

Table 8.2 Event Options

Event Options	**Description**
`StartDocument`	The `StartDocument` event reports the beginning of a set of XML events and encoding, XML version, and standalone properties.
`EndDocument`	The `EndDocument` event signals the end of the set of XML events.
`StartElement`	The `StartElement` event encapsulates information about the start of an element. It reports any attributes and namespace declarations declared in the start tag of the actual XML. It also gives access to the prefix, namespace URI, and local name of the start tag.
`EndElement`	The `EndElement` event corresponds directly to the end tag of an element.

Table 8.2 Continued

Event Options	Description
`EntityReference`	An `EntityReference` can be reported as its own event that allows the application programmer to resolve the entity or pass it through unresolved.
`Characters`	The `Characters` event corresponds to the following underlying XML entities: `CData` sections and `CharacterData`.
`ProcessingInstruction`	The `ProcessingInstruction` event reports both the target and the data of the underlying processing instruction.
`Comment`	The text of a comment is reported in a `Comment` event.
`DTD`	The `DTD` event encapsulates information about the Document Type Definition.
`Attribute`	Some XML processing situations (for example, XQuery or XPath query results) require that an attribute be reported as a standalone information item.
`Namespace`	`Namespace` declarations can also exist outside of a `StartElement` and may be reported as a standalone information item.

Comparison to SAX and DOM

To see how StAX compares to DOM and SAX, which are the other two parsers used extensively, take a look at how DOM and SAX would parse the `productcatalog.xml` file.

DOM is a tree-based parsing technique that builds up an entire parse tree in memory. Figure 8.10 shows how DOM parsing would look.

DOM parsing allows complete, dynamic access to a whole XML document:

```
DOMParser parser = new DOMParser();
parser.parse("productcatalog.xml");
Document document = parser.getDocument();
NodeList nodes =   document.getElementsByTagName("desc");
while(int i = 0;
  i < nodes.length(); i ++) {        Element descElem =
   (Element)nodes.item(i);
        Node childNode =
```

```
    titleElem.getFirstChild();
        if (childNode instanceof Text) {
          System.out.println("productID desc is: "
+ childNode.getNodeValue());
        }
}
```

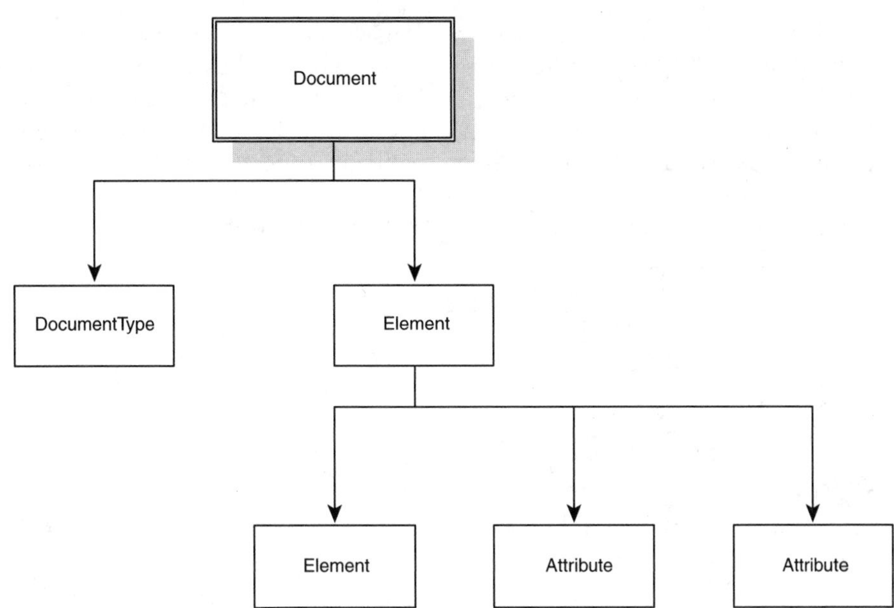

Figure 8.10 DOM parser

This program takes the XML filename, creates the DOM tree, and finds all the DOM element nodes for the `desc` elements by using the `getElementsByTagName()` method. Finally, it prints the text information associated with each of the `desc` elements by iterating over the list of `desc` elements and examining the first child that has the text contained between the start and end tags of the element, using the `getFirstChild()` method.

SAX is an event-driven push model for processing XML. Instead of building a tree representation of an entire document, as DOM does, a SAX parser uses a series of events as it reads through the document. These events are pushed to event handlers, which provide access to the contents of the document.

Figure 8.11 shows how the SAX parser reports events through a callback mechanism. The parser reads the input document and pushes each event to `ProductContentHandler` while processing the document.

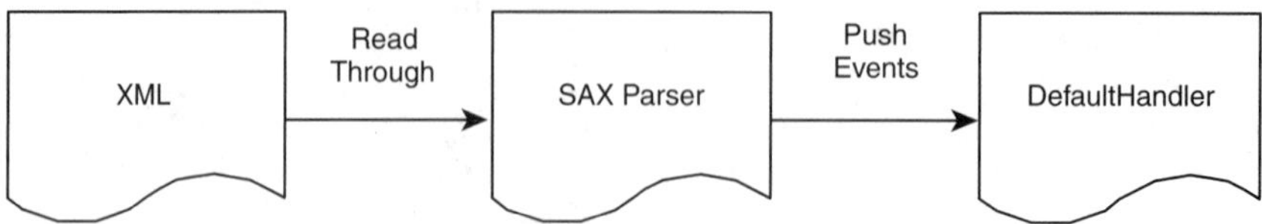

Figure 8.11 SAX parser

First, write the `ProductContentHandler` implementation class by extending the `DefaultHandler` class. This replaces the methods for the type of events in which you are interested. The code throws away any remaining events from the `DefaultHandler` class. The `ProductContentHandler` class provides the callback methods dealing with start element events, end element events, and character events for all the elements:

```
public class ProductContentHandler extends DefaultHandler {
        boolean isDesc;
        public void startElement(String uri, String localName,
String qName, Attributes atts) {
    if (localName.equals("desc"))
                    isDesc = true;
        }
        public void endElement(String uri, String localName,
String qName) {
          if(localName.equals("desc"))
               isDesc = false;
        }
        public void characters(char[ ] chars, int start, int length) {
     if(isDesc)

     System.out.println(new String(chars, start, length));
        }
}
```

Second, set the `ProductContentHandler` to the SAX parser. The parser begins to process the XML document. The parser generates the events and pushes them into the `ProductContentHandler` while reading the documents from beginning to end:

```
SAXParser saxParser = new SAXParser();
MyContentHandler myHandler = new
  MyContentHandler();
saxParser.setContentHandler(myHandler);
saxParser.parse(new File("productcatalog.xml"));
```

Table 8.3 shows a comparison between StAX Parser and SAX and DOM Parsers.

Table 8.3 Comparing StAX Parser to SAX and DOM Parsers

Criteria	StAX Versus SAX and DOM Parsers
Performance	The performance of the StAX cursor model is comparable to that of SAX parsing.
Ease of use	The application has control of the parsing, which makes the code easier to write and maintain. StAX also provides the iterator model for ease of use, but, in this case, creating event objects has a performance cost.
Filtering capabilities	The filtering capabilities of StAX are much more powerful than those of SAX.
Document-modifying capability	StAX's capability to modify a document is similar to that of SAX, in that a new document is created. Write-out APIs are provided in both the cursor and iterator models of StAX, but document modification is still quite difficult if you want to do anything beyond simple one-pass transformations.
Navigational support	In comparison to DOM, StAX has the same disadvantage as SAX in terms of lack of full navigational support. Forward navigation through a document is easier with StAX than with SAX, in that the application has control over which events it gets and when.

StAX parsing satisfies a majority of the SAX application's requirements. Therefore, if an application is well suited for SAX parsing, it can also benefit from the use of StAX. In addition, when applications need to take advantage of the streaming model for performance while maintaining full support for namespaces, StAX parsing is a good choice. Because the application controls parsing, it easily supports multiple inputs. StAX is especially useful in the new areas of web services and JAX-RPC, in which all of these features are required.

Summary

For web services to work, you need to encapsulate business logic and enable access to a diverse range of system resources. This can be done using Control Frameworks in WebLogic Workshop. The best approach is to build custom Controls and then connect to the built-in Java Controls, such as a database Control and an EJB Control. You can group related Controls for user within multiple projects and package them for sharing among the projects.

The other important aspect of building web services is XML-to-Java translation. This chapter described two approaches: XML-to-Java binding using XML Beans, and XML parsing using StAX parsers. The former is appropriate for nonstreaming situations, while the latter is best used for streaming environments. If you want to map most of your XML elements to Java objects or large documents, XML Beans is the better way to go. It is also appropriate if your architecture requires you to pass these Java objects through to other resources, such as JMS. For large documents, using parsers to get all the elements from the XML is very resource and time intensive. However, if you want to pull just a few elements out of an XML Schema, using a parser is the more efficient way.

XML Beans in WebLogic Workshop enables XML-to-Java binding. XML Beans provides a Java object-based view of XML data without losing access or integrity of the original XML structure. XML Schema is converted to XML Beans and represented in a hierarchical manner. `XmlObject`, `XmlCursor`, and `SchemaType` are three major APIs offered by XML Beans. `XmlObject` is at the top of the hierarchy, and beneath it are the user-defined types and built-in types. You can use XQuery, XPath, and XML Cursor expressions provided by XML Beans to access specific pieces of data in the XML.

The StAX parser uses an event-driven model for parsing XML documents and is well suited for web services. Two parsing models are used: a cursor model and an iterator model. Compared to SAX and DOM, the two other commonly used parsers, the StAX parser is easier to use and has better filtering capabilities. Its performance and capability to modify documents are comparable to that of SAX. Support for navigation is slightly inferior to that of the DOM parser.

9

Connecting to a Distributed Environment

The last chapter talked about Controls. This chapter looks at the next layer of technology that supports Controls: EJBs and the Application Integration Framework. Here, you will learn how to build EJBs in WebLogic Workshop, how to build entity and session beans quickly without much coding, and how to strengthen EJB deployment using WebLogic Server. This is the foundation for creating EJB Controls, which you used in Chapter 8, "Using Controls, Bindings, and Parsers."

Next, you will learn about the Application Integration Framework of WLI for integration to Enterprise Information Systems (EIS). The J2EE Connector Architecture specification defines how application servers such as WebLogic can be connected to EIS systems. WLI uses this specification and enhances it to connect to EIS. This chapter reviews the main components of the integration framework provided by WLI. You will also see the main components of the Adapter Development Kit. The Application Integration Framework interacts with the Control Framework to facilitate connection to EIS.

Building EJBs in WebLogic Workshop

Enterprise JavaBeans (EJB) is the primary server-side enterprise Java component architecture, enabling developers to design and develop customizable, reusable business logic. BEA WebLogic Server 8.1 supports EJB 2.0, which is the most recent version of the specification.

BEA WebLogic Server's built-in EJB container handles the underlying infrastructure services, such as multithreading, load balancing, clustering, object lifecycle, transactions, security, messaging, and persistence. The portability of the J2EE architecture enables EJBs written in Java to be deployed on any platform and operating system that support Java.

EJB 2.0 exposes four types of interfaces for session and entity beans:

1. Local home interface
2. Local business interface (or, simply, the local interface)
3. Remote home interface
4. Remote business interface (or, simply, the remote interface)

The local home and business interfaces define the methods that can be accessed by other beans, EJB Controls, web services, and page flows in the same WebLogic Workshop application. The remote home and business interfaces define the methods that can be accessed by other applications and web services.

Client applications can obtain an instance of the EJB with which to communicate by using the remote home interface. The methods in the remote home interface are limited to those that create or find EJB instances. When a client has an EJB instance, it can invoke methods of the EJB's remote business interface to do real work. The business interface directly accesses the business logic encapsulated in the EJB.

You use local interfaces for interactions between EJBs defined in the same WebLogic Workshop application, as well as interactions between EJBs and web services or page flows in the same WebLogic Workshop application. As you know, local interfaces offer a performance advantage over remote interfaces.

Message-driven beans do not have these interfaces because these beans' methods are not invoked directly by other beans or client applications. Instead, they process messages from client applications or other EJBs that are delivered via the Java Message Service (JMS). When a message is delivered, the EJB container calls the message-driven bean's `onMessage` method to process the message.

Example for Creating EJBs

This example uses the EJB Control in Chapter 8 that the `validateConfig` web service accessed for checking the configuration. The EJB Control is based on the session bean `ConfigSessionvbean`; it, in turn, references an entity bean. In the next few sections, you will see how to create the entity bean and the session bean that references this entity bean. The upcoming sections cover creating an EJB project, generating the EJB from a database table, building and deploying the entity bean, creating a session bean, referencing the entity bean, and building and deploying the session bean.

Creating an Entity Bean

When you want to expose existing database tables to an entity bean, WebLogic Workshop offers an easy way to generate the necessary entity beans. The first step in creating any EJB is to create an EJB project. Then you generate the entity bean from the database table, build it, and deploy it.

Creating an EJB Project

To build EJBs in WebLogic Workshop, you need to understand EJB projects. An EJB project is the development environment for session, entity, and message-driven beans; it is part of an application. An EJB project contains one or more EJBs.

An EJB project provides a design view, a Property Editor, building and debugging windows, and various wizards to facilitate the design and development of EJBs. Using design view, you can define business methods, CMP fields, and methods for local and/or remote interfaces (see Figure 9.1). Using a Property Editor, you can edit deployment descriptor settings and `ejbgen` tag settings. Using the various wizards, you can easily import EJBs into EJB projects, create `ejbCreate` methods, and define entity relationships. See Figure 9.1.

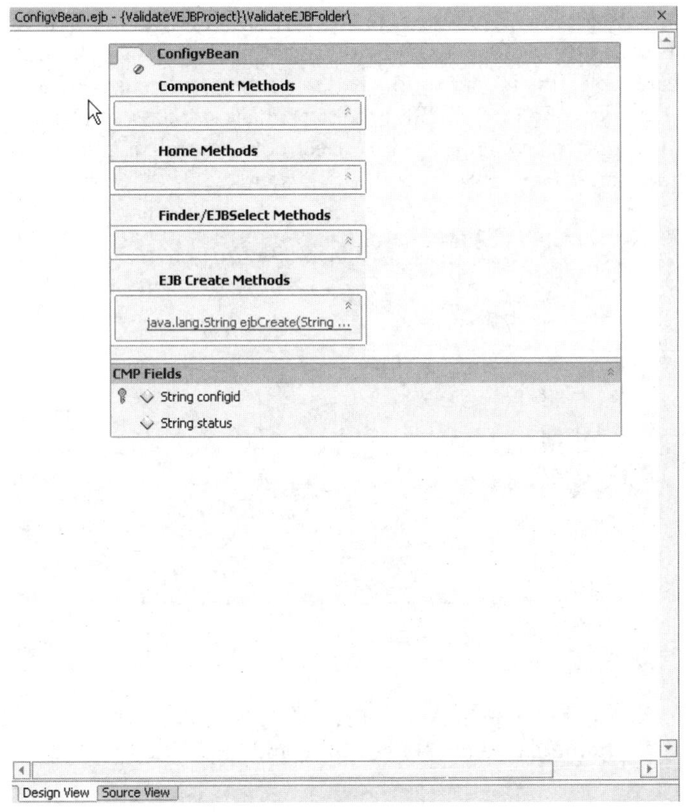

Figure 9.1 EJB in design view

A key advantage of developing EJBs in EJB project is that one file with the `.ejb` extension is used to represent an EJB. This file is created using `ejbGen`. In this file, the definition of the EJB class, its interfaces, and its deployment descriptor–specific settings are stored. Using a single file to store this information involves much less overhead than managing using several Java files.

Before creating a new bean, create and name a directory for it under the EJB project root. Create the bean within this folder. This is necessary because the newly created bean will be a package under the EJB project, and it needs a package name.

Generating Entity Bean from Database Table

Next, you generate an entity bean from a database table. To generate a CMP entity bean from a database table, you can use the option of creating an entity bean from a database table in the EJB Project menu. The database must be available from the domain you are using. This entity bean will later be used as a reference to a session bean; this session bean, in turn, will be used to create an EJB Control (described in Chapter 8).

This procedure is best illustrated through an example. First, you must select a data source; in this case, it is `cgSampleDataSource`. When you have selected the data source, you need to select the database table; this is `Config` for us. The `Config` table has two columns: `configID`, which is the primary key, and `status`. EJB needs a primary key class, so you should always have a primary key in your database. You need to select both columns and then provide the bean name and package name. Figure 9.2 shows the data source.

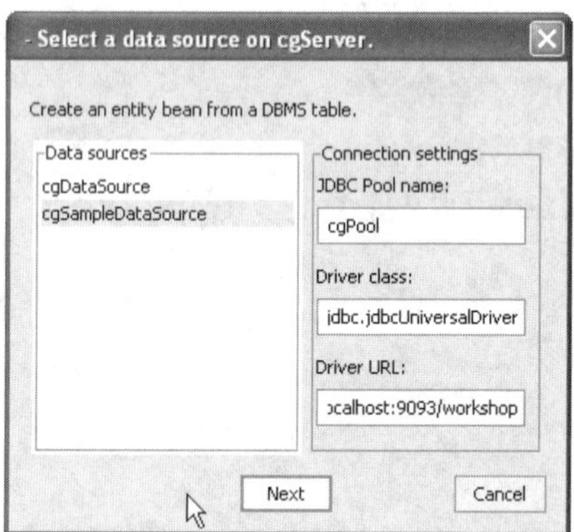

Figure 9.2 Data source

The local interface and remote interface are created, as shown in Figure 9.3. For each interface, you will see the home class name, JNDI name, and bean class name.

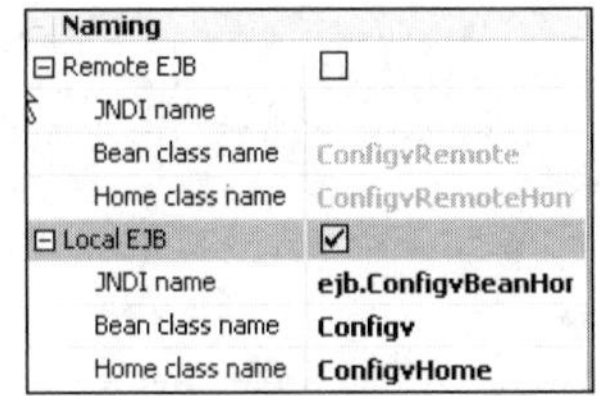

Figure 9.3 Local interface and remote interface of EJB

Understanding EJB Projects and `ejbGen`

EJB projects use `ejbGen` to generate and maintain EJBs. When you create an EJB in an EJB project and examine the source code in source view, you will notice special javadoc tags with the prefix `ejbgen`. These `ejbgen` tags are used to mark methods to be exposed in remote and home interfaces, store deployment descriptor settings, and store various other types of information. In many cases, you do not have to add these `ejbgen` tags directly. Instead, these tags are added when you define business methods to be local or when you create a primary key field for an entity bean. You can also use the Property Editor to edit `ejbgen` tag settings. When you build an EJB project, the build processes uses these tags to generate the various interfaces and to generate the appropriate deployment descriptor.

This is the code for the EJB generated from a database:

```
package ValidateEJBFolder;

import java.util.Collection;
import javax.ejb.CreateException;

import weblogic.ejb.GenericEntityBean;

/**
 * @ejbgen:entity
 *   ejb-name = "ConfigvBean"
 *   data-source-name = "cgSampleDataSource"
 *   table-name = "CONFIGV"
 *   prim-key-class = "java.lang.String"
 *
 * @ejbgen:jndi-name
 *   local = "ejb.ConfigvBeanHome"
 *
 * @ejbgen:file-generation local-class = "true"
➥local-class-name = "Configv" local-home = "true"
➥local-home-name = "ConfigvHome" remote-class = "false"
➥remote-class-name = "ConfigvRemote" remote-home =
```

```
"false"
➥remote-home-name = "ConfigvRemoteHome" value-class =
➥"false" value-class-name = "ConfigvValue" pk-class = "true"
 */

 public abstract class ConfigvBean
  extends GenericEntityBean
{

  public java.lang.String ejbCreate(String configid)
    throws CreateException
  {
    setConfigid(configid);

    return null;
  }

  public void ejbPostCreate(String configid)
    throws CreateException


  /**
   * @ejbgen:cmp-field column = "CONFIGID"
   *  primkey-field="true"
   * @ejbgen:local-method
   */
  public abstract String getConfigid();
  /**
   * @ejbgen:local-method
   */
  public abstract void setConfigid(String val);

  /**
   * @ejbgen:cmp-field column = "STATUS"
   * @ejbgen:local-method
   */
  public abstract String getStatus();
  /**
   * @ejbgen:local-method
   */
  public abstract void setStatus(String val);

}
```

Building and Deploying Entity Beans

Next, you need to build and deploy the entity bean. When you build an EJB project, the EJB's source code is compiled and checked for errors. The build output of an EJB project is an EJB JAR that contains the various Java and class files for the bean class, its interfaces, and any dependent value or primary key classes, as well as the deployment descriptor for these beans. When the build completes, the beans are (re)deployed on the server. You can also deploy, undeploy, and redeploy EJBs separately from the build activity.

During runtime, information about how EJBs should be managed by the EJB container is read from a deployment descriptor. The deployment descriptor describes the various beans packaged in an EJB JAR file and settings related to transaction management. Deployment descriptor settings can be changed without having to make changes to the actual beans, allowing for the fine tuning of EJBs.

Other Ways of Creating EJBs

If you have created EJBs in another development environment, you can create an EJB easily by importing the JAR file into the EJB project in the WebLogic Workshop environment. To do so, you need the EJB JAR and the source code files, and you need an EJB project in WebLogic Workshop. From the menu Create EJB, choose Import EJB from Jar. Locate the bean you want to import to your project.

You can also create an EJB from scratch. For this, first you need to create an entity bean in the EJB project; then you apply the home and remote interfaces.

Creating a Session Bean

Stateless session beans facilitate synchronous web services. First, you create a session bean with reference to the entity bean. Then you add an `ejb-local-ref` tag and the component methods. After that, you build and deploy the session bean.

This section uses the `validateConfig` web service as an example so that you can understand the steps for creating a session bean. You first create the session bean `ConfigvSessionBean` with reference to the entity bean `ConfigvBean`. The session bean invokes methods of the `ConfigvBean`. For the `ConfigvSessionBean` to invoke the `ConfigvBean's` methods, it must first locate and obtain a reference to the bean's home. You can modify the `ejbCreate` method in `ConfigvSessionBean.ejb` to locate and obtain a reference to the `ConfigvBean`, as shown in this code sample:

```
public void ejbCreate() {
 try {
      javax.naming.Context ic = new InitialContext();
      configvHome = (ConfigvHome)ic.lookup
➥("java:comp/env/ejb/ConfigvLink");
```

```
        }
        catch (NamingException ne) {
            throw new EJBException(ne);
        }
    }
```

Also include the following `import` statements, and define `ConfigvHome` as shown here:

```
import javax.naming.InitialContext;
import javax.naming.NamingException;

public class ConfigvSession
  extends GenericSessionBean
  implements SessionBean
{
  private ConfigvHome configvHome;
  public void ejbCreate()  ...}
```

Adding an ejb-local-ref Tag

In the previous `ejbCreate` method, use `ejb/ConfigvLink` to reference the `Configvbean`. At deployment time, this reference is mapped to the actual location of the `Configvbean`. This mapping is done in the deployment descriptor. In WebLogic Workshop, you don't modify the deployment descriptor directly; you use `ejbgen` tags inserted in the EJB file instead.

To map the reference to `ConfigvBean` in the `ConfigvSessionbean`, you need to insert an `ejbgen:ejb-local-ref` tag in `ConfigvSessionbean.ejb`. This implements the Session Facade design pattern, in which a stateless session bean is used as a facade to one or more entity beans. Remote clients interact only with the session bean, never directly with the entity beans. In Chapter 12, "Enhancing the Performance of Web Services," you will see how the Session Facade pattern improves performance: Only the calls between the client and the session bean go across the network, whereas calls from the session bean to the entity beans are local to the EJB container.

Add the properties in the Property Editor as shown here:

```
* @ejbgen:ejb-local-ref
 *   type="Entity"
 *   name="ejb/ConfigvLink"
 *   local="ValidateEJBFolder.ConfigvBean.Configv"
 *   link="ConfigvBean "
 *   home="ValidateEJBFolder.ConfigvBean.ConfigvHome"
```

Adding Component Methods

Now you add the business methods to the session bean that will be called by the client application. First, define the session bean's local interfaces by checking LocalEJB instead of RemoteEJB. Also add `ejb.ConfigvSession` as the JNDI name. Add a Component Method and make it local, this is indicated by a diamond as shown in Figure 9.4. Click the component method to go to source view, and modify the method:

```
/**
     * @ejbgen:local-method
     */
    public String getStatus(String configid)
    {
        try
        {
            Configv configStatus = configvHome.findByPrimaryKey(configid);
            String status = configStatus.getStatus();
            return status;
        }
        catch(FinderException fe)
        {
            return null;
        }
    }
```

Building and Deploying the Session Bean

Build the EJBs. When the build completes, the EJBs are deployed. The status bar at the bottom of WebLogic Workshop turns yellow with the message "Updating Server;" it turns green when the session beans are deployed.

To test whether the EJB has been properly deployed, you can use the Administration console. After you log on to the Administration console, you can select the EJB modules under deployment, as shown in Figure 9.5. Select the EJBs that you want to test, and run the test. If the test succeeds, you get the message "The `EJB_name` has been tested successfully" (with a JNDI name of `JNDI_name`). If the test fails, the message says, "The `EJB_name` has not been tested successfully. There was a problem determining the JNDI Name of the given bean." The EJB modules that are packaged in an enterprise application (`.ear`) are listed under Applications in the Administration Console.

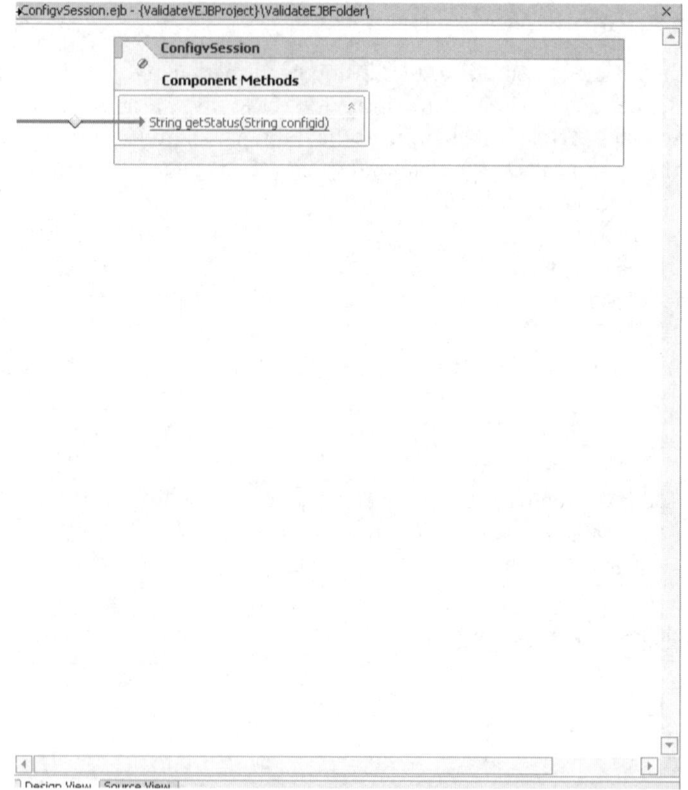

Figure 9.4 Local component method

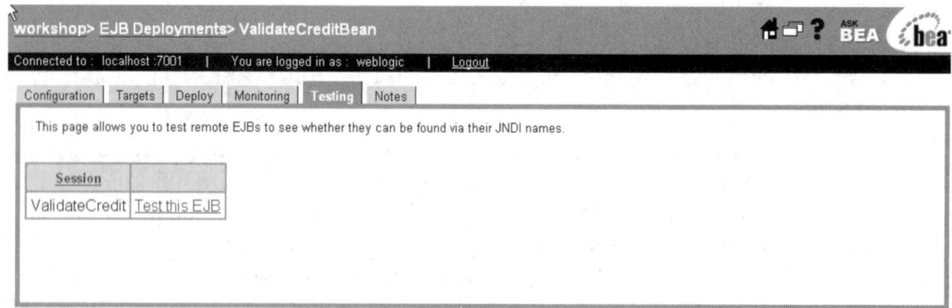

Figure 9.5 Administration Console

Strengthening EJB Deployment Using WebLogic Server

Beyond the basic EJB support, BEA WebLogic Server contains many high-end features that make EJB deployments robust:

- **Instance pooling**—WebLogic Server has a pool of session bean instances. It can allocate a new instance for each request. When a client is finished with an instance, the server puts it back into the pool for future reuse. This approach saves time because a new instance does not have to be created for each request, and it limits the load on the server by allowing the administrator to control the maximum number of session beans in the pool.
- **Clustering**—WebLogic Servers can be clustered to increase scalability and reliability. Beans can be distributed across the cluster using the naming and directory facility.
- **High availability with transparent failover**—WebLogic Server can replicate the state of EJBs across a cluster of separate WebLogic servers. This redundancy enables transparent failover to another WebLogic Server in the cluster when there is a failure.
- **Load balancing**—WebLogic Server allows for load balancing across the cluster of servers. The server can route requests from remote clients to EJB components using built-in or custom algorithms. This results in scalability beyond a single machine and can work with WebLogic Server's web server, as well as other vendors' web servers by using plug-ins.
- **EJB caching**—WebLogic Server stores a configurable number of EJBs in memory, to minimize database access. In case another instance of the server in the cluster updates the same bean, all the cached instances of the bean cached in the cluster are invalidated and reloaded with the next access. This feature increases performance and reduces the load on the database.

Connecting to EIS Using the Application Integration Framework

Web services expose functions and information from a variety of back-end Enterprise Information Systems (EIS), such as a Customer Relationship Management (CRM), ERP (Enterprise Resource Planning), Enterprise Resource Planning (ERP), or Human Resources (HR) application. One single web service might need functionality from a database, an ERP system such as SAP, and/or a legacy system. Examples of EISs include SAP, PeopleSoft, and Siebel. Merging and consolidating data from multiple sources is difficult. Very different and tedious code is required to access various EISs. The integration framework is based on the J2EE Connector Architecture specification 1.0. WebLogic Integration (WLI) provides adapters, application views, and application view Control for integrating with an EIS.

Understanding Elements of JCA

The J2EE Connector Architecture (JCA) defines a set of functionality that application server vendors can use to connect to EIS. The JCA has two basic components: the Common Client Interface (CCI) and a resource adapter that has a set of system-specific services: connection management, transaction management, and security management. See Figure 9.6.

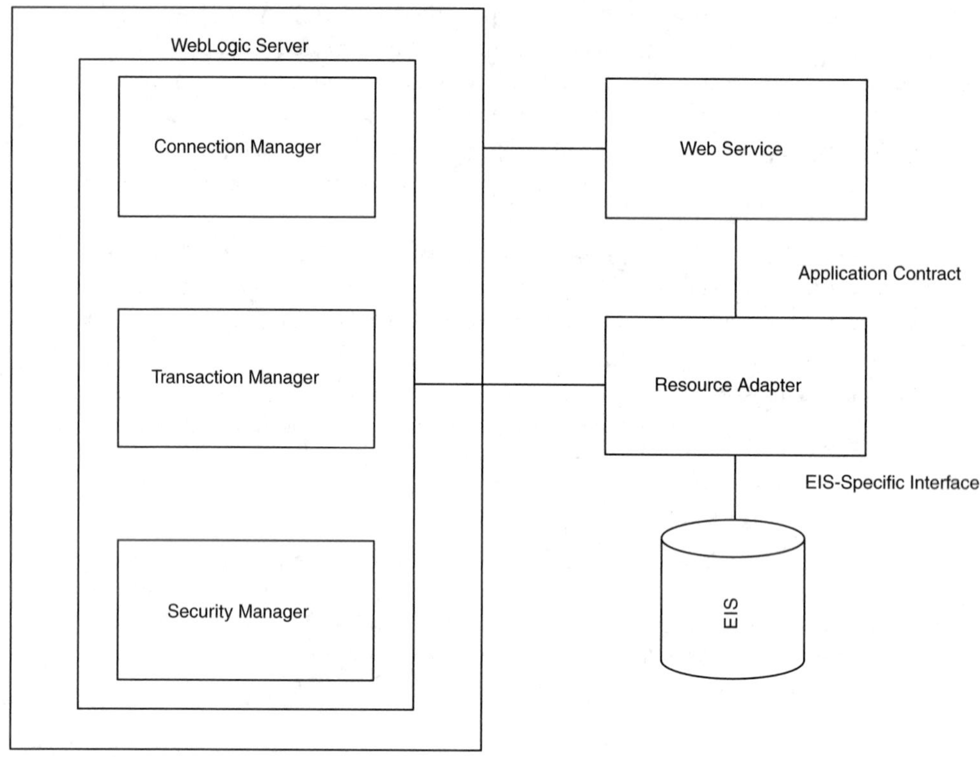

Figure 9.6 J2EE Connector Architecture

Common Client Interface

The CCI is a programming interface that client programs can use to connect to EIS. Using the APIs, you can enable a client application to interact with an EIS. The CCI APIs are composed of APIs for establishing connections to EIS, executing EIS commands, encapsulating the query results from EIS, and querying EIS metadata.

Resource Adapter

A resource adapter is a system-level software driver used by an application server to connect to the EIS. It is also referred to as a J2CA adapter. J2CA defines a set of service contracts that will be available to the adapter at application runtime. The three main services are connection management, transaction management, and security:

- **Connection management**—Enables the application server to create and manage connections to EIS. One important capability provided is support for connection pooling because connections to EIS are expensive. Connection-pooling connections with data and services are established, configured, cached, and reused automatically by the application server. This contract enables an application server to offer its own services for transaction and security management.
- **Transaction management**—Supports transactional access to underlying resource managers. This service enables the transaction manager provided within the application server to manage transactions across multiple back-end systems.
- **Security**—Enables the developer to define security between the EJB server and the back-end system. The specific security mechanism that is used depends on the security mechanism provided by the back-end system. For example, if a system requires Kerberos, the connection developer will include it. Under the contract, the connector provider must also support user authentication, user authorization, and any specific security contracts required by the back-end system.

Components of WLI

The Application Integration Framework in WLI consists of two parts: the Integration Framework and the Adapter Development Kit (ADK).

Integration Framework

The application framework provides additional functionality that the current J2CA specification lacks, such as support for bidirectional, asynchronous adapters and support for XML. WLI facilitates asynchronous, bidirectional interactions between WebLogic Server and EIS. WLI uses XCCI (XML CCI) for metadata in XML. It consists of adapters, application views, and application view Controls. See Figure 9.7.

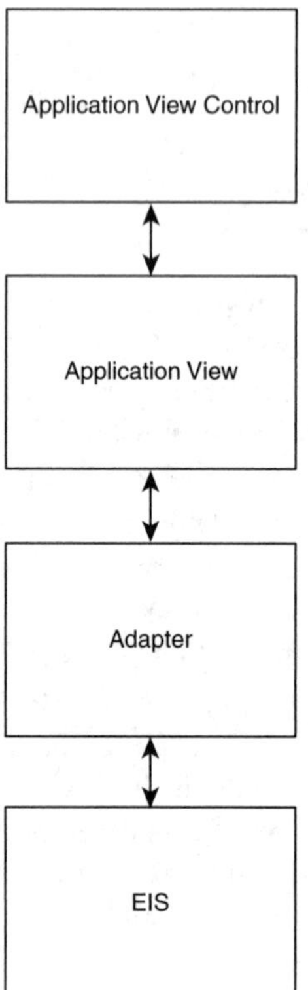

Figure 9.7 Adapters, application views, and application view Controls

Steps to Building an Integration Solution

Two examples help explain how the integration framework in WLI works. Here are the steps to building an integration solution:

1. First, define the overall integration solution In the first example, you will see how you can use a database adapter to find the configurations whose `status` is `yes`. This information is obtained from the `validateConfig` web service described in Chapter 6, "Designing Web Services." The EIS being used is a database; the adapter is a database adapter already bundled with BEA platform. The second example uses the Place order web service example in Chapter 7, "Developing and Deploying Web Services," where we talked about an asynchronous web service. When an order was placed through the Place order web service, the order was entered into the order-fulfillment system, such as SAP. WLI can provide the integration to SAP system through the SAP adapter.

2. Define an application view for each of these examples. This step includes defining the required services and events and testing the application view.
3. Publish the application view to the WebLogic Workshop application.
4. Define an application view Control that provides access to application view services.

The next few sections show you how to build these integration solutions and also describe in detail adapters, application views, and application view Controls.

Adapter Development

A *resource adapter* (or simply *adapter*) is a software component that acts as a connector between an EIS and BEA WebLogic Server. It corresponds to the resource adapter discussed in the J2CA specification. Adapters for popular EISs are available from applications vendors, from BEA Systems, and from third-party vendors. Each adapter provides bidirectional request/response integration with a specific application or technology.

Adapters handle two general types of operations: services and events. Services are request/response communications with the EIS. Client applications submit service requests to the EIS via the adapter, and the adapter returns the response. For example, a business process might invoke a SAP Business Application Programming Interface (BAPI) or execute a `SELECT` statement on a database. Responses are either synchronous or asynchronous.

Events are asynchronous, one-way messages received from an EIS. For example, the adapter can receive an Intermediate Document (IDoc) from a SAP system or a message from an MQSeries system. In effect, a service is a *request for some work to be done,* and an event is a *notification that some work has been done.*

The `ResourceAdapter` interface is new in WebLogic Platform 8.1. It unifies both event and service handling. In earlier WebLogic Integration releases, the event adapter and service adapter were treated as separate adapter components. Each was deployed and configured separately.

Configuration of event and service connections is now done under the umbrella of the `ResourceAdapter` interface. You will see the term *Resource Adapter* used in the Application Integration Design Console to represent a container of event and service connections.

Application Views

An application view provides a subset of services that is exposed by the adapter. Whereas adapters are closely associated with the specific functions available in the EIS, an application view is associated with business processes that must be accomplished by clients. The application view converts the steps in the business process into operations on the adapter. It communicates with EIS, including connection settings, login credentials, and so on. Events and services data is communicated via XCCI. Event and service metadata is provided via XML Schemas. These schemas describe events and services published by the view.

Interaction Between the Adapter and Application View

Each EIS uses its own interface to handle service requests and event notifications. Some interfaces are API based, while others use database or system calls. For example, SAP provides a BAPI interface that defines the parameters and syntax for BAPI requests and responses. For each EIS, the EIS interface defines the metadata that applications can use to integrate with the EIS. The EIS publishes data and expects requests in the format dictated by its interface rules. The adapter handles the data translation between XML documents in the application view and the EIS format, using schemas that map the data between XML and the EIS format.

For service requests, the request arrives at the adapter in the form of an XML document. The adapter uses the request schema associated with the service to translate the request to the format that the EIS expects. Similarly, when the adapter receives the response from the EIS, it uses the response schema associated with the service to translate the response to an XML document that the requesting application handles (see Figure 9.8).

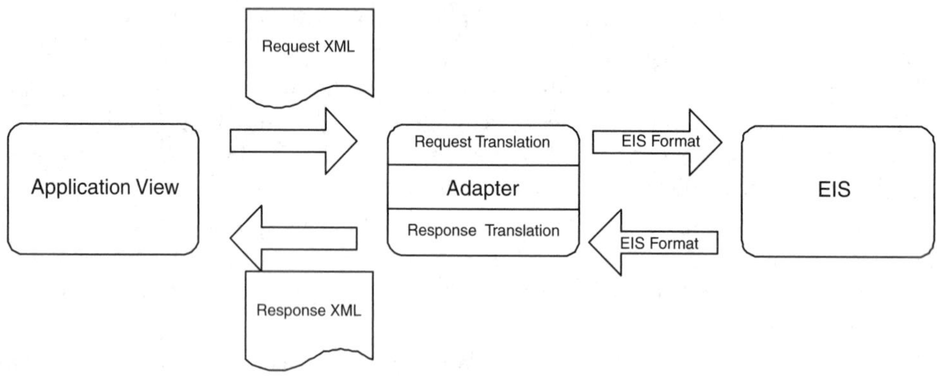

Figure 9.8 Service request/response

For event notifications, the message arrives at the adapter in the format that the EIS uses to publish the event. The adapter uses the event schema associated with the event to translate the response to an XML document that the subscribed application handles. See Figure 9.9.

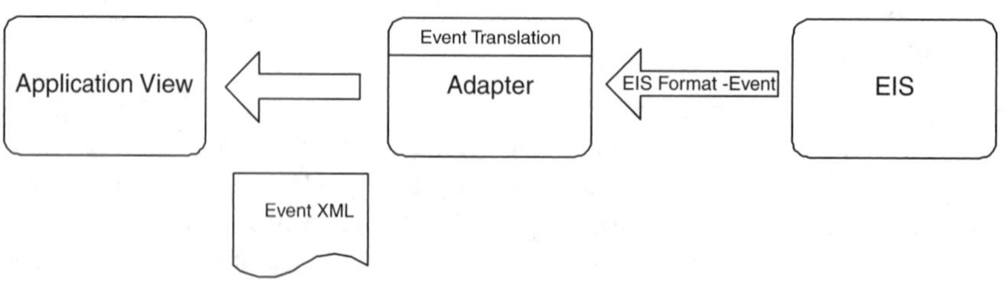

Figure 9.9 Event

Application Integration Design Console

You can create an application view using the Application Integration Design Console. To create an application view for the first example with a database adapter, you can follow these steps:

1. Log on to the WebLogic Integration Application View Console through the WebLogic Integeration menu in WebLogic Workshop.
2. Define the application context by selecting an existing application or specifying a new application name and root directory. This determines where the application view information is stored. This application uses the events and services that you define in your application view. The application view works within the context of this application.

Add folders as required to help you organize application views. Define a new application view for your adapter: `ConfigInfo`, the Description, and the Adapter. From the different choices for adapters, pick the database adapter. See Figure 9.10.

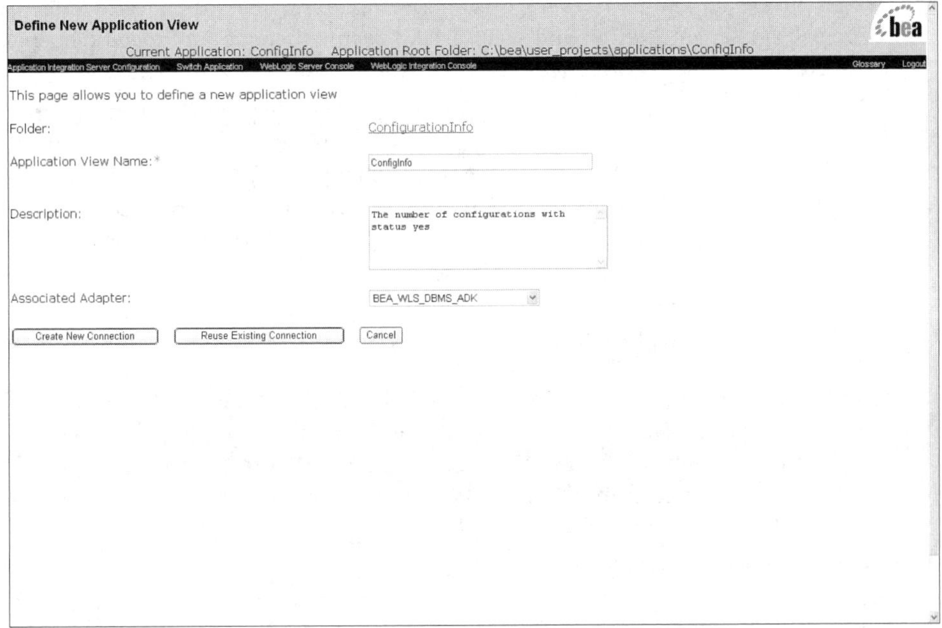

Figure 9.10 New application view

3. Add a new connection service or select an existing one. Here, you must choose the type of connection factory to associate with the application view. You can create a connection factory within a new adapter instance or select a connection factory within an existing instance of the adapter.

4. An adapter instance acts as a communications gateway between WebLogic Server and your EIS. An application view uses an adapter instance as a gateway for design-time browsing, event delivery, and service invocation. To enable design-time browsing and service invocation, you must also designate which connection factory the application view should use to get the connections used to communicate with the EIS. If you choose to create a new connection, WebLogic Integration creates the adapter instance for you. You define the connection properties, pool parameters, log level, and sign-on behavior of a new connection factory.
5. When you create a new connection, the browsing connection is also assigned as the service connection. Define the connection parameters for the browsing connection. See Figures 9.11 and 9.12. When you choose to reuse an existing connection, you select the adapter instance and factory by name, and you do not need to specify connection parameters directly. Using an existing connection factory can simplify server administration, especially when multiple adapters interact with a single EIS.
6. Add the events and services for this application view. The Add Service and Add Event pages enable you to add services and events that support specific business processes. An application view can have multiple services and events.
7. You can add the `ConfigInfo` service to the Add Service page. The `ConfigInfo` service queries the database table to obtain the information from the validate table. You add a SQL statement as shown in Figure 9.11. In many cases, this required information consists of a SQL statement for retrieving information from or updating information in a database. You can also add an event, as shown in Figure 9.12.

```
select * from WEBLOGIC.VALIDATE_TABLE
```

8. Perform final configuration tasks. When you have finished adding services and events and have saved your application view, you must complete the final configuration of connections and then test services and events. These configuration tasks are performed from the application view Administration page. If you want to edit the services or events, or create or edit browsing connections, you can use this step.
9. Test all services and events to make sure that they can properly interact with the target system. The purpose of testing an application view service is to evaluate whether that service interacts properly with the target EIS. Figure 9.13 shows how to test an application view service. Figure 9.14 shows the results of the test.

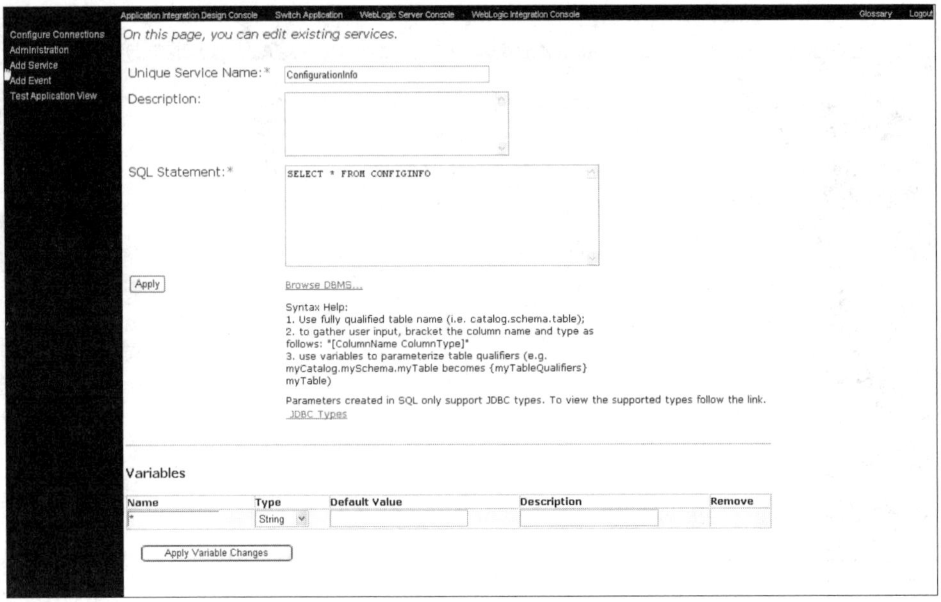

Figure 9.11 Add service

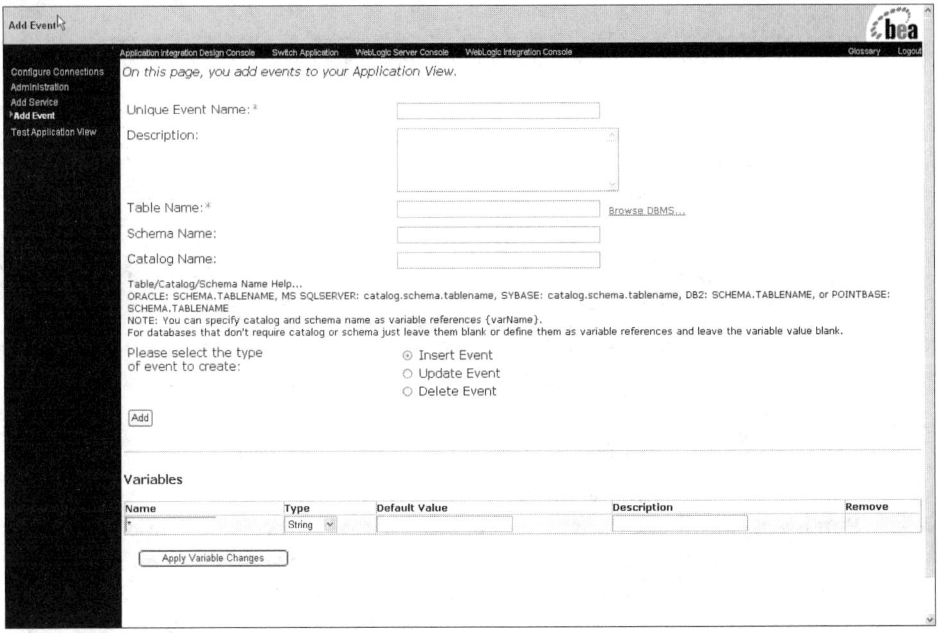

Figure 9.12 Add event

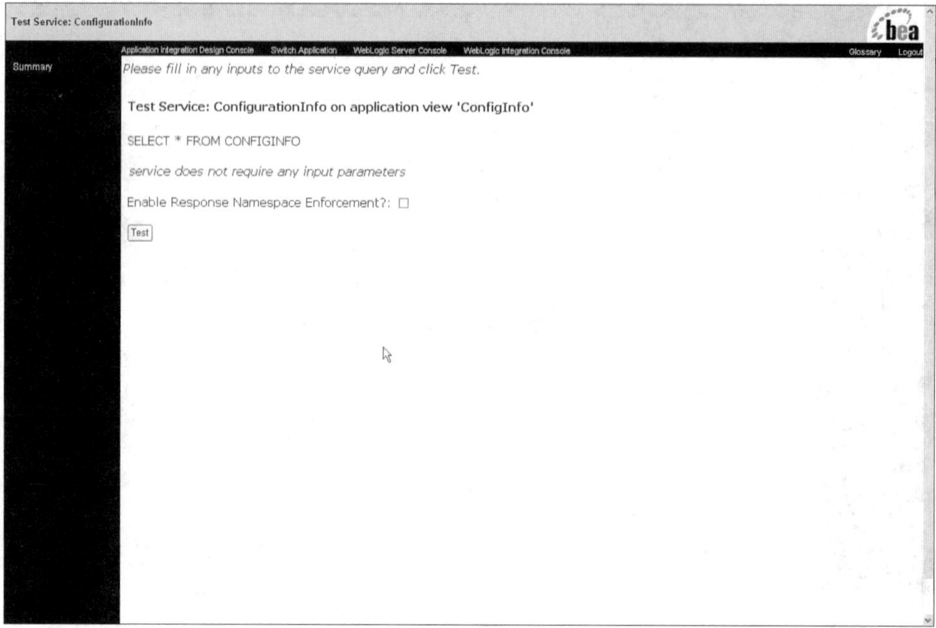

Figure 9.13 Test an application view

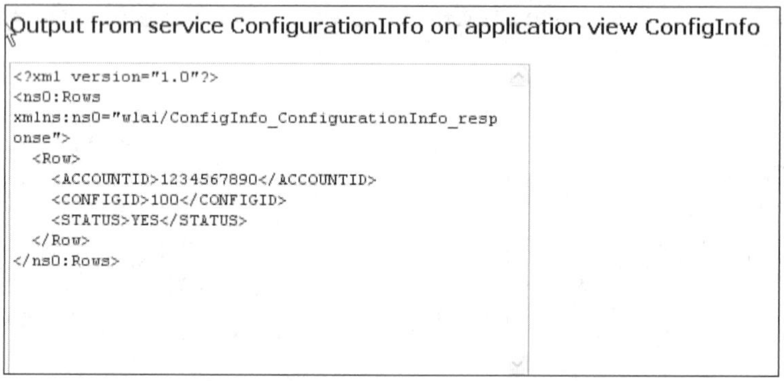

Output from service ConfigurationInfo on application view ConfigInfo

```
<?xml version="1.0"?>
<ns0:Rows
xmlns:ns0="wlai/ConfigInfo_ConfigurationInfo_resp
onse">
  <Row>
    <ACCOUNTID>1234567890</ACCOUNTID>
    <CONFIGID>100</CONFIGID>
    <STATUS>YES</STATUS>
  </Row>
</ns0:Rows>
```

Figure 9.14 Test results

10. Publish the application view to the target WebLogic Workshop application. Publishing the application views enables business process developers within the target application to interact with the newly published application view using an Application View Control. This makes the application view visible within WebLogic Workshop. The Application View Control wizard browses only published application views. Published application views can be monitored and managed using the WebLogic Integration Administration Console.

Application View Control

You use application view Controls in WebLogic Workshop to interact with an EIS through an application view. Application view Controls enable a business process engineer to browse the hierarchy of application views, invoke a service as an action in a business process, and start a new business process when an EIS event occurs. We look at business processes in the next chapter. You learned how web services can use Controls in the last chapter; similarly, a web service can act as an aggregator of other web services, EJBs, Java classes, and Controls that wrap adapters or EJBs.

To create an application view Control for the `ConfigInfo` application, add to your business process the Control shown in Figure 9.15. To test it, you can create the web service. When you run the test, you will see the results shown in Figure 9.16.

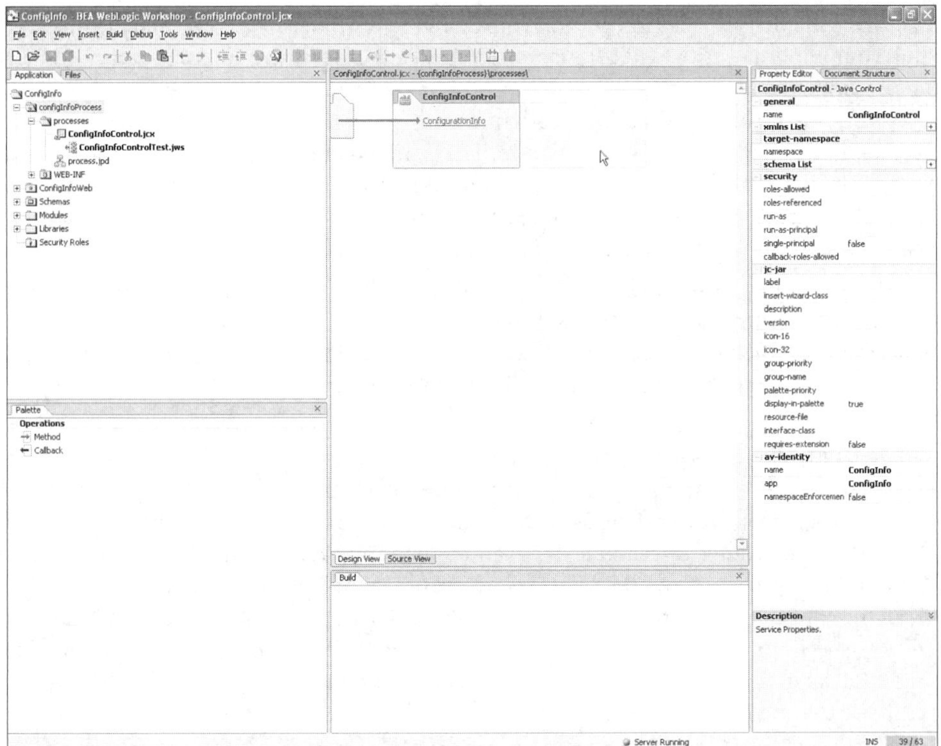

Figure 9.15 Adding an Application View Control

```
Service Response
Submitted at Sunday, May 16, 2004 3:10:57 PM PDT
 <Rows xmlns="wlai/ConfigInfo_ConfigurationInfo_response" xmlns:xsd="http://www.w3.org/2001/XMLSchema" xmlns:xsi="http://www.w3.org/2001/XMLSchema-
   instance">
   <Row xmlns="">
     <ACCOUNTID xmlns="">1234567890</ACCOUNTID>
     <CONFIGID xmlns="">100</CONFIGID>
     <STATUS xmlns="">YES</STATUS>
   </Row>
 </Rows>
```

Figure 9.16 Testing the web service for Application View Control

Application Integration Using the SAP Adapter

You will now see how to create an integration solution for the second example using the SAP adapter.

The SAP adapter provides integration with SAP BAPIs, which are interfaces that you can use to link your applications to SAP components. BAPI calls are synchronous and return information. This information is either error notification or a well-formed XML document containing the result of the BAPI call. The adapter also provides integration to IDocs; these calls are asynchronous and do not return any information. The third integration is to Remote Function Calls (RFCs). RFCs are calls in which the application establishes a connection to the SAP system using a valid user ID and issues a call to a SAP function. RFC calls are synchronous and usually return information.

To design an application integration solution with a SAP adapter, the first step is to download the SAP adapter from the BEA website and download the SAP JCo, which is SAP's Java Connector, from the SAP website. To place an order in SAP from BEA WebLogic, you need to generate schemas for the Create Sales Order BAPI. This BAPI facilitates the creation of the order in SAP.

To generate schemas for SAP business objects that will facilitate the creation of the order, you need to install BEA Application Explorer. To create schemas, first you need to either establish a new connection with SAP or use an existing connection. For a new connection, you need to name the connection (for example, D7b) and give the application server system number, the client number, the username, and the password, as shown in Figure 9.17. When you connect to SAP, all the application components, IDocs, and RFCs are pulled into the Application Explorer. Here, you specifically want to create a schema for the Create Sales Order BAPI. You can do that by right-clicking on the BAPI and creating the request and response schemas (see Figure 9.18). These schemas and `manifest.xml` file are stored in the working directory.

Next, you need to define an RFC remote destination in SAP. You must define a SAP remote destination so that the SAP system can send IDocs to the adapter and respond to RFCs and BAPIs. You must define this SAP remote destination before you add events to your application view.

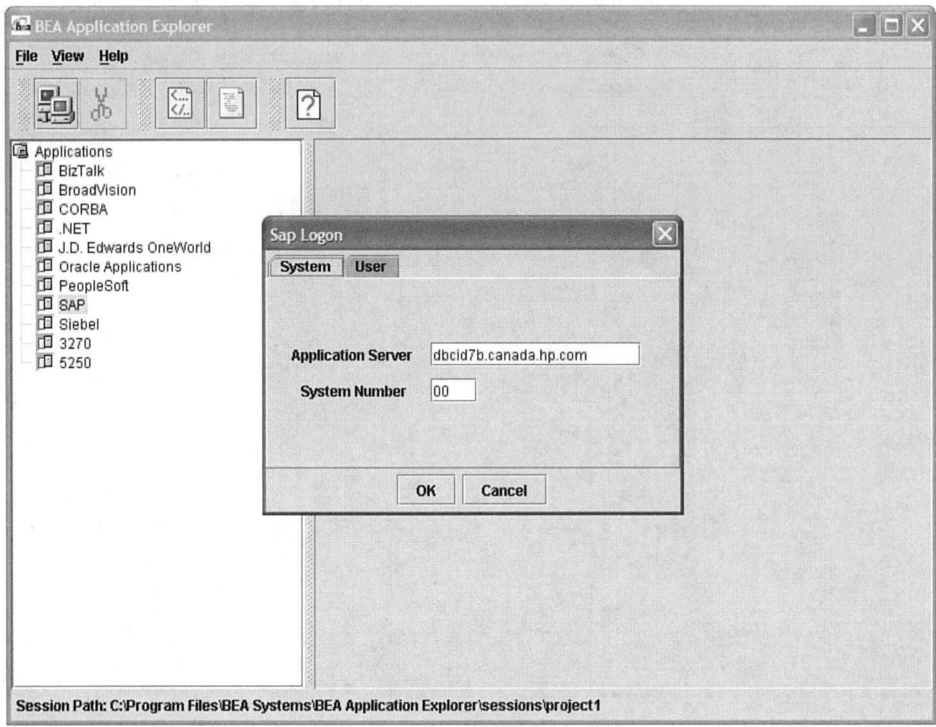

Figure 9.17 Connecting to SAP using BEA Application Explorer

Now create the application view; follow the same procedure as described earlier for the database connection. The adapter that you select is the SAP adapter. Then create a new browsing connection, as shown in Figure 9.19. Next, you need to configure your service with or without load balancing. Figure 9.20 shows an example of SAP without load balancing. To test a service, go to the application view Administration page and click the Test link beside the service to be tested. The Test Services page appears. In the Test Services window, copy the appropriate XML strings from the SAP request. When you click Test, the results appear in the Test Results window.

After you have created an application view to send and receive schemas, you can create a Control from this Application View. This SAP Control can be used in business processes.

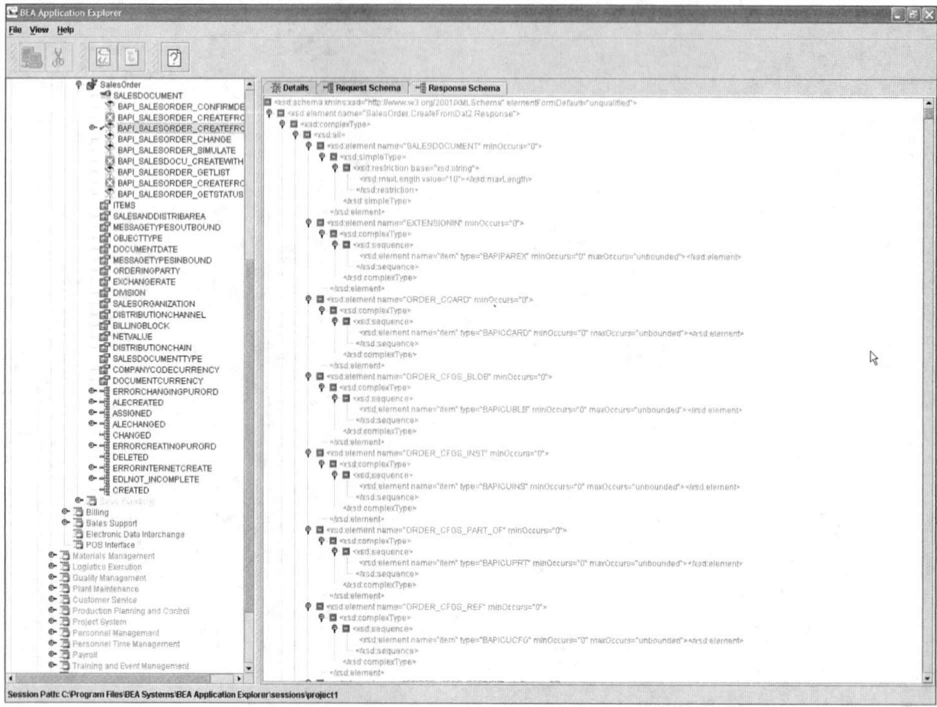

Figure 9.18 XSDs in BEA Application Explorer

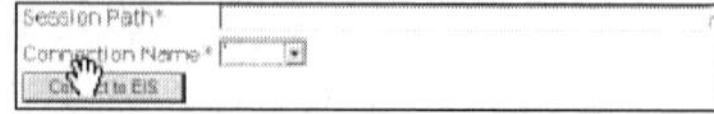

Figure 9.19 New browsing connections

Adapter Development Kit (ADK)

WLI's Application Integration Framework provides an ADK, which provides a collection of frameworks that support the development, testing, packaging, and distribution of resource adapters for WebLogic Integration. You can use ADK to create two type of adapters: service adapters and event adapters.

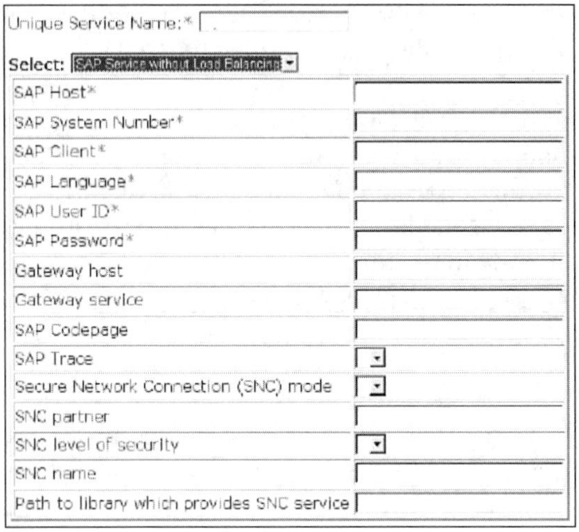

Unique Service Name:*
Select: SAP Service without Load Balancing
SAP Host*
SAP System Number*
SAP Client*
SAP Language*
SAP User ID*
SAP Password*
Gateway host
Gateway service
SAP Codepage
SAP Trace
Secure Network Connection (SNC) mode
SNC partner
SNC level of security
SNC name
Path to library which provides SNC service

Figure 9.20 SAP service

Specifically, the ADK includes frameworks for four purposes:

- A design-time framework provides tools for building web-based user interfaces that can be used to define, test, and deploy application views. Design-time operation is implemented as an extensible web application, using JSPs and JavaBean helper classes. A deployment helper framework is provided to facilitate the deployment of application views.
- A runtime framework is composed of a set of tools that can be used in developing adapters. It has adapter templates with prebuilt generic functionality and supporting service adapters and event adapters
- A logging framework provides ADK adapter classes and templates containing the appropriate logging calls. This framework leverages Log4J as it provides dynamic configuration for multiple targets, customized logging levels, and categories of logs.
- A packaging framework simplifies the creation of a J2EE Adapter archive (RAR), EAR and WAR file creation, and javadoc generation. This framework leverages Ant.

In the Integration Framework section, you used the DBMS sample adapters BEA_WLS_DBMS_ADK to create the `ConfigInfo` application view. DBMS sample adapters are J2EE-compliant adapters and include a JSP-based GUI. They provide examples of how an adapter can be constructed by using the WebLogic Integration ADK. A relational database is used as the adapters' EIS so that you can focus on the details of the adapters and the ADK instead of investing time to learn about a particular proprietary EIS. The DBMS sample adapters can help you understand the possibilities at your disposal as a developer when you use the ADK to build adapters.

To understand how the sample DBMS adapter was developed, you need to understand the two main steps of creating the adapter and designing the GUI. These are the detailed steps:

1. Complete the adapter setup worksheet. Use the worksheet to collect critical information about the adapter you are developing. The questions on the worksheet will help you define components, such as the logical name of the adapter and the basename of the Java package. Your answers to these questions will help you define your adapter before you start coding.
2. Implement the server provider interface package and the CCI.
3. Implement the event package.
4. Deploy the DBMS sample adapter.
5. The design-time GUI is an interface that enables a user to create application views, add services and events, and deploy an adapter that is hosted in a WebLogic Integration environment. This requires identifying the required JSPs from those provided as part of the sample, creating the message bundle, implementing the design-time GUI, and writing the server pages.

The details are elaborated at the BEA website (http://e-docs.bea.com/wli/docs81/devadapt/dbmssamp.html).

Summary

This chapter talked about the layer below the Control framework. It covered EJBs and the creation of entity and session beans. It showed how WebLogic Workshop facilitates the easy creation of entity and session beans. You created first an entity bean from a database table and then a session bean with reference to the entity bean. This session bean was used to create a Control in Chapter 8.

This chapter also covered the application integration framework and how it integrates with the Control Framework. You first learned in detail about the J2EE Connector Architecture. The application integration framework consists of adapters, application views, and application view Controls. Two examples were given of connecting to a database and to SAP through adapters and application views. This chapter described how to create an application view in the Application Design Console, and it ended with an overview of the Adapter Development Kit for developing new adapters.

10

Managing Business Processes

Web services represent different elements of a business process. In this chapter, you will learn how orchestration, choreography, and collaboration techniques are used for composing web services into a business process. You will also see how you can apply Business Process Management (BPM) and B2Bi integration with web services. You will see examples of how WebLogic Integration (WLI) supports both BPM and B2Bi. Different organizations are working toward different specifications in BPM—OASIS on the Business Process Execution Language for Web Service (WS-BPEL or, for short, BPEL); JCP on Process Definition for Java (PD4J) and BPELJ, a combination of WS-BPEL and Java, JSR 208—Java Business Integration (JBI); and the W3C on the WS-Choreography Description Language (WS-CDL). This chapter shows you how to model, run, and monitor a process in WebLogic Workshop and WLI. It also introduces B2Bi integration through ebXML and looks at WLI examples of ebXML messaging specifications. Business Processing Modeling Language (BPML) is a competitive specification in BPM put forth by BPMI.org; the first draft public in 2001. Figure 10.1 shows the evolution of business process standards.

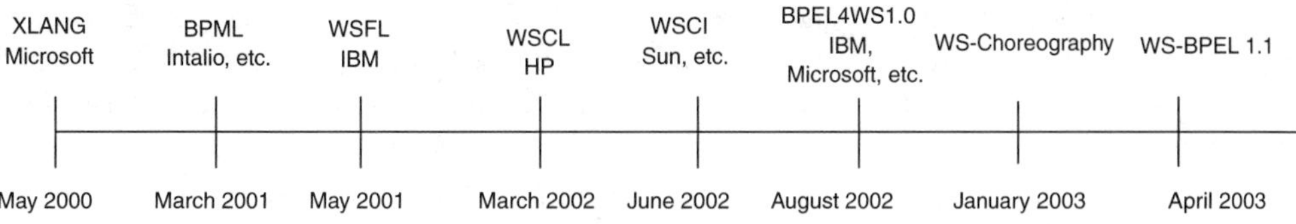

Figure 10.1 Evolution of business process standards

Web Services and Business Process Management

A business process can be defined as the execution of activities according to a defined set of rules to achieve a common goal between participants. IT systems work well as long as the processes they support have been modeled well and do not change. However, business processes change all the time, especially as the Internet easily links internal and external systems to enable businesses to rapidly adapt to a changing business environment.

Business Process Management

BPM systems can help in managing this complex and ever-changing processes. In simple terms, BPM provides the capability to model and measure the effectiveness of existing business processes. This helps a business understand how it currently operates, allows a business to identify where it can make improvements, and enables a business to test to see if the suggested improvements will provide the desired results before implementing them. BPM systems store and manipulate processes like data. They use workflow-type techniques to integrate existing applications, web services, and human processes, or to construct or deconstruct processes or subprocesses.

Orchestration, Choreography, and Collaboration

Web services represent different elements of a business process and, therefore, can be effectively managed within BPM systems. Orchestration, choreography, and collaboration are about composing web services into a business process. They offer different views and methods of the business process (see Figure 10.2).

Orchestration defines the rules for a business process flow. This is given to a business process engine to define and control the data flow. The OASIS Technical Committee for BPEL is chartered to work on WS-BPEL, which is the basis for web services orchestration. It is working toward a specification to formally describe interoperable business processes and business interaction protocols.

Choreography describes the sequence and conditions in which messages are exchanged between independent processes, parties, or organizations to realize some useful purpose. Choreographies need to be defined when two or more organizations or processes must cooperate because no single organization or process controls or manages the complete process. For example, a buyer cannot directly control what a seller does, and vice versa. If choreographies are not defined and agreed upon between the organizations or processes involved, those organizations and processes will not be capable of successfully interoperating to realize their shared objectives. The W3C WS-Choreography working group is chartered to define a language for describing choreography and determining the rules for the composition of web services and the interaction between web services.

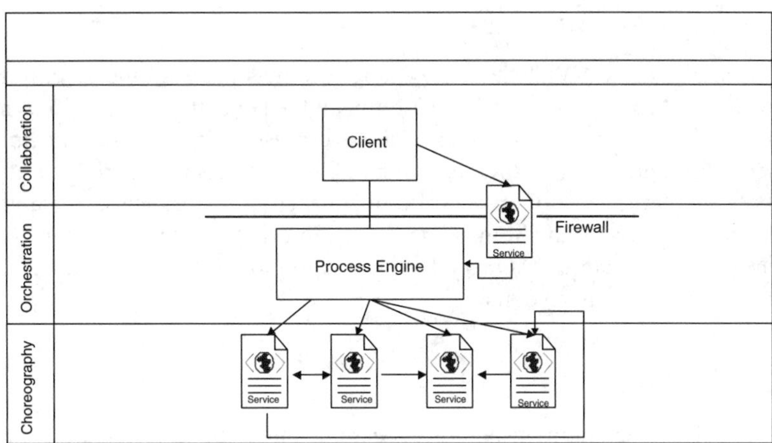

Figure 10.2 Orchestration, choreography, and collaboration

Collaboration defines an agreement between business process participants for achieving a business goal. ebXML's Business Process Specification Schema (BPSS) defines the collaborative process. It defines the message exchanges, such as the sequence of business transactions, message types, and message contents between partners. For example, to complete an order, you could have many business transactions between the partners: order reservation, acknowledgment for order reservation, placement of order, and acknowledgment of the order.

Traditionally, Electronic Data Interchange (EDI) has been used for collaboration between business partners. EDI uses many data formats and communicates through value-added networks VAN, which is very expensive. With the addition of security, reliability, and business semantics, web services now can be used for collaboration as a more cost-effective and more real-time alternative.

Using WLI for Business Process Management

WebLogic Integration (WLI) provides a robust and integrated BPM solution. Process modeling in WebLogic Workshop is based on PD4J, (JSR-207) and builds on Java Language Metadata technology (JSR-175). PD4J provides an easy-to-use syntax for describing a business process at the source code level for the J2EE platform.

Three Stages of a BPM Solution

A BPM solution has three stages: 1) modeling of the process, 2) execution or automation of the process, and 3) monitoring of the process.

Process Modeling

WLI has graphical tools to build, view, and change business process models with design and source views in the WebLogic Workshop environment. It enables the modeling of synchronous and asynchronous web services, as well as business process logic such as branching, nesting, looping, parallelism, grouping, and exception handling. WLI also enables integration of the business process with the Control Framework for connecting with databases, data files, HTTP, messaging, service brokering, and human interaction. You can use XML Beans for XML-to-Java transformation, and you can use XQuery Transformation Mapper for XML-to-XML, Java-to-XML, and non-XML-to-non-XML mapping.

Process Execution

WLI takes care of the execution of the process designed in WebLogic Workshop. Process execution also includes the autogeneration of J2EE code. As you design business processes using the graphical tools in WebLogic Workshop, WebLogic Workshop writes source code to a business process file (a JPD file). A JPD file is a Java file that contains code for a business-process Java class. JPD is the foundation technology for PD4J. When you need to write Java code, it is always available to you in the source view. WLI automatically builds and deploys the business process to a BEA WebLogic Server. You can upload test data in the test browser within WebLogic Workshop to test the execution of your process. You will see some examples of this later in the chapter.

Process Monitoring

Ongoing monitoring of a business process is very important as part of BPM. You can use the WLI console to monitor business processes (see Figure 10.3). WLI provides for the collection of statistical data in real time, SLA status monitoring and report generation of historical process information.

HP OpenView products have a Smart Plug-In (SPI) for monitoring the business processes in WLI. This is illustrated in Figure 10.4. At one end, WLI-SPI interacts with WLI using the JMX interface. At the another end, it interacts with various OpenView (OV) products using OV-specific interfaces.

Building a Business Process in Workshop

You can use WebLogic Workshop to model a real-world business process. As shown in earlier chapters, you can create Java controls and web services using WebLogic Workshop. Then, using the process nodes and control palettes in WebLogic Workshop, you can add web services, client requests, decision nodes, and Java controls to mimic a real-world process. As you add these various components, Workshop generates, in a separate tab, the source code and annotations to reflect the process logic, using the PD4J specification. After modeling this business process, you can test it by executing it within Workshop.

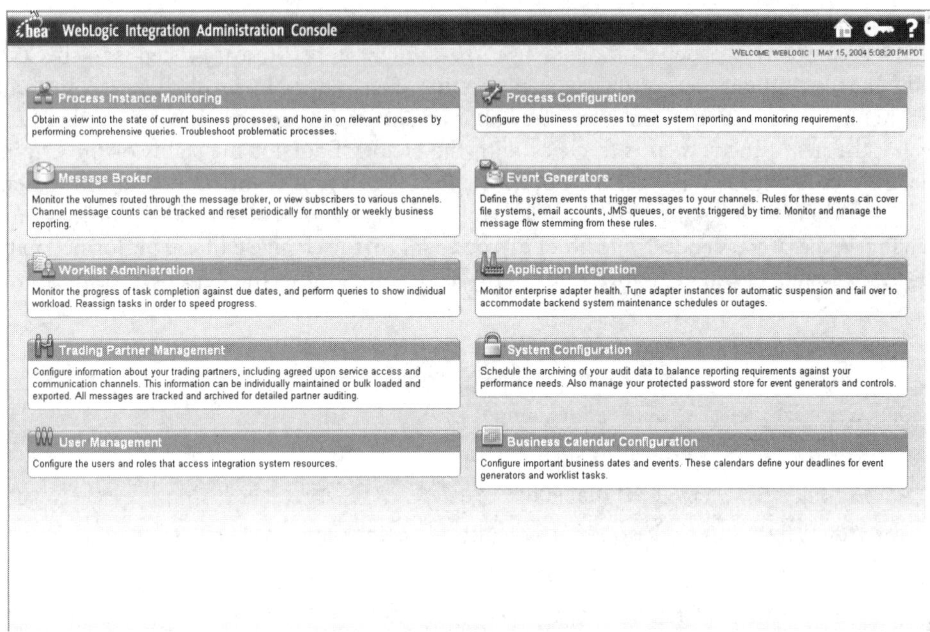

Figure 10.3 WLI console for process monitoring

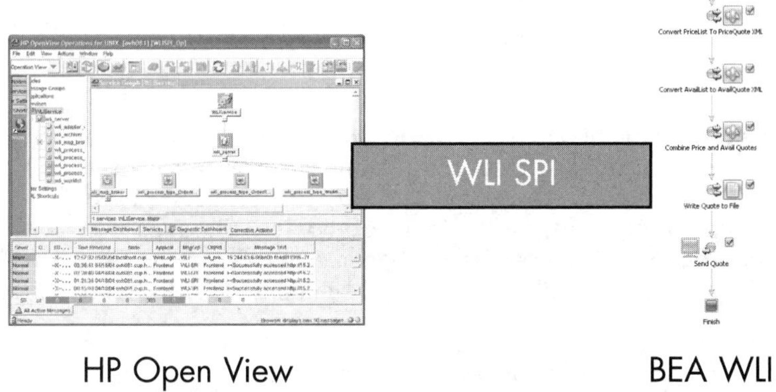

Figure 10.4 WLI SPI and HP OpenView suite of products

Example: Change Order Request Process

Here, we you take a look at a change order request within the order management business process for a vendor. A partner places a request to change the product configuration information of a previously placed order. To process the request, the web services application has to go through many process steps and decision points.

The first process step is the request from the web services client using the RosettaNet PIP (see the accompanying sidebar) for a change to an order. The next process step is to check the validity of the configuration of the changed product. This is done by invoking a web service to validate the configuration. If the configuration is invalid, the process ends. If the configuration is valid, the next process step is to check with the factory floor for the status of the original order and to determine if it can incorporate the reconfiguration of the product during assembly. This is done by invoking a database control to check the order status. If the order cannot be changed, the process ends. If the order can be changed, the change either is performed in the ERP-based system or can be written out to a file. Figure 10.5 shows the steps in the *change order request* process:

1. Creating a new application (`orderChangeprocess`).
2. Create a new process (`orderChange.jpd`).
3. Create a client request to start a process.
4. Add a web service (`validateConfig`).
5. Add a decision node to act on results from `validateConfig`.
6. Add a database control (`OrderStatus`).
7. Add another decision node to act on results from `OrderStatus`.
8. Write to SAP or write to a file using file control.
9. Conclude the process.

RosettaNet

The RosettaNet Implementation Framework specification is a guideline for applications that implement RosettaNet Partner Interface Processes (PIPs). These PIPs are standardized electronic business processes used between trading partners. To ensure that RosettaNet messages are structured and processed in a consistent manner, each PIP comes with a message guideline and XML Document Type Definition (DTD).

The RosettaNet Consortium is an independent, nonprofit consortium of major manufacturers of information technology, electronic components, and semiconductors that are working to create and implement industry-wide, open e-business process standards. These processes are designed to standardize the electronic business interfaces used between participating supply chain partners. You can read more about RosettaNet at www.rosettanet.org.

Now, we can examine in detail the steps to create this business process in WebLogic Workshop.

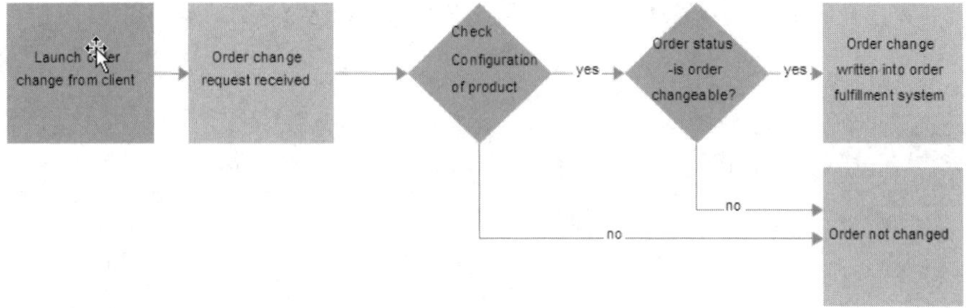

Figure 10.5 Steps in change order request process

Create New Application and New Process

First, you need to create a business process application called `orderChangeprocess` in which you build the business process `OrderChange.jpd` (see Figure 10.6).

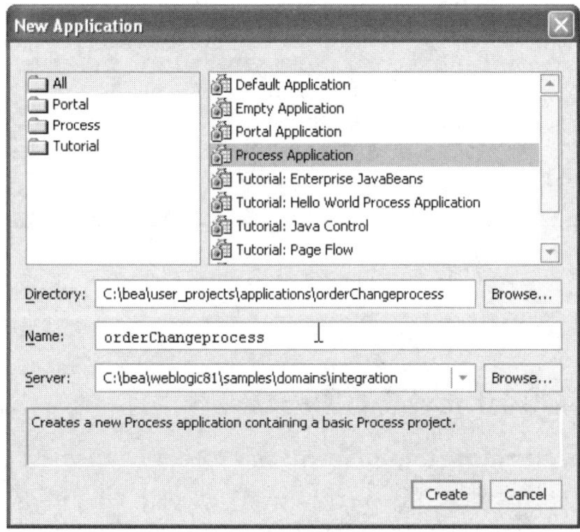

Figure 10.6 Create the new application `orderChangeprocess`

When you create `orderChange.jpd`, you will see in design view only the Start and Finish nodes (see Figure 10.7).

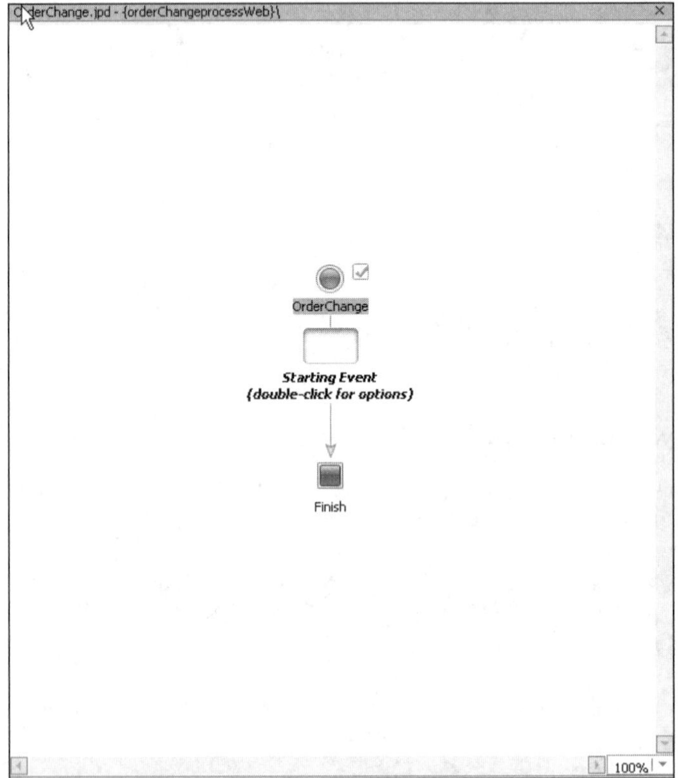

Figure 10.7 Design view of `OrderChange.jpd` file

Create Client Request to Start Process

In WebLogic Workshop, there are four different way to start a business process:

- Start a business process via a client request asynchronously.
- Start a business process synchronously using a client request with return.
- Start via an event (Timer, Email, File, Adapter, and so on) through a message broker.
- Start via an event synchronusly through a message broker.

In this example, the client requests a change order by sending an XML document with the changes. Therefore, you use the method invoked via a client request as the way to start the business process. The XML document has the format of RosettaNet PIP 3A8. You can call the client request `orderChangeRequest`.

Now you need to create the method and parameters that your client uses to trigger the start of your business process. First add `orderchange.xsd` to the schemas folder by importing it in the application. When you add the schema, XML Beans are created, as described in Chapter 8, "Using Controls, Bindings, and Parsers." Next, you need to specify the general settings, which specifies the method exposed by your business process to clients. Clients invoke this method to start and make requests on your business process. Specify a data type for the parameter to your `orderChange` method. Because XML is being used, the type was chosen from the XMLBean structure for `orderchange.xsd`. Map this to the parameter `orderChangeXML`, as shown in Figure 10.8. The General Settings tab is updated to indicate that you successfully specified a method name and parameters: indicates that a task is complete, and indicates that a task is not complete.

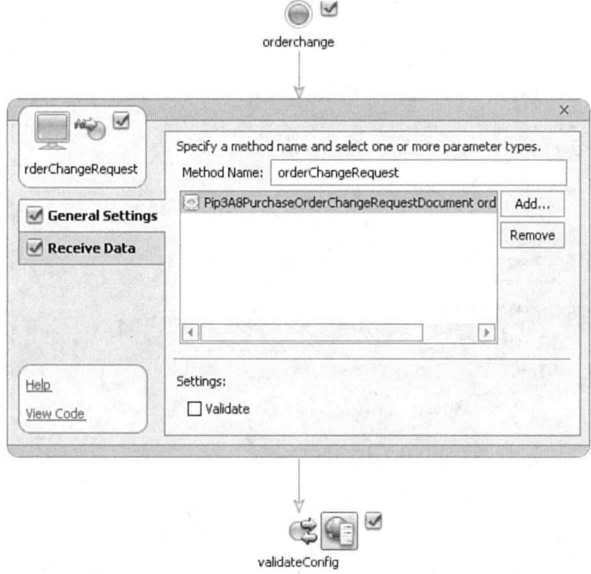

Figure 10.8 General settings

To specify Receive Data, you use Variable Assignment mode because you want to assign the XML message received from the client directly to a variable of the same data type. Create the new variable `orderChangexsd`. See Figure 10.9. The code for this process looks as shown below:

```
@jpd:process process::
 * <process name="orderchange">
*   <clientRequest name="orderChangeRequest" method="orderChangeRequest"/>
* </process>::
```

```
public class orderchange implements com.bea.jpd.ProcessDefinition
{
public noNamespace.Pip3A8PurchaseOrderChangeRequestDocument orderChangexsd;
public void orderChangeRequest(noNamespace.Pip3A8PurchaseOrderChangeRequest
➥Document orderChangexsd)
    {
        //#START: CODE GENERATED - PROTECTED SECTION - you can safely
➥add code above this comment in this method. #//
        // input transform
        // parameter assignment
        this.orderChangexsd = orderChangexsd;
        //#END  : CODE GENERATED - PROTECTED SECTION - you can safely
➥add code below this comment in this method. #//
    }
```

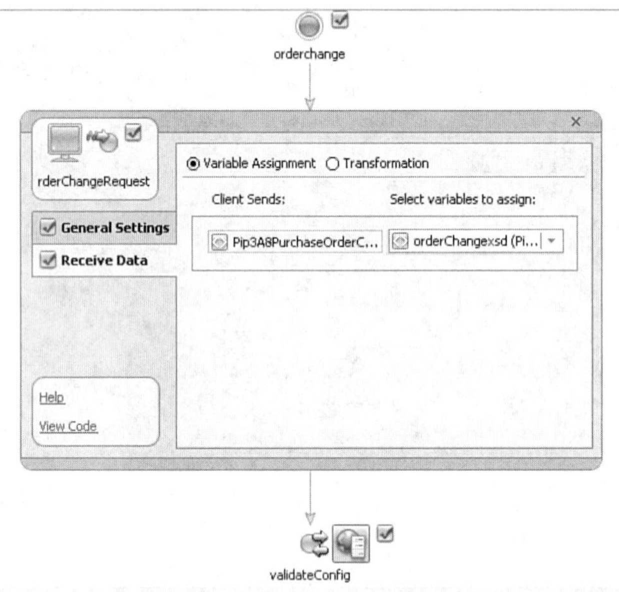

Figure 10.9 Receive Data

Add a Web Service

The next step is to call the `validateConfig` web service, which can be invoked through a web service control. You will use the same `validateConfig` web service used in earlier chapters, as shown in Figure 10.10.

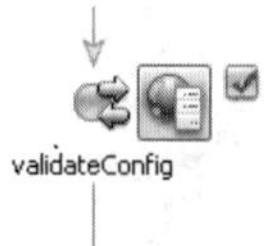

Figure 10.10 Insert web service control

Next, you need to specify the call to the `validateConfig` web service in the business process definition. On the General Settings tab, assign the method `validateConfig` (see Figure 10.11). You need to send data specified by the `validateConfig` method. To do this, you build a data transformation from the data received in `orderchange.xsd` to `validateConfig`, as shown in Figure 10.12. Do the same for the send data, as shown in Figure 10.13.

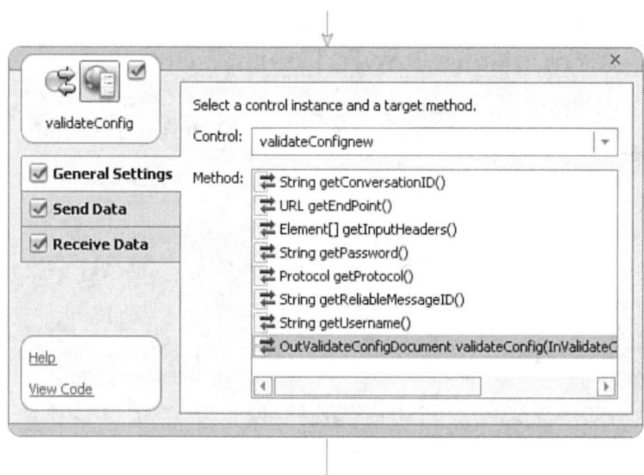

Figure 10.11 General settings for web service control

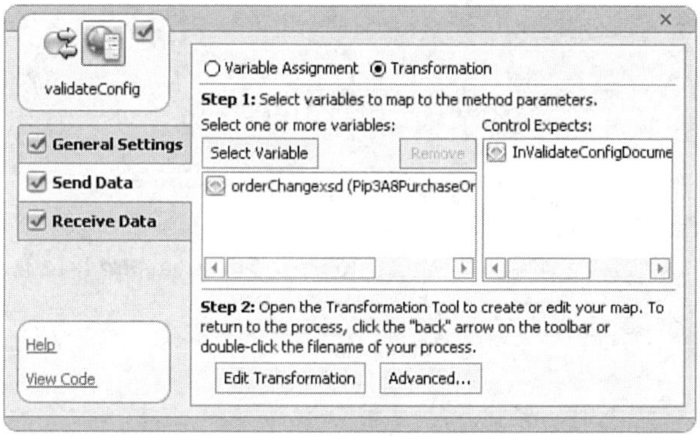

Figure 10.12 Receive data for web service control

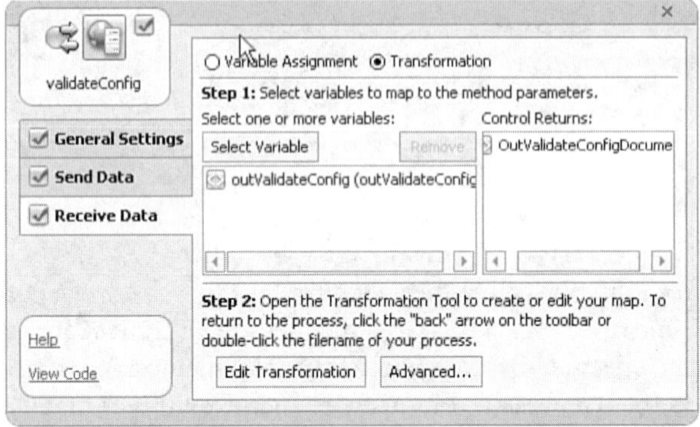

Figure 10.13 Send data for web service control

The code for the data transformation looks like this:

```
{-- processes/orderchangeTransformation.dtf#validateConfignew
➥ValidateConfigSend
--}

declare namespace ns0 = "http://production.psg.hp.com/types"

<ns0:inValidateConfig>
```

Here, the `model` element from `orderchange.xsd` is mapped to the `model` element in the `validateConfig` method:

```
    {
        let $Config := $orderChangexsd/Config
        return
            <ns0:Config>
                {
                    let $Model := $Config/Model
                    return
                        <ns0:Model RetailerProductID = "{
data($Model/@RetailerProductID) }"
                                    Key = "{ data($Model/@Key) }"/>
                }
```

Here, the `cstic` element from `orderchange.xsd` is mapped to the `cstic` element in the `validateConfig` method:

```
                {
                    for $Cstic in $Config/Cstic
                    return
                        <ns0:Cstic RetailerProductID = "{
data($Cstic/@RetailerProductID) }"
                                   Name = "{ data($Cstic/@Name) }"
                                   Value = "{ data($Cstic/@Value) }"/>
                }
            </ns0:Config>
    }
```

Figures 10.14 and 10.15 show how the data transformation looks in design view.

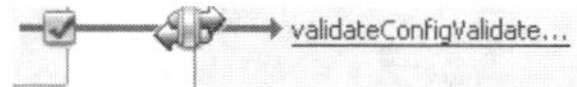

Figure 10.14 Data transformation

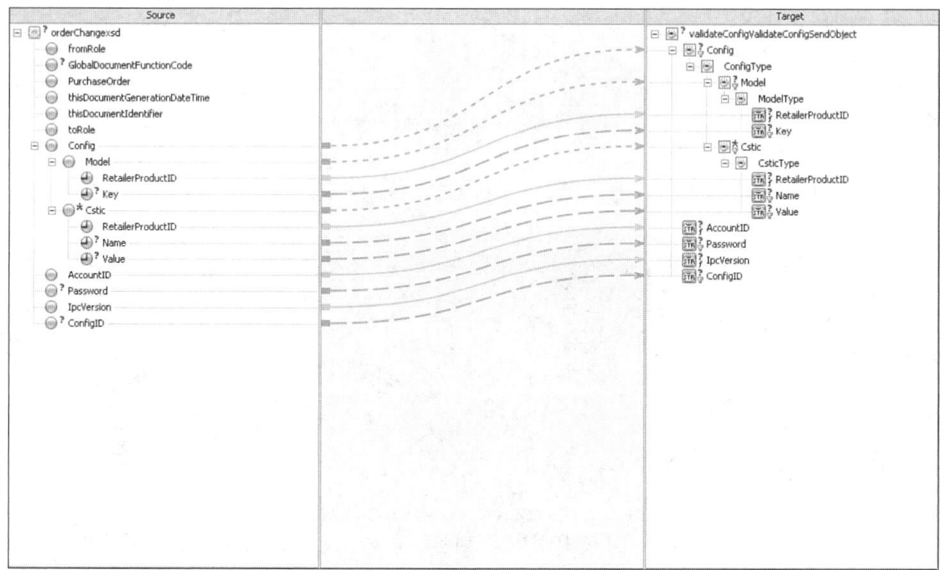

Figure 10.15 Mapping in design view

Add a Decision Node

Next, you need to add a decision node in the business process. If the configuration is valid, proceed; otherwise, end the process. To add this, click Decision in the palette, and drag and drop the decision node onto the business process in design view, as shown in Figure 10.16.

Figure 10.16 Insert decision node

You need to define a condition in this decision node. To do this, double-click the condition node to invoke the decision builder. Figure 10.17 shows that if the `validateConfig` status is `true`, you can go to the next step; if the decision is `false`, the process ends there.

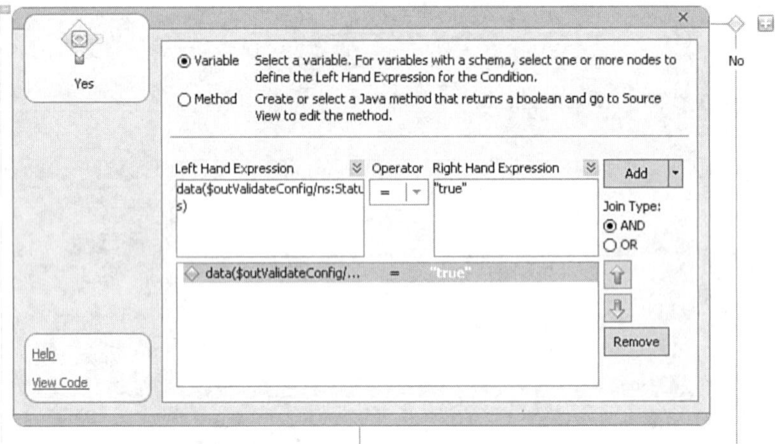

Figure 10.17 Decision node details

Add a Database Control

The next node is inserting an `orderStatus`, so you use a database control. This control sends the `AccountID` to the database table ORDERSTATUS, which sends a response to reflect whether the order is changeable. Again, data transformation is used here to send the `AccountID` to the database control. Figure 10.18 shows the general settings for this process node.

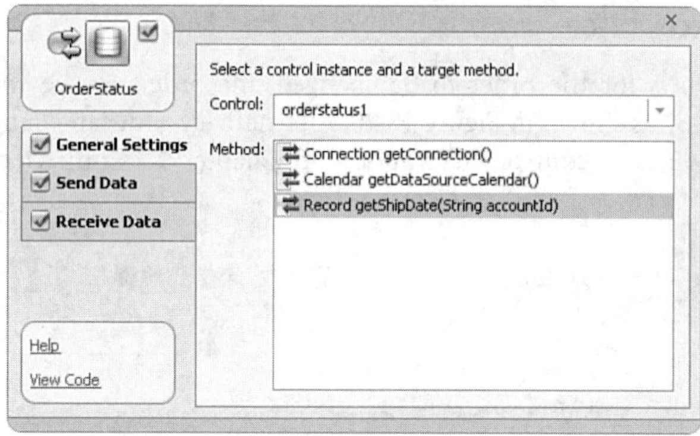

Figure 10.18 Database control

Add Another Decision Node

The next step is to check whether the `orderStatus` result allows for the order to be changed. For this, insert another decision point. To make the decision here, you can use a Java method condition whose return value is boolean, as shown in Figure 10.19. If the order is changeable, you go the next step; otherwise, the process stops.

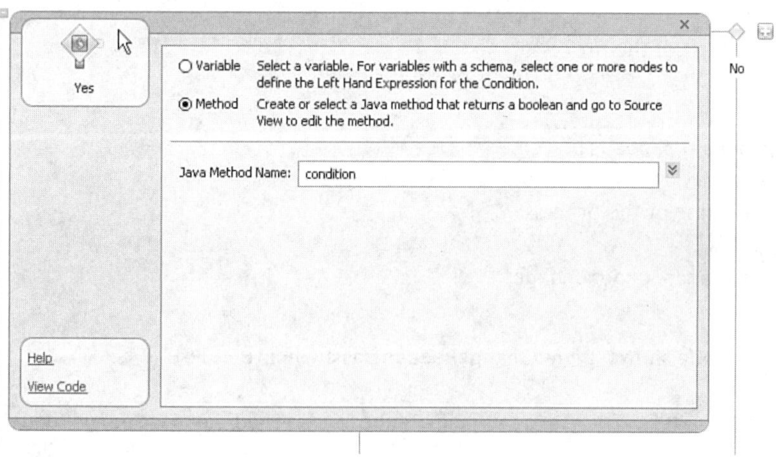

Figure 10.19 Second decision point

Write to SAP or File

If `orderStatus` allows for the order to be changed, the order can be written out to a file through a file control, as shown in Figure 10.20. Alternatively, you can change an order in SAP using the application view control that you saw in Chapter 9, "Connecting to a Distributed Environment."

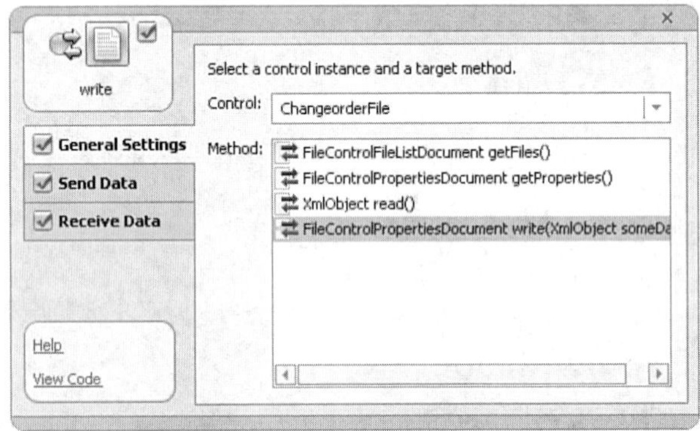

Figure 10.20 File control

This is the JPD for the `orderChange` business process and the code for the different parts of the process.

Here is the start of the process:

```
/**
 * @jpd:process process::
```

This is the name of the process:

```
 * <process name="orderchange">
```

The line of code shows `OrderChangeRequest` as a ClientRequest

```
*    <clientRequest name="orderChangeRequest" method="orderChangeRequest"/>
```

The process calls the `validateConfig` web service:

```
 *    <controlSend name="validateConfig"
➥method="validateConfignewValidateConfig"/>
```

This is the first decision point to check whether the configuration is valid:

```
 *    <decision name="Is configuration Valid?">
 *      <if name="true" condition=
➥"cond_outValidateConfig_1($outValidateConfig)">
```

The process calls the `order status` database control:

```
*        <controlSend name="OrderStatus" method="orderstatusGetJNDIName"/>
```

This is the second decision point to find out whether the order is changeable:

```
 *        <decision name="Is order changeable?">
 *          <if name="Yes" conditionMethod="condition"/>
 *          <default name="No"/>
 *        </decision>
 *      </if>
 *      <default name="No"/>
 *    </decision>
```

The business process writes the file through file control:

```
 *    <controlSend name="write" method="changeorderFileWrite"/>
 * </process>::
```

Execution of Process

When you execute the process, you will see the test SOAP message in the test browser. When you execute it, you will see that it goes through all steps of the process: client request, validate config web service, the first decision point, the order status information from the database, the second decision point, and then the end of the process. See Figures 10.21 and 10.22.

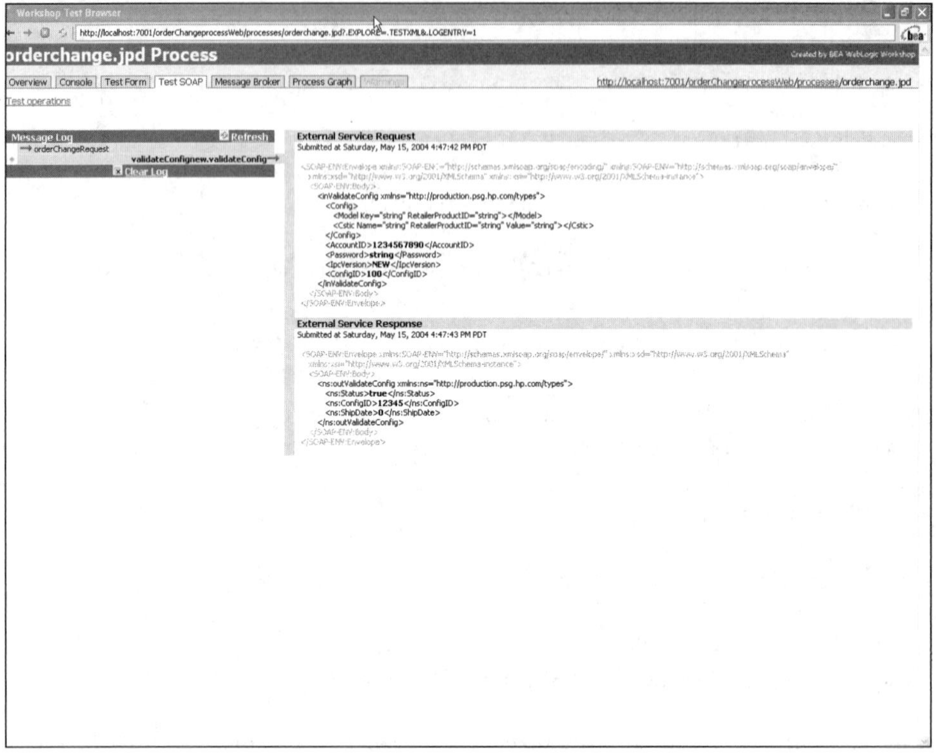

Figure 10.21 Test browser: `validateConfig` web service

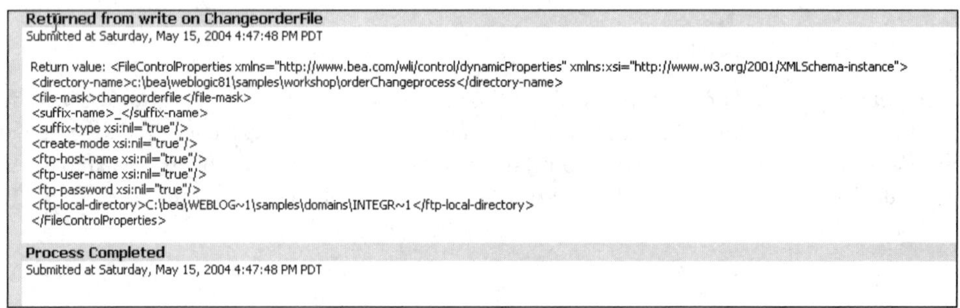

Figure 10.22 Test browser: end of process

Process Monitoring

You can monitor instances of your business process through the WebLogic Integration Administration Console in the WebLogic Workshop menu. Enter http://localhost:7001/wliconsole in a web browser; the default username and password for the sample integration server are weblogic and weblogic. Click Process Instance Monitoring to open a page that enables you to do the following (see Figure 10.23):

- View process instance statistics, including the number of instances in each state (running, suspended, aborted, and completed)
- View the summary or detailed status for selected instances
- Suspend, resume, or terminate selected instances

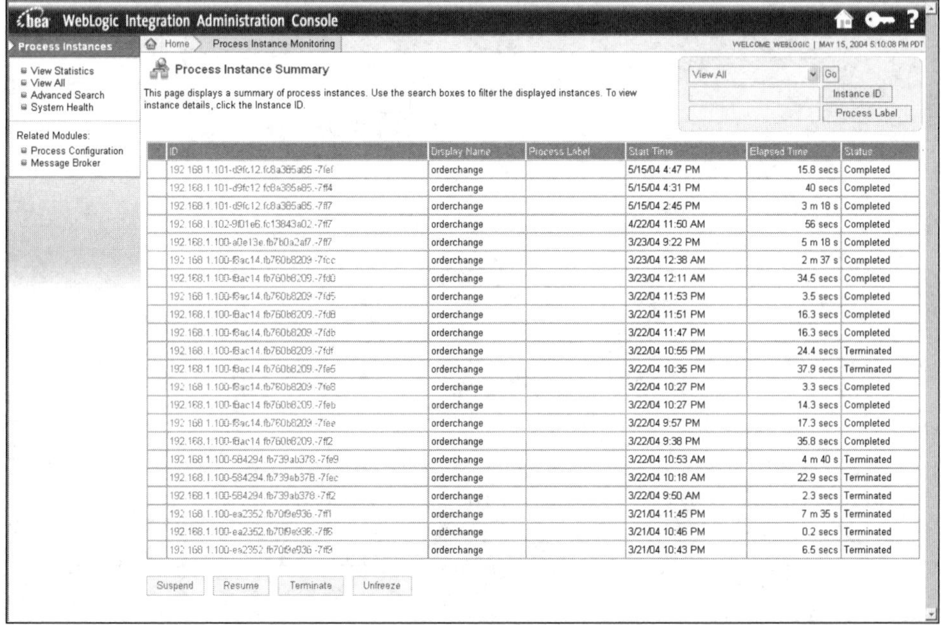

Figure 10.23 Process monitoring

WLI SPI from HP OpenView can be used to do the following:

- List business process types, instances, adapters, event generators, message channels, and the system archiver and their relevant attributes. Also, carry out management operations on these through OV.
- Monitor the performance of business processes and other relevant metrics in real time.

- Monitor critical events, such as failure conditions or violations of performance SLAs on business process execution time, through notifications.
- Generate historical reports on performance metrics.
- Customize the SPI to include application-specific monitoring and management capabilities.

Figures 10.24 and 10.25 show how a business process can be monitored.

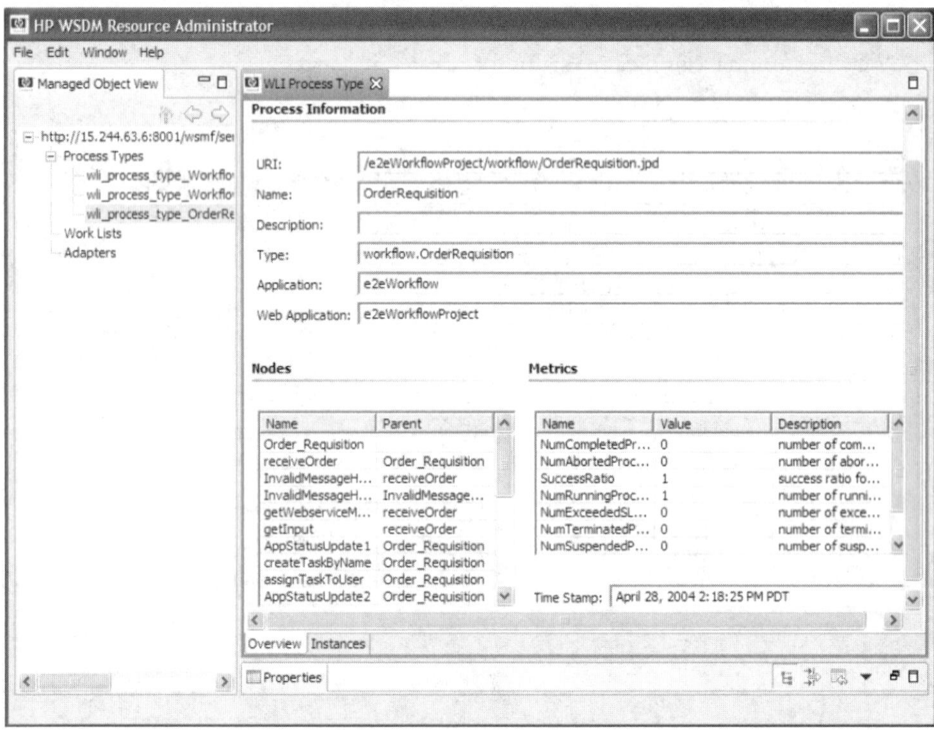

Figure 10.24 Business process monitoring in HP OV

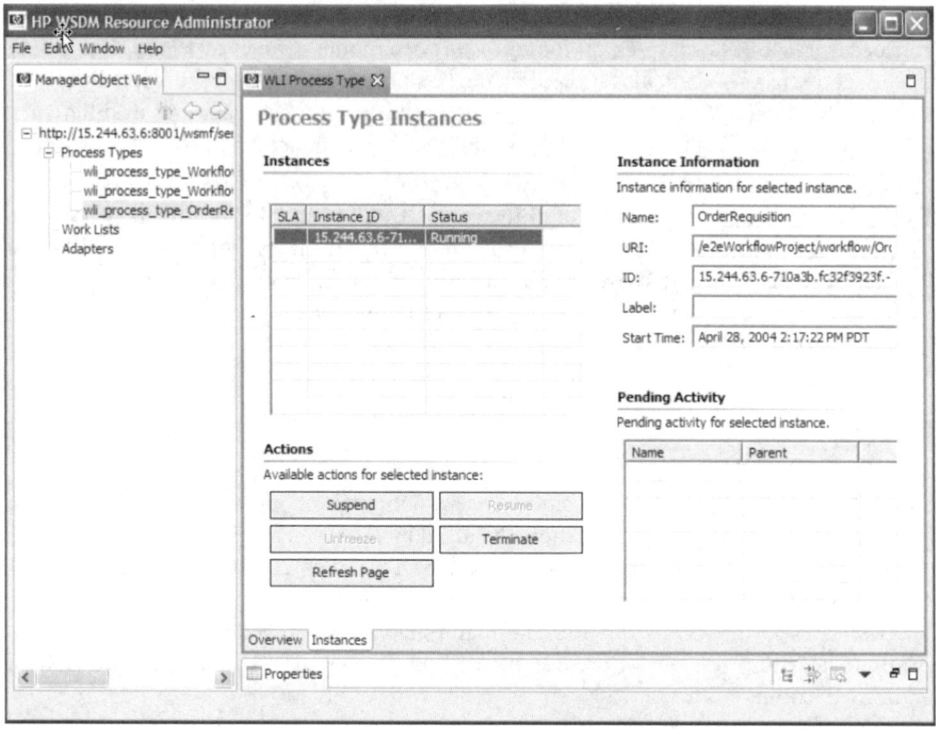

Figure 10.25 Business process instance monitoring in HP OV

Importing-Exporting PD4J ←→ WS-BPEL

In the section, "Building a business process in Workshop," you saw how to create a business process in WLI. WLI creates a JPD file based on the PD4J specification. WLI gives you the facility to export this file to a WS-BPEL through the BPEL exporter. This section discusses WS-BPEL first and then looks how the JPD file can be converted to BPEL.

The Business Process Execution Language for Web Services (WS-BPEL) defines a model and a grammar for describing the behavior of a business process based on interactions between the process and its partners. The interaction with each partner occurs through web service interfaces, and the structure of the relationship at the interface level is encapsulated as a partner link.

The WS-BPEL process defines how multiple service interactions with these partners can be sequenced and coordinated to achieve a business goal, and it also defines the state and the logic necessary for this coordination. In addition, WS-BPEL introduces systematic mechanisms for dealing with business exceptions and processing faults. It introduces a mechanism to define how individual or composite activities within a process are to be compensated when exceptions occur. This grammar can then be interpreted and executed by an orchestration engine. The engine coordinates the various activities in the process and compensates the system when errors occur. WS-BPEL is layered on top of the service model defined by WSDL 1.1. It defines the message-exchange protocols followed by the business process of a specific role in the interaction. It is a reusable definition that can be deployed in different ways and in different scenarios while maintaining a uniform application-level behavior across all of them.

Sometimes, your partners will specify the process using WS-BPEL. At other times, you might want to expose your process definition in WS-BPEL format to coordinate process interaction with your business partners. WLI provides a mechanism for importing WS-BPEL into WLI to create a PD4J format, as well as for exporting PD4J process model to the WS-BPEL format. For effectively using these mechanisms, it helps to understand the WS-BPEL specification, process definition, and grammar.

Specification

XLANG and WSFL were the early specifications for defining web services workflow. These were superseded by the WS-BPEL specification advanced by IBM, Microsoft, and BEA. WS-BPEL is layered on top of several XML specifications: WSDL 1.1, XML Schema 1.0, and XPath1.0. WSDL messages and XML Schema type definitions provide the data model used by WS-BPEL processes. XPath provides support for data manipulation. WS-BPEL provides extensibility to accommodate future versions of these standards, specifically the XPath and related standards used in XML computation.

The definition of a WS-BPEL business process follows the WSDL model of separation between the abstract message contents used by the business process and deployment information—namely, `messages` and `portType` versus `binding` and address information. A WS-BPEL process represents all partners and interactions with these partners in terms of abstract WSDL interfaces, such as `portTypes` and `operations`. No references are made to the actual services used by a process instance. The abstract part of WSDL does not define the constraints imposed on the communication patterns supported by the concrete bindings. Therefore, a WS-BPEL process might define behavior relative to a partner service that is not supported by all possible bindings, and some bindings might not be invalid for a WS-BPEL process definition.

Processes

WS-BPEL can be used to define an executable business process, which models the actual behavior of a participant in a business interaction. The specifics and the sequence of web service interactions conducted at each of the partners involved in an interaction are determined by the logic and state of the process.

WS-BPEL can be also used to specify *business protocols.* A business protocol specifies the sequencing of messages that are exchanged between partners to achieve the goal of the business. Depending on the business context, the business protocol defines the order of the sent and received messages. These messages exchanged between business partners are a result of internal processes, such as access to business logic or EIS.

WS-BPEL refers to business protocols as an abstract process because it is a process that is neither executable nor deterministic. It abstracts from the user the details of the complex internal process.

Because WS-BPEL can be used to define processes in two ways—either as abstract processes or as executable processes—there is continuity in the definition of the basic conceptual model between abstract and executable processes in WS-BPEL. This makes it possible to export and import the public aspects embodied in business protocols as process or role templates while maintaining the intent and structure of the protocols. This is one of the most attractive aspects for using WS-BPEL to increase the level of automation and lower the cost in establishing cross-enterprise automated business processes.

The two usage patterns of business protocol abstract description and executable business process description require a common core of process-description concepts. The WS-BPEL specification is focused on defining the common core and adds only the essential extensions required for each usage pattern.

Grammer of WS-BPEL

In this example of a BPEL process between two partners, a vendor and a customer, the customer initiates an order change request and the vendor sends back a confirmation.

The process includes namespaces to refer to the required WSDL and declares the parties involved. Roles refer to port types and how the partner and the process will interact, given the `serviceLinkType`:

```
<process name="orderChangeprocess " xmlns="...>
<partners>
<partner name="AccountID " serviceLinkType="tns1:orderChangeLinkType"
➥myRole="initiateChange"/>

<partner name="Vendor " serviceLinkType=" tns1:orderChangeLinkType "
➥partnerRole="acceptChange "/>
</partners>
```

Data is written to and from containers. Activities are executed sequentially, and messages are received from partner at the `portType`:

```
<containers>
<container name="changeRequest" messageType="tns2:orderChangemessage"/>
<container name="orderChangeInfo" |messageType="tns3: changeConfirmmessage"/>
</containers>
```

```
<sequence>
<receive name="receive1" partner=" AccountID "portType="tns3:confirmChangePT"
operation="change" container="orderChangerequest" createInstance="yes">
</receive>
```

Invoke the partner web service operation at portType:

```
<invoke name="invokevendor" partner="vendor" portType=" tns3:confirmChangePT "
operation="confirm" inputContainer=" orderChangerequest "
outputContainer="orderChangeInfo">
</invoke>
```

Reply with container data from the portType operation to the partner:

```
<reply name="reply" partner=" AccountID " portType=" tns3:confirmChangePT "
operation=" confirm " container=" orderChangeInfo ">
</reply>
</sequence>
</process>
```

BPEL and WLI

BEA and IBM have closely collaborated to work on a specification entitled BPELJ, which has been submitted to the JSR 207. BPELJ is a combination of BPEL with Java that allows these two programming languages to be used together to build complete business process applications. By enabling BPEL and Java to work together, BPELJ leverages the best from each language. BPELJ is implemented via extensions to the BPEL language, so any BPEL process is also a valid, executable BPELJ process. By standardizing these extensions, BEA and IBM are working to ensure that real-world automated business processes will be truly portable and interoperable across the J2EE platform. BPELJ has been designed specifically with JPD and JSR 207 in mind; consequently, BEA will be capable of providing an automatic and seamless migration experience from JPD to BPELJ.

This is the previous JPD file, now exported to BPEL:

```
<process name="orderchange"
➥xmlns="http://schemas.xmlsoap.org/ws/2003/03/business-
➥process/" xmlns:jpd="http://www.bea.com/wli/jpd"
➥xmlns:plnk="http://schemas.xmlsoap.org/ws/2003/05/partner-link/"
➥xmlns:bpws="http://schemas.xmlsoap.org/ws/2003/03/business-process/"
➥xmlns:wli="http://www.bea.com/workshop/bpel/wli"
➥xmlns:ctrl="http://www.bea.com/workshop/bpel/ctrl"
➥xmlns:xsd="http://www.w3.org/2001/XMLSchema"
➥targetNamespace="http://www.openuri.org/"
➥expressionLanguage="http://www.w3.org/TR/2003/WD-xquery-20031112/" >
```

This shows the partner information:

```
<partnerLinks>
    <partnerLink name="client" partnerLinkType="generated"
➥myRole="provider" partnerRole="client" />
    <partnerLink name="validateConfignew" partnerLink
➥Type="unresolved-type" />
    <partnerLink name="orderstatus1" partnerLinkType="unresolved-type" />
    <partnerLink name="ChangeorderFile" partnerLinkType="unresolved-type" />
</partnerLinks>
```

This is the start of the process:

```
<variables>
    <variable name="orderChangexsd" type="unresolved-type"   />
    <variable name="fileproperties"
➥type="com.bea.wli.control.dynamicProperties.FileControl
➥PropertiesDocument"   />
</variables>
```

The line of code shows `OrderChangeRequest` as a `ClientRequest`:

```
  <sequence>
    <receive jpd:name="orderChangeRequest" partnerLink="client"
➥portType="clientPT" operation="orderChangeRequest" variable="orderChangexsd"
➥createInstance="yes" >
</receive>
```

The JPD code is included as comments:

```
<jpd:javacode code="{
        //#START: CODE GENERATED - PROTECTED SECTION - you can safely add
➥code above this comment in this method. #//
        // input transform
        // parameter assignment
        this.orderChangexsd = orderChangexsd;
        //#END  : CODE GENERATED - PROTECTED SECTION - you can safely add
➥code below this comment in this method. #//
    }
">
      </jpd:javacode>
```

The process calls the `validateConfig` web service:

```
  <invoke jpd:name="validateConfig" partner
➥Link="validateConfignew" portType="unresolved-type"
➥operation="validateConfig" >
    </invoke>
```

This is the first decision point to see if the configuration is valid:

```
    <switch jpd:name="Is configuration Valid?">
      <case jpd:name="Yes" condition
➥="data($outValidateConfig/ns:Status) = &quot;true&quot;">
```

The process calls the `order status` database control:

```
        <sequence>
          <invoke jpd:name="OrderStatus" partner Link="orderstatus1"
➥portType="unresolved-type" operation="getShipDate" >
```

This is the second decision point to find out whether the order is changeable:

```
          </invoke>
          <switch jpd:name="Is order changeable?">
            <case jpd:name="Yes" condition="jpd:method"
➥jpd:method="condition">
    </switch>
```

The process writes the file through file control:

```
    <invoke jpd:name="write" partnerLink="ChangeorderFile"
➥portType="unresolved-type" operation="write" inputVariable=
➥"orderChangexsd" outputVariable="fileproperties" >
    </invoke>
  </sequence>
</process>
```

Implementing ebXML in WLI

Electronic Business XML (ebXML) refers to a technical framework and a set of specifications that will enable XML to be utilized in a consistent manner for the exchange of all electronic business data. ebXML specifically focuses on the business-to-business (B2B) market. The focus of ebXML is to develop a framework that makes it possible to automate the creation and the configuration of electronic relationships.

In 1999, OASIS and the United Nations Centre for Trade Facilitation and Electronic Business (UN/CEFACT) jointly established the Electronic Business XML working group for the development of a next-generation standard for electronic business. OASIS brought the technical expertise with XML and markup languages in general. The UN/CEFACT brought its experience in developing solutions for electronic business.

The ebXML architecture has the following different components. Figure 10.26 shows the ebXML technical architecture and how these components interact with each other.

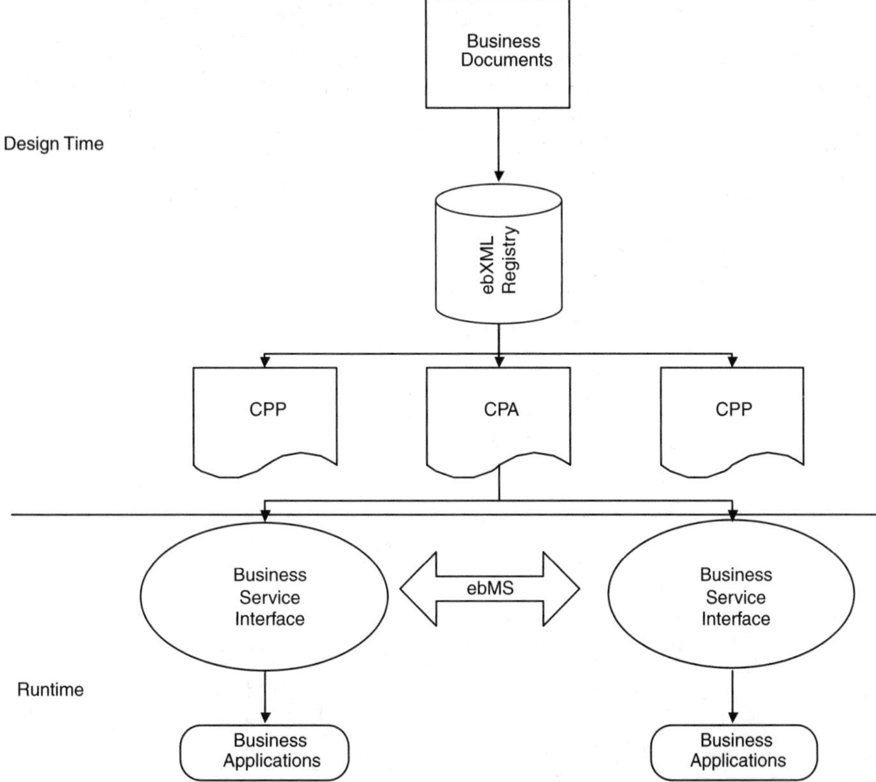

Figure 10.26 ebXML technical architecture

- **Collaborative Protocol Profile (CPP)**—The CPP defines XML data structures that describe what each trading partner supports and the components necessary to conduct electronic commerce, such as data communications, security, processes, document types, and telephone contacts.
- **Collaborative Protocol Agreement (CPA)**—The CPA is a special business agreement derived from the intersection of two or more CPPs. The CPA serves as a

formal handshake between two or more trading partners who want to conduct business transactions using ebXML.

- **Registry and repository**—This defines the access interfaces, security, and information storage format for any information that needs to be widely yet securely shared among trading partners or potential trading partners.
- **ebMS messaging**—This defines the means to move data between trading partners in a secure, reliable manner.
- **Business Process Specification Schema (BPSS)**—Using ebXML, you can extract and format the nominal set of elements necessary to configure an ebXML runtime system. The BPSS contains the specification of business transactions and the choreography of business transactions into business collaborations. This specification is used as input to the formation of ebXML trading partner CPP and CPA and to execute a set of ebXML business transactions. Figure 10.27 shows the steps for ebXML.

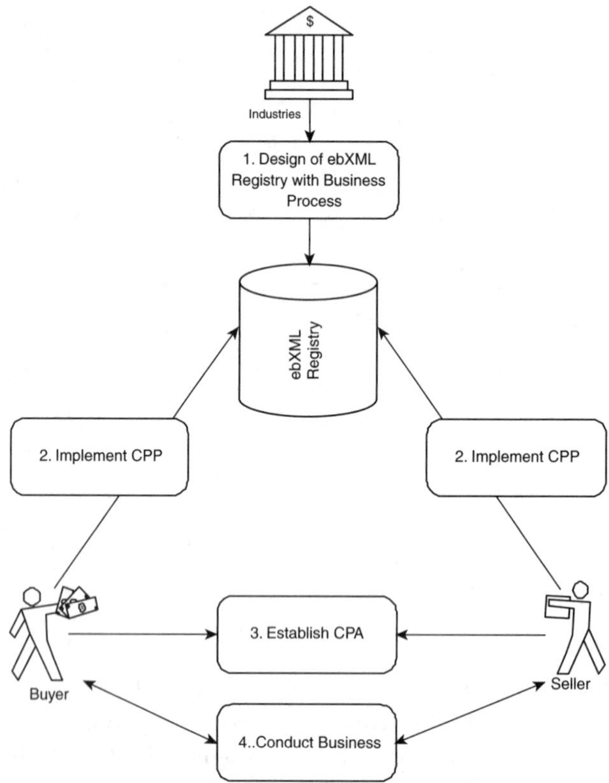

Figure 10.27 Steps for ebXML

ebXML and Web Services

You already learned the specifications for web services (SOAP, WSDL, UDDI, and BPSS) and for ebXML (ebMS, CPP/CPA, ebXML registry). Are these specifications complementary or competing? Table 10.1 gives a high-level comparison.

Table 10.1 Comparison of ebXML to Web Services

Components	Web Services	ebXML
Messaging	SOAP	ebMS Messaging (extension of SOAP)
Registry	UDDI	ebXML Registry and Repository
Definition of contract	WSDL	CPP/CPA
Process	WS-BPEL	BPSS

You need to design the system based on the integration scenario. Web services and ebXML are complementary.

In general, EbXML can be used in large B2B environments where you are extending or integrating enterprise SOAs. These situations require security and reliability, need high scalability, and are subject to trading partner agreements.

Web services can be used when there are simple request/response exchanges, there are no formalized commitments, and solutions can be augmented with ebXML middleware components to improve QoS.

WLI and ebXML

WebLogic Integration supports the ebXML Message Service Specification v2.0.This specification defines the message envelope and header document schema used to transfer ebXML messages with a communication protocol such as HTTP. They provide a set of layered extensions to the base SOAP and to SOAP Messages with Attachments specifications. The ebXML Message Service provides security and reliability features that are not provided in the specifications for SOAP and SOAP Messages with Attachments.

Take a look at an example in which a customer places an order on its partner through an ebXML transaction. Creating an ebXML process is very similar to creating a business process:

- First, create an ebXML application similar to the one created in the business process. Then create a process with an ebXML process called `customer.jpd`.
- Add a client request node to trigger the event of sending the order to the partner, as shown in Figure 10.28. Call the method `customerRequest`.

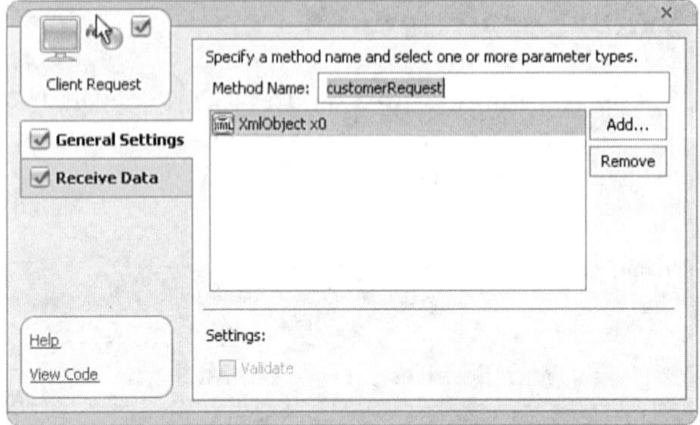

Figure 10.28 Customer request

- Create an ebXML control called `CustomerControl`, as shown in Figure 10.29. Specify the `ebxml-service-name` as `Partner`, which is the value of the business process on the partner's end. This service name corresponds to the `eb:Service` entry in the ebXML message envelope. To specify the business identifier of the initiator of the ebXML, leave it blank. It defaults to `000000001` at runtime. For the participant, enter `000000002`. This sets the participating trading partner ID as a static value.

Figure 10.29 ebXML control

- Use the method `void request (XmlObject` payload) of the ebXML control to create the `controlSend` node request for the customer process. The `send data` variable should be set to `order`. Here is the code generated for the ebXML control:

```
package ebXML.prototype;

import com.bea.jpd.JpdContext;
import com.bea.data.RawData;
import com.bea.xml.XmlObject;
```

This is the business process for the customer side, showing the customer sending the request:

```
/**
 * @jpd:process process::
 * <process name="Customer">
 *   <clientRequest name="Client Request" method="startCustomer"/>
 *   <controlSend name="request" method="partnerControlRequest"/>
 * </process>::
 */
```

This is the JPD code created in source view for the previous process:

```
public class Customer implements com.bea.jpd.ProcessDefinition
{
    public com.bea.xml.XmlObject order;

    static final long serialVersionUID = 1L;

    public Callback callback;


    /**
     * @common:control
     */
    private ebXML.prototype.CustomerControl customerControl;

    /**
     * @common:context
     */

    public void startCustomer(com.bea.xml.XmlObject x0)
    {
        //#START: CODE GENERATED - PROTECTED SECTION - you can safely add
➥code above this comment in this method. #//
        // input transform
        // parameter assignment
        this.order = x0;
        //#END  : CODE GENERATED - PROTECTED SECTION - you can safely add
➥code below this comment in this method. #//
    }
```

```
    public void partnerControlRequest() throws Exception
     {
        //#START: CODE GENERATED - PROTECTED SECTION - you can safely add
➥code above this comment in this method. #//
        // input transform
        // method call
        sellerControl.request(null);
        // output transform
        // output assignments
        //#END  : CODE GENERATED - PROTECTED SECTION - you can safely add
➥code below this comment in this method. #//
     }

     public interface Callback      {
     }

}
```

- To create the partner process, create `partner.jpd` and add an integration control to it. Then you can add an application view control if you want to write the order to a EIS system or you want to add a file control to write it to a file. A file control is used here. Use the Place order file as the `XMLObject` because it will store an XML.

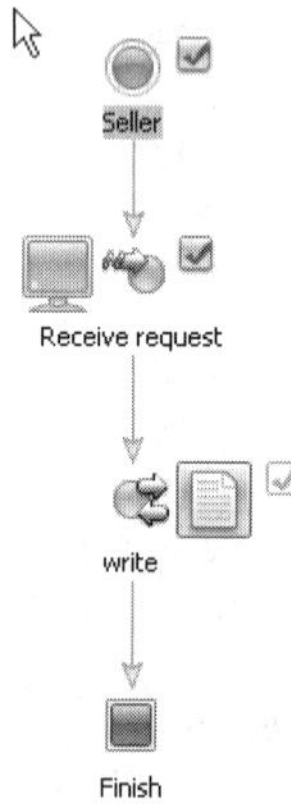

Figure 10.30 `Partner.jpd`

- Then test this ebXML process. You can also see a test SOAP message in Figures 10.31 and 10.32.

```
Operation request
Submitted at Tue Jan 20 14:17:07 PST 2004
 Method: ebXML.oneway.Seller.request
 Arguments:
    payload : <Order xmlns="bea.com/tutorial/order">
 <Order_Number>197992</Order_Number>
 <Customer_ID>000000001</Customer_ID>
 <Supplier_ID>000000002</Supplier_ID>
 <Customer_Name>FundCo</Customer_Name>
 <Requested_Provision_Date>08-17-02</Requested_Provision_Date>
 <Order_Items>
 <Item>
 <Part_Number>1001</Part_Number>
 <Quantity>1</Quantity>
 <Description>Pie</Description>
 <Price>3.14</Price>
 </Item>
 <Item>
 <Part_Number>1002</Part_Number>
 <Quantity>10</Quantity>
 <Description>Plank</Description>
 <Price>1.05</Price>
 </Item>
 <Item>
 <Part_Number>1003</Part_Number>
 <Quantity>22</Quantity>
 <Description>Charge</Description>
 <Price>1.60</Price>
 </Item>
 </Order_Items>
 <Product_Type>type</Product_Type>
 <Order_Amount>5.79</Order_Amount>
 </Order>
```

Figure 10.31 Test SOAP message

```
Operation write on Control file
Submitted at Tue Jan 20 14:17:07 PST 2004
 Method: ebXML.oneway.file.write
 Arguments:
    someData : <Order xmlns="bea.com/tutorial/order
 <Order_Number>197992</Order_Number>
 <Customer_ID>000000001</Customer_ID>
 <Supplier_ID>000000002</Supplier_ID>
```

Figure 10.32 Writing to file

- Confirm that the `order.xml` file was written out correctly to the C:\bea\... directory to confirm that you have received the file.
- You can monitor the process by clicking Monitor Process. You will see the WebLogic Administration Console, as shown in Figure 10.33.

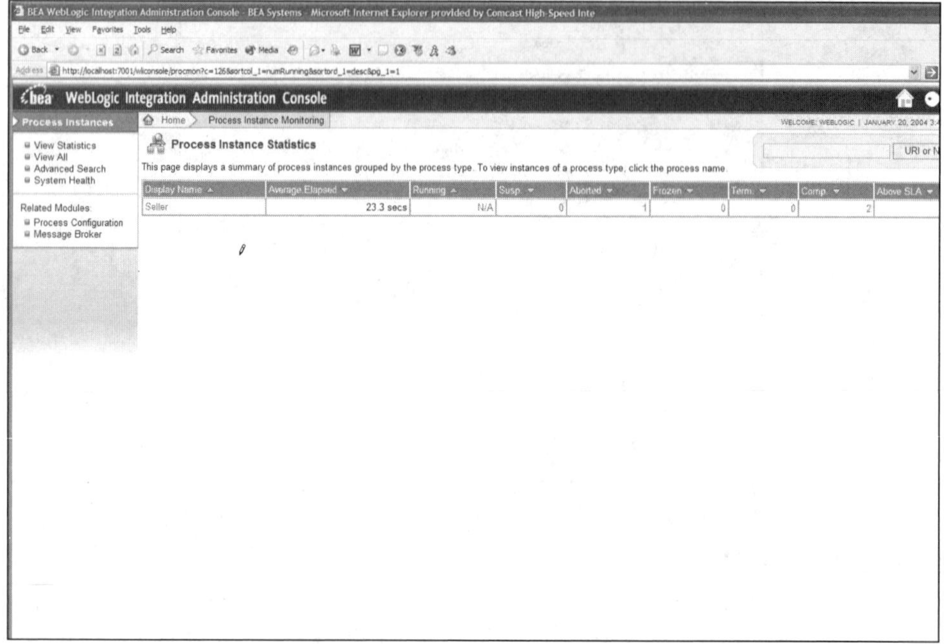

Figure 10.33 Process monitoring.

Summary

This chapter looked at Business Process Management and business integration. BPM systems provide the capability to model and measure the effectiveness of complex and ever-changing business processes. Orchestration, choreography, and collaboration are about composing web services into a business process. Orchestration defines the rules for a business process flow. Choreography describes the sequence and conditions in which messages are exchanged between processes. Collaboration defines an agreement between business process participants for achieving a business goal.

WebLogic Integration provides a robust and integrated BPM solution. It is based on PD4J, which provides an easy-to-use syntax for describing a business process at the source code level for the J2EE platform. WLI can be used for modeling, automation, and monitoring of a process. You saw an example of this in the development of the change order request process using WLI.

WS-BPEL defines a model and a grammar for describing the behavior of a business process based on interactions between the process and its partners. WLI provides a mechanism for importing WS-BPEL into WLI to create a PD4J format, as well as for exporting the PD4J process model into WS-BPEL format.

ebXML, which is targeted for the B2B market, refers to a technical framework and a set of specifications that will enable XML to be utilized in a consistent manner for the exchange of all electronic business data. Web services and ebXML are complementary. WebLogic Integration supports ebXML v2.0.

11

Security of Web Services

"Transition to web services was smoother in relation to earlier transitions to other systems. For the amount of money spent on this implementation, the benefits exceeded expectations"
—Sam Szteinbaum, VP and GM, North America Consumer Computing, Hewlett-Packard Co.

This chapter describes one of the biggest challenges for implementation of web services: security. Here, you review the security considerations—authentication, authorization, confidentiality, integrity, and nonrepudiation—required to properly secure an implementation. We look at how Two-Way SSL and other packaged security solutions such as XML firewalls can be used for ensuring security of web services.

The security specifications of web services have been ratified. This chapter describes WS-Security and the emerging standards from Liberty Alliance and SAML. We will also learn how Two-Way SSL and WS-Security can be used in WebLogic.

Overview on Security Considerations

When you are securing your web services, you should consider the security requirements from the following five perspectives:

- **Authentication**—Refers to the process by which you verify that users are who they claim they are
- **Authorization**—Involves finding out whether the person is permitted to access or modify the resource after being authenticated
- **Confidentiality**—Guarantees that only the intended recipient can see the information being exchanged

- **Integrity**—Ensures that the information arrives at its intended destination unaltered
- **Nonrepudiation**—Refers to the capability to trace a transaction so that neither the recipient nor the sender can deny receiving or sending that transaction

These aspects of security can be applied to a web services application in many different ways. These include leveraging the existing transport and infrastructure capabilities, as well as modifying the SOAP message itself. Each technique has certain advantages and disadvantages.

For example, using HTTPS for transmitting SOAP messages between client and server provides encryption (confidentiality) of the SOAP message, with very little programmatic work required by the developer. However, the disadvantage is the performance degradation encountered in encrypting every message that is exchanged, as well as the lack of flexibility in defining what service is permitted to decrypt the message.

In the same way, leveraging infrastructure services for authentication and authorization might mean less work for the programmer but runs the risk of vendor or platform lock-in. On the other hand, applying security to the message itself both provides the greatest flexibility for defining specifically what aspects of security are used and enables a higher degree of interoperability among services operating in a heterogeneous collection of platforms and programming languages.

Two-Way SSL

One of the simplest ways to ensure security for web services is to use SSL. SSL provides secure communication over the Internet, and Two-Way SSL provides additional authentication and low-level authorization. Two-Way SSL authenticates the requestor against a client certificate list and allows the client to authenticate the server to which it is making the request. This ensures that only users known to the web service provider can invoke the web services. SSL provides encryption for the data that is sent in the requests and responses. This encryption guarantees that the data passed from client to server is encrypted and unreadable by hackers. Therefore, all private information is kept safe during transmission over the Internet. Also, no connections are made unless the SSL handshake can be established. The web services provider can issue its own certificates or use third-party certificates such those issued by Verisign.

How Does SSL Work?

SSL is not a single, standalone protocol. It consists of a set of standardized routines that perform several security tasks. When a client and server communicate, SSL ensures that the connection is private and secure by providing authentication, encryption, and integrity. Authentication confirms that the SSL-enabled client knows the SSL-enabled server. Authentication can also be used to confirm that the server knows the client. Encryption creates a secure "tunnel" between the client and the server, preventing any unauthorized system from reading the data and thereby ensuring confidentiality. SSL also provides a mechanism for detecting if someone has altered the data in transit. These message-integrity checks ensure that the connection is reliable. If at any point during a transmission SSL detects that a connection is not secure, it terminates the connection, and the client and server establish a new secure connection.

SSL-enabled clients and SSL-enabled servers confirm each other's identities using digital certificates. Digital certificates are issued by trusted third parties called certificate authorities (CAs). They provide information about an individual's claimed identity, as well as that person's public key. By validating digital certificates, both parties can ensure that an imposter has not intercepted a transmission and provided a false public key for which he or she has the correct private key.

SSL server authentication enables a client to confirm a server's identity. SSL clients use standard techniques of public-key cryptography to check that a server's certificate and public ID are valid and have been issued by a CA listed in the client's list of trusted CAs.

SSL client authentication allows a server to confirm a client's identity. Using the same techniques as those used for server authentication, SSL-enabled server software can check that a client's certificate and public ID are valid and have been issued by a CA listed in the server's list of trusted CAs. The combination of server and client authentication using SSL is referred to as Two-Way SSL.

An encrypted connection requires that all information sent between a client and a server be encrypted, to provide a high degree of confidentiality to protect both parties of any private transaction. All data sent over an encrypted SSL connection is also protected with a mechanism for detecting tampering using a hash algorithm to ensure that the data has not been altered in transit.

Figure 11.1 illustrates the steps taken during an SSL negotiation. The steps are described next.

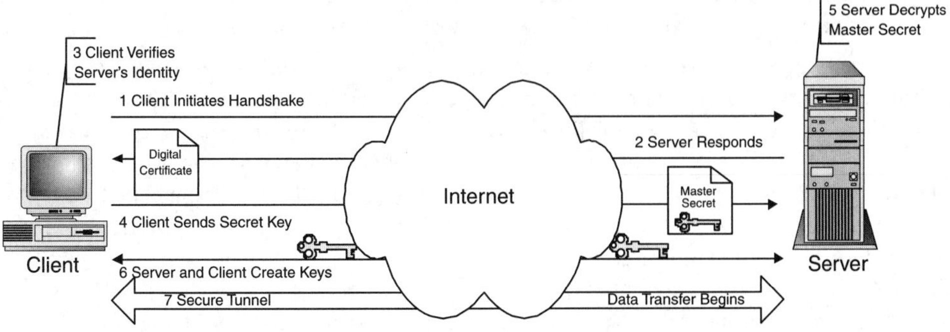

Figure 11.1 How Two-Way SSL works

1. The server sends the client its digital certificate. The certificate contains information about the server, including the server's public key.
2. When the client has the server's certificate, the client verifies that the certificate is valid and that a CA listed in the client's list of trusted CAs issued the certificate. The client also checks the certificate's expiration date and the server domain name. The same process happens in reverse for Two-Way SSL, in which the server authenticates the client.
3. After a client has determined that the server certificate is valid, the client generates a master secret key. This master secret key is encrypted using server's public key and is sent to the server.
4. Upon receiving the master secret key from the client, the server decrypts this master secret using its private key.
5. Now that both the client and the server have the same master secret key, they use this master secret key to create keys for the encryption. Because both participants used the same master secret key, they now have the same encryption.
6. They use the SSL encryption and authentication algorithms to create an encrypted tunnel. Through this encrypted tunnel, they can now pass data securely through the Internet.

In addition to Two-Way SSL, an access control list (ACL) can be used with the username and password for authorization. This helps define the role of the transaction accessing the web service and the level of service it has been authorized.

Two-Way SSL in WebLogic Server

You can configure WebLogic for Two-Way SSL. WebLogic Server always asserts the identity of the SSL certificate to ensure that it maps to a valid WebLogic user, even if the web service component doesn't require any special privileges. This identity assertion is a security check in addition to the default features provided by Two-Way SSL communication.

Identity asserters in WebLogic validate an outside identity token and map it to a valid WebLogic Server user. The default identity assertion provider, known as the `DefaultIdentityAsserter`, can validate WebLogic Security tokens, X.509 certificates, and IIOP CSIv2 tokens. The default identity assertion provider does its work via a `UserNameMapper` interface, which maps either an X.509 certificate array or an X.501 distinguished name to a username. The following steps show one way to configure WebLogic for mapping the identity token it receives to a WebLogic user:

- The default configuration of `DefaultIdentityAsserter` has to be changed to enable identity assertion for X.509 certificates.
- The default configuration of `DefaultIdentityAsserter` has to be changed to enable Default User Name Mapper.

- The Default User Name Mapper has to be configured to choose the Common Name (CN) field of the X.509 certificate to obtain the WebLogic username.
- Configure a WebLogic user corresponding to the CN of the client's X.509 certificate.
- Configure a WebLogic role and add the new WebLogic user to that role.

Issues with SSL Encryption

Two-Way SSL provides authentication, authorization, confidentiality, and integrity for the web services messaging. However, still a number of issues arise when using Two-Way SSL in transacting web services:

- This is a point-to-point implementation. As you implement it with each partner, you need to set Two-Way SSL with each partner. This affects scalability. Two-Way SSL does not align with an SOA architecture because it is point to point.
- Two-Way SSL operates only on HTTPS. You must stick to this protocol for web services.
- Implementation of SSL is vendor specific. This could cause issues with true interoperability between systems. When using a .NET client to access a Java web service in WebLogic, the Visual Basic code needs to be programmed for the location of the client certificate, and the Java client uses the default key store.
- When you use SOAP with Attachments, .NET supports only DIME attachment. This causes several issues with getting SSL set up on other application servers, such as Web Methods on the server side, and also if you are using Visual Basic on the client side.
- If you are using .NET on the client side with IIS servers, be aware that IIS supports only one certificate per server. If you use Two-Way SSL, issues arise if the server has to support a website that also requires a certificate.
- Performance is a big issue with Two-Way SSL. Table 11.1 compares performance numbers with and without Two-Way SSL. If you subject the Validate Config web service, which you developed in the last few chapters, to performance testing, you will see that without SSL, it takes 0.453 seconds to validate the configuration. With SSL, it takes 0.719 seconds. The `placeOrder` request in general takes longer because the XML is larger. In addition, it is a synchronous web service and the order is placed in SAP; this takes time to do all checks, such as a credit check or inventory check, before placing the order and sending back a synchronous confirmation.

Table 11.1 Performance of Web Services with and Without SSL

Transaction Name	Minimum	Average	Maximum	Std	90%	Pass
`Add Basket request`						
Without SSL	0.578	2.168	34.75	2.9	3.928	1,449
With SSL	0.625	1.799	39.77	2.8	3.045	2,323
`placeOrder_request`						
Without SSL	3.688	6.367	29.344	2.931	9.53	193
With SSL	3.734	5.591	16,469	1.972	7.465	19
`Validate Config_request`						
Without SSL	0.453	1.521	23.203	1.71	3.293	13,641
With SSL	0.719	2.172	24.078	2.252	3.804	10,080

These issues can be resolved by moving away from transport-level security to message-level security. If you want to use transport-level security, you can use Two-Way SSL with SSL accelerators, which we talk about in Chapter 12, "Enhancing the Performance of Web Services." Message-level security is part of the message and, therefore, is not point to point. With message-level security, you are not restricted to the HTTPS protocol used by SSL. New specifications published by OASIS—called WS-Security, described in the next section—look at message-level security. Ensuring interoperability is an important aspect of WS-Security. Therefore, different vendor-specific products are allowed to communicate in a standard fashion. In addition, moving away from attachments and more to doc-literal web services, as described in Chapter 7, "Developing and Deploying Web Services," helps alleviate the issues of DIME attachments.

XML Firewalls

You can also implement web service security using off-the-shelf tools, typically referred to as XML firewalls, offered by security tool vendors. These tools are network security appliances that act as a proxy and are deployed in the DMZ between internal and external network firewalls. They come as either a hardware or a software solution. The typical features of these tools are listed here:

- Authentication and authorization. The source of a message, as well as its content and headers, is compared to the requirements of the security policy before the request is authorized or denied.

- XML Encryption, a W3C Recommendation. This facilitates message-level encryption so both secure and nonsecure data can be exchanged in the same document. XML Encryption can handle both XML and non-XML (for example, binary) data.
- XML Digital Signature, a W3C Recommendation. XML Signature has the capability to sign only specific portions of the XML tree, not the complete document. When a single XML document is authored by many parties, those parties need to sign the part they authored. This is not possible when using transport-level security. It is important to ensure the integrity of certain portions of an XML document, while leaving open the possibility for other portions of the document to change. Consider, for example, a signed XML form delivered to a user for completion. If the signature were over the full XML form, any change that the user made to the default form values would invalidate the original signature. XML signatures add authentication, data integrity, and support for nonrepudiation to the data that they sign.
- XML Schema validation. This checks for well-formedness of and conformance to specified schemas.
- Validation of standards such as WS-Security, SAML, and WS-I.

Some companies offer packaged tools for security as hardware or software solutions (see the accompanying sidebar for examples).

Packaged Tools from Vendors: Reactivity and Vordel

Reactivity XML Firewall is an XML proxy designed to secure XML and web services traffic. The Reactivity XML Firewall typically sits in the DMZ and scales behind a load balancer. It is a hardware solution. It provides security through authorization, such as X.509, username-password authentication through for LDAP.

This solution provides auditing, logging, and exception handling. It can be deployed as an appliance package, and it has a security-hardened OS, rack and stack scalability, dedicated hardware for enhanced security, SSL acceleration, and secure hardware key storage.

Vordel is a software solution with features similar to that of Reactivity. It can be deployed in two ways: as an XML gateway or as an agent model.

The XML gateway enforces access-control rules by processing security tokens contained within incoming SOAP messages. It ensures that the

continues

XML format and content are appropriate for the target. It provides security adapters to existing security technologies such as LDAP directories, traditional firewalls, and PKI.

The interceptor or agent communicates with a centralized XML security server that performs the processing of security rules. Its architecture puts the security enforcement closer to the web services application. Security is enforced at the web service endpoint itself, instead of requiring XML traffic to travel through an infrastructural device to be secured.

WS-Security

The OASIS Web Services Security (WSS) technical committee has issued WS-Security as an OASIS standard. You can use WSS for authenticating web services and ensuring message-level integrity and confidentiality. Interoperability is ensured when using WSS.

WS-Security Documents

Three documents describe WS-Security:

- **WSS Core**—SOAP Messaging Security document
- **WSS**—Username Token Profile document
- **WSS**—X.509 Certificate Token Profile document

WSS Core: SOAP Message Security Document

This document proposes a standard set of SOAP extensions that can be used when building secure web services to implement message content integrity and confidentiality. It is flexible and is designed to be used as the basis for securing web services within a wide variety of security models, including PKI, Kerberos, and SSL. Specifically, this specification provides support for multiple security token formats, multiple trust domains, multiple signature formats, and multiple encryption technologies. This specification provides three main mechanisms: the capability to send security token as part of a message, message integrity, and message confidentiality. These mechanisms by themselves do not provide a complete security solution for web services. Instead, this specification is a building block that can be used in conjunction with other web service extensions and higher-level application-specific protocols to accommodate a wide variety of security models and security technologies.

Message integrity is provided by leveraging XML Signature in conjunction with security tokens, which might contain or imply key data, to ensure that messages are transmitted without modifications. The integrity mechanisms are designed to support multiple signatures, potentially by multiple actors, and to be extensible to support additional signature formats. The signatures can reference a security token.

Similarly, message confidentiality is provided by leveraging XML Encryption in conjunction with security tokens to keep portions of SOAP messages confidential. Three elements of the XML Encryption standard—`xenc:RefernceList`, `xenc:EncryptedKey`, and `xenc:EncryptedData`—have been leveraged. You need to encrypt only parts of a message, so you can reduce response times by encrypting only the most needed sections of the payload. For example, in a `placeOrder` web service, you might need to encrypt only the customer name, address, telephone number, and credit-card information. The other key point about XML Encryption is that you can encrypt different keys. This is important for XMLs that are passed among multiple services, with each service privy to only one piece of the information. The encryption mechanisms are designed to support additional encryption technologies, processes, and operations by multiple actors. The encryption might also reference a security token. Two XML Schemas are considered part of the WSS Core.

WSS: Username Token Profile Document

This document describes how to use the `UsernameToken` with the WSS specification. More specifically, it describes how a web service consumer can supply a `UsernameToken` as a means of identifying the requestor by username and, optionally using a password to authenticate that identity to the web service producer.

WSS: X.509 Certificate Token Profile Document

This document describes the use of the X.509 authentication framework with the Core WSS specification. An X.509 certificate can be used to validate a public key that can be used to authenticate a WSS-enhanced message, or to identify the public key with which a WSS-enhanced message has been encrypted.

WS-Security and Interoperability

WS-Security can be used in the .NET and J2EE implementations of web services. This promotes interoperability. A .NET client can sign and encrypt a request to a Java web service and vice versa, allowing a common method of ensuring security across platforms.

The OASIS WS-Security technical committee has conducted two interoperability testing sessions in which a simple ping web service is secured and encrypted in three scenarios to test interoperability. The results of the testing lab are available in the public documentation for the group; 12 companies, including BEA and Microsoft, took part, and all 144 combinations of interoperability were tried and were successful. These three tests were used:

- In the first, the request header contained a username and password.
- In the second, the request header contained a username and password that were encrypted using a public key.
- In the last one, the request body contained data that was signed and encrypted. The certificate used to verify the signature was provided in the header. The certificate associated with the encryption was provided out-of-band. The response body was also signed and encrypted, reversing the roles of the key pairs identified by the certificates.

WS-I is also currently working on the Basic Security Profile, an interoperability profile involving transport security, SOAP messaging security, and other security considerations implicated by the Basic Profile 1.0. WS-I will provide clarifications and guidance designed to promote interoperability of WS-Security.

Designing for Security Using WSS

Taking the WSS specification, you can use the following tips to design a flexible security system for your web services:

- Define access privileges based on identity using authentication and granular authorization.
- Use the certificate that the partner might have already been using for Two-Way SSL, and pass it as an identity token in the SOAP header.
- Passing the token at the message level enables you to programmatically link the identity to an authorization mechanism.
- Validate the document at the message level by checking the integrity of the SOAP request (or at least the SOAP body) with XML Digital Signatures, which is part of the WSS.
- Ensure the privacy of all or parts of the body of the SOAP message using XML Encryption, which is part of the WSS. You can get granular control over what elements of the message are encrypted and can selectively encrypt different elements for different potential recipients.
- If you are using only WSS without Two-Way SSL, use it in conjunction with an XML firewall solution (described later in this chapter) to prevent random attacks on the service. WS-Security implements security at the message level, not the transport level. Therefore, the box might still be vulnerable to attack, even if the messages or payload is secure.

WS-Security in WebLogic

WS-Security is controlled in WebLogic as WS-Security policy files. One part of a WS-Security policy determines the security requirements for SOAP messages coming into a web service or web service control. This part of the policy determines what sorts of security mechanisms must be present in an inbound SOAP message to pass the security gate. The other part of a WS-Security policy determines the security enhancements to be added to outgoing SOAP messages before they are sent out over the wire. This part of the policy file determines the kinds of security mechanisms that a web service or web service control adds to SOAP messages. We show examples in WebLogic for both these parts of the WS-Security policy.

WS-Security policies are configured in WSSE files, which is an XML file with the .WSSE extension. The `<wsSecurityIn>` element describes the security requirements for incoming SOAP messages; the `<wsSecurityOut>` element describes the security enhancements added to outgoing SOAP messages.

To apply a WS-Security policy to a web service, add the annotations `@jws:ws-security-service` and `@jws:ws-security-callback` to the web service file:

```
/**
 * @jws:ws-security-service file="MyWebServicePolicy.wsse"
 * @jws:ws-security-callback file="MyWebServicePolicy.wsse"
 */
public class MyWebService implements com.bea.jws.WebService
```

If the web service communicates synchronously with its clients, you need to use only the `@jws:ws-security-service` annotation. If the web service sends callbacks to its clients, you must use both annotations.

To apply a policy file to a web service control, use the control annotations `@jc:ws-security-service` and `@jc:ws-security-callback`:

```
/**
 * @jc:ws-security-service file="TargetControlPolicy.wsse"
 * @jc:ws-security-callback file="TargetControlPolicy.wsse"
 */
public interface TargetControl extends
➥com.bea.control.ControlExtension,
➥com.bea.control.ServiceControl
```

If your web service control communicates synchronously with its target web service, you need to use only the `@jc:ws-security-service` annotation. If the control receives callbacks from its target service, you must use both annotations.

Figures 11.2 and 11.3 show an example of applying the WS-Security policy file `placeOrderPolicy.wsse` to the `placeOrder` web service. It shows that the tag `<wsSecurityIn>` requires the account and password for security in the incoming SOAP message.

CPDWebService
placeOrder.jws
placeOrder.wsdl
placeOrderControl.jcx
placeOrderClient.java
placeOrderPolicy.wsse
ceOrder.jws - {WebServices}\CPDWebService\
package CPDWebService;
/**
* @jws:wsdl file="#IoPlaceOrderSessionServiceWsdl"
*/
/**
* @jws:ws-security-service file="placeOrderPolicy.wsse"
*/
public class placeOrder implements com.bea.jws.WebService
{
/**
* @common:operation
* @jws:protocol soap-style="rpc" form-post="false" form-get="false"

Figure 11.2 Example of a WS-Security policy file in the `placeOrder` web service

```
CPDWebService
    placeOrder.jws
    placeOrder.wsdl
        placeOrderControl.jcx
    placeOrderClient.java
    placeOrderPolicy.wsse
laceOrderPolicy.wsse - {WebServices}\CPDWebService\
<wsSecurityPolicy xsi:schemaLocation="WSSecurity-policy.xsd" xmlns="http://www.bea.com/2003/03,

    <wsSecurityIn>
        <!--
        Incoming SOAP message must be accompanied by a valid username
        and password.
        -->
        <token tokenType="username"/>
        <!--
        Incoming SOAP messages must be encrypted with mycompany.jws's
        public key. The alias and password to access the mycompany.jws's
        decrypting private key in the keystore are provided by
        the <decryptionKey> element below.
        -->
        <encryptionRequired>
            <decryptionKey>
                <alias>account</alias>
                <password>password</password>
            </decryptionKey>
        </encryptionRequired>
        <!--
        Incoming SOAP messages must be digitally signed with the sender's
        private key.
        The sender's public key is used to validate the signature.
        -->
        <signatureRequired>true</signatureRequired>
    </wsSecurityIn>

    <wsSecurityOut>
        <!--
        Accompany the SOAP message with a valid username and password
        -->
        <userNameToken>
                <userName>weblogic</userName>
                <password type="TEXT">weblogic</password>
        </userNameToken>
        <!--
        Encrypt the SOAP message with the recipient's public key.
        Only the recipient's private key can decrypt it.
        Ensures the confidentiality of the SOAP message.
        (This process requires that the sender's keystore already contains
        a digital certificate containing the recients public key.)
        -->
        <encryption>
            <encryptionKey>
                <alias>client1</alias>
            </encryptionKey>
        </encryption>
         <!--
```

Figure 11.3 Example of a WS-Security policy file

Security Standards in Identifying Management

A number of security standards are currently being developed by consortiums and standards bodies for sharing security information such as login information and security policies. Here, we look at Liberty Alliance and SAML, which are the two leading efforts for identity management.

Liberty Alliance

Liberty Alliance has developed an open standard for federated network identity through open technical specifications. The vision of the Liberty Alliance Project is to protect the privacy and security of vital identity information when individuals and businesses conduct transactions online. The standard is intended to accomplish the following objectives:

- Support a broad range of identity-based products and services
- Enable commercial and noncommercial organizations to realize new revenue and cost-saving opportunities that economically leverage their relationships with customers, business partners, and employees
- Provide consumers with a choice of identity provider(s), the capability to link accounts through account federation, and the convenience of simplified sign-on when using any network of connected services and devices
- Increase ease of use for consumers to help stimulate e-commerce

Individuals have various accounts with different service providers. Associated with each account are attributes with information such as name, phone number, social security number, address, credit record, and payment information. Network identity refers to the global set of attributes that are contained in these accounts. For individuals, it is the sum of their financial, medical, and personal data, all of which must be carefully protected. For businesses, network identity represents their capability to know their customers and constituents and to reach them in ways that bring value to both parties.

Today, the burden of maintaining identity information across all the accounts falls on the individual. The individual is responsible for remembering the multiple username/password pairs for each online account, and the individual must manage the information that each website maintains to ensure that it is both up-to-date and appropriate. To alleviate the problem of remembering all their usernames and passwords, users typically either try to use the same combination (which isn't always possible because of the varying requirements imposed by service providers) or record these values elsewhere. Many times, individuals simply forget and repeatedly go through the effort of resetting the information.

Overall, the result is a reduction in the level of security that the usernames and passwords were designed to provide. A problem even before getting to deal with usernames and passwords is filling in information during registration for an online account. During registration at a site, the user is asked for information deemed necessary and relevant to a transaction at hand. Most users are tired of filling in forms and shy away from even creating an account in the first place.

Federated identity will address these issues, removing from web users some of the burden of creating and maintaining their identity on the web and allowing businesses interacting with these users to offer new holistic experiences. Understanding and creating the best technical infrastructure to enable these relationships to work in a digital world is the goal of the more than 160 member companies within the Liberty Alliance.

SAML

The Security Assertion Markup Language (SAML) is an XML-based framework for exchanging security information. It is being developed by the OASIS XML-Based Security Services Technical Committee (SSTC). In SAML, security information is expressed in the form of assertions about subjects:

- The subject is an entity, either human or computer, that has an identity in some security domain. For example, a person identified by e-mail address in a particular Internet DNS domain is a subject.
- Assertion conveys information about authentication acts performed by subjects, attributes of subjects, and authorization decisions about whether subjects are allowed to access certain resources.

XML constructs are used to represent assertions. They can have a nested structure, in which a single assertion might contain several different internal statements about authentication, authorization, and attributes. Assertions containing authentication statements describe previously completed authentication events.

Assertions are issued by SAML authorities such as authentication authorities, attribute authorities, and policy decision points. Using a protocol defined in SAML, clients can request assertions from SAML authorities and get a response from them. SAML authorities can use various sources of information, such as external policy stores and assertions that were received as input in requests, in creating their responses. Thus, whereas clients always consume assertions, SAML authorities can be both producers and consumers of assertions (see Figure 11.4).

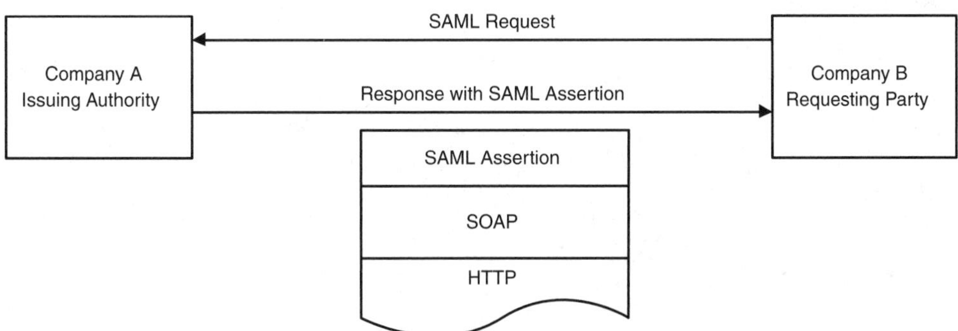

Figure 11.4 How SAML works

The SAML protocol consists of XML-based request and response message formats. SAML currently defines one binding of these message formats for use with SOAP over HTTP. These message formats can be bound to many different underlying communications and transport protocols.

Summary

In this chapter, you have seen how you can use different ways of securing your B2B web services. Authentication, authorization, integrity, confidentiality, and nonrepudiation are the five considerations that you have to address to properly secure your web service implementation. You can leverage existing transport and infrastructure capabilities, as well as modification of the SOAP message itself, to implement security.

Two-Way SSL is the simplest way to apply security to web services. It works at the transport level and provides authentication, low-level authorization, confidentiality, and integrity. You can configure Two-Way SSL in WebLogic Server. Two-Way SSL has a few issues because it is point to point, and it also has interoperability and performance issues.

Another way of implementing security is to use XML firewalls, which are security solutions offered by vendors.

WS-Security is an OASIS standard, which will provide better flexibility and interoperability for securing web services. You can use WS-Security for authenticating web services, ensuring message-level integrity and confidentiality. Using WSS also ensures interoperability between J2EE and .NET environments. WS-Security is controlled in WebLogic as WS-Security policy files to establish security mechanisms for inbound and outbound SOAP messages.

Liberty Alliance has developed an open standard for federated network identity through open technical specifications. SAML is an XML-based framework for exchanging security information, where security information is expressed in the form of assertions about subjects. Assertions, which convey authentication information, are issued by SAML authorities.

12
Enhancing the Performance of Web Services

In the last chapter, we covered one of the biggest challenges in implementing web services. This chapter describes the other big challenge: performance of web services. Concerns about poor performance of web services is one big factor why companies shy away from implementing web services, especially in the B2B arena. For B2B transactions, especially the ones that enable websites for retail consumers, performance is very important. Many factors influence the performance of web services, and this chapter covers some of them, including how to track performance bottlenecks and how to improve performance in all the building blocks of web services.

First, you will examine the inherent factors—HTTP, XML, SOAP, and security—constraining the performance of a web service implementation. Then, you will learn how to identify the performance bottlenecks in the web services tiers and the underlying systems running the web services; you also will learn how HP OpenView Transaction Analyzer can help in this role. This chapter then looks at a variety of ways to improve performance: SOAP implementation options, XML parsers, XML Beans, XML compression, XML and SSL accelerators, patterns and tuning EJBs, and databases and JVM.

Understanding Performance Constraints

The only performance guarantee that you have in dealing with the Internet is that performance will vary wildly from one time to the next. Besides that, when you are using web services, four fundamental factors constrain the performance of web services: the HTTP transport protocol, XML messaging, the SOAP messaging protocol, and security.

Creating and Terminating HTTP Connections

Web services generally rely on HTTP as the transport protocol. HTTP was designed to enable one server to handle hundreds of requests quickly by not maintaining a long-term stateful connection between the clients and the server. The HTTP communication transaction enables the server side to handle many clients. However, it also means that a lot of time is wasted creating and terminating connections. This performance cost is exaggerated for clients that need to perform a large number of calls between the client and the server. Other technologies, such as DCOM, CORBA, and RMI, don't have this problem because they maintain the connection throughout the application lifecycle.

Converting to and from XML

Conversion to and from XML during the communication process is another performance consideration that must be taken into account with web services. Depending on how complex your data is and how much of it there is, the time taken for this conversion can become a serious issue. This overhead isn't too bad when you consider a simple string or number to be encoded. Binary data, such as images, tend to be much larger and take a lot longer to convert. XML tends to take more bytes (by an average of fivefold) to encode data than the equivalent binary representation. Both XML size (transfer rate) and XML marshalling can pose performance problems. Excess data due to XML tags is another disadvantage. This certainly is not as fast as transferring the image across the wire in its original format. Although this sort of time penalty occurs with other architectures such as RMI and CORBA, it can be especially bad for web services implementations.

Processing SOAP Messages

All web services communication takes place as XML messages encoded in a SOAP envelope. SOAP overheads include extracting the SOAP envelope, parsing the contained XML information, setting type information in every SOAP message, and encoding/decoding the message. SOAP overhead also results from the fact that a SOAP message itself is in XML format and needs to be parsed by a SOAP server before even the XML message or payload can be parsed.

Securing Web Services

Web services' performance is affected by the different options, such as message-level security, one-way SSL plus authorization, and Two-Way SSL, which can be used to securely access the web service. For example, Two-Way SSL can result in a 30 percent degradation in performance after it is added to the web services application to make it secure as we saw in Chapter 11, "Security of Web Services."

Identifying Performance Bottlenecks

Despite the inherent performance hits from using HTTP, XML, and SOAP, there are ways to improve the performance of a web service implementation both at the application level and at the system level. You can do this by looking at the web service application from end to end to determine the performance bottlenecks and where performance can be improved.

Factors Impacting Performance

A number of factors impact application performance. It is useful to break down performance measurements into time spent on components in different tiers, time spent marshalling and unmarshalling data sent between different tiers, and time spent on network transfers (see Table 12.1).

Table 12.1 Performance Bottlenecks in Each Tier

Layer	Performance Bottlenecks
Web services layer	SOAP parsing, security handshake
Business logic layer	EJBs, XML parsing
Back-end systems	Databases, EIS
Other	Network, garbage-collection cycles by JVM

This is a general checklist of possible system factors to measure:

- CPU usage on machines running the application
- CPU usage on the database server
- Disk and memory usage on the database server
- Memory used by WebLogic Server
- Network traffic between different tiers
- Latency times as compared to acceptable response times
- Throughput or transactions per second
- Frequency and length of garbage-collection cycles by the JVM

You can use tools that help with identifying system- and application-specific bottlenecks. One such tool is the HP OpenView Transaction Analyzer (OVTA).

HP OpenView Transaction Analyzer

OVTA helps diagnose performance bottlenecks in an application or web services. It fully supports the BEA WebLogic Server platform. It provides transaction monitoring for web and application servers. OVTA automatically tags and traces transactions from the client to the web server, from the web server to the application server, through the application logic, and out to the database. The types of transactions traced include HTTP requests, web container transactions, EJB container transactions, and database (JDBC or ADO) transactions (see Figure 12.1).

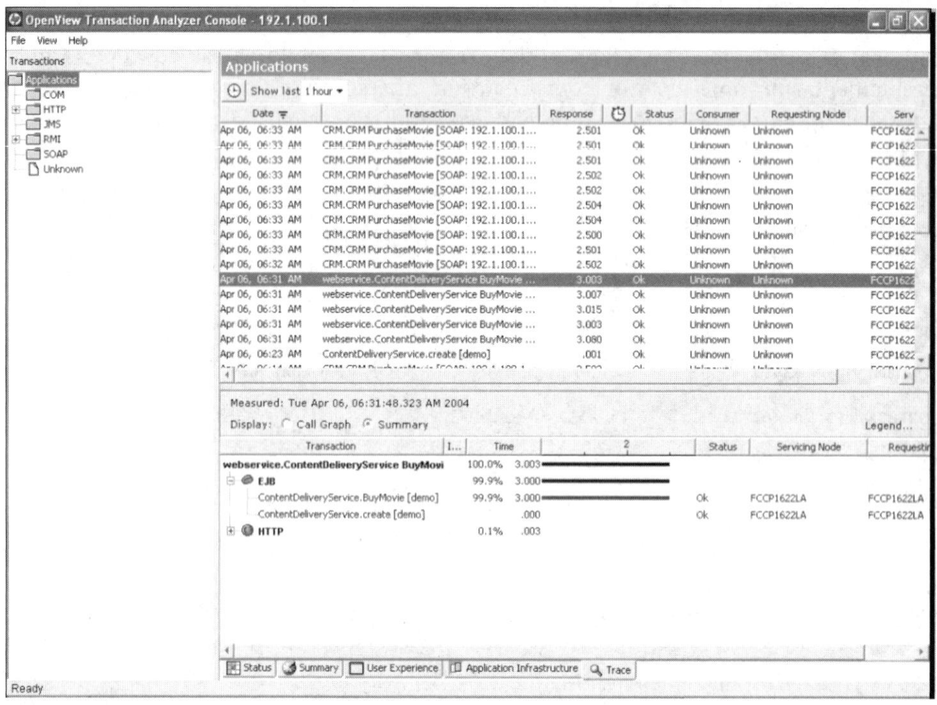

Figure 12.1 OVTA

To deliver application performance and end-to-end transaction response times, OVTA uses a tag-and-trace capability to discover, intercept, identify, monitor, and correlate all the components of the end-to-end transaction. During installation of OVTA, transaction agents, consisting of special monitoring classes and communications software, are placed on user-specified servers (called managed nodes). Then, as applications are loaded into the application server, OVTA automatically inserts the monitoring classes into the application to monitor J2EE method invocations and correlate their end-to-end behavior.

The OVTA transaction agents forward the data gathered to a measurement server, where it is saved in a database and where the entire transaction path is reconstituted using the unique transaction correlator. You can use the OVTA Console to get different representations of the transaction data collected at the time a problem was identified, from a high-level overview of the transactions for a selected web host to trace information and call graphs for a particular J2EE component.

OVTA identifies performance bottlenecks whether the problem is in the network layer, the web server and web container, the EJB layer, the JDBC layer, and so on. Either you can see from the aggregated data which particular component is over the baseline and is the cause of the problem, or you can turn on trace mode to drill down to the actual method causing the bottleneck. OVTA traces transactions across managed nodes and process boundaries, including many JVMs, load balancers, and failover servers. OVTA monitors at the byte code level, without requiring any source-code modification or recompilation or repackaging of applications.

Improving Web Service Performance

At the web service application level, you can evaluate how performance is affected by a variety of factors. The design of security for accessing the web service, design of the SOAP layer, and choice of XML parser all influence the overall performance.

SOAP Implementation Options

SOAP processing performance varies a lot based on the length and complexity of the messages exchanged. Here are some options that you should consider for your SOAP implementation.

SOAP Engines

SOAP engines with streaming XML parsers are faster because they reduce memory required to run large messages. Pull parsers are optimized for processing SOAP messages and mapping XML document components to application objects. In general, many commercial products run two to three times faster than open-source implementations. Using BEA SOAP gives better performance results than Apache Axis, an open-source SOAP implementation. The response time for the Validate Config service which we have used in the earlier chapters with the Axis SOAP engine was 0.469 seconds compared to the SOAP engine in BEA, which was 0.336 seconds which is a 72% increase in performance. When you select a SOAP engine, you need to run performance tests to simulate the requirements of your applications and establish internal benchmarks. The benchmarks should address a variety of different messages, in a variety of different configurations, and with different user load levels.

By default, WebLogic Server is configured to use the built-in parser to parse XML documents. In release 8.1, the built-in XML parser is based on Apache Xerces. You can configure your system to use another parser instead of the built-in parser through the WebLogic Console.

You can configure a new XML Registry by entering a unique Registry name in the Name field and setting the Document Builder Factory, Sax Parser Factory fields to the appropriate Factory parser classes.

For example, to use WebLogic FastParser, enter the following information:

```
Name: WebLogic FastParser
DocumentBuilderFactory:
SAXParserFactory: weblogic.xml.babel.jaxp.SAXParserFactoryImpl
TransformerFactory:
```

If you want to directly specify the Apache Xerces parser, enter this:

```
Name: Apache Xerces/Xalan Registry
DocumentBuilderFactory: org.apache.xerces.jaxp.DocumentBuilderFactoryImpl
SAXParserFactory: org.apache.xerces.jaxp.SAXParserFactoryImpl
TransformerFactory: org.apache.xalan.processor.TransformerFactoryImpl
```

After you have selected the parser, you need to fill in the options for the When to Cache list box. Here, you can specify either Cache on Reference, in which WebLogic Server caches the external entity referenced by a URL the first time the entity is referenced in an XML document; Cache at Initialization, in which WebLogic Server caches the entity when the server starts; or Cache Never, in which WebLogic Server never caches the external entity.

Finally, select the server on which you want to deploy this XML Registry.

SOAP with Attachments

SOAP with Attachments instead of document-style can lead to improved performance. This is because document-style takes more time to process than SOAP with Attachments. If there is a large payload, you might want to consider sending it as a SOAP attachment instead of sending it as an XML payload because XML conversion takes extra processing time. We can see in Table 12.2 the performance numbers for a Product Catalog web service used to deliver catalogs of HP PCs to retailers. Using SOAP with attachment is faster than using document-literal web service. But as described in Chapter 7, "Developing and Deploying Web Services," attachments might not be a good choice because of issues with interoperability. You must weigh the project requirements of interoperability and performance in making this choice.

Table 12.2 Performance Comparison Between Document-Literal and SOAP with Attachments

Transaction	Min. (sec)	Max. (sec)	Avg. (sec)
Product Catalog (document-literal)	10.5	19.27	12.65
Product Catalog (as attachment)	8.6	11.74	9.73

Simple SOAP Data Types

Using simple SOAP data types such as String, Int, Float, and NegativeInteger is better than using complex data types such as XML documents and objects. When you create and use new data types, SOAP introduces a serializer to convert the data from the XML value into a Java value and back again, which can impact performance.

XML Parser Selection

Most existing XML parsers support type checking and conversion, checking how well the XML is formed and resolving ambiguities. These activities make the parsing slower than optimal. Consider using a stripped-down XML parser that performs only essential parsing and has a small code size and memory footprint.

DOM, SAX, StAX, and JAXB are some of the commonly used XML parsers. The performance of these parsers depends on the situation.

Comparison of DOM, SAX, STAX, and JAXB

DOM-based parsers are slower than SAX-based ones. The performance of the StAX cursor model is comparable to that of SAX parsing.

SAX is the best choice for single-pass processing, efficient parsing, and validation. DOM can build a document tree quickly. JAXB is very effective for element access. Figures 12.2, 12.3, and 12.4 show performance measurements using DOM, SAX, and JAXB. Figures 12.2, 12.3, and 12.4 are from a Java One 2003 (Optimizing XML Processing for Performance, Rob Ruyak, Lalit Mathwani, Biswadeep Nag, Sun Microsystems) presentation.

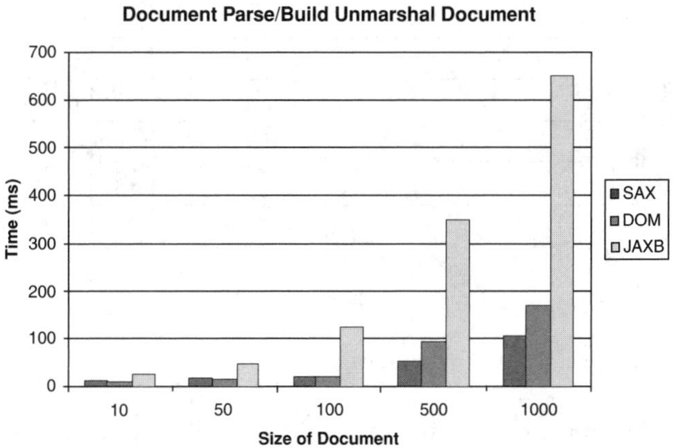

Figure 12.2 Document parse/build/unmarshal time

Figure 12.3 shows the comparison among SAX, DOM, and JAXB to parse and create an in-memory model. JAXB is the slowest.

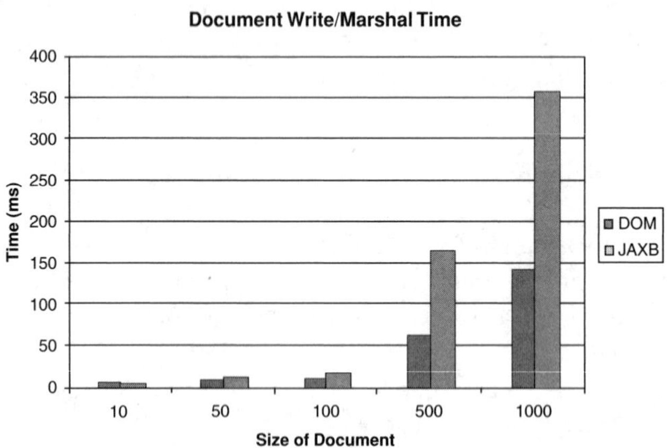

Figure 12.3 Document write/marshal time

Figure 12.3 shows the same comparison to serialize this to text form. JAXB is the slowest.

Figure 12.4 shows the time to access data elements and change them. DOM takes the most amount of time.

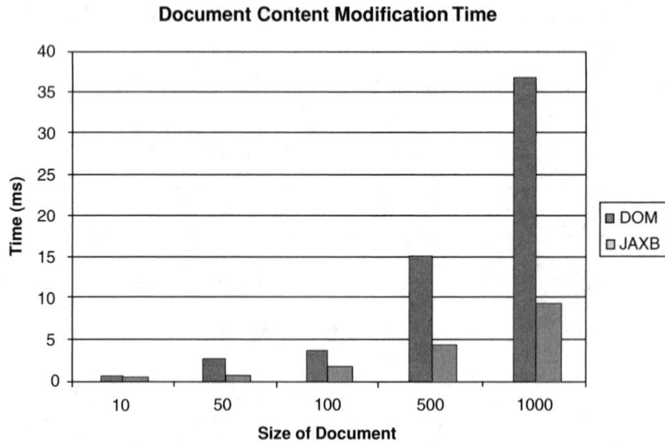

Figure 12.4 Document content-modification time

As you can see, the choice of XML parser should be made based on the specific characteristics of your web services.

Performance Enhancement with XML Beans

XML Beans, which was initiated by BEA, was designed with performance in mind. It has been submitted to the Apache open source. The XML Beans architecture provides two efficient ways to access XML information. When fine-grained access and control is required, you can use the `XMLCursor` interface to navigate the XML document and go directly to elements, attributes, and content. Alternatively, XML Beans generates Java classes from XML Schema and keeps them in synch with the underlying XML. This can be used for strongly typed documents. Compared with typical DOM parsers, XML Beans generates far fewer objects and creates them only when needed. This leads to significant performance enhancements and dramatically decreases memory consumption.

What differentiates XML Beans from other Java-binding technologies such as JAXB and Castor is the fact that XML Beans supports two synchronized XML access models, one to the underlying XML content and one to the strongly typed Java classes (see Figure 12.5).

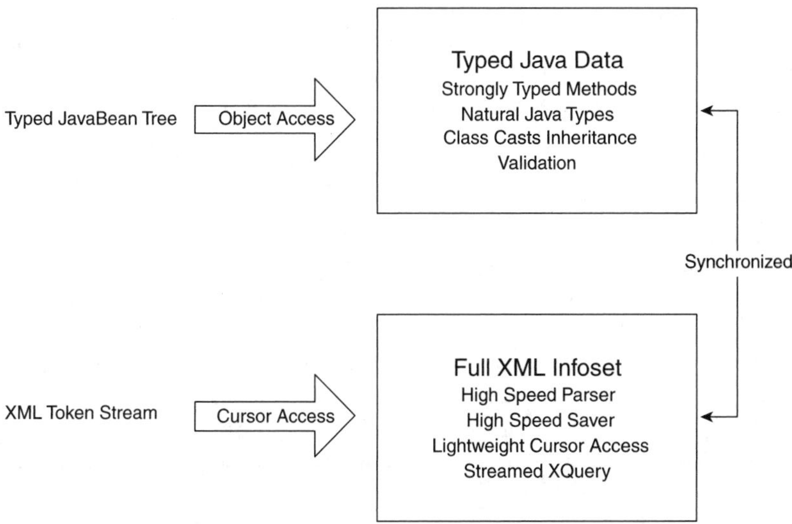

Figure 12.5 XML Beans architecture

Marshalling is incremental. If you don't touch an element of the underlying XML data, that element never gets marshaled into a Java object. Additionally, the parsing and serialization processes are fast and comparable in runtime performance to hand-parsed solution.

Table 12.3 shows the performance numbers for parsing XML payload based on the Purchase Order Example Schema described in the W3C XML Schema The performance numbers across different XML parsers were observed through internal measurements by BEA. These numbers are for general informational purposes only. These tests were done on a 2GHz Intel Xeon with 1G of RAM.

Table 12.3 Load and Read a Document: Time (Milliseconds)

	XML Data Size			
Parser	**1KB**	**10KB**	**100KB**	**1MB**
XML Beans Cursor	0.191	1.56	16.2	159
Xerces 2.3 DOM	0.302	1.88	17.9	215
XML Beans	0.302	2.64	26.4	320
JAXB 1.0 Beta	0.862	10.10	86.0	768
Castor 0.9.4.3	2.740	8.08	55.8	534

BEA has tried to make XML Beans compatible with the JAXB specification. However, JAXB does not share the design goals of 100 percent schema coverage or full preservation of XML, so XMLBeans needed to modify and expand on the standard JAXB API. BEA is working with Sun and the Java Community Process to converge JAXB and XML Beans over time through JSR 222.

XML Compression

Various compression schemes can be used with web services SOAP traffic. Compression packs the content into smaller packages and, therefore, shortens the network transmission latency. You can apply XML compression to web services application endpoints or at various intermediate nodes. Compression/decompression algorithms must be deployed at both ends of a network connection or web services interaction. Multiple algorithms exist, and the web service should negotiate the applicable algorithm for a given session or transmission. Compression tools are available from many vendors, as well as from various open-source communities.

Sending Binary Data in XML Message

XML encodings are much larger than the equivalent binary encodings. CDATA, a feature of the core XML 1.0 standard, can be used to encapsulate binary data within XML data structures. Similarly, SOAP with Attachments can point to binary data files encapsulated within the surrounding HTTP packet. Typically, you can use CDATA or SwA to pass binary data (such as an image) in the XML document, not in the SOAP message payload.

Using XMill for Large Files

XMill is a compressor for XML documents that typically can deliver large compression rates. XMill is an open-source XML compressor maintained by SourceForge.net. For large files, compression rates are twice as good as gzip's compression rate (gzip is a utility that compresses files). XMill works at the command-line level and does compression on a file-by-file basis. After compression, the file extension is changed from `.xml` to `.xmi`.

XMill is based on a grouping strategy that groups and compresses text items based on their semantics. For example, a sequence of `<Product>` elements with `<Description>`, `<Size>`, and `<features>` in an XML document could be rearranged by grouping all descriptions, all sizes, and all features together. This leads to high compression because each group contains text items with high similarities.

The items are grouped according to the parent label. In some cases, a label has different meanings in different parts of the document. For example, `<Title>` in `<Person>` has a different meaning than `<Title>` in `<Book>` or when different labels have the same meaning, like a `<ChildName>` in `<Person>` contains a person name like `<Name>`.

In XMill, each text item is reached through a path of labels from the root of the XML document. If you want to group by employee number for employees in a company, the path to the text item is /Root/Company/Employee/@employeenumber.

After the grouping is done in containers, conventional compressors, such as gzip, are applied to the containers and exploit those similarities. When the overall size of the containers reaches a certain user-specified memory window, the containers are compressed and stored in the output file. The compressed content of the memory window is called a run. After the run is stored in the output file, the containers are filled with data again.

In addition to path expression, the user can specify how to "precompress" a specific text item. XMill enables the user to specify additional "user compressors" to precompress the text items before they are stored in the containers. Note that the gzip compression is still applied to the containers afterward. XMill provides an interface for writing your own user compressors in C++.

XMill compression can be achieved in WebLogic Server by adding a filter. You can define filters in the context of a web service. A filter intercepts a request for a specific named resource and executes the code of XMill compression in the filter. When a filter intercepts a request, it has access to the `javax.servlet.ServletRequest` and `javax.servlet.ServletResponse` objects that provide access to the HTTP request and response, and a `javax.servlet.FilterChain` object. The `FilterChain` object contains the filter for the XMill compression.

XML Accelerators

XML accelerators offload XML processing from application servers and web servers. The benefits of XML accelerators are faster response times and lower project costs. The contents of incoming XML messages are examined and matched against user-defined patterns. XML documents matching a specific pattern can be sent to a corresponding server for further processing, while those matching another pattern can be "redirected" to another server. This lets application developers and network administrators exercise tight control over which transactions are processed on which servers.

Before you configure the XML accelerator for XML operations, you should determine which of the several common formats or varieties of XML will be used in the client application; which XML elements, attributes, or text and HTTP fulfillment locations contained or identified in the anticipated XML traffic should be used for XML pattern matching; and which servers will be assigned the XML patterns that you create.

HP E-Commerce/XML Accelerator

HP offers an E-Commerce/XML Accelerator SA 7150 that manages XML traffic using XML patterns, pairs of URI expressions and XML expressions. URI expressions serve as "coarse" filters, allowing the system to determine whether an HTTP `POST` request is targeted at an XML-enabled server. If no URI match is found, the XML accelerator does not bother to examine the document for XML content; it simply passes the document to the mapped server—that is, the one with the IP address and network port of the incoming message. XML expressions are the "fine" filters—those to be applied to the content and context of the XML data embedded in the HTTP `POST` request. XML patterns are assigned to servers identified by IP address and server port. When a match between a pattern and an incoming request occurs, the XML accelerator sends data to the appropriate server.

Multiple XML accelerators can be connected in a series, or cascaded, to multiply your site's XML processing and availability capabilities. HP's XML accelerator uses XPath syntax. It works with any XML application that supports XML 1.0 and that is transported via HTTP or HTTPS `POST` request methods. You can purchase these XML accelerators from HP's website.

SSL Accelerators

SSL encryption and decryption can use a lot of processor overhead, limiting a web server to as few as 5 or 10 SSL transactions per second. When using SSL for security, you can increase a web service's performance by offloading SSL processing from the server to a specialized coprocessor. Hardware implementation of SSL encryption and decryption is significantly faster than a software implementation.

The factors that influence the choice of SSL accelerator are whether you have a single web server or a web farm, and whether you already have load balancing or you need it as part of the SSL accelerator setup and cost.

Three devices that are representative of the most common methods of doing this are the nCipher nFast 800 SSL Accelerator PCI card or AXL300 Accelerator PCI card from HP, the Radware CertainT 100 SSL Accelerator 800 appliance, and the BIG-IP 5000 IP application switch, a Layer 7 load-balancing switch with SSL acceleration capabilities. All three products are accelerators in the sense that they take over processing of SSL traffic. In terms of SSL functionality, they're actually in-line processors that handle SSL encryption and decryption. They examine all traffic, decrypt HTTPS traffic, and typically leave the rest alone.

Each of these products has its place, and only one is likely to be appropriate for a given network. Nevertheless, all have approximately the same level of performance in terms of SSL encryption and decryption—between 750 and 840 SSL handshake transactions per second. If you have a single web server, you'll need the nFast or AXL300 Accelerator PCI card from HP. The AXL300 adds a dedicated coprocessor to a ProLiant Server, offloading cycle-consuming cryptographic processing. Up to eight cards in a single SSL-secured server provide linear, scalable performance. If you've already implemented a web farm, the CertainT is an appliance that sits in front of a load-balancing device, decrypting incoming traffic and encrypting outgoing traffic. If you plan to upgrade to a web farm but haven't set up the infrastructure yet, the BIG-IP can provide load balancing and SSL acceleration, as well as several other functions.

Performance Tips

Repeated SOAP client calls to access server state can choke a network and degrade the server performance. It is best to cache data on the client side whenever possible, to avoid requests to the server. Ensure that the client data remains up-to-date by using a call to a server service that blocks until data is changed.

Stay away from using XML messaging to do fine-grained RPC (for example, a service that returns a single stock quote). When the transport is slow and/or unreliable, or the processing is complex and/or long-running, consider an asynchronous messaging model. Cache the WSDL in a centralized database and periodically check for newer versions; also cache schema definitions for scalability.

XML caching can also be used to save performance. By analyzing requests against a cache, you might be able to identify whether this request has been seen before so that you can just send a cached response instead of processing the transaction.

Improving the Business Logic Layer and Database Performance

To improve the overall performance of a web service, it is critical to look at J2EE components in the business logic layer and also the back-end systems such as databases. You can improve the performance in different ways. This section cover the most relevant ones: J2EE patterns and tuning EJBs and databases.

Leveraging Patterns

Performance improvement can be achieved by patterns in J2EE. The Service Locator, Session Facade, Value List Handler, and Data Access Object patterns are some of the patterns used in web services to improve performance.

Service Locator

To access different resources such as `EJBHome` objects, `DataSource` objects, JMS `ConnectionFactory`, and JMS Topic/Queue, the J2EE specification mandates the use of JNDI.

An EJB client needs to initially get the `EJBHome` object from JNDI to manage the lifecycle of `EJBObjects`. JMS clients need to get the ConnectionFactory and Topic/Queue from JNDI for processing messages. JDBC clients need to get a `DataSource` object to get a database connection. JNDI lookup process is expensive because clients such as web services servlets need to get a network connection to the JNDI server. If the JNDI server is located on a different machine and you need to go through a lookup process every time for each of the different resources, it can be redundant and expensive. Figure 12.6 shows the JNDI lookup process.

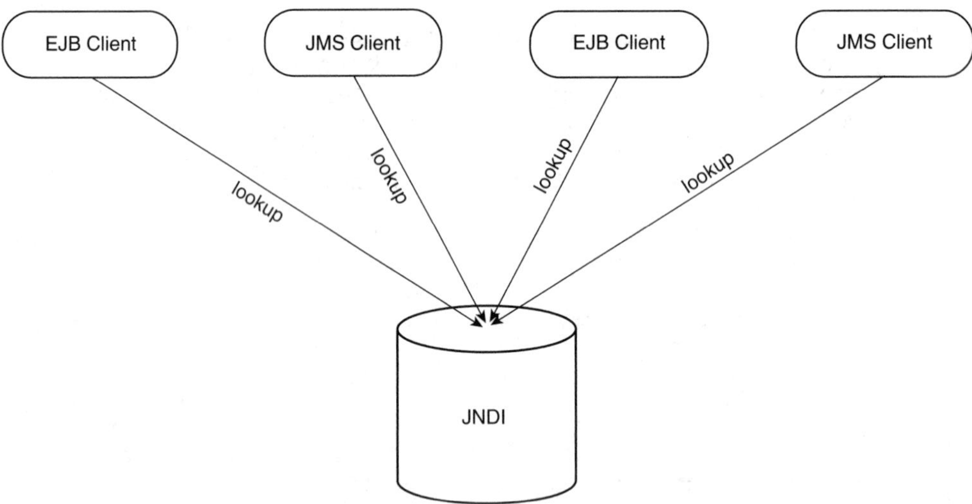

Figure 12.6 JNDI lookup process

You can use the Service Locator pattern, which has a class to cache service objects, methods for JNDI lookup, and methods for getting service objects from the cache. When the first JNDI lookup is done, it can be cached for later lookups. This technique reduces redundant and expensive JNDI lookup processes, thus increasing performance significantly. Figure 12.7 shows the `ServiceLocator` class intercepting the client request and accessing JNDI only once for a service object.

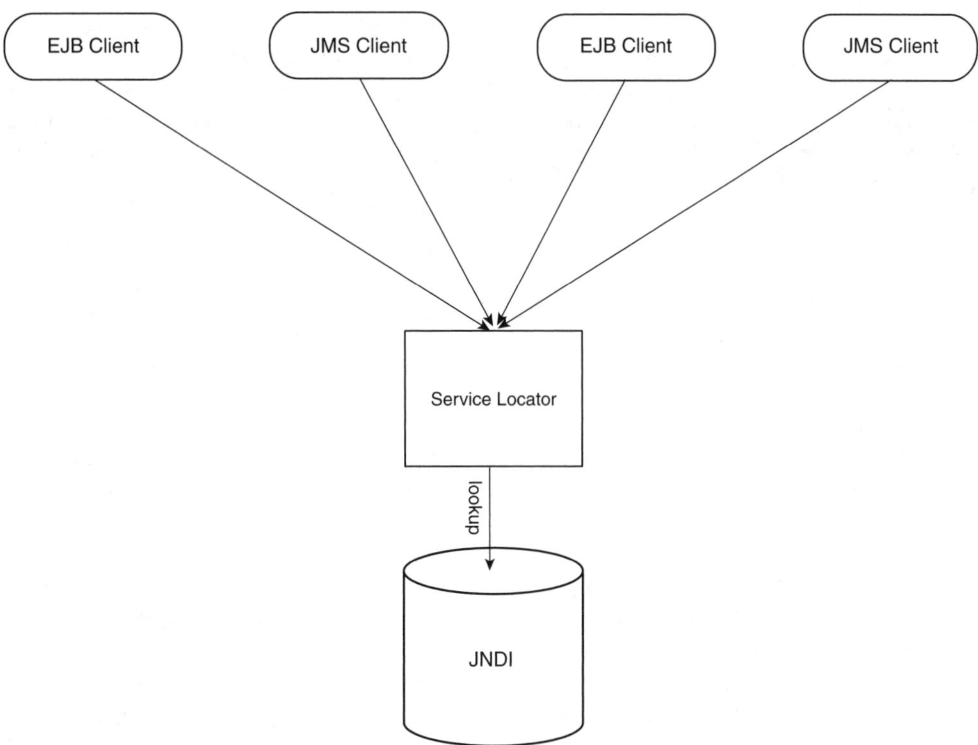

Figure 12.7 Service Locator pattern

Session Facade

EJB clients, such as web services servlets, can access entity beans directly. This takes more network calls and imposes network overhead. Figure 12.8 illustrates this process. The web service servlet calls multiple entity beans directly to accomplish a business process, thereby increasing the number of network calls.

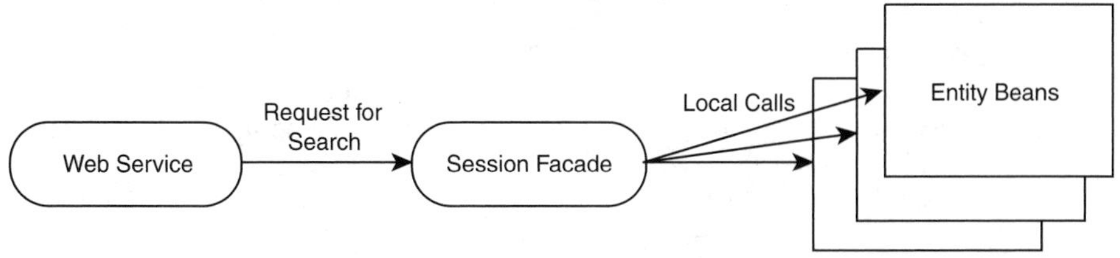

Figure 12.8 Entity bean calls

You can wrap entity beans with a session facade to decrease the network traffic of web services to entity beans. To accomplish a business process, a coarse-grained method call can be made from the web service to the session facade. In this approach, to process a business method, instead of fine-grained calls being placed to entity beans, a coarse-grained method calls the session facade, which, in turn, calls the entity beans to process the client request (see Figure 12.9).

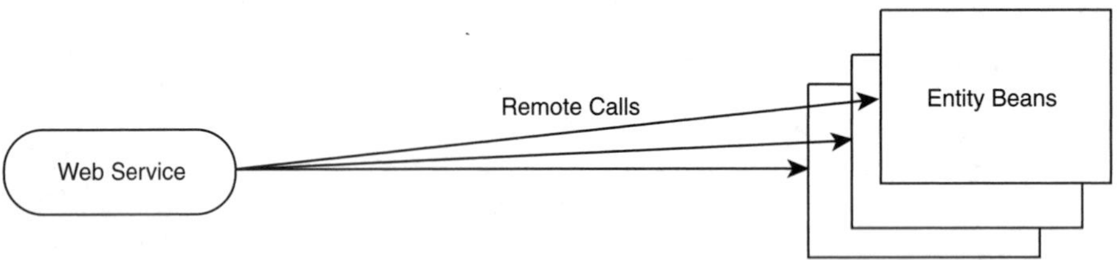

Figure 12.9 Session Facade pattern

The first important benefit of the Session Facade pattern is that the web service has a simpler interface to the entity beans and is abstracted from the details of which entity beans it needs to connect to. The second important benefit of the Session Facade pattern is that it improves performance because calls from the session bean to the entity beans are local to the EJB container. Performance can be further enhanced through the use of local interfaces, introduced as part of the EJB specification, version 2.0. Local interfaces provide support for lightweight access from within the EJB container, avoiding the overhead associated with a remote interface.

You need to use the Session Facade pattern in conjunction with the Data Transfer Object and Version Number patterns. The Data Transfer Object pattern provides a means of transferring serializable information from one or more entities behind the session facade to other components outside of the EJB container. When a change is requested to the information within it, the version number for instances is used to check for old data transfer objects. The component always ensures that the value of the version number matches the version number for the entity to be modified.

Value List Handler and Data Access Object Patterns

When web services are used to search large amounts of data and retrieve results, the client takes a long time to retrieve that data and use entity beans to search the data. This has an impact on performance largely because, by nature, EJB has overhead when compared to normal Java objects. Figure 12.10 illustrates this process.

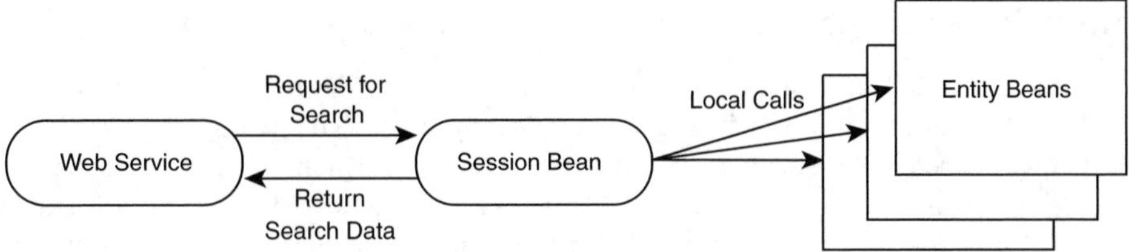

Figure 12.10 Search process

You can reduce overhead due to entity beans and huge data by using Data Access Objects (DAO) instead of entity beans and the Value List Handler pattern to cache a list of `Value` objects that are retrieved through the DAO. When a client wants to search data, it calls Value List Handler, which, in turn, is responsible for caching the data and returning it to the client iteratively. Figure 12.11 illustrates how the Value List Handler intercepts a client search request and returns data iteratively.

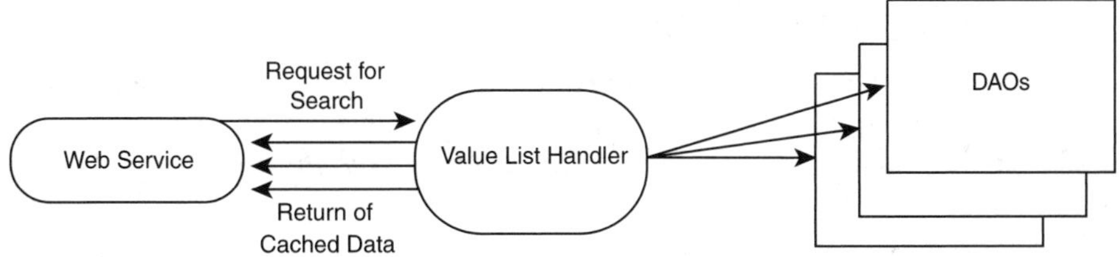

Figure 12.11 Value List Handler and Data Access Object pattern

The DAO manages the connection with the data source to obtain and store data. The data source can be a persistent store such as an RDBMS, an external service such as a B2B exchange, or a repository such as an LDAP database. The DAO completely hides the data source implementation details from its clients. DAO provides a simplified interface for performing complex JDBC operations and for encapsulating data-access logic. This improves the performance of transactions with the sources of data.

Tuning EJBs

You can improve the performance of web services that use EJBs for providing business logic by using some of the patterns described in the earlier section. WebLogic Server provides ways to tune EJBs that will yield additional improvement in performance. The use of container-managed persistence (CMP) rather than bean-managed persistence (BMP) can help utilize the built-in performance-optimization facilities.

Setting EJB Pool Size for Session and Message-Driven Beans

When EJBs are created, an instance of the session bean is created and given an identity. When the EJB client, such as a web service, removes a bean, the bean instance is placed in the free pool. When a subsequent bean is created, it reuses a previous instance that is in the free pool. WebLogic Server maintains a free pool of EJBs for every stateless session bean class. The `max-beans-in-free-pool` element of the `weblogic-ejb-jar.xml` file defines the size of this pool. Use the default setting `max-beans-in-free-pool` element for the best performance for stateless session and message beans because it enables you to run beans in parallel, using as many threads as possible.

You can specify a value for `initial-beans-in-free-pool`. WebLogic Server then populates the free pool with the specified number of stateless session bean instances at startup. This improves the initial response time for the EJB because initial requests for the bean can be satisfied without generating a new instance, `initial-beans-in-free-pool` defaults to `0` if the element is not defined.

Setting Caching Size for Stateful Session and Entity Beans

Use the `setSessionContext()` or `ejbCreate()` methods to cache bean-specific resources. Release acquired resources in the `ejbRemove()` method. Allow stateful session beans to be removed from the container cache by explicitly using the `remove()` method in the client.

Activation and Passivation of Stateful Session EJBs

Passivation is the transfer of an EJB instance from memory to secondary storage. The EJB container performs passivation when the cache becomes full. When the EJB session object is needed again, the bean is activated by the container. Activation is the transfer of an EJB instance from secondary storage to memory. Set the appropriate cache size with the `max-beans-in-cache` element to avoid excessive passivation and activation. Tuning `max-beans-in-cache` too high consumes memory unnecessarily.

Configuring the Deployment Descriptor

Declare nontransactional methods of session beans with the `Not Supported` or `Never` transaction attributes in the `ejb-jar.xml` deployment descriptor file. Transactions should span the minimum time possible because transactions lock database rows. Set the transaction timeout in the `ejb-jar.xml` deployment descriptor file. You can set the `trans-timeout-seconds` in the transaction descriptor of the `weblogic-ejb-jar.xml` deployment descriptor file:

```
<transaction-descriptor>
    <trans-timeout-seconds>20</trans-timeout-seconds>
</transaction-descriptor>
```

Tuning the Database

You can tune the database in different ways to achieve better performance.

Deferring Database Locking

WebLogic Server supports few locking mechanisms: database, optimistic, and exclusive locking mechanisms. The default and recommended mechanism for EJB 1.1 and EJB 2.0 is database locking, which improves concurrent access to entity EJBs. The WebLogic Server container improves concurrent access by deferring locking services to the underlying database. Unlike exclusive locking, with database locking, the underlying data store can provide finer granularity for locking EJB data, in most cases, and can provide deadlock detection.

Tune the Connection Pool Size

You should tune the connection pool size to minimize the creation and destruction of database connections. When using a JDBC connection pool, modify `DriverName`. Set `InitialCapacity` to equal the `MaxCapacity` value. Set the `MaxCapacity` value to at least equal the `ThreadCount` value and then, if necessary, increase it again until you find the right number.

Tuning the JVM

After you tune the application, tuning the Java Virtual Machine (JVM) can result in one of the biggest boosts in overall performance. The performance of JVMs can vary across vendors as well as between minor versions of the JVM from the same vendor. To test the relative merits of different JVMs, it is a good idea to benchmark your application against different JVMs. The performance of JVMs can also vary between different operating systems and hardware. Therefore, benchmarks and performance tuning should be done on the same hardware and software on which you expect to deploy the application.

You can use HPjmeter, from Hewlett-Packard, to do performance diagnostics on the JVM. It runs on HP-UX, Solaris, Windows, and Linux platforms. You can download this free utility from www.hpjmeter.com. Coupled with the standard profiling interfaces available in the Java Virtual Machines, HPjmeter visually displays the internal performance of your Java application. Quick data collection and display make iterative application performance improvements fast. HPjmeter features include CPU time; clock time, including a list or call tree; process or thread; call count; object creation; heap heuristic memory leak detection; thread-based metrics; and program heuristics.

When using WebLogic Server, you might want to consider JRockit as the JVM; it provides optimal running performance for applications and web services developed in WebLogic Server. JRockit is optimized for Intel architectures—especially the 32- and 64-bit Itanium. Four garbage-collection modes allow for optimal memory management. High-performance threading allows Java optimized thread scheduling, switching, and synchronization to run more threads at higher speeds. The management console enables real-time monitoring, management, and fine-tuning of applications.

Summary

Performance of web services is important, especially in B2B implementations. Several inherent factors constrain the performance of web services, such as creating and terminating HTTP connections, converting to and from XML, processing SOAP messages, and securing web services. Despite the inherent performance hits, there are ways to improve the performance at both the application and system levels. Tools such as HP's OpenView Transaction Analyzer help with determining the performance bottlenecks at each web service tier, as well as the system factors such as CPU, disk, memory usage, and network traffic.

SOAP performance can be improved by using SOAP engines with streaming XML parsers, attachments instead of document-style, and simple data types. XML performance can be improved by choosing the right XML parser among DOM, StAX, SAX, JAXB, and XML Beans, depending on the specific characteristics of your web services. XML compression and XML accelerators offer two additional ways of improving XML performance.

Performance improvement can be achieved by using patterns in J2EE. The Service Locator pattern uses caching to speed up JNDI lookups. By using the Session Facade pattern, you can decrease the network traffic of web services to entity beans. You can reduce overhead due to entity beans and large datasets by using Data Access Objects (DAO) and the Value List Handler pattern to cache a list of `Value` objects retrieved through DAO. WebLogic Server provides ways to tune EJBs and databases for higher performance. Tuning the JVM can result in one of the biggest boosts in the overall performance.

13
Testing of Web Services

In this chapter, you will learn about the unique requirements of testing web services and how you must extend current traditional testing methods to test web services. This chapter discusses how to build a comprehensive test suite that covers unit, functional, integration, interoperability, regression, performance, load, and stress testing. Automated tools can be used very effectively to test web services. This chapter provides an introduction to some performance tools such as Empirix e-TEST and e-load, and HP OpenView Internet Services.

Approach to Web Services Testing

After you have developed the web services, you need to test them before deploying to the production environment. Testing web services is similar to testing applications, but with some key differences. You must build on top of traditional testing methods to address the unique attributes of a web services solution built on an SOA. You first must understand the differences that need to be addressed, know the extensions that you have to make to current testing methods, and use certain tools to help in your testing efforts.

Differences from Traditional Testing

Before delving into web services testing concepts, it's important to explore the unique aspects of web services that pose a challenge when you try to apply traditional testing models. Three key aspects to web services used in an SOA are worthy of mention.

First, a web services–based architecture results in a distributed, loosely coupled system with dependent stakeholders. Although this architecture holds great benefit in terms of scalability and extensibility of the system, it presents a great challenge for the tester. No longer is each component of the system necessarily constructed and deployed by a single corporate entity. The overall system might actually be derived from components that are constructed, tested, and hosted by multiple stakeholders. As such, it is difficult to establish consistent code quality, availability, and quality of service (QoS) across these entities.

Second, validation of end-to-end transactions is significantly more difficult in the SOA system because of the difficulty in tracking message routes through intermediaries. Yet, without the capability to monitor and validate effectively, it would not be possible to tune, debug, and optimize the system.

The third difference in the web services solution is that it provides a standards-based, service-driven model to integration. Whereas earlier object technologies such as CORBA provided facilities for building distributed architectures, they did so via complex programmatic interfaces. With web services, standards for data format (XML), communication (SOAP), and the programmatic interface (WSDL) are data driven and share a common XML-based foundation. Traditional testing tools must evolve to fully support these standards for effective testing to occur.

The use of web services standards has other implications for current testing tools. Web services–based integration highlights the importance of validating interface points and message formats instead of simply testing at the graphical user interface level. Using testing tools that utilize GUI-driven automation is simply inadequate for a web services project. The biggest challenge to testing your web services is that there is no user interface, so all the testing must be accomplished programmatically. Your strategy should be to develop a test suite, or set of tests, that can be run both automatically and by nondevelopment testing personnel.

Testing for interoperability also differentiates web services from the testing of web applications. WS-I Basic Profile gives recommendations for web services to be interoperable. Testing tools need to have the capability to check the compliance of web services against the WS-I Basic Profile.

Business processes might involve a human factor as well, which must be accounted for during testing. These processes also support asynchronous web services. Testing should cover human factor testing in addition to testing synchronous and asynchronous transactions.

Extending Current Testing Methods

Based on this discussion of the differences in web services testing, it is reasonable to assume that current testing methodologies should be extended to support the use of web services in an SOA solution. Here are a few key practices to consider as part of this extended model.

Establish Service-Level Agreements (SLA)

The interenterprise SOA system spans multiple stakeholders and intermediaries. Hence, it is important to establish service levels such as high-availability metrics, web service response times, and security policies upfront, during the requirements phase. After they have been established, these service levels should be incorporated into test plans. Doing so proactively is not only politically expedient when dealing with multiple stakeholders, but it also is less costly from a development standpoint.

Perform Component-Level Validation and Benchmarking

Establishing the SLAs upfront facilitates the capability to perform component-level testing. Instead of benchmarking the service level of the overall system when integrated, strive to perform testing of the individual web service components before integration to ensure that they meet acceptable parameters.

Mandate Stress Testing

When dealing with a distributed system with multiple intermediaries, it is important to perform stress/load testing in a predeployment mode. Testing should be performed for steady stream throughput and for peak traffic.

Extend Test Scenarios to Address Web Services Functions

Test cases need to be extended to support the web services paradigm and its accompanying functionality. This includes testing for SOAP message format validation; the publish, bind, and find functionality; service location independence; validation of interfaces as defined in WSDL; and testing for interoperability between SOAP platforms.

Invest in Testing Tools

Because web services are programmatic interfaces to functionality, they are good candidates for automated testing tools. Developers can quickly simulate thousands of virtual users accessing the web service under different system conditions. Things to look for in a testing tool include the following attributes:

- **Performance testing**—This involves the capability to measure the performance and scalability of a web service. A good testing tool can help find performance bottlenecks. This includes the capability to test that the web services functionality is executed and is accurate and valid even under high load.
- **Autogeneration**—This involves the capability to generate different combinations of input and different test scenarios randomly. This can help with regression testing as well.
- **WSDL support**—This refers to the capability to automatically generate a set of starting test cases based on the data types, methods, and operations defined within a WSDL.
- **Build integration**—The concept of continuous integration implies that you should build, deploy, and test as often as possible. To do this, the testing tool must be capable of being run both inside an environment and as a standalone process from the command line. Developers and testers must be able to execute a single command-line script to run through the test cases. For example, with a non-GUI build solution, you could integrate testing with Ant.

- **Use as proxy server**—A proxy server is a server that in some way evaluates, filters, modifies, or otherwise interjects some function between two end-user programs. This feature is useful when requests from clients to services need to be viewed and verified. One use of this approach is as a security filter for testing security. You can establish and verify specific patterns contained in the SOAP message. As messages are sent from a client, use the proxy server to check for consistencies and send the messages on to the appropriate service. If a message is inconsistent with the established pattern, a SOAP fault is returned to the client, thereby ensuring security across the service.

  Another use of a proxy server is during integration testing as a translator of a web service between multiple endpoints. Each endpoint might require different forms of an XML message. Use the proxy server to receive a client request, translate that request into different messages using XSLT, and then deliver each message to the corresponding endpoint. Certain vendors offer proxy server testing. Proxies can also be used to host a web services management broker, which can intercept web service messages and help to manage them in production.

Other factors to look for include interoperability tests, GUI support for XML editing, load-testing capability, and code profiling. Several vendors already offer web services testing tools that include some or all of these features. For example, Empirix has a set of testing and monitoring tools, including FirstACT, an automatic test-case generator. Another testing tool, Parasoft SOAPtest, is an automated intermodule testing tool that emulates both the SOAP client and the SOAP server and allows early module testing. Testing tools for interoperability are Web Service Monitor and Web Service Profile Analyzer from WS-I group.

Building Your Test Suite

The test suite consists of all the different testing that must be done for web services. The testing lifecycle consists of the following phases of testing (see Figure 13.1):

- Unit testing generally is done by the development team.
- Functional testing tests the web services in functional units. Examples of functional units are the XML parsing and the business logic.
- Integration testing is very critical for B2B-based web services. This is testing from the partner's client invoking the web service to your SOAP engine to the business logic and any interfaces to legacy/ERP applications.
- Interoperability testing is an important part of integration testing.
- Performance testing is extremely important for web services. This is one of the critical problems plaguing the adoption of web services.
- Finally, regression testing ensures that the functionality being introduced does not affect functionality already in production.

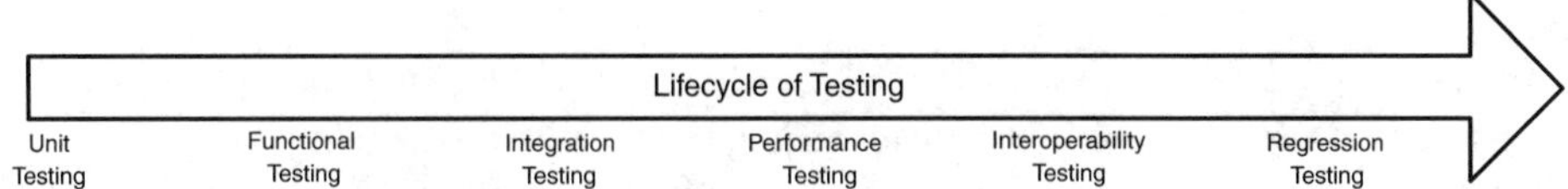

Figure 13.1 Lifecycle of testing a web service

Test View in WebLogic Workshop

After you have developed your web service in WebLogic Workshop and when you want to do a quick test to see if the web service works, WebLogic Workshop provides a test environment, called test view, for the web services you develop.

Test view provides a way for you to invoke a web service's methods from a browser and view the XML messages that are exchanged. Test view keeps a log of activity while testing a web service so that you can examine the details of the interaction between the client and the web service at any point.

Test view can be reached directly via the Start or Start with Debug actions in WebLogic Workshop's user interface. You also can enter test view directly by entering the URL of your web service in the address bar of a browser. See Figure 13.2.

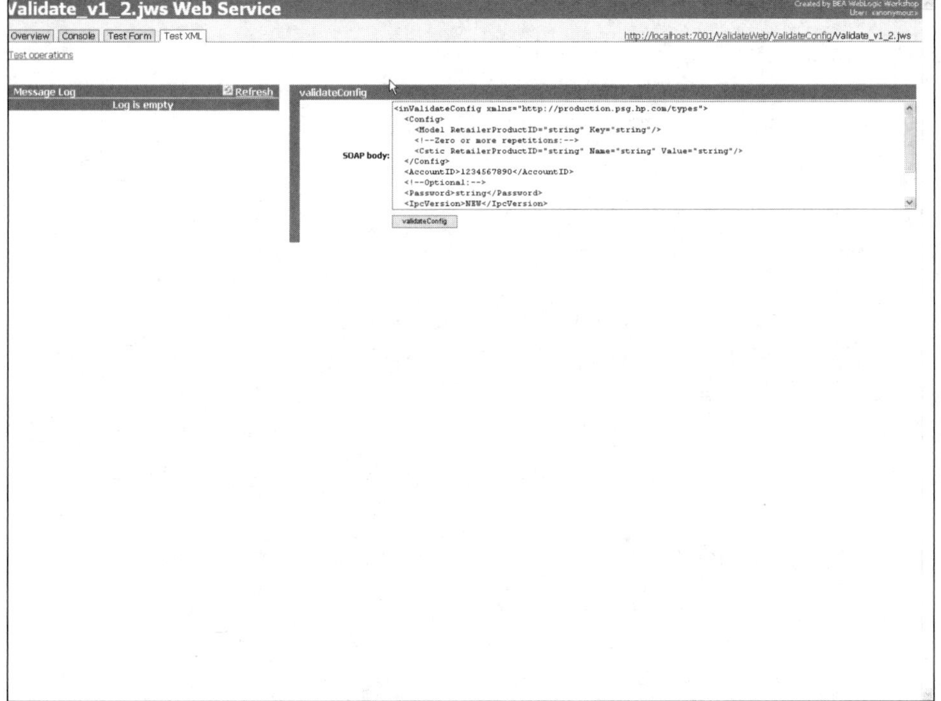

Figure 13.2 Test view in WebLogic Workshop

Unit Testing

Unit testing involves the development team testing the code before handing it over to the testing team. This type of testing generally tests a block of functionality, such as a Java class, instead of how different blocks of functionality work with each other. The tests are intended to test every aspect of the class that could conceivably not work.

A popular unit-testing tool is JUnit, an open-source Java testing framework used to write and run repeatable tests. JUnit brings synergy between coding and testing, enabling the programmer to write new code when a test is failing. Using JUnit, you can write quality code faster.

You should run your tests every time you run the compiler. The compiler tests the syntax of the code, and the tests validate the integrity of the code. JUnit tests can be run automatically and give simple and immediate visual feedback as to whether the tests passed or failed. JUnit tests can be organized into test suites containing test cases. The composite behavior of JUnit tests enables you to assemble collections of tests and automatically conduct regression testing using the entire test suite. To run a simple test in JUnit, first create a subclass of `TestCase`:

```
package junitfaq;

import java.util.*;
import junit.framework.*;

public class UnitTest extends TestCase {

    public UnitTest(String name) {
        super(name);
}
```

Next, write a test method to assert expected results on the object under test:

```
public void testEmptyCollection() {
        Collection collection = new ArrayList();
        assertTrue(collection.isEmpty());
   }
```

Write a `suite()` method that uses reflection to dynamically create a test suite containing all the `testXXX()` methods:

```
public static Test suite() {
        return new UnitTestSuite(UnitTest.class);
    }
```

Write a `main()` method to conveniently run the test with the textual test runner:

```
public static void main(String args[]) {
        junit.textui.TestRunner.run(suite());
    }
}
```

To run the test with the textual test runner used in `main()`, type the following command:

```
java junitfaq.SimpleTest
```

The passing test results in the following textual output are displayed:

```
Time: 0
OK (1 tests)
```

To run the test with the graphical test runner, type the following command:

```
java junit.swingui.TestRunner junitfaq.SimpleTest
```

The passing test results in a green bar are displayed in the graphical UI.

Functional Testing

This type of testing ensures that the functionality of the web service is as expected. Is the business logic handled correctly? Does your web service implement security and authentication as it is meant to? Does your web service support all the communications protocols it is meant to? Because your web service can be accessed by clients that you can't control, what happens if those clients make requests that you aren't expecting? Bounds testing and error checking are especially important.

Server functional testing ensures that the server delivers appropriate responses for the given requests. However, due to the complexity of web services, this task is far from simple. With most web services, it is impossible to anticipate exactly what types of requests clients will send. Enumerating all possible requests is not feasible because the space of possible inputs is either unbounded or intractably large. As a result, it is important to verify that the server can handle a wide range of request types and parameters.

Testing Tools: SOAPtest and Empirix e-Tester

Testing tools make this task easier. For example, you can use Parasoft's SOAPtest and Empirix's e-Tester to test the functionality of a web service server. They facilitate server testing by automatically creating a test suite from a WSDL document or SOAP message for the service you want to test. When you click the Run Tests button, a suite of test cases covering all possible methods is created and executed. With SOAPtest or Empirix, you can also direct the tool to an external database or spreadsheet to "feed" the input for functional testing of the service. SOAPtest and e-TEST can be used for web services developed in Workshop.

Testing Your Web Service Using SOAPtest

Client testing verifies that the client can correctly send a request and that the client behaves correctly when it receives a response. SOAPtest provides a web service deployment feature that lets your workstation function as the server in your client/server relationship. SOAPtest can emulate a server based on new or already-deployed web services, letting you test client functionality and emulate server-supplied responses. Emulating the server is especially useful when the server is still being implemented, when it has bugs, or when it should not be accessed during testing.

Testing Your Web Service with Empirix's e-Tester

Here, you learn how to test the `validateConfig` web service in e-TEST by supplying a `validateConfig` SOAP message. Here are the steps you need to follow:

1. Build a script to run the test by simulating the test. Open e-Tester to create a new script, as shown in Figure 13.3. For `validateConfig`, select the second radio button, Provide a Raw HTTP Request Header and Let e-Tester Build My Navigation. Load the `validateConfig` input file. The box shown in Figure 13.4 should appear populated with the information from your input file. You can change the URL to `https` if you want to test with SSL. Save this script.

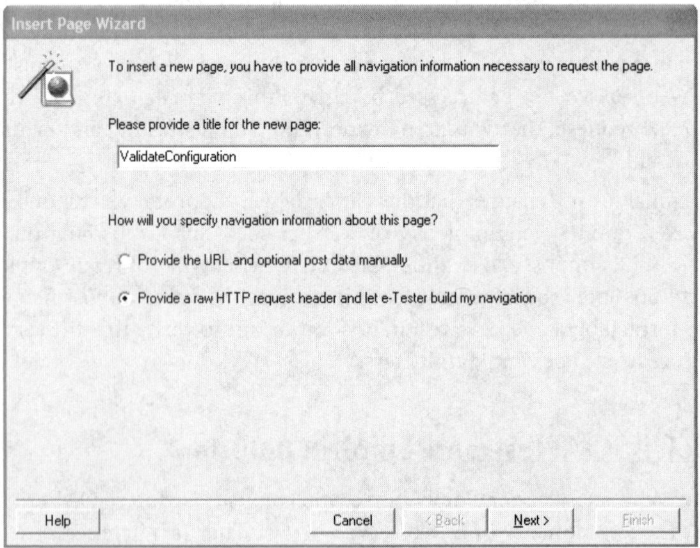

Figure 13.3 Create a new script

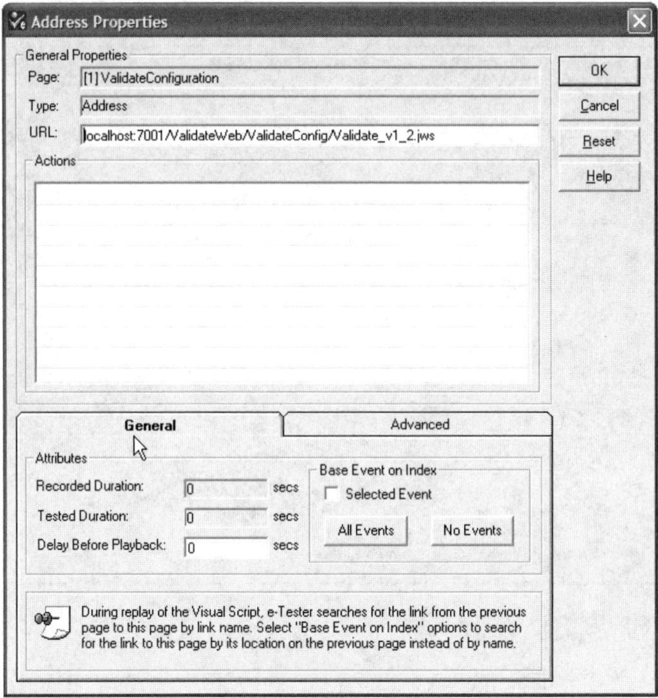

Figure 13.4 Information from the input file

2. To set up SSL certificates, go to the Authentication Manager and set it up as shown in Figure 13.5.
3. Supply e-TEST with a file with all the values for the test. You can supply e-TEST with values of different files for `validateConfig` and their corresponding SSL certificates by entering this data into an Excel sheet and saving as a CVS file. This file can be uploaded in e-TEST, as shown in Figure 13.6.
4. Run the test. You can iterate through the scripts by running the script. It will run through all the values and give you a result. The output shows the time taken for each iteration, the result of the test, and any comments.

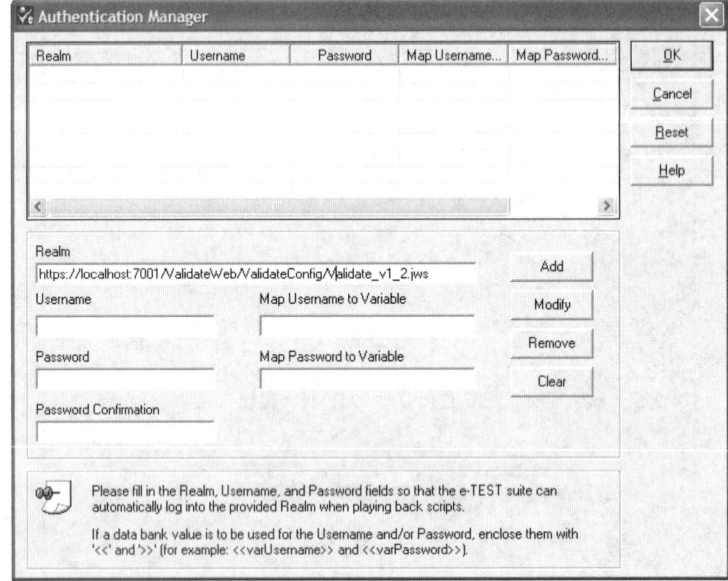

Figure 13.5 Set up SSL certificates

Integration Testing

Integration testing is testing from the real client intranet or Internet. The purpose of integration testing is to test the whole cycle of the web service with the business logic. Testing should be done between the partners. The testing scenarios should go through the total flow: The partner client requests the web service and the web service executes, along with the business logic and connection to any back-end system. Test scripts must be written to test all the possible test scenarios, including positive and negative scenarios. Table 13-1 shows examples of test scripts for the `placeOrder` web service flow.

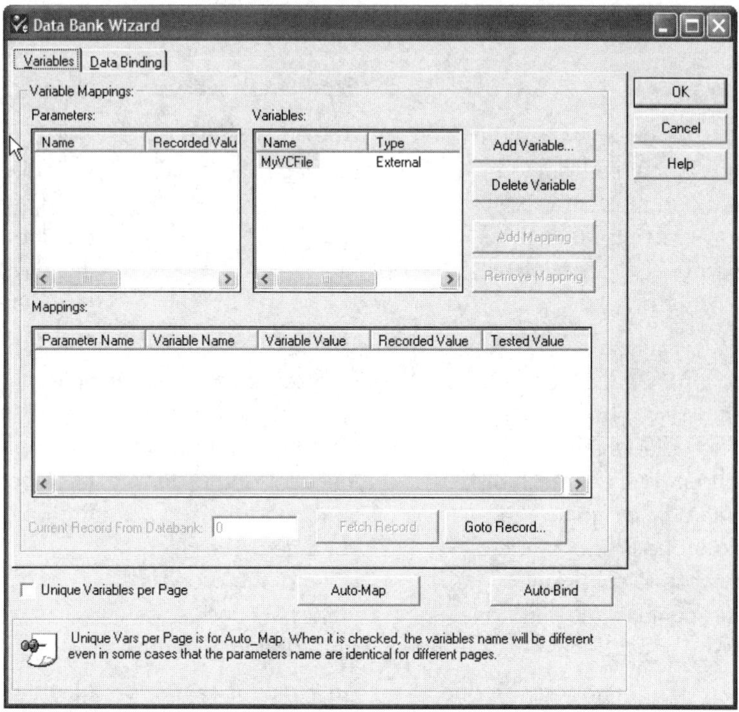

Figure 13.6 Input of CVS file to e-Test

Table 13.1 Example of Test Scripts for `placeOrder` Web Service

Step	Description	Expected Results	Notes
1	The `placeOrder` web service receives the file from the client and parses the XML file to create an `Order` object (which contains all the order data).	An `Order` object is created.	This is not a validation point for testing, but you can look for files in this directory (troubleshooting).
2	The `placeOrder` web service invokes the `validateConfig` web service. This web service checks the order configuration details in the `Order` object against the data in the Product Catalog database to confirm that the order contents meet the rules in Web Logic Server.	The `validateConfig` web service (against the Product Catalog database) is invoked, and order configuration is validated. The rules are that the order is valid only under prescribed conditions.	This is not a validation point for testing, but you can look for files in this directory (troubleshooting).
3	If the order configuration does not meet any of the configuration rules, an e-mail is generated and sent to Business Operations team.	An e-mail is sent and received by the Business Operations team.	Negative testing on this is not necessary.
4	If the order is a duplicate (check is on the PO#), an e-mail is generated and sent to the Business Operations team.	An e-mail is sent and received by the Business Operations team.	
5	For all orders except duplicates, the `placeOrder` web service calls the SAP Java Connector (jCO). The jCO triggers the BAPI table parameters to be imported, which, in turn, allows the order object to be mapped to the BAPI table parameters. This then invokes a Remote Function Call from the WLS to trigger an SAP program to accept the data from the WLS and map it to an IDOC template to create the IDOC.	IDOC (Intermediary document) is created in SAP.	

Step	Step Description	Expected Results	Notes
6	The IDOC number is returned to the WLS from SAP, which triggers the order information from the `Order` object to be written to the Order database. The IDOC number is also passed to the Order database.	Order, Configuration, and Customer tables in the Order database are updated with data from the `Order` object.	

Interoperability Testing

As part of integration testing, you should also do interoperability testing. The WS-I has two testing tools for interoperability assessment with the WS-I Basic Profile. The tools, with implementations in both C# and Java, can be used on any web services platform.

The testing tools and their supporting documentation and processes were developed by the WS-I Test Tools Working Group. The tools have been designed to allow for expansion and extension, so they can accommodate the Basic Profile as well as future profiles. They can be configured to specifically address whichever profile definition they need to verify. Testing results help developers ensure that their web services meet the WS-I interoperability guidelines.

Part of the WS-I tool set is the Web Service Communication Monitor (called simply Monitor here), which captures messages exchanged between web services and the software that invokes them and stores them for later analysis. The Web Service Profile Analyzer (referred to here as Analyzer) evaluates messages captured by Monitor and also validates the description and registration artifacts of the web service. See Figure 13.7.

This includes the WSDL documents that describe the web service, and the XML Schema files that describe the data types used in the WSDL service definition and the UDDI registration entries. The output from Analyzer is a report that indicates whether a web service meets the interoperability guidelines of the WS-I Basic Profile 1.0. The report provides details on the specific deviations and failures so that users know which requirements of the WS-I Basic Profile were not met. Furthermore, many of the testing tools incorporate the WS-I verification tool. For example, SOAPtest from Parasoft verifies the Web Services Description Language (WSDL) and Simple Object Access Protocol (SOAP) traffic for conformance to Basic Profile 1.0 using Testing Tools 1.0 developed by WS-I. The testing tools have been seamlessly coupled with SOAPtest.

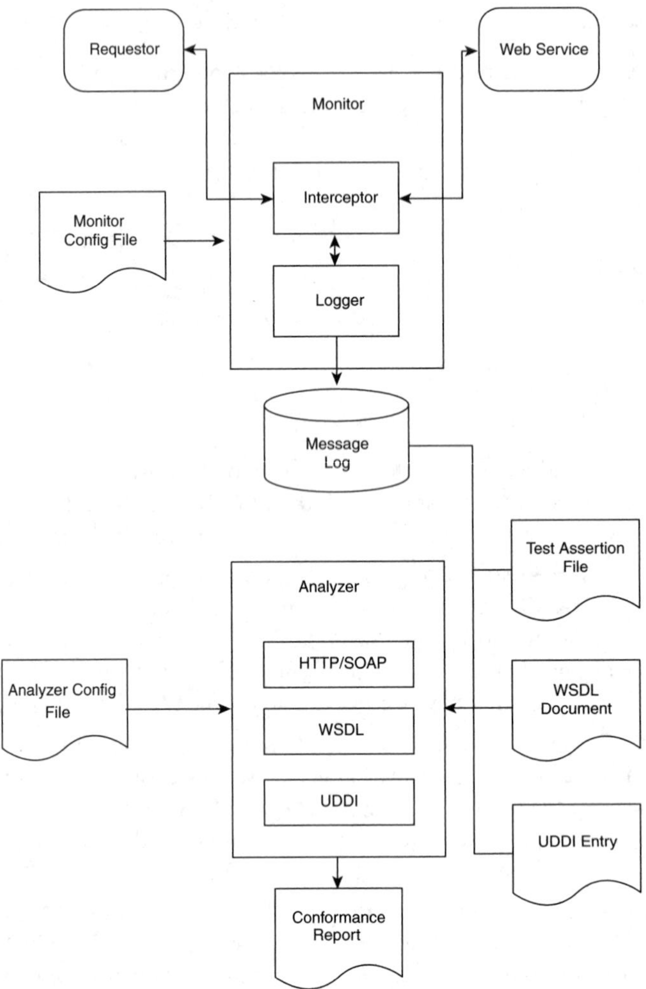

Figure 13.7 Monitor and Analyzer of WS-I testing tool

The following shows parts of the output from WS-I Analyzer tool for the Validate Config service, if the particular section passes the test, you will see this:

```
<entry type="portType"
➥referenceID="{http://production.psg.hp.com/types}validateConfig">
                    <assertionResult id="WSI2010" result="passed">
       </assertionResult>
</entry>
```

If the section fails, it will look like the following:

```
➥referenceID="{http://production.psg.hp.com/types}validateConfig">
                  <assertionResult id="WSI2115" result="failed">
                        <failureMessage xml:lang="en">A wsdl:message
➥element containing a wsdl:part element that uses the &quot;element&quot;
➥attribute does not refer, via that attribute, to a global element
➥declaration.</failureMessage>
                        <failureDetail
xml:lang="en">{http://production.psg.hp.com/types}validateRequest

Element Location:
  lineNumber=7
      </failureDetail>
```

Regression Testing

A regression test is normally a cut-down version of a functional test. Its aim is to ensure that the web service is still working between builds or releases. It assumes that some area of functionality was working in the past, and its job is to check that it still does. Because regression testing is, by its nature, a repetitive task, it must be automated. This is true for traditional applications and websites; it is even more true for web services. Save the test case input values for all the tests, and check whether the same test case outcomes are produced in subsequent test runs. By reproducing and repeating these tests, you can determine whether the functionality of your server changes over time. When investing in a regression tool, ensure that it has the capability to import SOAP requests already developed by hand into the automated testing tool. SOAPtest and Empirix e-Tester provide fairly robust support for regression testing.

Performance Testing

Two factors make performance testing critical. First, organizations tend to develop web services that transfer a sizable amount of data within each transaction by passing in user-defined XML data types as part of the SOAP request. Second, organizations are using web services to exchange information between business partners and have SLAs in place specifying guaranteed performance metrics. Organizations need to test performance of their implementations against these SLAs to avoid financial and business penalties.

HP OpenView Internet Services

You can use HP OpenView Internet Services (OVIS) for performance testing. OVIS measures the response times for transactions. Although OVTA, described in Chapter 12, "Enhancing the Performance of Web Services," monitors real transactions through the application, OVIS can generate synthetic transactions to help measure and test the application performance.

You can use this tool to test the application after fixing a performance problem by simulating the activity that identified the problem in the first place. OVIS uses OVTA to show response times, down to the code level. Figure 13.8 shows how OVIS integrates with OVTA and the WLS. It can help predict problems in the code before it goes into production. By setting up transaction activity that a normal user would go through, you can get some metrics on how well your application responds during the testing phase. If you want to do more robust load testing or regression testing, you must to incorporate other testing vendors for a complete testing solution.

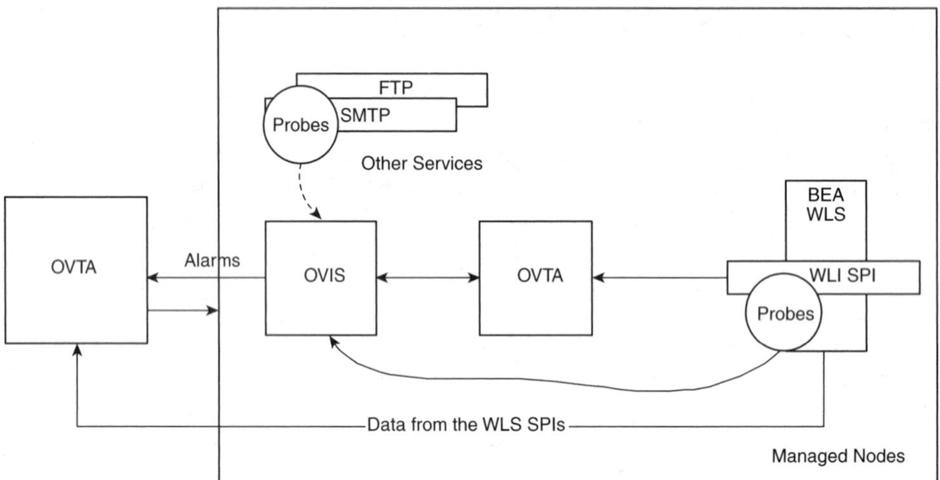

Figure 13.8 OVIS, OVTA, and WLS

To simulate business activity and gather performance measurements, OVIS uses software probes. These software probes test the services by executing typical request/response transactions. OVIS uses a Web Transaction Recorder to build a probe for the application that you want to test. The software probes forward the data to the OVIS measurement server and store the data in a database. A graphical dashboard (see Figure 13.9) displays the data, such as average number of seconds taken to complete each service transaction. With the integration of OVTA, you simply choose the transaction with a high response time, and OVTA runs and shows the actual method causing the problem. This information can provide you with a starting point in fixing any performance bottlenecks in the application.

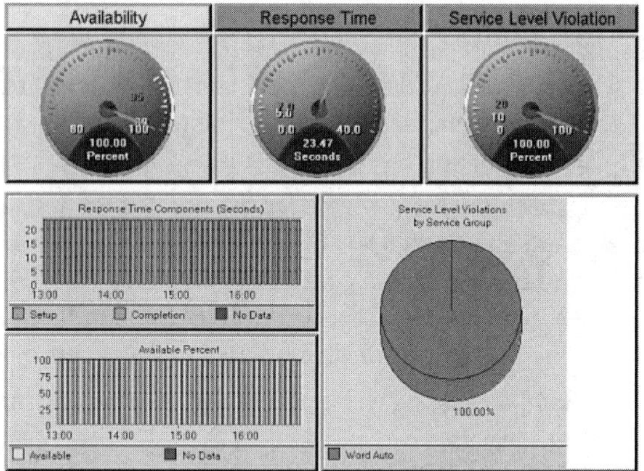

Figure 13.9 Dashboard for OVIS

Performance Profiling

Profiling usually means timing how long methods take to execute. This helps identify which methods are performance hogs. These methods can be examined in more detail, going down to the line level of code, to determine whether that amount of time is appropriate or whether you can cut the time by recoding that piece.

Performance analysis is different from profiling because it is a more complex and comprehensive process in which you obtain detailed timing information that enables you to track the overall flow of your application. You can observe and investigate how long methods take to execute, what combination of methods execute to accomplish a specific task, and where there might be a bottleneck holding up the application's response to the user. We talked about performance analysis in Chapter 12 and showed how you can use OVTA to analyze performance bottlenecks.

Other Performance Test Tools

TestMaker is a public-domain tool available for performance testing. It is a utility specifically designed to test web services for scalability and performance. It can look at Java and .NET web services, as well as HTTP, HTTPS, and SOAP protocols.

TestMaker includes a scripting language to create intelligent test agents, a Test Object Library that contains software objects that simulate user actions to drive a web service, a graphical interface for creating and editing agents, and a utility to run agents concurrently. TestMaker can import an existing web services project into the IDE and conduct an initial performance run in less than an hour. The results are simple and easy to understand.

You can use Empirix e-load for testing web services performance by simulating between several hundred to several thousand users.

Load Testing

Load testing is necessary to understand the impact of varying web service transaction loads on the web service application and infrastructure. Performing a good load test is an important step in ensuring the scalability of the web service, as well as the impact of other infrastructure pieces such as database servers, firewalls, load balancers, the network, application servers, and web servers. One of the standard load tests can serve as a baseline for comparing all future releases and configuration changes.

Using Empirix for Load Testing

The scripts created in the functional test can be used for doing load testing in Empirix's e-load. You can submit the scripts as scenarios. For each script, you can specify the number of virtual users using the web service. You can submit more than one script per scenario. If it is done this way, all virtual users from each script are started together at the ramp-up speed that you define. You can also start another scenario after the first one has completed its ramp-up. Empirix offers many controls that help with simulating the test:

- You can choose to start a scenario one of three ways: immediately, at a specified delay, or at a certain time.
- You can stop a scenario one of four ways: not at all (the test runs indefinitely), after iteration count (the test runs for a certain number of iterations), at a specified time (the test runs until a specified time), or after a delay (the test runs for a specified time).
- You can set the ramp-up specifications. The ramp-up can be specified by percentage, which starts scenarios at the specified percentage, or a specific number, which starts a certain number of scenarios.

- You can set the iteration count and the delay time. For this example, the settings are to start after a delay of 2 minutes, stop after a delay of 20 minutes, and ramp up one user every 15 seconds.

After you start the scenarios, you can monitor them in the TEST console, which enables you to monitor response times, the number of transactions completed, performance graphs, and so on. To analyze the performance, go to the eReporter/Query Wizard in the eTest console and select the session that you ran to view the load graphs. In the Select Query section, highlight Add Data Versus Time, and press Next. See Figure 13.10.

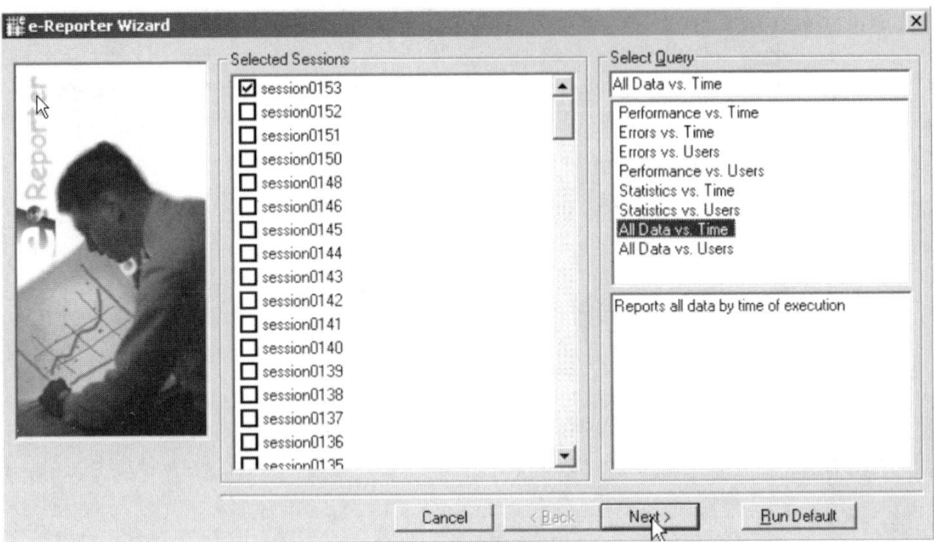

Figure 13.10 eReporter/Query Wizard

Choose the Available Data Series that you want and press the >> button to move them to the Selected Data Series. The most relevant are Kb Rcvd/sec, Trans/sec, Overall Number of VUs (virtual users), and Average Performance. Two examples of graphs that you can view are "All Data Versus Time" and "Average Performance" of the `validateConfig` web service. In "All Data Versus Time," you can see all the data recorded, such as the overall hits and the overall number of virtual users (see Figures 13.11 and 13.12).

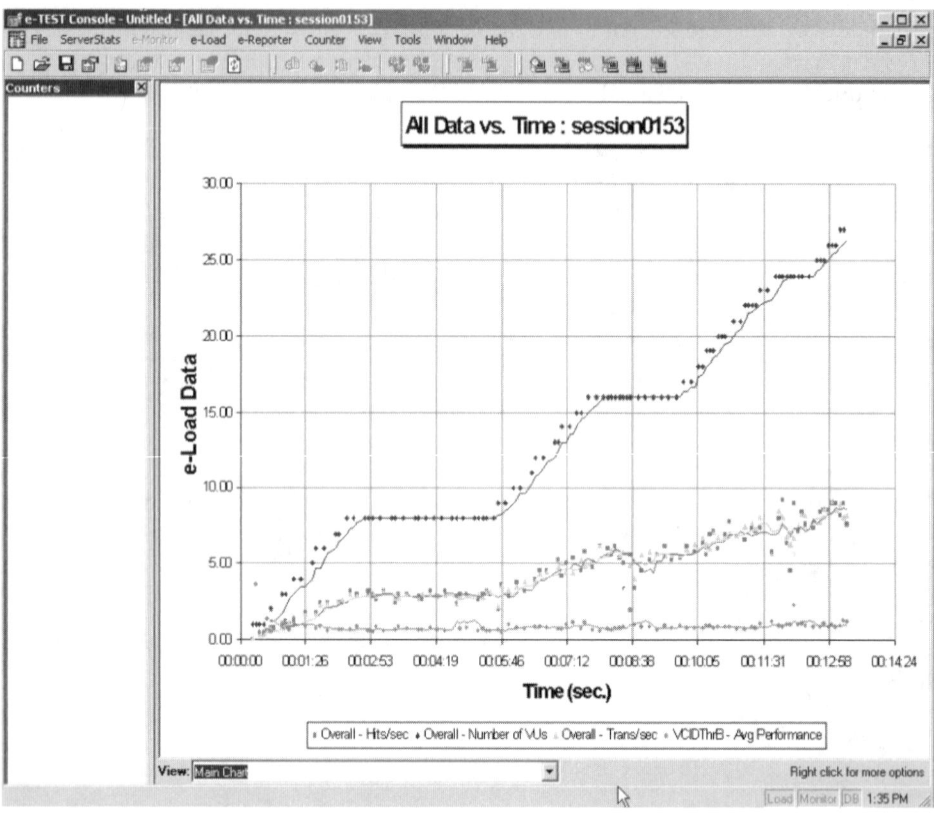

Figure 13.11 All Data Versus Time graph

Stress Testing

Stress testing is necessary to determine how many simultaneous users can use the web service before the performance degrades. Apply steadily increasing load until the web service breaks. This tells you how well the web service will handle unexpected loads from unplanned events. Generate real-world load and maintain the load over period of time. This tells how exactly how your web service will degrade and break under sustained load. By closely monitoring server memory consumption during the testing runs, you will be able to determine whether any memory leaks are present in the system.

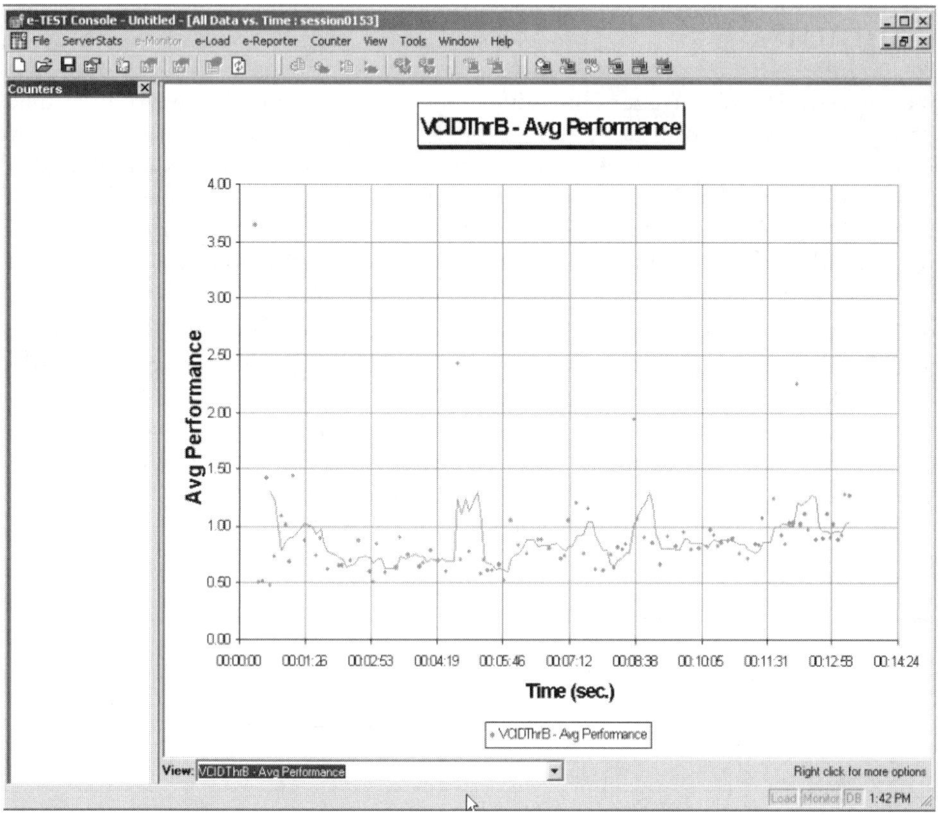

Figure 13.12 Average Performance graph

Capacity Planning Testing

Planning helps to determine the hardware and software configuration required to adequately meet present and future needs. Capacity planning testing can help you define how many transactions per hour your system can support, identify the acceptable response for the system, and determine the hardware and network infrastructure needed to deliver those numbers.

After the first iteration of testing/tuning, you can establish a baseline from the results of a meaningful test. Use this baseline to compare subsequent test results with the first test. Creating a baseline gives you concrete proof of the impact of major changes, such as a JDK upgrade, a WLS upgrade, back-end system updates, DB upgrade, and hardware upgrade.

Summary

Testing web services is different from testing traditional applications because of three unique aspects of web services: a distributed, loosely coupled system with dependent stakeholders; validation of end-to-end transactions that spans traffic through intermediaries; and a standards-based, service-driven model for integration. You can address these unique challenges by applying the following practices: 1) establish service-level agreements, 2) perform component level validation and benchmarking, 3) mandate performance testing, 4) extend test scenarios to address web service functions, and 5) invest in testing tools designed for web services.

A comprehensive test suite should include unit tests, functional tests, integration tests, interoperability tests, regression tests, performance tests, and load tests. WebLogic Workshop provides an environment for unit testing called test view. JUnit, an open-source Java framework, provides good capabilities for programmers to do unit testing. Automated tools can be easily used for testing web services. Empirix and Parasoft's SOAPtest can be used for functional, integration, regression testing, load and performance testing. HP OpenView Internet Services works well for performance characterization. WS-I has two testing tools for interoperability assessment: Monitor and Analyzer.

14
Managing Web Services

This chapter discusses web services manageability. You will see why web services offer a different challenge in manageability compared to traditional management. You will explore the manageability stack to see how you can meet the challenges of web services management. You also will explore the JMX architecture used in the WebLogic platform with OpenView. In addition, you will examine the concepts of the WS-Resource Framework, WS-Notification, WSDM, and grid computing; these are some of the efforts in the industry to have standard specifications for web services manageability. This chapter also looks at HP's strategy in the area of web services manageability and how Lifecycle for Management of Web Services (LCM4WS) helps you to manage the changes in the lifecycle of web services.

Why Managing Web Services Is Different

Today, more web services are under development than in production. Often, developers don't give sufficient consideration to the management aspects of the web service during development. Your IT organization should be designing in manageability from the beginning. If you wait until after deployment, costs associated with adding manageability are much higher. You should build suitable management functionality into the web service for it to be manageable. Doing so can make these web services more successful than those that are not well managed. If management concerns are not attended to early, the problems that operational personnel with the right tools otherwise could have fixed easily end up putting a drain on the development resources.

Managing at Different Levels

Management refers to the supervisory and administrative actions performed on the applications and web service components. Management needs to occur at multiple levels (see Figure 14.1). Managing the health of a business process includes sending alerts when exceptions arise, rerouting service requests based on predefined policies, and so on. It includes managing an individual service for availability and performance, managing the individual components such as EJBs that make up the service, managing the underlying IT infrastructure such as web servers and database servers.

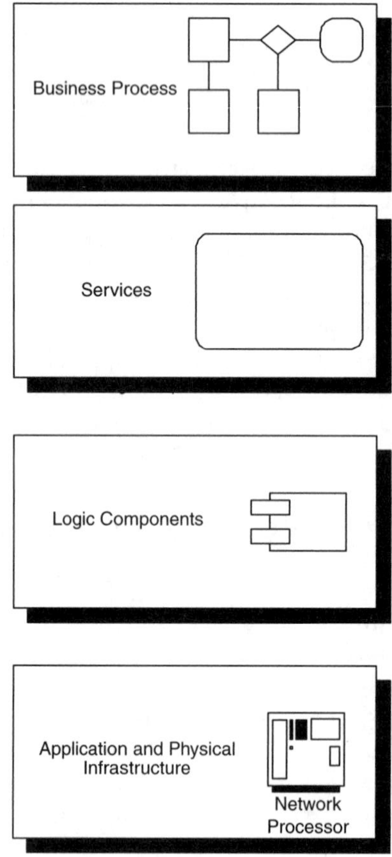

Figure 14.1 Management at different levels

The key tasks that need to be carried out in a web services environment are very similar to those in traditional IT management. They include making services available to the right users; using authentication and authorization policies; capturing information about usage so that resources can be allocated and the right users can be billed; measuring the quality of service, such as response time against service-level contracts; and acting upon SLA violations by defining how the system should respond if an SLA is violated, how IT resources should be adjusted in case of an SLA violation, and how refunds should be processed. For example, HP OVIS enables customers to support SLA management and can proactively monitor a network. Combing OVIS data via threshold alerts to HP OpenView operations greatly enhances the customers' capability to do capacity planning, to proactively alert IT operations on problems before they occur, and to provide summary data meaningful to an end customer. To monitor web services, HP OVIS provides support for SOAP services via an HP-supported probe. But although the requirements are similar to those of managing a traditional IT environment, execution is very different.

Comparing with Traditional IT Management

Traditional infrastructure management takes place behind a corporate firewall, where every component is under the IT department's control. With web services, the big challenge is managing an environment that is outside your control. A typical web services deployment spans multiple enterprises. The magnitude of the challenge depends on the degree of difficulty to get the necessary information about the different web services resources. The specific issues are as follows:

- Identifying applications that cross boundaries
- Gaining visibility between corporations
- Managing service agreements
- Determining the causes of IT problems

Another major difference is that many aspects of management in traditional environments are carried out in a proprietary manner. This clearly doesn't work for a standards-based web services environment, where multiple types of applications need to communicate with one another. Currently, there is no standard approach to managing web services. What management solution vendors can offer is instrumentation at the SOAP endpoints and intermediaries. This provides information about the web services as they use these applications. However, this management view is incomplete and does not have critical information on the state of the web service as it executes messages among various endpoints.

Evolution of Management Stack

As applications have evolved to a more service-oriented architecture, the management of applications is evolving from Java to J2EE to web services–based management. Most of the application management is done through the JMX architecture, which is being extended now to web services.

Web services management is being seen as a part of an overall management and security strategy. That management of the underlying infrastructure stack, from systems and network to databases and applications, is as relevant to the web services that it supports as it is to the traditional IT environment. This perspective is built on the concept that end-to-end management is critical.

Web services technologies themselves are most suitable to be the platform for management because of language and platform independence, interoperability through standards, industry momentum, and the capability to expose interface and hide implementation. This chapter shows the evolution of the management stack through the following:

- JMX architecture
- J2EE Management Specification
- Web services distributed management and its relation to the Web Services Resources Framework (WSRF), Web Services Notification (WS-Notification), and grid computing

Using JMX Architecture

You can use the Java Management Extensions (JMX) architecture to manage or monitor web services. By using JMX within your application design, you can realize the following benefits:

- JMX enables a Java application or resource to be managed without significant investment by simply embedding a managed object server and making the functionality available via one or more managed beans.
- JMX can scale from small to large implementations because of its component-based nature.
- The JMX APIs are open interfaces that enable management-solution vendors to integrate JMX into their solution.
- JMX leverages existing standard Java technologies such as JNDI, JTA, and JDBC.

The components of the JMX architecture are shown in Figure 14.2.

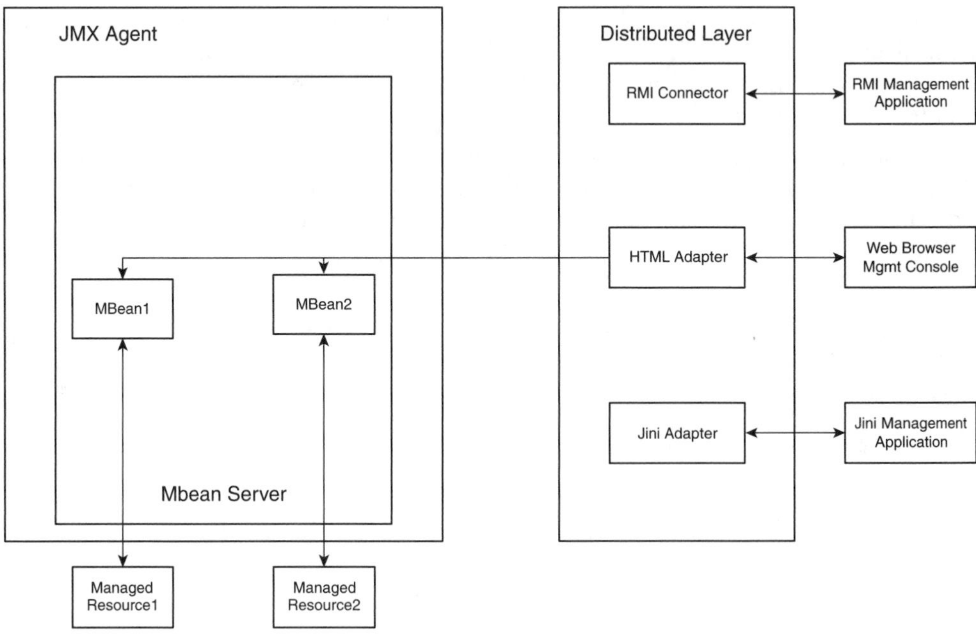

Figure 14.2 JMX architecture

MBean is a wrapper to your web services and is used for managing the web services. MBeans live within an MBean server. An MBean server lives within a JMX agent. You can communicate with MBeans either via a custom Java program that connects to the MBeans or via a JMX adapter or connector using HTTP, RMI, or Jini.

MBean Methods

MBean has getter, setter, and notification methods. Getter methods are used for receiving information on resources. For example, they tell the number of requests that are waiting for a JDBC pool entry to become available. Setter methods are used for setting thresholds for alerts. For example, using a setter method, you can change the minimum acceptable cache hit ratio before an alert is raised. Notification methods that are fired when an event in your managed resource occurs. For example, when a threshold is exceeded, a notification method is executed in the MBean. Other programs and monitors can register as listeners to the MBean notifications.

Types of MBeans

WebLogic has two different types of MBeans: configuration and runtime MBeans. Configuration (or config) MBeans expose attributes and operations for configuring a managed resource. When the admin server starts, it builds config MBeans from the information in the `config.xml` file. When a managed server starts, it creates local replicas of the config MBeans for its managed resources. The config MBeans on the admin server are called administration (or admin) MBeans, and the replicas on the managed server are called local configuration MBeans.

Runtime MBeans provide information about the runtime state of a managed resource. Runtime MBeans are not replicated; they exist only on WebLogic Server because their underlying managed resource local MBeans exist only inside an MBean Server.

MBean Server

Each WebLogic Server has its own MBean Server. All WebLogic Servers provide a local `MBeanHome` interface through which JMX calls access the MBeans that are hosted on its MBean Server. For managed servers and the admin server, the local MBeanHome interface provides access to the local config MBeans and runtime MBeans for the current server only. The admin server provides an additional instance of the `MBeanHome` interface called the Administration `MBeanHome`. This provides access to admin MBeans along with all other MBeans on all server instances in the domain. You can also build your own custom JMX MBeans to manage and monitor your customer J2SE/J2EE applications.

Using JMX on WebLogic Server

WebLogic Server implements the JMX 1.0 specification to provide open and extensible management services. All WebLogic Server resources are managed through these JMX-based services. Web services that run within WebLogic Server can be managed through them as well. WebLogic can manage resources in three different ways:

- WebLogic admin console
- WebLogic command-line utility
- Custom Java programs using JMX using Conf2admin

You can build your own management utilities that use these JMX services to manage WebLogic Server resources and applications.

WebLogic Admin Console

You can access the WebLogic Admin Console by directing your web browser to http://localhost:7001/console. Figure 14.3 shows how management commands (setters) and runtime queries (getters) are sent from the browser through the admin server to the WebLogic Admin MBean.

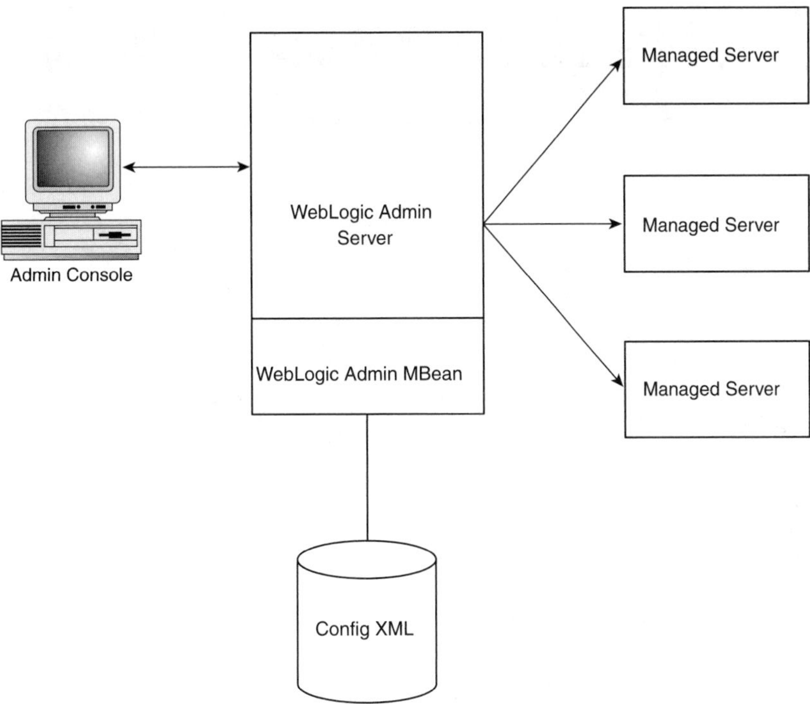

Figure 14.3 Management through WebLogic Admin Console

Figure 14.4 shows the WebLogic console showing a JDBC connection pool.

Figure 14.5 shows the details of the MBean. It shows the MBean class `weblogic.management.configuration.JDBCConnectionPoolMBean` and the MBean attribute.

At runtime, WebLogic Server automatically supplies an MBean object for internal services and for each application servlet and EJB that are part of your web service under its control. These are the runtime MBeans, and they become management-oriented proxies for their companion application objects. These generated runtime MBeans are registered in the internal MBean Server. Therefore, the user can see and adjust the allowed attributes of these MBeans through the WLS Admin Console. As each servlet and each EJB is represented as an MBean, the web service is visible for management down to these levels of granularity. The developer can now work with the MBean logic to add new functionality as required.

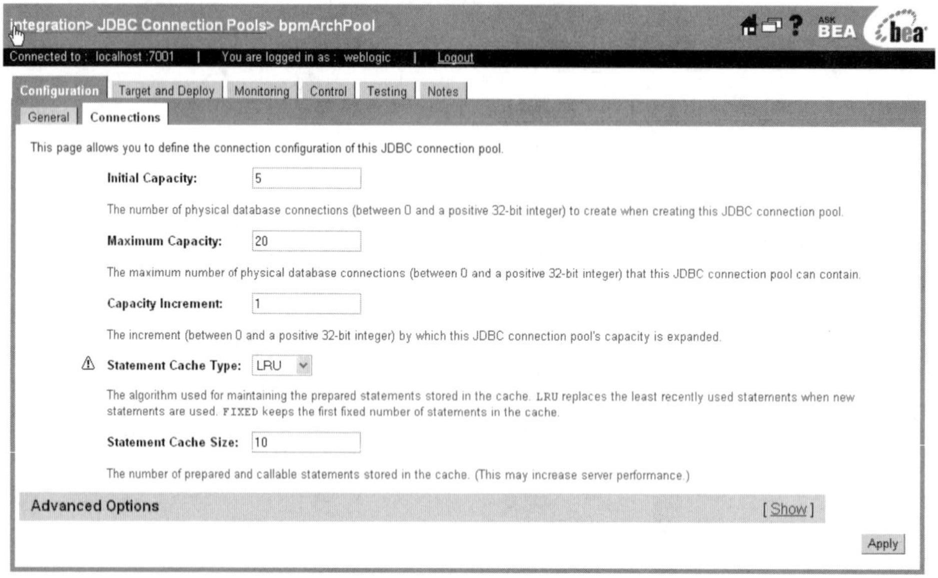

Figure 14.4 JDBC connection pool

WebLogic Command-Line Utility

This is a command-line interpreter that connects to a WebLogic Server and translates user commands to JMX calls. These calls are applied to those MBeans registered in the MBean Server supplied by BEA, but they can also be applied to user-defined MBeans that have been registered with the MBean Server.

Conf2Admin

This is a script-generation utility that can generate `Weblogic.Admin` commands from a `config.xml`. These script commands can then be used to re-create elements of a WebLogic Server domain in another WebLogic Server domain. This also alleviates some burden of understanding all the syntax associated with a scripting language.

Using JMX with HP OpenView

HP enhances the BEA WebLogic Server (WLS) management by providing a BEA WLS-specific Smart Plug-Ins (SPI) module that integrates the management of the BEA WLS and any associated applications that depend on it. This SPI integrates information from many sources into one screen. It gathers data from any supplied MBeans supplied by WebLogic Server and interprets it to be more meaningful to the end operator. It has a 100 percent JMX architecture. HP OpenView also has a WLI SPI that is also based on JMX; it was covered in detail in Chapter 10, "Managing Business Processes."

Attributes

Table 113-1

Attribute Label	Description	Value Constraints
Initial Capacity	The number of physical database connections to create when creating the connection pool. *MBean:* `weblogic.management.configuration.JDBCConnectionPoolMBean` *Attribute:* `InitialCapacity`	*Minimum:* 0 *Maximum:* 2147483647 *Default:* 1 *Dynamic:* yes
Maximum Capacity	Maximum number of physical database connections that this connection pool can contain. Different JDBC Drivers and database servers may limit the number of possible physical connections. *MBean:* `weblogic.management.configuration.JDBCConnectionPoolMBean` *Attribute:* `MaxCapacity`	*Minimum:* 1 *Maximum:* 2147483647 *Default:* 15 *Dynamic:* yes
Capacity Increment	Increment by which the connection pool capacity is expanded. When there are no more available physical connections to service requests, the connection pool will create this number of additional physical database connections and add them to the connection pool. The connection pool will ensure that it does not exceed the maximum number of physical connections as set by `MaxCapacity`. *MBean:* `weblogic.management.configuration.JDBCConnectionPoolMBean` *Attribute:* `CapacityIncrement`	*Minimum:* 1 *Maximum:* 2147483647 *Default:* 1 *Dynamic:* yes
Statement Cache Type	The algorithm used to maintain the statement cache: • LRU - After the `statementCacheSize` is met, the Least Recently Used statement is removed when a new statement is used. • Fixed - The first `statementCacheSize` number of statements is stored and stay fixed in the cache. No new statements are cached unless the cache is manually cleared. *MBean:* `weblogic.management.configuration.JDBCConnectionPoolMBean` *Attribute:* `StatementCacheType`	*Default:* LRU *Valid values:* • LRU • FIXED *Dynamic:* no
Statement Cache Size	The number of Prepared and Callable Statements stored in the cache for further use. WebLogic Server can reuse statements in the cache without reloading them, which can increase server performance. Setting the size of the statement cache to 0 turns it off. Each connection in the pool has its own cache of statements. *MBean:* `weblogic.management.configuration.JDBCConnectionPoolMBean` *Attribute:* `StatementCacheSize`	*Default:* 10 *Dynamic:* yes

Figure 14.5 MBean class and MBean attribute

The HP OpenView SMART Plug-In can help IT operations in many ways. A number of screens, reports, and graphs are supplied in HP OpenView Operations (OVO). The value gained from using OVO over the WebLogic Admin Console is that OVO is about managing your entire IT infrastructure, from network to systems, to devices, to applications. When you talk about management, problems could occur because of multiple factors and system problems. A comprehensive management platform such as OVO enables you to get this end-to-end view, not a view isolated to one particular platform, such as WLS.

OVO monitors networks as well as WebLogic Server and the applications and web services running on it on the same console. Using one set of tools, you can present information in existing MBeans or new custom-built MBeans in addition to OpenView-supplied metrics. Fifty-five metrics are available out of the box, including servlet execution times, JDBC connection pool rates, EJB and JMS utilization, and JTA rollback rates.

You can define new user-defined metrics (UDMs). UDM is an XML-based file that exposes metrics that can be monitored through HP OpenView. You can enable custom calculations to show business information. Figure 14.6 shows UDM in HP OpenView. When have the MBean created and registered in WebLogic, you can look at the steps required to integrate it with OpenView. OpenView provides built-in support to manage a number of JMX-based metrics from WebLogic. To have OpenView recognize custom metrics, you need to build a custom or user-defined metric. This metric can then be used in OpenView to create alarms, graphs, and reports. The first step is to create a user-defined metric file, an XML file defining what JMX components to access. To view this file here, you use a JMXSPI mapping tool from HP that enables a developer to build metric definitions from existing JMX MBeans.

In the UDM `ConversionRate` shown, you can get a better sense of how the MBean is being used. First, create two base metrics: `OrdersCreated` and `ValidateConfigs_Created`. With these two metrics, you can build a composite metric using calculations. In this case, you want to find out the conversion rate of configurations into valid orders. To do this, create the metric `ConversionRate` that divides the `OrdersCreated` by the `ValidateConfigs_Created` and multiplies by 100 to get a percentage:

```
<Metric id="OrdersCreated" alarm="no">
     <MBean instanceType="single">
          <FromVersion server="6.0 update"1"/>
          <ObjectName>*:Name=MyOrdersCreationManager</ObjectName>
               <Attribute>OrdersCompletedCount</Attribute>
   /MBean>
</Metric>
<Metric id="ValidateConfigs_Created" alarm"no"/>
     <MBean>
          <FromVersion server="6.0" update="1"/>
          <ObjectName>*:=MyOrdersCreationManager</ObjectName>
               <Attribute>ValidateConfigsCreatedCount</Attribute>
   /MBean>
</Metric>
<Metric id="WLSSPI_810" name =B810_Orders" alarm="yes" graph="yes">
     <Calculation>
          <FromVersion server="6.0 update"1"/>
               <Formula>( OrdersCreated/ValidateConfigs_Created)*100</Formula>
   </Calculation>
</Metric>
```

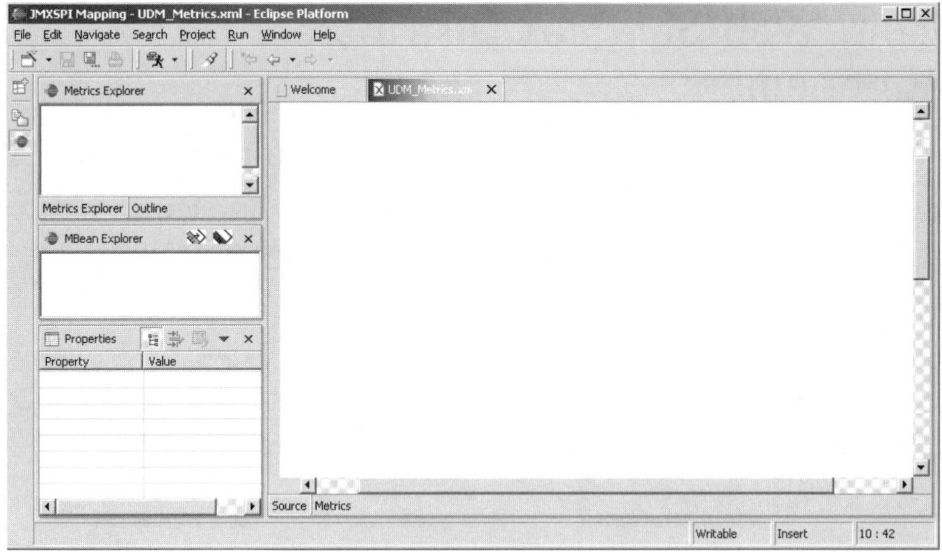

Figure 14.6 UDM in HP OpenView

Using J2EE Management Specification

The JSR 77 specification proposes a standard management model for exposing and accessing the management information, operations, and parameters of the J2EE platform. JSR 77 is part of the J2EE 1.4 specifications. The J2EE Management Specification abstracts the manageable parts of the J2EE architecture and defines an interface for accessing management information. This helps system administrators integrate J2EE servers into a system-management environment and also helps application developers create their own management tools. The J2EE management specification is based on JMX. JMX defines only the general mechanism for managing a Java-based system; it doesn't define the management of a concrete system. A J2EE server is a concrete system, and JSR 77 defines a concrete object model. The J2EE management model defined in JSR 77 contains managed object models for JVM, Enterprise JavaBeans (EJBs), and the EJB module. You need access to the managed objects defined by the model. Therefore, the specification requires the server vendor to provide a management EJB (MEJB) that must be deployed on the server. The MEJB uses some of JMX's classes and interfaces, and acts as an interface to access managed objects as JMX MBeans.

Using Web Services Distributed Management

OASIS has a technical committee for Web Services Distributed Management (WSDM). It is chartered to define web services management, including web services to manage distributed resources and develop a model of a web service as a manageable resource. WSDM is defined by two specifications: the Management Using Web Services specification (MUWS) and the Management of Web Services (MOWS) specification. The architecture of WSDM is shown in Figure 14.7.

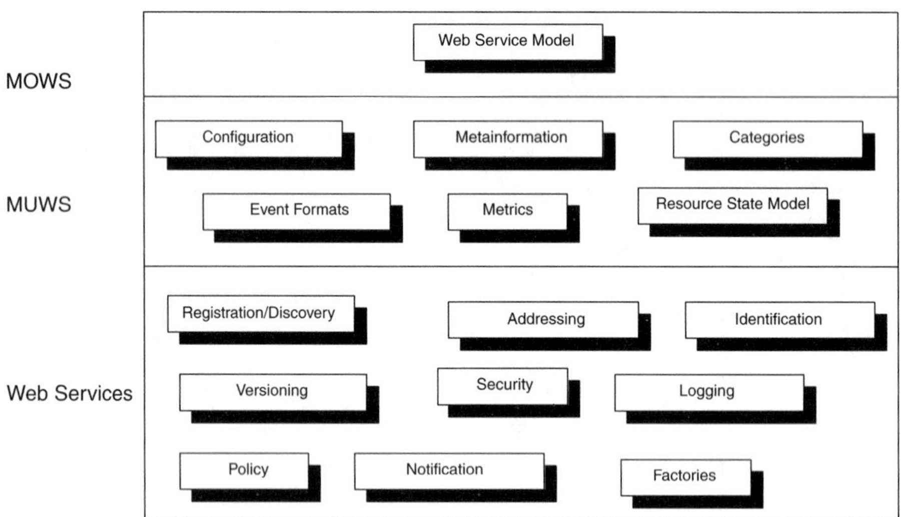

Figure 14.7 WSDM architecture

Management Using Web Services (MUWS) Specification

MUWS is a specification for managing distributed resources by using web services technologies. The management capabilities are defined by a WSDL. MUWS is based on existing standards: XML, SOAP, WSDL, and UDDI. The MUWS architecture makes use of the web services architecture shown in Figure 14.8.

MUWS is also based on WS-Resource Framework (WS-RF), mainly WS-ResourceProperties (WS-RP) and WS-Addressing. WS-RP enables you to expose properties. It doesn't know whether these properties are metrics, state information, or something else (WS-RP is discussed more in the next section). MUWS comes on top of WS-RP and provides a categorization of resources into identity, metrics, state, and control:

- **Identity**—Provides a unique identifier for the manageable resource, along with a description and version. Web services elements can optionally have version information that includes a version date and a version number: major/minor/release/build. Each version has list of changes made since the last update. MUWS helps with managing the version capability. The identification capability is used to help establish the web service endpoint being managed. The identity capability can be used to determine whether two manageability providers manage the same resource.
- **Metrics**—Provides a current system time and mechanism to categorize properties as metrics along with some initial, limited metadata.
- **State**—Provides a base operational state model for interoperable semantics, a current state, and a set of standards operations to enable and disable the operational state of the resource.

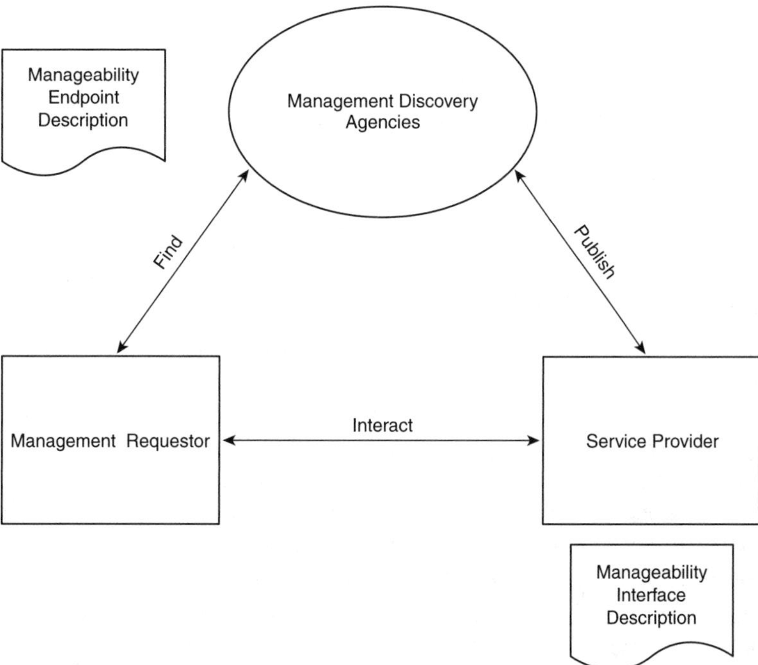

Figure 14.8 MUWS architecture

WS-Resource Framework

An earlier section discussed MUWS based on WS-Resource Properties and WS-Addressing. You should first understand how a WS-Resource is defined.

Web services are stateless, but they make changes to stateful resources, such as adding a row in a database. A WS-Resource is defined as a composition of a web service and a stateful resource. It is used in the execution of web service message exchanges. The state of the WS-Resource can be queried and modified via web service message exchanges. It can be created and destroyed.

WS-Addressing is be used to designate the stateful resource component of the WS-Resource to be used in the execution of message exchanges. WS-Properties is the XML document that defines a particular view or projection of the state data implemented by the WS-Resource. The WS-Resource Framework encompasses these two specifications.

WS-Notification

The WS-Resource framework works with the WS-Notification family of specifications for notification. For example, after a contract has been defined in WS-Resource Framework, WS-Notification can publish a notification of contract changes that require an action by a partner or supplier.

The event-driven or notification-based interaction pattern is a commonly used pattern for interobject communications. Examples exist in many domains in publish/subscribe systems provided by message-oriented middleware vendors, or in system- and device-management domains. This notification pattern is increasingly being used in a web services context. WS-Notification includes the following types of messaging:

- Standard message exchanges to be implemented by service providers that want to participate in point-to-point notifications.
- Standard message exchanges for a notification broker service provider, allowing the publication of messages from entities that are not themselves service providers.
- Operational requirements expected of service providers and requestors that participate in notifications.
- XML model that describes topics of subscription. There are three normative specifications: WSBaseNotification, WS-Brokered Notification, and WS-Topics.

WSRF and WSN combine the management of systems, business applications, and grid computing through a single web services–based framework. WSRF and WSN are designed to satisfy the requirements of management communities in systems (Distributed Management Task Force, DMTF), grids (Global Grid Forum, GGF), and web services (OASIS, WSDM).

They will enable systems-management applications to manage multivendor hardware and software, grid infrastructure and applications to be built with the same standards, as well as business applications using publish-and-subscribe notification based on stateful resources across corporate boundaries.

These specifications have support from the Global Grid Forum (GGF), which means that this effectively marries web services and grids. Grid computing applies the resources of many computers in a network to a multiple problems at the same time, usually to a scientific or technical problem that requires a large number of computer processing cycles or access to large amounts of data.

Management of Web Services (MOWS)

MOWS defines a model for managing web services.

The web service specific management aspects modeled by MOWS are the web service lifecycle state, management metrics such as message count and rate, the types of relationships to aid in discovery and root cause analysis, events to notify changes (in attribute values, lifecycle state, metrics, relationships, and metainformation about the model).

MOWS also addresses management operations of web services using several categories: monitoring, control, configuration, discovery, and performance.

MOWS is being modeled to be accessible in a way consistent with MUWS.

Selecting a WSM Tool

Mainstream management players are expanding into the web services arena along with pure-play specialists, who lead the way in services management today. You also have the option of waiting for your current management vendor to flesh out its product suite with web services capabilities.

You can evaluate a Web Services Manageability (WSM) tool from several dimensions. Based on your business needs, some of these dimensions are more important than others. We have listed in the following sections several criteria in each area that you can use for evaluating and selecting the right WSM tool suitable for your business.

Some of the leading vendors offering web services management solutions are Hewlett-Packard, Actional, and AmberPoint.

Core Capabilities

You need a core set of management capabilities in a WSM tool: runtime monitoring alerting and logging (see Table 14.1). These capabilities provide raw information on the overall functioning of the web service. This also becomes the foundation on which other management capabilities can be built.

Table 14.1 Core Capabilities in a WSM Tool

Functionality	Criteria for Evaluation
Runtime monitoring	Monitor the latency of web service components and the web service as a whole.
	Monitor items such as uptime, the health of the service (for example, ping for responsiveness), the total number of web service requests, and the number of web service requests by each requestor.
	Monitor successes and failures and security access denials.
	Measure quality of service (QoS).
Alerting	Send notifications based on exceeding threshold levels (for example, handling *n* number of SOAP requests within a given *delta* time).
	Send alerts based on metrics defined by SLAs (for example, when a service takes too long to fulfill a request).
	Send alerts based on errors within the web service. This is for both errors from the SOAP layer and the errors propagated up from underlying components (such as security violations, XML errors, and service errors).
Logging	Log each SOAP call. The details should include the time of invocation, the identity of the service, the identity of the caller, the time that a call is completed, and the message size.
	Log at different levels of detail.

Business Monitoring

A WSM tool can also provide business-level information. This is useful to understand how the business functions are being performed and to track against key business objectives. See Table 14.2.

Table 14.2 Business Monitoring in a WSM Tool

Functionality	Criteria for Evaluation
Runtime monitoring	Capability to accept tracking information from the a web service Business Process Management (BPM) tool throughout an orchestration/process with visibility of content and activity at each stage.
Alerting	Real-time information gathering based on the data held in the XML payload of the message in the request. This could be used for triggering events (for example, notification to someone when a large order arrives or billing).
	Based on contractual agreement violations (for example, the exceeded number of requests per month).
Logging	Capability to define and log content-centric or message-centric concerns (for example, purchase orders over a certain amount).

Controlling Management Functions

Another important capability to consider is the level of control and flexibility in tweaking the management functions to suit the business and IT requirements. See Table 14.3.

Table 14.3 Controlling Management Functions in a WSM Tool

Functionality	Criteria for Evaluation
Alerting	Capability to alert via multiple interface types (for example, e-mail, pager, and call-tracking systems).
	Capability to filter duplicate alerts, group multiple alerts of the same type, or linked alerts to eliminate overalerting.
Logging	Capability to set or modify monitoring and logging levels at runtime.
	Capability to specify the level (verbose, debug, production, and so on) of logging being done for a service or application as flexibly as possible at the web service or orchestration level.

continues

Table 14.3 Continued

Functionality	Criteria for Evaluation
Configuration	Dynamic routing based on load-balancing schemes, subscriber priority, and current service performance.
	Rule-based configuration capabilities.
	Profiles for provisioning at different levels.
Component management	Web service versioning and obsolescence without impact to subscriber.
	Fail-safe mechanisms (for example, switch to a backup web service if one fails).
	Capability to determine dependencies between managed web services and infrastructure components that they rely on. This can be used to analyze the impact of failures.
	Capability to manage internal and external web services. This includes external networks such as Grand Central and JamCracker.
	Client device detection.
	Capability to translate or check incoming and outgoing messages for conformance to different data.
Analytics	Retention of monitoring and tracking information and statistics for later analysis, querying, and/or auditing.
	Query of historical information, preferably with standard tools such as RDBMS and reporting tools with ad-hoc report-generation capabilities.
	Capability to drill down to determine what dependencies web services have on lower-level entities such as EJBs and server machines.
	Capability to drill up to determine what web services are affected by a particular lower-level component.
	Capability to drill down on particular steps within a process to see detailed information regarding failures and so on, but also to be able to see the data flowing between process steps.

Table 14.3 Continued

Functionality	Criteria for Evaluation
	Web service modeling capability, which can take as input accumulated statistics such as hits by requestor and component latencies, and can help evaluate stress limits on the infrastructure and software components that make up individual or composite web services. This is of great value in the area of capacity planning.

Other General Evaluation Criteria

You should also look at other general considerations, such as security, interoperability, and platform requirements, when evaluating a WSM tool. (See Table 14.4.)

Table 14.4 Other Evaluation Criteria for a WSM Tool

Functionality	Criteria for Evaluation
Interoperability	Integration with other management consoles, such as OpenView
	Capability to incorporate other management interface information (for example, JMX) into the monitoring and alerting mechanisms
	Capability to interface with translation services
	Support for multiple platforms, such as .NET and J2EE, and multiple operating systems, such as HP-UX, Linux, and Windows
	Capability to integrate with web services from ERP (for example, SAP) solutions using their UDDI or equivalent registries
	Integration with XML Schema repositories, such as Contivo, for message checking
	Compatibility with existing web services standards (for example, can use UDDI information to configure manageability parameters)
Security	A security access mechanism to limit capabilities and access within and to web services
	Compatibility with emerging web service security standards and mechanisms

Table 14.4 Continued

Functionality	Criteria for Evaluation
General	Technology that is noninvasive to the web services
	No requirement for any additional software to be installed in the service infrastructure
	Insignificant (<100ms) performance impact to web service invocation

Lifecycle Management for Web Services

Organizations must be responsive to change if they are to take advantage of the flexibility of web services. These call for tools that will help align IT and business to become more agile. To create this alignment, operational and business metrics need to be exposed from the various infrastructure, services, and processes management, and need to be tied back to the specific business-related services that are enabled by the technology. For example, you can extract the business information contained within a SOAP message—such as the size of an order—and package it for real-time business activity monitoring. Business activity monitoring (BAM) provides relevant and timely information about business activities inside your organization and those involving your customers and partners by aggregating, analyzing, and presenting this information. BAM provides more accurate information about the status and results of various operations, processes, and transactions so that you can make better decisions, more quickly address problem areas, and reposition your organization to take full advantage of emerging opportunities.

As another example, rather than merely reporting a problem with a network, you can warn users that the outage will affect a specific application. Alert business users that the application is part of a particular business process and that a network outage will cost the business $1 million and create a huge business impact.

Web services management moves beyond the people who manage IT resources and addresses the people who manage the business. But to leverage this kind of capability, you need to have visibility and control over the resources and service levels. Hewlett-Packard has taken the approach proposed in the specifications, WSDM, and driven a business-relevant view of managing web services into its Lifecycle Management for Web Services (LCM4WS) solution. This solution aligns different groups within the enterprise together to more effectively manage lifecycle changes for web services applications. LCM4WS is comprised of four components that have been integrated to provide a complete solution for web services: Web Services Management (WSM), the Management Integration Platform (MIP), the Business Service Catalog and Designer, and Identity management.

Conceptually, LCM4WS looks at managed objects at three different levels: at the business service, the web service level, and the web service container level.

Concept of Business Service

The business service plays the role of a single entity that represents a business application. For example, order fulfillment is a business service that represents functions represented by different parts of the enterprise. It is a virtualized resource and includes various metrics, operations, and events.

It is represented as a standards-based managed object that can be integrated into current management products. In the example from the HP case study, it can consist of web services such as Product catalog, Validate config, Place order, and Order status. Each web service can be hosted in different web service containers.

Figure 14.9 shows the business service, web service, and web service container as part of the management channel. The first component, Management Integration Platform (MIP), is used in the management channel. In the example scenario, the business manager monitors the order-fulfillment service; the architect monitors the web service, such as the Product catalog; and the operations staff monitors that instance of the Product catalog web service in the web service container.

WSM

Figure 14.9 also shows the application channel that hosts the web services. The second component of LCM4WS, Web Services Management (WSM), is used here to extract information from the web service application channel and direct it into the management channel. It does this through WSM Broker, WSM J2EE Agent, and WSM .NET Agent. WSM J2EE Agent provides the capability to integrate with existing J2EE application servers. Currently, an agent is provided for the BEA WebLogic Server environment. The agent uses JMX to manage the web services in WebLogic Server. Platform vendors who embrace WSDM do not require agent deployment; it is expected that agents will disappear over time as the standardization of the management interfaces is offered directly from the web service container.

WSM also provides WSM handlers whose capabilities are performance monitoring, logging and tracing for support purposes, payload auditing, business content monitoring, and security monitoring and integrations. Finally, WSM provides for every managed web service a published management object that exposes the management capabilities for that application component. This model is consumable by management tools that embrace the WSDM specification.

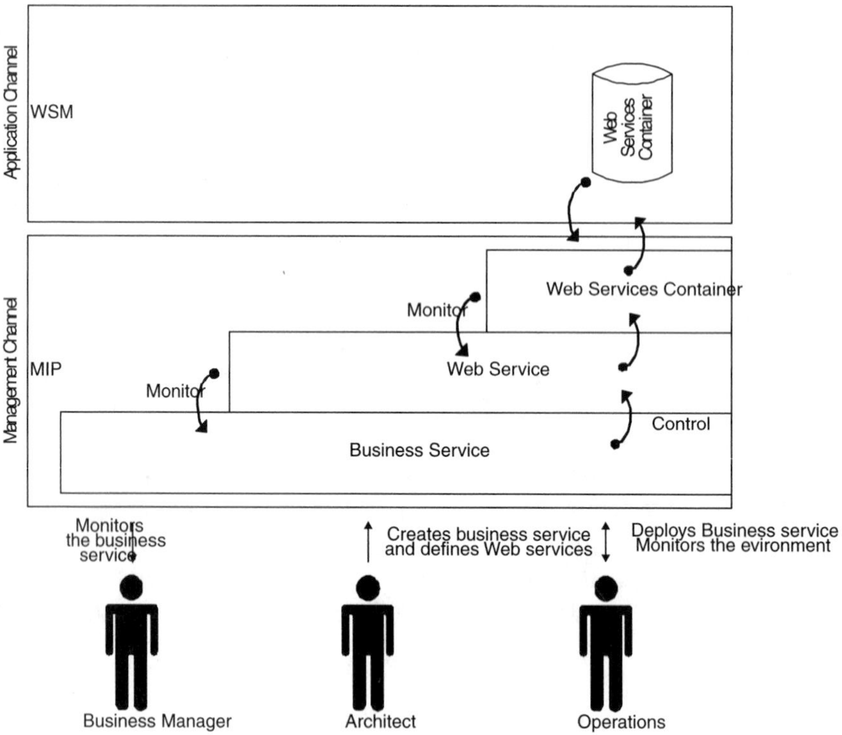

Figure 14.9 Business service, web service, web service container

Effective Improvements Using LCM4WS

Figure 14.10 shows how the deployment of the order-fulfillment service can be done so that it is managed by LCM4WS. First you define the order-fulfillment service in the business service catalog. The business service catalog and designer is the third component of LCM4WS. The Catalog service populates the management channel. Then the operation staff deploys the order-fulfillment service on WebLogic; this triggers the Catalog service to deploy. Now the monitoring information flows from the application channel to the management channel, and the resources can be monitored. The resources in the application channel are reflected in the management channel, and any change to those can be easily reflected in the management channel. You will see an example of this next.

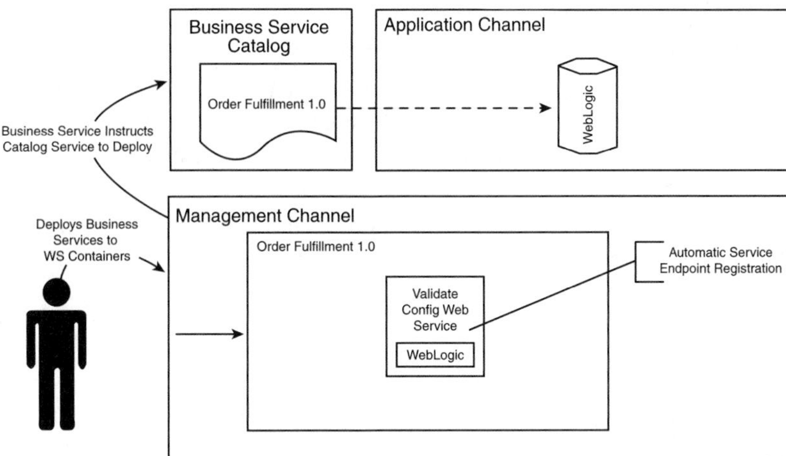

Figure 14.10 Deployment of the order-fulfillment business service

Consider an example scenario to explain how LCM4WS can help with changes to your business service. The business manager monitors the performance of the order-fulfillment service and needs to increase it (in particular, for the Validate config web service). The operations staff determines that adding another web service container—in this case, a WebLogic server, would improve the performance. The new resource in the application channel is reflected in the management channel, as shown in Figure 14.11.

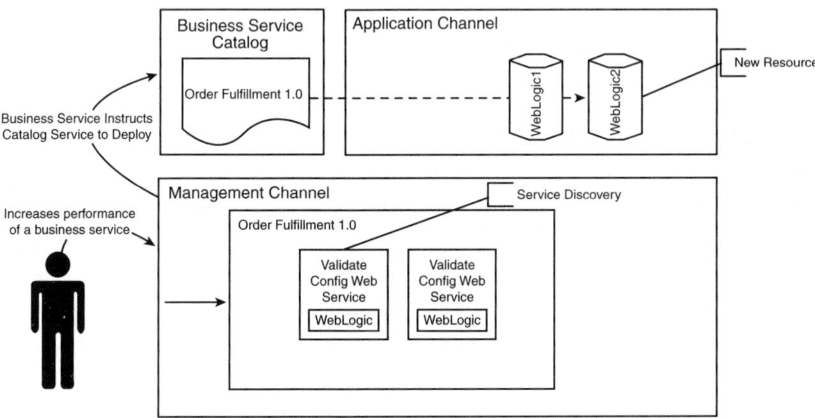

Figure 14.11 Performance increase of order fulfillment

The performance improvement now can be measured at the order fulfillment service level, and you can immediately get business metrics such as ROI and revenue increases.

The last component of LCM4Ws is identity management. It provides end-to-end security for web services by leveraging one or more existing enterprise user identity stores. This allows the solution to naturally plug into the existing security infrastructure, such as PKI and key management, while extending those security solutions to include web services.

The key difference between the LCM4WS solution and other pure-play WSM point products is that the model-based approach allows for alignment between IT and line-of-business managers, and also allows for automation and coordination of complex tasks throughout the deployment lifecycle of the web services.

Web Services Network Monitoring

You have learned how web services are different and must be managed as a distributed environment. Web services network monitoring is a technique by which a third party provides a neutral framework for enterprises to participate and provide shared visibility into the transactions occurring across the network. The third party's framework should offer mechanisms to gain the trust of the participating enterprises. Using a third party to provide independence and visibility is key to building trust when exchanging goods or data. Web services management can be done in addition to management at the producer and consumer of services.

The monitoring of web services offered by the third party will help achieve shared visibility and enable your business to respond more proactively to your customers in the following ways:

- **Highly available network**—A guaranteed 99.95 percent uptime of the third party's service network can ensure that the service network will always be capable of responding to your enterprise messages, even if the partner systems are down. This enables your applications to more elegantly handle error conditions associated with your partner's connection difficulties.
- **Real-time activity monitoring**—You can access the third party's web services for activity reports to review performance history or to inspect the details of any transaction.
- **Exception handling**—Through the third party, you can route faults to e-mail, pagers, cellphones, and even fax machines, or to other web services. Doing so enables you to respond more proactively with your partners and those using your services.
- **Alerts**—The third-party service can issue alerts when error conditions occur on the network, such as when SOAP faults are returned, when delivery fails, when someone fails to connect to the network, or when a security policy violation occurs.

- **Translation**—A third party can help in translating messaging format and version, communicating between different security layers or between different systems. An enterprise with a web services architecture might have to interact with enterprises that do not use web services but instead use EDI. The third party can translate the EDI to a web service and mediate the interaction. This shields your enterprise from having to deal with multiple-partner environments and avoids the need for point-to-point deployments.

Grand Central and Blue Titan are two companies that provide web services networking. Figure 14.12 shows the web services networks.

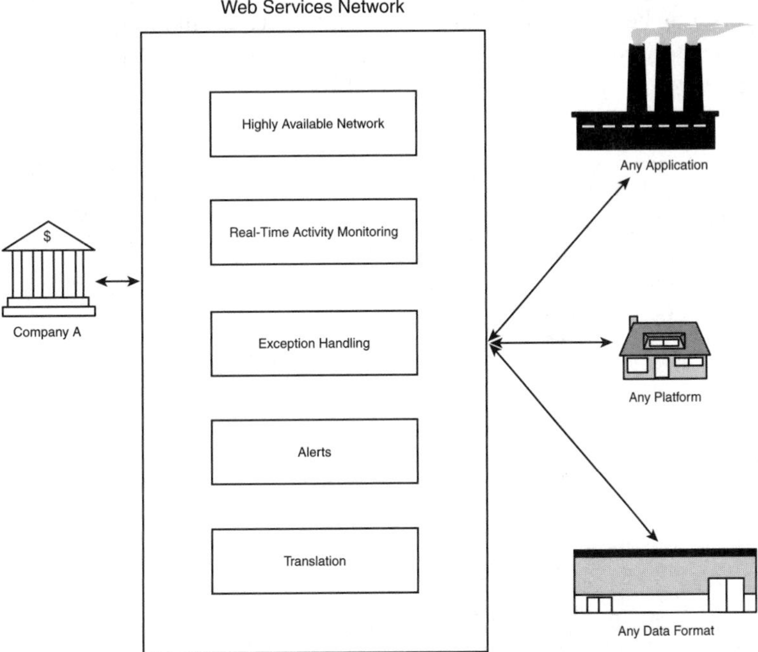

Figure 14.12 Web services network

Summary

This chapter first defined web services manageability and the need for managing web services. It described how managing web services is different from managing web applications. It covered the evolution of the management stack, through the JMX architecture and J2EE management specification, including JSR77 and WSDM for managing web services. WSDM consists of MOWS and MUWS. MUWS is built on WS-Resource Framework and WS-Notification. You also learned about the criteria for selecting a WSM tool, and you were introduced to LCM4WS, proposed by HP, which looks at the lifecycle management of web services and introduces the concept of a business service. LCM4WS essentially consists of four components: WSM, MIP, the business service catalog, and identity management. Finally, this chapter covered how web services networks can be managed through web services network monitoring.

Index

Symbols

A

C

D

E

K-L

M

N

O

T

U

V

W

X-Z